A WORLD IN CHAOS

Social Crisis and the Rise of Postmodern Cinema

CARL

TOM

BOGGS and POLLARD

ROWMAN & LITTLEFIELD PUBLISHERS, INC.
Lanham • Boulder • New York • Oxford

ROWMAN & LITTLEFIELD PUBLISHERS, INC.

Published in the United States of America
by Rowman & Littlefield Publishers, Inc.
A Member of the Rowman & Littlefield Publishing Group
4501 Forbes Boulevard, Suite 200, Lanham, Maryland 20706
www.rowmanlittlefield.com

PO Box 317
Oxford
OX2 9RU, UK

British Library Cataloguing in Publication Information Available

Library of Congress Cataloging-in-Publication Data

Boggs, Carl.
   A world in chaos : social crisis and the rise of postmodern cinema / Carl Boggs and
Tom Pollard.
      p. cm.
   Includes bibliographical references and index.
   ISBN 0-7425-3288-7 (hardcover : alk. paper)—ISBN 0-7425-3289-5 (pbk. : alk.
paper)
   1. Motion pictures—Social aspects—United States. I. Pollard, Tom, 1947– II. Title.
   PN1995.9.S6B64 2003
   302.23'43'0973—dc21   2003004675

Printed in the United States of America

♾™ The paper used in this publication meets the minimum requirements of American
National Standard for Information Sciences—Permanence of Paper for Printed Library
Materials, ANSI/NISO Z39.48-1992.

For Cynthia Boresoff
—CB

For Sue Dickey
—TP

CONTENTS

PREFACE

This book is an exploration of several powerful trends in Hollywood filmmaking that we refer to as "postmodern cinema"—trends we believe both reflect and influence the larger sociohistorical environment within which movies are produced, distributed, viewed, and critically assessed. We do not argue that such trends are necessarily predominant (much less monolithic), but they do carry forward some of the most creative and influential artistic forms of our period, going back to the 1960s. Nor do we insist that "postmodernism," in film or any other realm, amounts to anything resembling a pure, undistilled cultural expression; the very diffuse and multifaceted nature of the postmodern shift militates against such homogeneity. On the contrary, we find in present-day filmmaking—as in the mass media and popular culture—a rich, complex, indeterminate *mixture* of elements incorporating both "modern" and "postmodern," although we do argue that the latter is clearly ascendant within parameters of the film industry. In approaching the study of cinema in this fashion, we embarked on this project less as an exercise in conventional academic "film studies" than as an exploration of the complex developmental interaction between film and its broader environment, between art and society. From this standpoint, we look to critically investigate American film culture along many dimensions: as an aesthetic form, a mode of entertainment, a vital component of the mass media, and a crucial and highly profitable industry with an increasingly globalized setting. Our excursion into postmodern cinema does not privilege any of these elements.

The interpretation of Hollywood filmmaking we develop here, with emphasis on the period from the late 1960s to the beginning of the twenty-first century, revolves around a fundamental shift in the material and ideological life of the country, bringing to the fore drastically altered images of social reality, new filmmaking techniques, and a whole panorama of changing sensibilities around the family, sexuality, personal relationships, work, politics, and so forth. We do not insist that there is anything smooth, uniform, or necessarily predictable about this shift—indeed, such a premise would fly in the face of what postmodern culture has come to represent within the matrix of historical conditions. Our interpretation of postmodern cinema calls into question certain stereotypes of the Hollywood film industry, above all the notion that it merely perpetuates conservative or hegemonic values in the service of corporate domination. There is of course more than a kernel of truth to this, but a more comprehensive look at movies produced over the past three decades shows a richer, more complex, and indeed a more conflicted legacy that runs counter to such facile generalizations. We argue that the propaganda model or "inculcation thesis" so often applied to media culture simply fails to hold up to close scrutiny. What we find instead are strong countervailing trends that include, among other things, something of a *revolt* against long-standing Hollywood methods, formulas, and themes. Without doubt, the corporate structure, now more powerful and globalized than ever, sets limits to the cinematic enterprise, but this structure imposes no more rigorous limits on filmmaking than it does on book publishing or popular music (where an extremely wide range of products is available). Our goal in this study is to investigate the different, often conflicted and contradictory currents at work in a film industry that long ago departed from the ritualized practices and norms of the classical studio system.

We suggest that postmodern culture embellishes a strong pull toward diversity, critique, marginality, and even rebelliousness as it is reproduced largely within confines of the mainstream culture industry. This is one of the great paradoxes of Hollywood filmmaking today, which helps account for its peculiar aesthetic and political idiosyncrasies. It is within such a culture, oriented toward power, profits, mass audiences, and market standing, that films of such maverick directors as Oliver Stone, Woody Allen, Martin Scorsese, Robert Altman, John Sayles, the Coen brothers, Tim Burton, and John Waters have been regularly produced and distributed since the 1970s. While this stratum of directors (and affiliated producers, writers, and editors) might properly be described as a cultural elite, it is a stratum nonetheless keenly responsive to conditions of everyday life in post-Fordist, globalizing, socially atomized capitalist society. This is a society and culture, moreover, where elements of modernity (crisis ridden as they are) and postmodernity coexist within a tense and uneasy equilibrium.

We trace the evolution of postmodern cinema through its multiple and overlapping expressions: films that fit the blockbuster-spectacle mode beginning in the mid-1970s (*Star Wars* and *Titanic*), the theme of existential angst and despair (the movies of Woody Allen), the narrative of American historical decline and "loss of innocence" (Oliver Stone's *JFK*), the celebration of social mayhem and violence (Quentin Tarantino's *Pulp Fiction*), and a "ludic" preoccupation with farce and playfulness (John Waters's *Serial Mom*). What postmodern films share in common is an irreverence for authority and convention—a rebellious spirit, dystopic views of the future, cynical attitudes toward the family and romance, images of alienated sexuality, narrative structures deprecating the role of old-fashioned heroes, and perhaps above all, the sense of a world filled with chaos. These features are often combined with a romantic turn toward nostalgia, a longing for the past that encapsulates so much postmodern culture, along with a harshly critical, even nihilistic attitude toward politics, reflected in such 1990s films as *Bob Roberts*, *JFK*, *Enemy of the State*, *Wag the Dog*, *Falling Down*, *Primary Colors*, and *Bulworth*. Not surprisingly, films produced within the postmodern arc rarely embrace any coherent politics; their often well-developed cultural radicalism scarcely enters the realm of *political* radicalism. From such perspectives we conclude that an understanding of American film culture must incorporate yet go beyond scholarly discourses such as film studies, poststructural cultural criticism, neo-Marxism, critical theory, and those mainstream texts that strive to isolate the study of cinema from its sociohistorical context. Such methodologies, useful to a point, present film as a separate cultural medium with its own esoteric aesthetic and technical characteristics, or they reduce what is a complex and diverse cinematic enterprise to the workings of a monolithic culture industry

To investigate the historical and social meanings of postmodern cinema, we have chosen to incorporate but also supplement the fields of academic film studies and cultural criticism, bringing in discourses associated with sociology, history, economics, and literature as well as communications and popular culture. A complex, mediated phenomenon like film requires a critical, multidisciplinary approach engaging the dialectical interplay of cinema and larger trends at work in a rapidly changing, post-Fordist, globalized society. Strict attention to specific "texts," "codes," and "discourses" divorced from their totality can never be adequate to this task. Further, to understand the dynamics of film *culture*, we need awareness of developments within the general culture (and on the edge of that culture)—in contrast to the familiar film studies emphasis on artistically elevated but marginal works quite distant from the world of mass audiences and broad societal concerns. By fixing our conceptual lenses on vital changes taking place within the Hollywood film industry, we do not concede that the works in question are nothing more than the commodified output of a profit-driven corporate system, although this problem looms large indeed. On the contrary: The films we explore in this book are part of the most creative, engaging, and influential moviemaking to come out of the century-long cinematic tradition. Moreover, the very division separating mainstream and independent, conformist and innovative tendencies has broken down with the emergence of postmodern cinema, with its novel aesthetic and technical flourishes. It is in precisely this spirit that we have chosen to focus so much attention on surrounding arenas of contemporary life: mass media, popular culture, politics, and the family. This requires many tools and insights derived from critical social theory, a framework crucial to unraveling the complex interplay of cinematic techniques, literary narratives, social themes, and hidden meanings that permeated the film legacy from its very inception.

We have chosen to write about film—most of all postmodern film—in the belief it represents an excellent medium for studying important shifts in American cultural and political life. In 2002 more Americans went to the movies—attended showings in theaters—than at any time since immediately after World War II. When video sales are included in the mix, it seems obvious that filmgoing has reached its all-time peak, at precisely the moment when competing media forms (cable television and the Internet) have taken off in popularity. The attendance figures for 2002 were 1.5 billion, compared with a low of 820 million in 1971. Studio revenues for the same year totaled nearly $10 billion, well beyond any previous year. At a time when the video revolution might have threatened to overtake the theaters, the number of screens nationwide actually *increased* to a high of 36,000. With movies remaining firmly a centerpiece of popular culture, Americans flocked to see such blockbusters as *Spider Man* and *Lord of the Rings*, no doubt part of an undercurrent of escapism resulting from the aftereffects of the terrorist attacks (including fear of future attacks). Perhaps for similar reasons, postmodern cinema thrived during the same period.

We live in a paradoxical time when stifling elements of commodity production and media culture reign supreme yet when explosively creative artistic trends are on the upswing, giving rise to a public sphere in which "politics" (that is citizenship and popular decision making) has deteriorated while diversity, multiculturalism, and subversive discourses are more visible in the general life of the country. Such paradoxes and conflicted outcomes help explain our fascination with postmodern cinema as it has evolved and achieved new meaning over the past two or three decades.

A good many definitions of "modern" and "postmodern" have been freely and sometimes glibly framed within scholarly (and some popular) literature in history, social theory, and cultural studies, and we set forth our own departures at different points in the text, always striving to remain both respectful toward and critical of what has preceded us. Our main priority is to trace the shift, historically and theoretically, from the long era of modernity to an emergent postmodernity, above all where it intersects with the realm of film culture. We explore the developmental basis of this epic shift, identify its central features, and then specify the multiple thematic patterns and modalities within postmodern *cinema* going back to the late 1960s and early 1970s, locating the shift within the sociohistorical conditions of the period.

There can be little doubt that postmodern culture, however widely studied, revisited, and debated over the past two decades, is difficult to theorize, in part because of its relative novelty and in part because of a diffuse and fragmentary character rendering linear, structured, categorical schemas apparently obsolete. What distinguishes postmodernism from earlier grand traditions, ideologies, and discourses is its self-conscious rejection of integrated paradigms or structures of thought, its refusal to adopt "modern" forms of instrumental rationality. At the same time, postmodernism does embrace a wide range of philosophical claims and conceptual departures—with far-reaching political and cultural implications—that we believe have strongly influenced the trajectory of contemporary American cinema.

We assume that discourses of postmodernity make sense only with reference to what came before—namely, modernity—and more specifically to the intensifying *crisis* of modernity. In historical terms, we view *modernism* as rooted in Enlightenment rationality, industrialism; the idea of human progress tied to science, technology, and material growth; and diffusion of universalistic ideals that, in the United States, have long been associated with the liberal-capitalist mode of development and civilization. Modernity achieved its most coherent expression in the work of such epic theorists as Marx, Comte, J. S. Mill, Durkheim, and Weber. It has run into a series of well-known challenges throughout the twentieth century, never greater than in the past few decades—the product of its deep internal flaws, limits, and contradictions. The consequences of this increasingly "dark side" of the Enlightenment are by now rather familiar: massive global poverty, harsh social inequalities and dislocations, escalating military conflict and civic violence on a world scale, bureaucratic domination, demise of the nuclear family, and ecological crisis. The catastrophic terrorist attacks of September 11, 2001, when seen as part of a larger deadly global dialectic of military violence and blow-back, simply added to this matrix; the crisis of modernity has assumed new apocalyptic dimensions, with all its fearsome implications for American political and cultural life. Surely, no discussion of American cultural life today can adequately proceed without fully taking into account this complex historical backdrop.

With this in mind, we argue that *cultural* modernism (and with it post-modernism) must be situated within a series of economic, political, intellectual, and cultural transformations occurring over a period of many decades. "Culture" or aesthetics cannot be viewed separately from those sociohistorical forces that give it meaning and set its parameters—a methodological premise we assume is just as valid for cinema as for other art forms. In the United States, cultural modernism moved along somewhat diverse paths, then recently became more fully integrated into the corporate-dominated culture industry, which in Hollywood inevitably refers to some variant of the studio system. The social themes, aesthetic flourishes, and technical styles we understand here as "modernist" correspond to the broad panoply of institutions, values, and interests associated with historically modernist development grounded in the Enlightenment, industrialism, urban society, and faith in human progress through material growth. If this approach departs from some views of modernism, we believe the perspective adopted here makes good theoretical sense in helping to situate or contextualize precisely what ultimately challenges and supersedes modernism, namely, postmodernism.

Our focus on the long historic shift from modernism to postmodernism, from established Hollywood conventions to bold and experimental forays into new cultural territory, is not meant to indicate any fundamental "break" or rupture with the past. We see a gradual, uneven, partial, *incomplete* process where elements of both modern and postmodern remain intertwined at all levels of the economy, politics, and cultural life. We agree with the notion that postmodern aesthetics would indeed be unthinkable in the absence of a supporting "modern" infrastructure replete with vital institutional, technological, and human resources. This interweaving of the two paradigms means that postmodern culture has not reached anything close to hegemony—nor will it do so in the foreseeable future, given an entrenched corporate structure that tolerates only so much "diversity" and "ambiguity." Despite great bursts of creative energy within postmodern cinema, modernism remains the dominant force in Hollywood as in media culture as a whole.

Our view that cinematic innovations, creative autonomy, and (limited) cultural subversion can appear and even flourish in an age of corporate colonization may seem paradoxical, indicating as it does that overriding commercial imperatives can coexist with strong aesthetic priorities. As we argue throughout this book, notably and most emphatically in chapter 6, the process of commodification has never been absolute or total, nor has it always crowded out creative autonomy as long as it seems to adhere to minimal rules of the game. In some ways undermining the thrust of commodification, the very scope and complexity of media culture today tend to short-circuit any movement toward one-dimensionality. Insofar as elements of the media system have evolved into a kind of contested terrain, the flourishing of a cultural phenomenon like postmodern cinema is not as paradoxical as might appear on the surface.

For this and other reasons, the stylistic and technical features often associated with postmodern cinema are not always unique to it; they cut across the now hazy boundaries dividing film genres just as they traverse the modern/postmodern distinction. We refer here to the role of sophisticated technology such as digital imaging, along with the familiar use of pastiche or nostalgia and the adoption of specific types of montage sequences. Such "technical" modalities are compatible with disparate cinematic forms, narratives, and themes, although some methods (such as digital technology, sophisticated animation, and rapid-fire editing) do help define the postmodern enterprise for many directors. Similarly, the question of whether a film contains narratives or themes critical of dominant institutions and values runs across the dividing line separating the modern and the postmodern.

This latter point cannot be stressed enough: We conclude that the innovative technical, stylistic, and narrative departures of postmodern cinema—that is, its distinctive *cultural* radicalism—rarely if ever give rise to a *political* radicalism that offers a systemic critique of the status quo, depicts forms of collective action, or embraces an alternative vision of social progress. On the contrary, postmodern filmmaking rejects both the possibility and the desirability of such coherence, linearity, unity, and optimism, all ways of thinking crucial to oppositional politics. More often, postmodernism cuts across familiar ideological discourses such as liberalism, socialism, and nationalism, or it winds up debunking them altogether. And it is still the legacy of modernism we most closely associate with a cinema of radical critique and change, as in the case of Marxism, social realism, and cinema verité.

Some critics might argue that what we call postmodern cinema—inclusive of particular cultural and aesthetic trends of the past few decades—should not be viewed as especially novel any more than the Hobbesian world of disorder, chaos, and violence it presumably inhabits and reflects. There is some validity to such a response, but we need to take into account the wider ensemble of factors at work. To be sure, many older "discourses"—the Gothic novel, existentialism, surrealism, German expressionism, and film noir, to name the most important—did contain themes and motifs we regard as integral to the postmodern shift: tragedy, death of the hero, tormented personal relations, ambiguity, dystopic views of the future, unhappy endings, and so forth. All this, moreover, has been a familiar staple of murder mysteries, thrillers, horror pictures, tragedy-laden dramas, and the like throughout the entire history of moviemaking. It is equally true that the present-day world, disorderly and crisis ridden as it might be, has no special lock on chaos, violence, or cynical popular moods, as any quick reference to earlier phases of twentieth-century history will reveal. We are still living against the backdrop of two world wars, a holocaust, the advent of nuclear weapons, and plenty of ongoing economic misery, racism, military violence, and terrorism.

We do not refute such observations but rather suggest they ultimately *reinforce* the underlying thesis and spirit of our work. The last few decades of the twentieth century have witnessed an intensifying buildup and mounting impact of these developments—visible in politics and culture—as part of the growing crisis of modernity that informs our cinematic interpretations. Countermodernizing trends become more heightened, more fully crystallized, as they feed into the postmodern shift, achieving probably their most exaggerated definition in the United States over the past few decades. If there is nothing fundamentally new in the themes and motifs we explore in this book, their cultural articulation and power take on dramatic new meaning at a time when Hollywood filmmaking itself is experiencing far-reaching transformations. Postmodern cinema gives expression to a "syndrome" of modalities previously visible only in the most highly impressionistic form. Meanwhile, if Hobbesian trends have been in motion for a long time, surely the end of the twentieth century has given new meaning to these trends: widespread economic misery, a culture of violence, growing social polarization, stifling bureaucratic controls and surveillance, rampant corporate power, global ecological crisis, the rapid spread of military weaponry, terrorism, and deepening personal alienation in all spheres of daily life. For the United States, of course, one can add to this list the destabilizing consequences of 9/11 and its aftermath. In a word, American society is in the throes of increasing civic turmoil, political disaffection, and generalized social decay—a worsening state of affairs that postmodern cinema illuminates and no doubt helps foster.

This book is the product of a lengthy intellectual evolution and gestation, spanning a period of several years and moving through a number of drafts, revisions, and phases of articulation and rearticulation. Throughout this process, we have been blessed with the invaluable assistance and support of many colleagues and friends. Carl Boggs wishes to acknowledge the strong intellectual contributions and personal encouragement of Douglas Kellner, who took an interest in this project from the very outset and provided a close and critical reading of many parts of the text. Ray Pratt has been for three decades a constant source of scholarly and emotional support; it was his infectious love of film—especially the politics of film—that furnished so much of the initial impetus for this project. George Dolis, a colleague at Washington University in St. Louis during the 1970s, can take credit for being the first person to bring me into the orbit of film studies—though it would be at least another two decades before that interest would begin to bear fruit. Steve Kovacs, a longtime friend who is a unique combination of filmmaker and film scholar, has been a wonderful source of inspiration, inviting Tom Pollard and me to San Francisco State for our first full-length presentation of the main arguments contained in this book. Steve Best has read a good portion of the manuscript in its different stages of evolution and has offered many insightful comments and suggestions. Darrell Hamamoto, whose seemingly unlimited knowledge of American popular culture (including film) has provided a wellspring of useful information and new ideas, is owed abundant thanks. Several colleagues at National University and elsewhere—Mona Afridi, Monica Carbajal, Barbara Epstein, Doug Hadsell, Teresa Larkin, Peter McLaren, Laurie Nalepa, Karen Offitzer, Michael Parenti, John Sanbonmatsu, and Igor Subbotin—have given generously of their support. Deepest thanks are owed to Cynthia Boresoff, whose boundless energy, commitment, and support have done so much to give this project added vitality.

Tom Pollard wishes to thank Sue Dickey for her unwavering support throughout the entire research and writing process. Both Colleen Pauze and Edna Espanol provided valuable assistance and support at different stages of the project. Gratitude is also due Jessie Lawson, formerly of the University of California, Berkeley Center for Media and Independent Learning, for encouraging the decision to write "The Art of Film" course, which served as a major inspiration for this book, and to Eva Wunderman for the generous insights she was able to provide from the viewpoint of an outstanding film director.

1

THE NEW
CINEMATIC SOCIETY

The art and business of filmmaking, along with the experience of film viewing, are today integral to the discourses of modernity and postmodernity that have both reflected and shaped virtually every realm of social life in North America over the past few decades. Thanks in part to significant new advances in technology (from videotapes and cable television to DVDs and the Internet), American cinema has reached broader audiences, both in the United States and around the world, than probably any other cultural medium; it has become more dynamic, aesthetically integrated, and multi-faceted than other media such as music, architecture, painting, literature, and television. A major defining characteristic of the film enterprise today is its capacity to assimilate most all these other forms into its increasingly wide scope of aspirations, technical powers, and aesthetic sensibilities. As a vital element of media culture, film has done much to transform—for better or worse—the general public sphere, constituting in the process what Norman Denzin calls a "new visual legacy"[1] and what George Ritzer refers to as one of the "new cathedrals of consciousness."[2] Viewed in historical terms, cinema occupies a space where the global forces of industrialism, consumerism, technology, and popular culture merge into a hegemonically powerful *ensemble*.

Both within and outside the film legacy, what can be defined as the postmodern shift represents—in all its enormous complexity and diffuseness—a fundamental historical trend in American society, first taking hold in the 1970s as a deep response to ongoing structural changes: the post-Fordist economy, globalization, the information revolution, heightened patterns of consumption, and growing social atomization. This shift was readily visible in the spheres of art and architecture, academia, mass media, popular culture, and even politics, going back to at least the 1960s.[3] Perhaps nowhere has it become more detectable than in the world of cinema, which, through its innately elaborate celebration of images, glamour, and spectacles, arguably embraced features of postmodernity from its very inception at the turn of the century. The well-chronicled history of Hollywood moviemaking has been one long testimony to the immense power of visual images to evoke emotional responses among popular audiences—indeed, to reflect and influence processes of social change—within a seemingly endless parade of texts, discourses, narratives, thematic flourishes, and technical innovations.

This book explores the unique role of film in shaping contemporary history, politics, and culture within an unfolding mélange of forces that both illuminates and helps mold the popular consciousness, stretching from the 1970s to the start of the new millennium. Cinema inevitably enters into the main cultural, political, and even philosophical discourses of the period, even if those discourses do not always find their way into overt statements by producers, directors, writers, and other creative figures within filmmaking. As Mas'ud Zavarzedeh points out, cinema, by virtue of its great cultural power in American society, tends to revolve around "sites of ideological investment"[4] insofar as it represents particular images of the social life-world: class and material relations; gender, romance, and sexuality; politics and governance; race and ethnicity; the allure of collective beliefs; a vision of hero–protagonists; the understanding of violence in society; and so forth. It upholds and sometimes glorifies a sense of the past, present, and future—directly, indirectly, or only metaphorically. What seems rather noteworthy about the postmodern shift, however, is that long-standing boundaries and divisions associated with modernity have become increasingly blurred or refracted, a motif that underlies much of this book.

The sociohistorical context of postmodern cinema is a highly rationalized yet simultaneously turbulent world dominated by multinational corporations with enough reach in power and wealth to control the bulk of the world's resources, labor markets, flow of capital, and the long-term fate of the planetary environment. These same corporations possess unbelievable colonizing power over mass media and popular culture, especially in the industrialized nations and most particularly in the United States. The capacity of sprawling business empires, banking systems, governments, and international agencies to manage economic, political, and cultural life coincides, paradoxically, with a civic life that is anything but stable and orderly. On the contrary, stabilizing processes of institutionalization at the commanding heights coexist with growing *disorder* and even chaos within a civil society increasingly rife with anarchic planlessness, social dislocation, class polarization, poverty, violence, and ecological crisis. As global capitalist patterns of production and consumption responsible for this Hobbesian morass veer toward ever more predatory and destructive outcomes, international or domestic outcomes that could block or reverse such trends are nowhere to be found. In the absence of even minimal international Keynesian structures, the huge multinationals are free to further globalize, downsize, technologically restructure, and merge while continuously sharpening their exploitative capabilities. In this milieu, we are bound to encounter intensifying social and "natural" contradictions giving rise to popular moods of anxiety, fear, pessimism, and cynicism about a future increasingly filled with images of doom and apocalypse. Born out of historical crisis and the sharpening contradictions of modernity but also shaped by the contours of corporate colonization, postmodern cinema both mirrors and helps reproduce the mood of the time, lending it an aesthetic aptly described by Mike Davis as the "glamour of decay."[5]

THE CRISIS OF MODERNITY

The gradual appearance of postmodernism in cultural, intellectual, and political life—and specifically within Hollywood cinema—is perhaps best understood as part of an intensifying crisis of modernity linked to the epochal decline of Enlightenment rationality. For at least two centuries, modernity has been forged through a coherent set of beliefs and norms shaped by the industrial revolution and tied to the idea of progress achieved through sustained scientific, technological, and economic development—a schema that reached its pinnacle at the time of the English, French, and American Revolutions, inspiring struggles for individual freedom and rights, popular governance, a rational-legal administrative order separated from the ancien régime and its hegemony located in the aristocracy, the Church, and state bureaucracy. Modernity was always an optimistic, forward-looking, secularizing, rationalizing ethos, part of the "great transformation" that overtook the traditional order with its rapid spread of market relations to every corner of society. By the mid-twentieth century, this modernizing impulse, no longer strictly grounded in the liberal-capitalist order, followed the route not only of commodity production but also of bureaucratic and technological expansion, whether under the aegis of U.S. corporate capitalism, European Social Democracy, fascism, or Soviet-style communism. Nineteenth-century ideologies of liberalism, nationalism, and Marxian socialism, whatever their differences, converged within a matrix of assumptions regarding a more or less linear, progressive view of history grounded in sustained industrial and technological development, erosion of Church power, the domination of nature, and optimistic expectations about the future. Where Enlightenment beliefs and attitudes gained a powerful stronghold, as in the United States, modernization would inexorably shape and reshape the entire social terrain along lines anticipated by such diverse thinkers as Marx, Comte, J. S. Mill, Durkheim, Veblen, and Weber. It would be a universe in which the main protagonists stood for a clear set of rational beliefs and agendas linked to continuous material growth, institutional expansion, and national regeneration.

Within this historical labyrinth, cultural modernism meant a break with time-honored preindustrial traditions combined with a somewhat hesitant move toward (still limited) mass constituencies that would, fitfully and unevenly, attach themselves to the rationalizing and commodifying impulses of urban, industrial society. Whether in photography, art, architecture, literature, or music, cultural modernism became deeply inscribed in forms of (generally elite or avant-garde) artistic creativity if not yet of popular consciousness. In the world of cinema, which achieved a mass audience no earlier than the period during and immediately after World War I, modernism took hold not only in the United States (with the innovations of D. W. Griffith) but also in Europe (with the breakthroughs of directors like Eisenstein, Pudovkin, Murnau, and Renoir), being loosely though never consistently allied with an ethic of social realism where filmmakers sought to capture vital elements of social reality on screen—for example, in the epic struggles of the Russian Revolution; classic depictions of poverty, exploitation, and upheaval within capitalist society; scenes from the American Civil War and later military conflicts; and the seemingly endless corruptions and machinations of ruling elites. Over time, both modernism and realism followed the broad path of photographic representation, visible in a large output of documentaries, quasi-documentaries, docudramas, historical dramas, and similar forays into cinema verité.

We explore the "modernist" paradigm here within its broader sociohistorical context as part of a series of transformations covering a few hundred years extending into every sphere of human activity—intellectual, social, political, and economic as well as cultural. From this standpoint, historical forces, social conditions, and cultural forms are deeply interconnected, meaning that any interrogation of *cultural* modernism (or postmodernism, for that matter) must be situated within this totality. "Culture" never stands alone, independent of particular developmental forces, institutional constraints, economic interests, and political values, although it cannot be mechanistically reduced to any of these factors either. Looking at the twentieth century, we view the evolution of American cinema within the intricate web of modernity that includes Enlightenment values, industrialism and urbanism, liberal-capitalist ideology, patriarchy, bureaucracy, and the expansion of technology—all this tied to an optimistic view of human progress that was deeply imbued with national traditions and became integral to the studio system that marked the classic style of Hollywood filmmaking. In this context, modernism augured a historic breakdown of the distinction between "high" and "low" art, a polarity that in any case was always less meaningful within cinema than other art forms. Indeed, film generally entered the daily lives of Americans as a distinctly *mass* phenomenon, devoid of the pretenses of European *haute culture*, allowing for its later commodification within a studio system that was well equipped to capitalize on new business opportunities. Thus, any early claims of elevated cultural status or hostility to the commercial impulse ultimately gave way to strong capitalist imperatives, just as in other realms of social life. Of course modernism, even in the film industry, did champion some avant-garde notions, including uniqueness of the artist, cultural authenticity, and the special impact that works of art can have on popular consciousness—notions that persist to this day despite myriad references to "the death of the author."

While Hollywood modernist fare such as Westerns, gangster films, combat movies, detective thrillers, historical dramas, and some sci-fi works usually entered into the business of mythmaking, in the end films of this sort usually incorporated a mixture of visual images, literary narratives, and purported social "facts" or "experiences" said to be dug out of actual everyday life, enabling the viewer to identify (often subliminally) with protagonists, narratives, and ideals encoded within definite ideological messages. (Historically, of course, we know that the vast majority of Hollywood films gave representation to mainly status quo ideals and messages.) The power of film to evoke deep, visceral, emotional responses by means of deft screen writing, directing, cinematography, special effects, and acting performances was surely one of its most appealing qualities. The modernizing ethic spawned by Enlightenment rationality and then twentieth-century industrialism intersected roughly and unevenly with a *cinematic* modernism that remained firmly hegemonic in the film industry through at least the 1960s. What might be considered a loosely defined cinematic modernism drew from the seminal influence of Griffith, Chaplin, Eisenstein, Pudovkin, and then later such widely divergent filmmakers as Ford, Capra, Huston, Visconti, De Sica, and (in a very mixed sense) Welles. Tied to the emergent studio system, it was an ethic that set out to depict historic struggles between good and evil in a world where (typically white male) protagonists stood for a coherent, progressive set of values and where redemption (individual and collective) always seemed possible. It was a world inhabited by characters whose embellishments of modernity were shaped by their sense of historical mission—a mission most graphically visible in the classic Western and combat genres popular from the 1920s through the 1960s. Within modernism, the hero (however flawed or tragic) was invested with the power to decisively influence or transform society, or at least to stand tall against enormous odds, exemplified by Capra's *Mr. Smith Goes to Washington* (1939) and Ford's *Grapes of Wrath* (1940).

At its core, modernity was linked to the process of industrialization and its myriad consequences: exchange relations, commodification, hierarchy, urbanism, instrumental rationality, and universalistic notions of progress. The postmodern shift, of course, entails a profound critique and rejection (but never full transcendence) of modernity, made resonant by a growing crisis of the Enlightenment and industrial paradigm that was already set in motion during the nineteenth century. Postmodernism gathers strength by virtue of the increasing fissures and contradictions within modernity, fueled by economic globalization, corporate domination, bureaucracy, ecological crisis, and the personal alienation that pervades everyday life. The shift from modernity to postmodernity, from norms and values of industrial order to those of indeterminacy, difference, and (in some ways) *disorder*—never amounting to a rupture or break with the past—has become increasingly visible in the cultural world, including perhaps above all cinema. The postmodern sensibility captures a range of experience, knowledge, and subjectivity that the modern has either repressed or obliterated insofar as modernity, previously thought to be the crowning achievement of human progress, instead generated massive disaffection that over time led to higher levels of disillusionment, cynicism, and insecurity that came with disempowerment and alienation. Nowhere has this phenomenon been more visible than in the United States.

One strategy for exploring the crisis of modernity within highly industrialized societies is to interrogate the epochal decline of ideological discourses associated with historically modernizing forces such as the nation-state, industrialism, urban life, bureaucracy, and material growth—namely, liberalism, nationalism, socialism, and communism. In different ways, these ideologies celebrated the historic impetus toward economic, technological, and bureaucratic rationalization that, since the 1960s, has generated a series of localized counterresponses visible in the New Left and counterculture, the new social movements (notably feminism and ecology), identity politics, various modes of populism, and finally postmodernism itself. These counter-responses were made possible by deep fissures and contradictions arising out of the crisis and eclipse of modernity: class divisions and social disloca-tions, turbulence of urban life, mass society, bureaucratic domination, and the global ecological crisis. Long-established ideological discourses, origi-nating in the early phases of capitalist development, affirmed an optimistic, transformative view of history inspired by visionary ideals and programs, while the backlash against modernity moved through a less certain, more am-biguous, often dystopic understanding of historical process; in any event, the supposedly positive consequences of modernity were thrown into question.[6] These sentiments came to permeate much of political and intellectual life in the United States and ultimately its cultural life as well.

While there is little evidence to suggest that the "age of ideology" is totally exhausted, as writers like Fukuyama and Schwartzmantel argue,[7] it seems reasonable to conclude that those ideologies connected with modernity have been on a downward spiral for many decades. What seems equally obvious is that cultural and aesthetic impulses connected in some way to modernity are likewise in profound crisis—a major reason postmodern forms of culture (including perhaps above all cinema) have taken off in so many directions through the 1980s and 1990s. While modernism as such has scarcely disap-peared from any area of life, creative and influential filmmakers of this period (such as Coppola, Scorsese, Altman, Allen, Stone, Lee, Tarantino, and Wa-ters) have been drawn to postmodernism in one form or another—a move that we argue corresponds to the transformed sociohistorical situation.

Here postmodern film discourses build on a revulsion against tightly structured, formulaic, narrowly commercialized methods traditionally linked to the studio system, although the question of working independently of cor-porate production, marketing, and distribution has never been fully resolved or even confronted. The breakdown of hierarchical studio control by the 1960s ushered in a new era of filmmaking that opened up new creative space for writers, directors, cinematographers, actors, and editors even as corpo-rate power was being reconsolidated. Given extraordinarily deep changes at work in American society, it was now possible for innovative, experimental movie production to develop alongside the quest (often successful, as it turned out) for mass audiences. These audiences were increasingly receptive to novel, pathbreaking, sometimes offbeat cinematic methods and themes, such as those pioneered by independent filmmakers like John Cassavetes; indeed, the dividing line between "mainstream" and "independent" produc-tions often became blurred, as reflected in the work of experimental direc-tors able to maintain a strong creative presence (and perhaps even celebrity status) within a Hollywood film industry that had been for some time under critical assault. The postmodern shift tore down, gradually but inexorably, some well-established boundaries—not only between "low" and "high" culture (a questionable distinction from the outset, especially where film is concerned) but also between realism and formalism, between establishment and progressive, and between and among the many conventional genres, such as drama, comedy, thriller, gangster, and combat.

If postmodern cinema became subversive of many long-standing Hollywood codes, methods, and rituals, its distinctly *social* or political meaning was typically more ambiguous: In certain ways it cuts across familiar bipolar divisions of left versus right, liberal versus conservative, oppositional versus conformist, and innovative versus traditional—a major reason postmodern auteurs have always been so difficult to classify along familiar ideological or political lines. What can be said, however, is that the same trends underlying post-Fordist transformations in general (such as workplace and social differentiation, civic privatization, high-tech innovations, consumerism, and urban dislocation) have been simultaneously behind the postmodern shift in cinema. In a universe of fragmentation, dispersion, and ambiguity have appeared scores of films, including some of the best, calling into question basic conventions tied to corporate, family, religious, and patriotic values, though few of these films affirm genuinely radical impulses. At the same time, where this unfolding postmodern ethos can be understood as part of a deepening aesthetic revolt—much like cubism or German expressionism in painting or cinema verité in film—its cultural *and* political consequences could in time turn out to be rather explosive. We know that the many artistic and intellectual precursors to the postmodern turn go back many decades, incorporating tendencies such as German expressionism; dadaism; surrealism; existentialism; the earlier cinematic work of Fritz Lang, Orson Welles, and Alfred Hitchcock; film noir; and the neo-noir revival that took off in the 1970s.

Today it is the larger sociohistorical context that so obviously endows postmodern cinema with its great abundance of cultural exuberance and creativity. As Fredric Jameson observes, there is an undeniably powerful linkage between globalization of the capitalist economy (greatly intensified since the 1970s) and growing concentration of corporate power within the film industry, a linkage that recasts virtually every cinematic development in the United States and elsewhere. Viewed thusly, the development of postmodern cinema must be situated within a framework of corporate mergers, economic restructuring, and product diversification—structural processes that force adoption of novel production and marketing strategies that demand technological innovation, thematic difference, and thematic diversity within a greatly competitive international market.[8] Whereas postmodernism reflects a condition and outlook attuned to indeterminate change and turbulence, it further signifies creative *responses* and in some ways *adaptations* to the essentially coherent, rationalized workings of a mature corporate order. From this standpoint, Linda Hutcheon is correct to point out that "postmodern film does not deny that it is implicated in capitalist modes of production, because it knows it cannot."[9] Still, modernism generally assumed that human progress would follow the path of what is systemically rational, while postmodernism revolves instead around what is localized, "micro," and diffuse. If modernism embraced the positive, visionary, transformative side of Enlightenment ideology and the industrial revolution, postmodernism follows the path of its crisis and (potential) transcendence. Whereas modernism envisions a powerful transformative role for specific agencies of change (such as leaders and collectivities), postmodernism more or less denies such agency in its embellishment of a decentered, unstable, changing self or social identity.

The breakdown of cultural modernism and the simultaneous emergence of postmodern film discourse coincide with the appearance of a full-blown cinematic age where the restless search for new epistemological and aesthetic paradigms—a search often taking its architects in the direction of chaos and even apocalypse—has infused the spirit of much contemporary filmmaking. This quest makes abundantly good sense in a crisis-ridden world of urban chaos, civic violence, hyperreal media culture, ecological crisis, and a progressively disordered international politics. Here the diffuse conditions of postmodernity involve nothing less than development (or refinement) of new ways of seeing the world, including a new cinematic "voyeurism" (to use Denzin's reference)[10] appropriate to the society of the spectacle and hyperconsumerism.

The larger sociohistorical context of postmodern cinema referred to earlier requires further elaboration in the aftermath of the 9/11 terrorist attacks on the World Trade Center towers and the Pentagon. In much the same fashion as the sinking of the *Titanic*, the holocaust of World War II, and the nuclear annihilation of Hiroshima and Nagasaki, the September terrorist episode and its aftermath must clearly be seen as a blow to modernity, as both reflecting and exacerbating global Hobbesian disorder. Viewed within the deadly cycle of U.S. militarism and international terrorism, now elevated to new levels, 9/11 has given further impetus to what is becoming the prototype war of the twenty-first century, a series of frightening skirmishes that promise to be endless, costly, and devastating, that can only help to legitimize organized forms of violence around the world. The largest single act of terrorism by far on American soil, the attacks produced shock effects that continue to reverberate throughout the United States and the world. What was most novel about 9/11 was that the hegemonic superpower became for the first time the target of such awesome violence, carried out with unprecedented efficiency.

We know that catastrophes like 9/11 never occur in a social or historical vacuum; in this case, the event can be understood only as a particularly virulent form of "blowback," that is, a blow against empire carried out by groups proclaiming specific grievances against the U.S. economic, political, and military presence in the Middle East and elsewhere—a presence that has escalated since the end of the Cold War and the military assault on Iraq in 1991. As Chalmers Johnson wrote even *before* 9/11, terrorism must be seen as the inevitable product of U.S. global domination—violent reactions borne of horrendous imperial deeds and spurred by the deep alienation and sense of powerlessness felt among the diverse victims of empire that could be (indeed *were*) foreseen well before September 2001. Johnson argues that terrorist adventures undertaken against the United States "are all portents of a twenty-first century crisis in America's informal empire, an empire based on the projection of military power to every corner of the world and on the use of American capital and markets to force global economic integration on [U.S.] terms, at whatever costs to others."[11] He adds, "There is a logic to empire that differs from the logic of a nation, and acts committed in service to an empire but never acknowledged as such have a tendency to haunt the future."[12] In the case of the al-Qaeda terrorist network most likely responsible for the 9/11 operations, it would be difficult to interpret these events as anything but the vengeful payback for mounting U.S. involvement in the Middle East: longtime support for Israeli occupation of Palestine with the displacement of tens of thousands of people from their homeland; decade-long bombings and sanctions against Iraq costing up to a million lives; military bases set up in Saudi Arabia, Turkey, and elsewhere in the region; massive weapons sales to many governments; covert actions going back several decades; and the taken-for-granted machinations of oil politics. Indeed, a number of terrorist attacks had already taken place before 9/11, including an earlier attempt to destroy the World Trade Center, in the wake of the Persian Gulf War.

Still, 9/11 hit the United States and the world like a mammoth shock wave. As Tariq Ali observes, "The complacency of this world was severely shaken by the events of 11 September. What took place—a carefully planned assault on the symbols of U.S. military and economic power—was a breach in the security of the North American mainland, an event neither feared nor imagined by those who devise war games for the Pentagon. The psychological blow was unprecedented. The subjects of the Empire had struck back."[13] Aside from the enormous human casualties, which exceeded the toll at Pearl Harbor, the blow resulted in a great disruption in the routines of daily life in the United States, including damage to an economy that even one year later had not fully recovered. Among its many repercussions, 9/11 resulted in vast corporate downsizing and job loss, drastic alterations in travel and tourism, erosion of physical mobility, renewed emphasis on law enforcement and surveillance, strengthening of the authoritarian security apparatus, and expansion of military power along with the scope of armed intervention, all accompanied by a rise in generalized insecurity, fear, and distrust. At this point, U.S. foreign policy rests on the premise that its military can intervene virtually anywhere in the world, largely outside the realm of international law and customs and beholden to no higher authority, with minimal harmful consequences—at least until the effects of blow-back are measured. It might be argued that 9/11 has reinforced conditions of postmodernity exemplified by a world of heightened atomization, chaos, violence, and dystopia. A new sense of vulnerability overtook American culture. Raul Mahajan observes that 9/11 "forever ended the idea that the United States could somehow float above the rest of the Earth, of it and not of it at the same time. Americans can no longer foster the illusion that what happens to the rest of the world doesn't affect them."[14]

From a strictly global standpoint, the cycle of militarism and terrorism has produced a milieu of chaos, instability, and violence threatening to engulf the United States in a way that seemed largely unthinkable throughout the Cold War years—a threat where, as Caleb Carr writes, "brutality, massacres, terrorism, and even genocide have become daily facts of international life."[15] One reason for this new state of affairs is that "international terrorism has taken a sudden, significant leap in strategy and particularly in tactics in order to match the dominant American military role in the world."[16] One problem here is that the United States has increasingly relied on deadly military force to protect its hegemony within the New World Order. In part, this has involved a willingness to engage in debilitating wars of attrition (Korea and Vietnam); a sophisticated use of techno-war, including above all strategic bombing campaigns (Iraq and the Balkans); and an overwhelming monopoly of weapons of mass destruction (including the ever-present nuclear option). Defense of empire has brought to the fore barbaric war methods that regularly flout the canons of international law.[17] When pushed to its extremes, as has often been the case, U.S. pursuit of unconditional objectives has wound up obliterating long-valued distinctions between military and civilian targets.

Terrorism easily and predictably becomes part of this imperial labyrinth, part of a Hobbesian global milieu in which poverty, social polarization, ecological decay, crime, militarism, and powerlessness are the norm, especially in huge megacities like Cairo, São Paolo, Bombay, Mexico City, Seoul, Bangkok, Karachi, and Djakarta. Where such conditions fester, the descent into chaos may not be far off, particularly given the wide availability of sophisticated weapons. Walter Laqueur writes, "Traditional terrorism will certainly continue; for years to come it will remain the prevalent mode of conflict, sometimes in its 'pure' form, at other times in the framework of civil wars or general lawlessness."[18] It is likely to be an era of recurrent mass violence where wanton destruction of civilian targets (or "infrastructures") becomes rather commonplace, facilitated by the spread of high technology and erosion of the familiar "rules of engagement." The social impact of this dynamic can be horrendous, as we have already seen. Laqueur suggests that "the consequences of mass panic in both material and human terms can be huge; they can lead to a paralysis of normal life, epidemics, post-traumatic stress, and tremendous anxiety, especially if the nature and extent of the danger is unknown." He adds, "They may exceed the fantasies depicted in the most ghastly horror movies."[19] Moreover, a turbulent, violent world inescapably spawns a wide variety of Mafiosa groups, mobs, gangs, death squads, terrorist cells, private armies, and of course secret-police networks along with the requisite forms of surveillance and control maintained by authoritarian governments. What defines so much of this dystopic landscape, according to Hans Magnus Enzensberger, is the very randomness of violent conflicts that now seemingly have no coherent ideological or class objectives. Thus, "in today's civil wars there is no longer a need to legitimate our actions. Violence has freed itself from ideology. . . . Where the state can no longer enforce its monopoly on violence then everyone must defend himself."[20] Written several years before 9/11, Enzensberger's commentary powerfully resonates with the transformed international situation.

Despite its relatively unchallenged global domination, the United States has become increasingly absorbed into this dialectic, more vulnerable with each extended reach of empire; clearly this is one of the most salient historical meanings of 9/11. The crisis of modernity, already dramatized in the cinematic legacies of noir and neo-noir, has now entered the lives of American citizens with a vengeance, mirroring a world of powerful, menacing forces veering out of control—surely beyond the control of ordinary citizens. What noir portrayed as part of the dark side of daily modern life—the claustrophobia, alienation, fear, and violence—has indeed emerged as a more generalized manifestation of the cycle of militarism and terrorism, exacerbated by the *end* of the Cold War, which, ironically, further deepens the Hobbesian labyrinth. The "noir city" has been transformed into something of a "noir nation," at a time when the old familiar ideological backdrops seem to have vanished from sight. The culture has become saturated with images of violence, insecurity, dystopia, and blow-back, the empire having come home. Reflecting on the film noir legacy, Nicholas Christopher writes, "That an American city is now more likely to be devastated by the nuclear weapon which a terrorist can plant in a car trunk than the intercontinental ballistic missile that screams through the sky from eastern Russia is surely cause for more, not less, angst. That the terrorist may as easily be an American citizen—with far more lethal capabilities than the old Cold War saboteur—as a foreign national ought to be the source of even greater angst."[21]

The media and popular culture images of the postmodern environment reflect and help reproduce precisely this chaotic universe where civic violence, corruption, rampant white-collar crime, poverty, and urban deterioration are the order of the day. The psychological consequences involve a sense of displacement, dread, and paranoia that, sooner or later, find their way into the contemporary narratives, styles, and spectacles of American film. Ray Pratt writes of a postmodern condition typified by the "age of paranoia," where distrust and fear correspond to an authoritarian, programmed world of bureaucratic and corporate domination breeding widespread alienation and powerlessness. In this context postmodern cinema— examples include *The Conversation, Blade Runner, Brazil, Enemy of the State,* and *The End of Violence*—offers terrifying visions of an emerging society shaped by total surveillance and institutional controls obliterating the realm of privacy, free spaces, and social autonomy historically championed by American liberalism. Here "paranoia is increasingly a binding force for the whole nation."[22] In a universe where events seem totally beyond any popular decision-making inputs, generalized feelings of suspicion, distrust, and fear predictably mount. One result is the ongoing search for enemies and scapegoats that allows people to "interpret" their predicament, their horrible frustrations by focusing hatred on outsiders, aliens, and other "enemies": communists, drug traffickers, rogue states, terrorists, and demonic leaders who, in the aftermath of 9/11, appear very much as a *genuine* threat, often viewed through an ethnocentric or racist prism. As Pratt notes, "Hysterical public construction of enemies, suspicion of outgroups, and general paranoia have been distinctive elements of American politics since the early 1800s."[23] Yet paranoia today, as Pratt goes to great lengths to emphasize, is increasingly grounded in the reality of a Hobbesian state of nature—that is, it has a legitimate basis in reality. One need look no further than the intensification of domestic authoritarian politics in the wake of 9/11: Law enforcement, intelligence agencies, and the military have experienced unprecedented rebirth within the war on terrorism. In establishing a new Homeland Security Department, the Bush administration has fought for far-reaching legislation enabling it to skirt established bureaucratic and legal rules; elites want a "new flexibility" to carry out policies of surveillance and control. "War rooms" focusing on potential terrorist (and other) dangers have appeared at the local, state, and federal levels, linking more than 100,000 law enforcement officers within a single political agenda. Video cameras now track students, workers, shoppers, and other citizens around the country more systematically than ever, further obliterating the boundary between public and private life.

In the United States during the postwar years, economic development, the worship of technology, growing corporate domination, militarism, and a domestic culture of violence have been deeply intertwined, so that trends at work after 9/11 were already established decades ago as the crisis of modernity began to advance. William Gibson writes of an increasing fascination in American culture during the 1990s with guns, warriors, violence, and war—a fascination that found its way into dozens of Hollywood movies before and after the terrorist attacks. Such a "new war mythology," exemplified in part by the rise of paramilitary groups and domestic terrorist incidents, has filled a psychological void for millions of men who feel disenfranchised.[24] Consonant with the paranoid style, many look to apocalyptic visions and scenarios much like those that captured the fancy of Timothy McVeigh and his cohorts.[25] In his harsh critique of contemporary American politics, William Ophuls argues that liberal capitalism, with its obsessive devotion to "amoral individualism" and its absence of any commitment to a long-term public good, is so intellectually and morally bankrupt that it cannot begin to address urgent social problems; the very sense of citizenship has imploded. Thus, America is a "society ground down into atoms" where "solitary and powerless individuals suffer from a spiritual vertigo that few have the intellectual or moral resources to withstand, so they resort to pathological means of coping." Echoing the dystopic outlook we here associate with postmodernism, Ophuls concludes that we are facing "not a sudden and dramatic fall into an Orwellian nightmare but rather a more gradual descent . . . into a monolithic regime of media manipulation and bureaucratic centralism resembling Huxley's *Brave New World*."[26] These words were written several years *before* the catastrophe of 9/11.

The great promises upheld by modernity inspired by Enlightenment rationality have run aground on the most powerful trends at work today: globalization, corporate expansion, bureaucratic and technological controls, eco-logical crisis, social atomization, and, perhaps most of all, militarism. The events surrounding 9/11 have no doubt exacerbated such trends, but they are hardly new. Postmodern culture (including film) both mirrors this predicament and remains trapped within it.

FILM AND THE POSTMODERN ETHOS

The postmodern assault on Enlightenment values and modernity has called into question the familiar tendency to universalize simple moral or episte-mological truths that might be distilled from historical experience. In the United States of the late 1960s and early 1970s, a popular mood of angst and insecurity began to take hold, mirroring all the fear, paranoia, and cynicism of a noir world defined by the specter of the Cold War balance of nuclear ter-ror, political assassinations, post-Vietnam syndrome, social conformism, and continuous deterioration of urban life.[27] Such images, of course, seemed rather appropriate to the thoroughly modernized yet socially fragile world of late capitalism—resonating with new forces at work in American society: post-Fordism, the information revolution, economic globalization, ecologi-cal and urban crisis, and the previously mentioned collapse of religious and ideological metanarratives. At this juncture, postmodernism constituted much less a unified theory or world outlook than an extremely amorphous congeries of attitudes, feelings, and reactions, occasionally informed by philosophical discourses that unfortunately resist facile theoretical or politi-cal conceptualizations. This shift would profoundly reshape much of intel-lectual, cultural, and political life in the United States, thus remapping (in Stam's words) the whole terrain of possibilities.[28] It would be felt nowhere more than in the film scene.[29] If postmodernism lacks the coherence and specificity of many earlier discourses, we can still identify within it several critical themes and trends that provide the main organizing structure of this book.

Here we make use of the term "postmodernity" as a conceptual vehicle for exploring the complex processes that grow out of and supersede—but again, do not yet fully transcend—modernity, for investigating fundamental trends that depart from entrenched modernist theories, practices, movements, and artistic expressions. Insofar as the postmodern shift brings forth a critique of Enlightenment ideals, universalism, master discourses, and the search for ba-sic foundations of knowledge and truth, it rejects modernist assumptions re-garding social cohesion, strict causality, and determinacy in favor of multiple outlooks, plurality, fragmentation, and ambiguity—a shift that would have a dramatic impact on film culture. In the words of Steven Best and Douglas Kellner, "Such a [postmodern] play with different styles suggests yet another crucial characteristic of postmodern cultural forms: the rejection of structure, order, continuity, cause-effect relations in favor of disorder, chaos, chance, discontinuity, indeterminacy, and forces of random or aleatory play."[30] The fact that this process has been partial and uneven, with elements of the modern and postmodern commonly mixed within specific experiences, practices, and texts, scarcely denies its enormous cultural impact.

As might be expected, postmodern cinema has developed along manifestly diverse lines in a setting where the filmgoing public will be scarcely aware of the cinematic distinctions employed here. If postmodernity remains an elusive concept with variable interpretations and applications, efforts to further specify and concretize this hybrid phenomenon must nonetheless be undertaken for the sake of analytical clarity. This imperative relates just as much to film studies as to any other field of study. We identify five general trends within an emergent (but not yet hegemonic) cinematic postmodernism, as follows: 1) the blockbuster spectacle (the *Star Wars* episodes, *Batman*, *Jurassic Park*, and *Titanic*), featuring hyperreal, super-commodified media spectacles extending well beyond the movie experience itself; 2) the theme of existential morass pervasive in earlier film noir and neo-noir films (*Out of the Past*, *Touch of Evil*, *Taxi Driver*, and *Chinatown*) and more recently given fuller articulation in the work of Woody Allen; 3) emphasis on the uniquely American slide into historical quagmire and with it the vanishing of classic hero–protagonists, most visible in the dystopic films of Oliver Stone (*Born on the Fourth of July*, *The Doors*, *Salvador*, and especially *JFK*); 4) a turn toward the motif of Hobbesian disorder and chaos reflected in the work of directors like Scorsese (*Mean Streets*, *Taxi Driver*, and *Casino*), DePalma (*Dressed to Kill*), and more recently Quentin Tarantino (*Reservoir Dogs* and *Pulp Fiction*); and 5) embellishment of a "ludic" or theatrically playful cinema where little is valued or held sacred, where conventional norms and rules are subject to irreverent mockery, as in the cinema of John Waters (*Hairspray*, *Cry Baby*, and *Serial Mom*). While these large (and sometimes overlapping) patterns cover a significant cultural terrain, some common narrative structures and social themes do recur throughout—a turn toward nostalgia and romantic pastiche, death of the hero, a disintegrating social milieu, images of tormented or tragic personal relationships, and dystopic (pessimistic, fearful, or mordant) visions of the future. Consistent with the postmodern ethos, it would be hard to arrive at *political* generalizations that might cut across these divergent motifs; ideological coherence of any sort is almost entirely lack-ing. What can be said, however, is that recent technical and stylistic innova-tions in cinema have generated a body of work that is unquestionably ex-perimental, irreverent, eclectic, and at times even subversive in its cultural sensibilities. While such departures may not always be associated with our understanding of postmodern culture, they have surely come to permeate the filmmaking landscape of the past two or three decades.

Within this epic transformation, the classic opposition between "real" and "unreal" has lost its relevance as older cinematic schemes and methods have increasingly loosened their hold—witness, for example, the downward trajectory of cinema verité that was historically one of the cornerstones of modernism. Evolving largely within but also on the periphery of mainstream filmmaking, postmodernism served to broaden the space for creativity and self-reflection, difference and pluralism, and critique of and resistance to hierarchy—though typically within parameters of a corporate studio system that is still hierarchical but more globalized. Here the somewhat glamorized role of the auteur, continuously visible and influential within postmodern diffuseness, provides new creative leverage even as it performs its work un-der the watchful eye of profit-hungry but always cautious business interests. One noteworthy phenomenon today is that the most prolific auteurs have become recognized as "public intellectuals" in a modality essentially un-known throughout the studio era, as demonstrated by the careers of Cop-pola, Scorsese, Altman, Lee, Allen, Stone, Sayles, Burton, and Tarantino, among others. Yet if the new generation of auteurs is free to make films con-taining provocative aesthetic and social statements, its creative autonomy re-mains limited, falling well short of cinematic architectonics of the sort cele-brated by classic auteur theory. If postmodern values encourage wider zones of creativity, novelty, and difference, they join a cultural process that is surely more collaborative than ever, reflecting in part the growing power of pro-ducers, actors, writers, cinematographers, and editors and in part the en-hanced role of sophisticated techniques.[31]

This blurring of directorial functions, as with eroding distinctions be-tween the real and the illusory, form and content, the mainstream and the al-ternative, and the historical and the present, is magnified by the familiar postmodern murkiness concerning narratives, plot structures, editing tech-niques, and the defining power of cinematic images. The well-known ambi-guity and relativism of postmodern culture inevitably enter into and help re-shape contemporary filmmaking, whatever the style or "genre" in question. This helps explain why, at a time of expanding corporate power in the U.S. culture industry as a whole, we find an abundance of films standing apart from long-established Hollywood formulas and codes, often inspired by hostility to one or another cornerstone of the status quo. American films of the 1980s and 1990s frequently exhibited a jaundiced view of hallowed institutions, as conservative critics of Hollywood never tire of repeating: the family, big business, law enforcement, the military, patriotism, and religion.[32] Some commercially successful Hollywood fare also dwelled critically on U.S. military adventures abroad, corruption in city hall, the false promises of electoral politics, the ruthlessness of Wall Street culture, or the corporate assault on the environment, such as *Born on the Fourth of July* and *JFK* (Stone), *Silkwood* (Mike Nichols), *The Milagro Beanfield War* (Robert Redford), *Bob Roberts* (Tim Robbins), *Wag the Dog* (Barry Levinson), *Erin Brockovich* (Steve Soderbergh), and *Lone Star* (Sayles).

Yet only rarely do such films, governed by deeply critical sensibilities as they might be, move toward distinctly *political* conclusions or alternatives; like so much of American society itself, movies are depoliticized to the extent their cultural radicalism is rarely translated into *political* radicalism. While postmodernism is often associated with a strongly pessimistic turn in social and political life, it offers no exit from the deepening contradictions of post-Fordist capitalism where the prevailing mood is one of fear, anxiety, and powerlessness. Of course, the ethos itself disparages any such attempt, lest it be assimilated into universal (and hence potentially transformative) discourses tied to ideological metanarratives. As popular disaffection with modernity intensifies, trends toward privatized lifestyles along with a retreat from social and political life are reinforced as civic culture disintegrates.[33] We should be rather surprised if this mood did not enter the canons of postmodern cinema, even its most "radical" side—witness the often virulently antipolitical content of such films as *Bob Roberts*, *Dave*, *Wag the Dog*, *Primary Colors*, and *Bulworth*. The cynical, politically morbid, and ultimately depressing character of even the best contemporary American filmmaking coincides with the politically amorphous nature of postmodern art in general, from the work of Andy Warhol to punk rock, the music of Philip Glass, the architecture of Robert Venturi, and the literature of William Burroughs. Much the same could be said of the European intellectual founders of postmodernism (starting with Michel Foucault, Jacques Derrida, and Jean Baudrillard), who, though at one point emphatically theorists of the left, wound up attached to discourses calling into question the very *possibility* of radical politics. Earlier cinema that appears to correspond with postmodern thematics, including the work of such auteurial giants as Fellini, Truffault, Godard, and Fassbinder, fits much the same pattern.

The emergence of postmodern cinema has so transformed ways of making, seeing, and interpreting film that old conceptual distinctions (auteur theory, realism versus formalism, genre theory, and semiotics) now require fundamental rethinking. Take "auteur" theory, which first gained currency in Europe during the 1950s: What does our understanding of the director as single galvanizing force in filmmaking mean when media culture and communications are today, far more than ever, shaped by far-reaching expert collaboration, diversification, and the ubiquitous power of the commodity? In the postmodern era, a new stratum of highly paid superstar actors, for example, has achieved seemingly unlimited power to influence script and performance. Cinematographers, sound technicians, and especially film editors can have a decisive influence on the final cut of a movie, while producers and directors—now forced to adapt to globalized and highly competitive markets—must combine efforts out of fear their project will atrophy. Meanwhile, filmgoing audiences have grown increasingly fond of graphic images and spectacles that, given the wide availability of sophisticated technology, can be brought to the screen by even the most limited directors. Many contemporary American directors have achieved great status, but few possess the auteurial nobility of domineering figures like Chaplin, Ford, Hitchcock, Welles, Hawks, and Wilder, all of whom managed their sets with near dictatorial powers. Neither the authority nor the style of even the most auteur-like present-day directors can be said to reach such levels because neither the culture nor the technology will seemingly permit it. While directors whom we broadly locate within the postmodern shift can obviously still aspire to the status of generally recognized and well-paid directors, perhaps even "public intellectuals" in the tradition of Welles and Hitchcock, their creative autonomy and decision-making capabilities are usually more restricted. From this standpoint, "auteur theory," while retaining much of its utility because of the undeniable achievements and idiosyncratic styles of many filmmakers, requires significant reconceptualization. Auteurism clearly underestimates the importance of production conditions today, where the overwhelming need for material resources subordinates requirements for independent directorial status.[34] We argue that it is now possible to speak of a *modified*, somewhat attenuated auteur theory in which the director, still obviously a figure of great stature, shares more power with other creative influences while maintaining a strong integrative role.

Whether the focus is modernism or postmodernism, there is of course no ignoring the dynamic and integrative function of directors who manage to carve out space within a highly rationalized culture industry, many of whom operate in that nebulous terrain where mainstream Hollywood and indie fringes overlap. It might even be argued that the power of directors relative to producers has in some ways been *magnified* since the breakdown of the old studio system, for they surely have greater access to financial, technical, and human resources—not to mention enhanced artistic flexibility—than before. While mass audiences have been drawn more to actors or "star" performers than to directors or writers, the majority of film *critics* (following the seminal influence of François Truffaut and Andrew Sarris) have paid more attention to directors as prime movers of the cinematic process, as the innovative force shaping both film style and content. Classical auteur theory viewed directors as movie "authors" in much the same way literary writers are the authors of books or architects the designers of buildings, occupying a special niche within the total field of activity while harmonizing diverse functions (such as writing, performance, cinematography, and editing) into an artistically cohesive whole. Here the director is celebrated as enjoying nearly total freedom to determine the final outcome, a freedom that for many decades was blocked by stifling conformism at the major studios. Directorial autonomy, wherever it could be gained, meant continuous struggle against studio executives, producers, and corporate elites whose agendas were above all hitched to commercial success. From the 1920s through the 1960s, "success" on these terms went hand in hand with a conservative ideology linked to patriarchal family values, middle-class individualism, patriotism, and so forth. Only a few directors—those reaching the stature of Ford, Welles, Hitchcock, and Wilder—were able to make inroads into the heavily conformist factory system presided over by stodgy mainstream studio heads.[35]

The breakdown of traditional studio power, along with transformations growing out of European influences, the 1960s counterculture, and new social movements, helped pave the way toward wider directorial freedom in many areas of filmmaking. The 1970s witnessed the emergence of a new generation of Hollywood auteurs whose cinematic impulses departed radically from the assembly-line products of the mainstream film industry; they brought a creative, experimental, rebellious flair to film production that kept its distance from, and in some ways countered, the all-consuming business imperative. New Hollywood directors brought a variety of "alternative" and "independent" impulses to mainstream filmmaking, reflected in a body of late 1960s/early 1970s works that included *Bonnie and Clyde* (Penn), *The Graduate* (Nichols), *The Godfather* (Coppola), *American Graffiti* (Lucas), *One Flew over the Cuckoo's Nest* (Forman), *2001: A Space Odyssey* (Kubrick), *Nashville* (Altman), *Taxi Driver* (Scorsese), *Annie Hall* (Allen), and *Coming Home* (Ashby). Even at the peak of this cinematic revolution, however, directors won acclaim only when their films (like those just mentioned) made big money at the box office. Filmmakers were forced to mix aesthetic and commercial objectives while they protested against infringements on their autonomy, as in many cases where producers dictated significant cuts in the final version. In reality, of course, compromises were imposed all along the way, from script development to endless technical and shooting decisions to the all-important process of editing. Even at this high point of directorial power, the "author" theory made sense only to a limited degree, depending on the amount of independent financing available (an issue that became more salient in the 1980s as costs escalated). Whereas more strictly "indie" filmmakers like Cassavetes or documentary producers like Barbara Kopple could retain auteur status by refusing to yield to commercial pressures, no such option was available to more established directors hoping to win over mass audiences. The very decision to remain at least partly within studio production and distribution networks imposed sharp limits on cinematic "authors," but this was a price major directors were nearly always willing to pay.

The declining role and influence of the original stratum of New Hollywood auteurs by the early 1980s occurred just as large-scale studio power was being reconsolidated.[36] Corporate domination reached new heights during the 1990s, although this development in itself did not signify the eclipse of auteurial creativity or semiautonomy. For one thing, the growth of corporate power coincided with strong *countervailing* trends in the form of product diversification, resource dispersion, and expanded local centers of innovation and creativity resulting from efforts of culture industry giants to solidify their footholds within a competitive globalized economy. It follows that many directors could, and did, work successfully within this setup during the 1980s and 1990s, as shown by the thriving careers of Allen, Stone, Lee, Sayles, Altman, the Coen brothers, Levinson, Burton, and Waters. We suggest that the combined artistic and commercial success of these filmmakers endows them with the aura of (postmodern) critical public intellectuals—a rare status in twentieth-century American culture. Yet if the auteur perspective continues to have validity (and we believe it does), the classical understanding of this concept needs to be jettisoned in favor of a more "balanced" approach taking into account the complexities of postmodern culture. Several factors enter into this more attenuated view of the director, most of them resulting from the postmodern shift: the "networked" character of collaboration made possible by the information revolution and hyperspecialization of professional work, pluralization of markets allowing for creative independence to be more easily absorbed within the corporate system, erosion of "master discourses" undercutting architectonic designs of any single creative figure, and the impact of post-1960s multiculturalism, "local knowledge," a more open and diversified workplace, and social fragmentation. Gallant efforts to resist these postmodernizing trends—visible in such grandiose projects as Coppola's *Apocalypse Now* (1979)—turn out to be exceptions to the general trajectory. Elevated auteur status is retained by only a few directors actively involved in production and other phases of moviemaking or by purely indie directors like Nicolas Roeg and Peter Greenaway, satisfied to remain fully outside the scope of mass recognition. It has become increasingly difficult for filmmakers in Hollywood (and elsewhere) to mobilize the vast financial, technical, and human resources required for ambitious cinematic visions.

As filmmaking becomes even more integrative and collaborative than in the classic studio period, efforts to pinpoint multiple sources of creativity will be correspondingly difficult. While "authorship" is still usually attributed to the director, the role of performers, writers, cinematographers, music directors, editors, and even technicians—not to mention producers—is becoming more and more recognized. As always, the director confronts the onerous task of unifying tremendously diverse inputs, but here too the contribution of producers often turns out to be decisive, especially where large budgets and expansive set locations or technical requirements come into play (as with action pictures and blockbusters). While producers may yield significant artistic control to directors, writers, and others, they only rarely give carte blanche to the creative side as long as important financial and/or narrative issues are at stake. Producers and studio executives will minimally insist on control over such crucial areas as budgeting and the final cut, generally fearful that either style or content will stray too far from established conventions—the type of restraints satirized in Altman's *The Player* (1991). Of course, producers' interests lie in generating the best rate of return on what is usually a large investment, and this remains just as true in the postmodern era as before. Such pressures enforcing artistic conformity are reduced, however, where the director is involved as a producer or is able to find sufficient independent resources.

Since the 1970s, a number of well-known film directors (including some within the "postmodern" orbit) have achieved renown as celebrities who occupy a special niche in the cultural, social, and sometimes political life of the country; their scope of recognition goes well beyond the world of film itself. Any list of such influential filmmakers would surely include Woody Allen, Oliver Stone, Martin Scorsese, Francis Ford Coppola, Robert Altman, Steven Spielberg, George Lucas, Spike Lee, and the late Stanley Kubrick. In his classic essay "What Is an Author?" Michel Foucault argues that efforts to interrogate the author's role in society must refer precisely to "how the author was individualized in a culture such as ours, the status we have given the author . . . [and] the system of valorization in which he was included; or the moment when stories of heroes gave way to the author's biography."[37] With this conceptualization in mind, we can place the evolution of American filmmaking, including its directorial functions, within the historical context of postmodern cinema—a context that, as we have seen, simultaneously *elevates* and *diminishes* the status of auteur. Our gaze is placed not only on the director's integrative and creative role but also on his or her relationship to mass audiences and, by extension, to the broader social environment. This is yet another way of reformulating the classic auteur theory to meet shifting conditions of postmodern cinema.

If the notion of total auteurial mastery seems rather overstated today, so too does the familiar concept of film *genre* that still appears in most texts and commentaries on Hollywood film. The idea of genre suggests a mode of looking at films based on vital shared characteristics: subject matter, plot, social themes, visual techniques, directorial style, and so forth. The narrative structure takes on particular meaning here, following along such lines as melodrama (sci-fi, Westerns, thrillers, action, youth rebellion, and historical dramas) and comedy (slapstick, romantic, satirical, and black comedy). Stories told within the framework of particular genres or subgenres can be viewed at one level as cinematic reconstructions of ancient myths of the sort found, for example, in the familiar saga of heroes faced with tremendous obstacles who ultimately win redemption by slaying dragons or rescuing helpless damsels in terrible distress. Insofar as modernist cinema especially depends so much on rearticulation of these myths, we can conclude that films will typically reveal much insight into the values, beliefs, and rituals of the society in which they are produced.[38] Narratives built around heroic exploits of protagonists up against seemingly hopeless odds are perfectly suited to any number of mythological interpretations—and of course this is the stuff of modernist cinema. Here the concept of film genre reaches a considerably high degree of narrative and possibly also social unity that so often endows cinema with its powerful emotional meaning and appeal. At the same time, the stylization often accompanying genre productions has usually functioned to establish distance between viewer and subject matter.

While genre distinctions may have been useful through the 1960s, when studios produced films under factory conditions according to clearly identifiable formulas and codes, the usefulness of such distinctions begins to evaporate once we enter the more amorphous domain of postmodern cinema. If some easily recognizable categories (action films, docudramas, romantic comedies, and horror movies) still resonate in the minds of both industry producers and movie viewers, today we can see a profound trend toward the *breaking down* of cinematic distinctions and labels that once seemed rather airtight. Since the 1970s, both Hollywood and indie films have increasingly resisted facile labeling, often cutting across established genres to combine aesthetic and narrative elements of more than one film "type." How do we categorize a film like Ridley Scott's *Thelma and Louise*? A straightforward drama? A thriller? A feminist road movie? Or Altman's *The Player*? A drama? A comedy? A thriller? A critique of the studio system? The answer of course is that the films in question fit all these categories and more. The same could be said of *Casino*, *JFK*, *Do the Right Thing*, *Hannah and Her Sisters*, *Chinatown*, and *Pulp Fiction*, to mention just a few, since they resist singular definitions appropriate to modernist cinema in which narratives and themes are more tightly structured, more coherent, more linear. Even the once readily identifiable gangster picture has been muddied by films like *Married to the Mob*, *Bugsy*, *Miller's Crossing*, *Analyze This*, and the previously mentioned *Casino*. The entire art and technique of postmodern filmmaking throws into question categorical, fixed, totalizing labels insofar as neither the narrative nor social thematics is moved forward by any sort of particular formula or truth-seeking epistemology. As Gary Crowdus observes, we find today a "masterly blend of film genres which playfully and self-reflexively mirrors the conventions of the industry while at the same time parodying them."[39] The visual images, moreover, are frequently rapid, juxtaposed, fleeting, disconnected, and refracted—a style hardly conducive to formulaic genres. Hardly anything in the world of cinema, including the role of director and narrative flow, can be regarded as fixed or coherent today as it was in the past. The very architectonics of the cinematic enterprise has, for better or worse, been thoroughly reconfigured as part of the postmodern cultural turn.

Following this line of argumentation, it is easy to see that the traditional demarcation between "realist" and "formalist" canons loosely employed by both film scholars and critics needs to be revisited. This separation revolved around a certain polarity of cinematic schemes, with its simple opposition between efforts to capture or "represent" reality on screen and attempts to convey a realm defined by visual and technical illusions. Even at the height of the classic period, motion pictures generally combined elements of *both* realism and formalism because the medium itself demanded perpetual juxtaposition of images, sounds, and technical effects, so that depictions of "reality" and forays into symbolic impressions coexisted to one degree or another within the unfolding mise-en-scène. Leaving aside such fare as newsreel-style documentaries, we can say that strong components of realism and formalism tend to merge within the broad ensemble of visual representations. It might be argued that formalism constitutes a much needed embellishment of even the most starkly "realist" enterprises as it provides added emotional depth and visual power on screen. As can be detected in such films as *JFK* and *The Milagro Beanfield War*, historical experience depicted through cinema can be expertly magnified by forays into the illusionary, mystical, or spectacular. At the other end, distinctly postmodern fare (*Zelig* provides a good example) does in fact confront history but in manifestly ironic fashion, with irony serving as a vehicle of reflection and satire.[40] If we closely revisit conventional genres—Westerns, combat movies, film noir, historical epics, and sci-fi adventures—we see a complex interweaving of realist and formalist elements where each operates to supplement and reinforce the other. While the notion of purely realist or formalist filmmaking was probably always mistaken, such a distinction has even less currency today given the manner in which postmodernism subverts the very quest for undistilled truth, knowledge, and "reality."

Since the late 1960s, many film scholars and even a few critics have gravitated toward semiotics as a methodology promising to help unravel the deep, underlying meaning of cinematic projects. Grounded in the structural linguistics of Ferdinand de Saussure, which holds that artistic motifs, symbols, and signs require systematic analysis, Christian Metz and other disciples of semiotics argue that films constitute special "texts" with their own distinct "language" or discourse embracing both visual and aural elements.[41] Introduced as a literary theoretical tool, semiotics calls attention to the playing out of disparate cinematic "codes"—articulated, for example, through narratives or storytelling—that inform a filmmaker's attempt to present a story, embellish its motifs and symbols, and build toward a literary and thematic denouement. Some codes depart from or subvert established norms of thought and action, while others reproduce elements of "common sense"—part of the dominant system of beliefs, or what Antonio Gramsci called "ideological hegemony."[42] At this juncture, the main objective of film analysis is considered to be the deciphering of linguistic or discursive logic underlying both cinematic style and content. All films possess various, typically multiple, "deep structures" of meaning—oppositional, rebellious, conformist, repressive, redemptive, and so forth. Distilling specific linguistic patterns or codes within cinematic discourse can therefore be useful in theorizing and unraveling these deep structures. At the same time, linguistics—a highly abstract and not always precise methodology—can take us only so far and in fact can easily obscure more than it illuminates. As Dudley Andrew suggests, there can be no distinct "grammar of cinema" given its reliance on images. He writes that "the common meaning of a cinematic signifier can be only determined by the context which not only modifies the sign but instructs us to read it at such and such a level."[43] Its utility is more noticeably flawed in the realm of postmodern cinema where marriage of the commodity, technology, and hyperreal media culture can overwhelm even the most intricate exercises in discursive analysis. Semiotics assumes a readily decipherable, structured, coherent framework, but this can hardly be taken for granted when it comes to a wide range of contemporary filmmaking. Nor can discursive analysis itself be compelling where it is not grounded in concrete historical and social processes. No doubt various methods can help uncover certain "deep structures" of meaning, but films like *Stardust Memories*, *Blade Runner*, *Pulp Fiction*, and *JFK* will be inhospitable to strictly semiotic or structuralist interpretations. The enormously complex structure of most films, incorporating a shifting balance between storytelling and style or technique, renders them far too elusive for any single theoretical framework to fully "deconstruct."

The postmodern assault on entrenched traditions and discourses calls forth a thorough reconsideration of modernist theories and concepts—in film as in other regions of social and cultural life. Defenders of the modernist faith, whether in politics or aesthetics, are forced onto an ever narrowing terrain as transformative optimism growing out of the Enlightenment gives way to sharpening conflicts, fissures, and challenges not likely to soon disappear. The age of postmodern cinema, though hardly monolithic or even dominant in its own right, is marked by novelty in part because of vast economic, technological, and international changes. To thoroughly grasp this phenomenon, we need more than an analysis of "texts," "codes," and "signs" that, in semiotic theory, so frequently appear detached from the all-important flow of historical conditions and events. Further adding to this predicament is the fact that postmodernism cannot be said to constitute a unified philosophical or cultural alternative to modernism since the very tenets of postmodernism inevitably undermine any such coherence: local knowledge, decentered universe of meaning, multiperspectival outlook, rejection of master discourses, and so forth.

Modernism in the sphere of art both reflects and transcends the broader legacy of modernity tied to industrialism, technology, urban life, and bureaucratic structure—a legacy elaborated by classical social and political theorists over the several decades between 1850 and 1930. Cultural modernism first embraced and then began to question the power of the commodity and, to a lesser extent, the role of science and technology. But it is also true that modernity entered into daily life through the goods, artifacts, and processes of consumer society—the system of mass production, a large mainstream audience, and dynamic modes of technological reproduction—all destined to strongly impact media culture. Yet these same rationalizing forces soon developed to the point of near implosion, generating *countertrends* favoring discourses of fragmentation, localism, and diversity. Seen from the extreme fringes of postmodernism, these new conditions gave rise to a historical paradigm of novelty and difference suggesting new categories of analysis along lines initially framed by Guy Debord, Marshall McLuhan, Baudrillard, Foucault, and (more recently) Fredric Jameson. If historical novelty is associated with far-reaching cultural change, there can be no turning back to simpler unmediated discourses of modernism that, in film, recalls the Hollywood studio system and the work of classic auteurs like Griffith, Ford, Hawks, Capra, and Kazan.[44] Deep sociohistorical transformations are bound sooner or later to generate a series of changes in aesthetics and culture. With post-Fordist capitalism, we have an increasingly commodified aesthetics that goes hand in hand with the expansion of media culture, which in turn expresses the dynamics of corporate colonization throughout the larger society. As for postmodern cinema, it appears today as a truly conflicted form unable to transcend its own historical immediacy. As Christopher Sharrett writes, "The cinema of postmodernity suggests a society no longer able to believe fully its received myths (the law of the father, the essential goodness of capitalism, the state, religious authority, the family). Yet it is also unable to break with these myths in favor of a historical materialist view of reality."[45]

MASS AUDIENCE AND MEDIA CULTURE

The full expansion of media culture in the United States has its origins in the post–World War II era, when rapid technological change gave rise to a sophisticated communications apparatus destined to impact all forms of artistic life. Although the culture industry was critically deconstructed as early as the 1930s by Frankfurt school theorists Walter Benjamin, Max Horkheimer, and Theodor Adorno,[46] in actuality a more developed and sophisticated media system did not appear until the maturation of television, until a much wider variety of "cultural" products began to dominate the social landscape. Since the 1950s, American society has experienced a multitude of technological novelties: big-screen television, cable and satellite television, video recorders, multimedia consumer products of every sort, and more recently the Internet with its unlimited online entertainment possibilities. Within this panoply of consumer items and aesthetic outlets, film culture too evolved and matured over a period of several decades, greatly extending both the quality of its product and the scope of its audience.

Media culture has evolved into a full-scale commodified system of production and distribution in which virtually everything is done for profit by giant corporations seeking mass audiences and expanded market shares. It is a culture saturated with the steady flow of images, sounds, and spectacles, where relatively passive consumers are routinely bombarded with media transmissions. Identities, loyalties, and leisurely preferences are shaped by hegemonic values—increasingly reproduced through media culture—to a degree rarely imagined in human history. Owners and managers of media conglomerates like Disney, Time-Warner, Sony, and Viacom, obsessed with reaching large audiences in highly competitive markets, strive to avoid offending significant constituencies that, in the end, could erode their market standing. The predictable result is an overwhelmingly formulaic, conformist industry that has become ideologically sanitized, sensing it must deflect "political" or socially aware concerns altogether. But this is only part of the story: As Ritzer argues, the spread of media culture—of mass consumption in general—serves to "reenchant," to make more humanly comfortable, an everyday social existence that is otherwise cold, rationalized, and bureaucratic. Reenchantment enables the system to open itself up to novelty, leisure, entertainment, experimentation, and even new kinds of eroticism at precisely the moment when commodity production (and specifically media culture) intensifies its hold over an increasingly passive and cynical citizenry.[47] At the same time, reenchantment forces the capitalist market to open itself up to powerful new influences and pressures, including diversification. As Kellner points out, "Precisely the need to sell their artifacts means that the products of the culture industries must resonate to social experience, must attract large audiences, and must thus offer attractive products which may shock, break with conventions, contain social critique, or articulate current ideas that may be the product of progressive social movements."[48] This duality lies at the very heart of postmodern cinema.

It is this very duality that helps explain why, at a time of intensified corporate colonization of social and cultural life, the film industry has been able to nourish emergent (including postmodern) countertrends against established traditions and codes, suggesting how media culture can be understood as something of a contested terrain. Many risk-taking producers, directors, writers, and actors have sufficient autonomy to push their own agendas that, in some cases, run up against bottom-line priorities of the megacorporations. It is hardly surprising today to see films with subversive or radical content produced and/or distributed within the Hollywood studio structure: *Malcolm X*, *The Player*, *JFK*, *Bulworth*, *Norma Rae*, *The Milagro Beanfield War*, *The Insider*, and *Erin Brockovich*, to name only a few. In the face of unprecedented corporate media power, postmodern cinema breaks with simple formulas and genres, adopting a decidedly mixed orientation toward film as commodity. This shift, however, falls short of any genuine assault on corporate domination or market imperatives—impossible within the existing setup in any case. The point here is that a film culture appealing to larger, more diversified audiences and possessing a strong variety of artistic impulses manages to coexist with corporate priorities, as in the case of book and music production. The postmodern shift illuminates a system of film production shaped more by a wide base of consumerism than by a tightly administered managerial structure, a reality that clashes with audience-manipulation/propaganda models of the culture industry.

Media culture embraces the main features of liberal-capitalist order: hierarchy mixed with extreme individualism, commodification fused with diversity, and urban industrialism combined with growing social atomization and psychological alienation. Representations of decay, violence, and turbulence endemic to Hobbesian disorder are conveyed through every media form—television, music, graphic arts, theater, and perhaps most of all film. While modernity is shrouded in such myths as individual heroism, worship of technology, democratic citizenship, and national redemption, cultural modernism has yielded to a "post" ethos questioning most everything before it, consistent with the darker impulses of anti-Enlightenment ideology. In cases where critique of the status quo is given clear expression, such critique may be attenuated through depictions of rampant egoism, pessimism, or nihilism. Trapped in the social immediacy of the present, images attached to media culture tend to eviscerate a collective sense of both past and future. A culture thriving on fabricated images and sounds detached from *historical* context and meaning, it subverts a deeper understanding of social patterns as they unfold over time. Whether the cinematic moment is *Star Wars* or *The Truman Show* or *Titanic* or *Pearl Harbor*, all attention is riveted on the momentary, fleeting, and spectacular even where possibly intended social content is somewhere assimilated into the whole. Personalities, melodramatic scenes, surface images, outlandish actions, and technical flourishes easily crowd out historical narrative, whatever the purported ideological substance. The much celebrated information revolution ends up short-circuited by the colonizing power of all-consuming images intrinsic to contemporary media culture—and to much of what we refer to as postmodern cinema.

Film enters into and reproduces media culture, with the cinematic enterprise now established as a dramatic, visual, and technological medium increasingly oriented toward marked *rapidity* of shot sequences, hyperimage manipulation, and highly innovative montage constructions playing on viewers' sensory impulses. In some ways, of course, this dynamic is an inherent part of cinema itself, visible from the earliest Hollywood classics, but has now achieved its fullest expression with the flourishing of postmodern cinema. Each modality of postmodern filmmaking we identify here—blockbuster spectacle, existential morass, historical impasse, Hobbesian chaos, and ludic playfulness—finds its expression in one dimension or another of media culture. Yet media culture also involves an objectification process reinforcing audience passivity with cultural experience shaped by and through the commodity, geared to receptive consumers, thus inevitably undercutting audience sense of engagement. Viewed from this perspective, media culture and postmodern cinema are twin expressions, indelible signs of a deteriorating public sphere in which popular involvement (democratic participation in its myriad forms) winds up more subverted than bolstered. The progressive side of economic and technological change is strongly countered by a darker, mordant side that (implicitly) rejects any historical mission grounded in universal values and goals.

Along these lines, Baudrillard has theorized that historical events and experiences are now transformed into hyperreal spectacles by the mass media and culture industry, blurring the distinction between fact and fiction, reality and perception, and subject and object to the extent where all conceptual boundaries disappear. Following Debord's *Society of the Spectacle*, Baudrillard's work approximates and underlines what today is understood as "postmodern" in both politics and culture. With his monolithic view of media culture, Baudrillard offers insights into an American cultural scene that he locates squarely within commodity production.[49] Events like the Persian Gulf War, the O. J. Simpson trials, the Unabomber saga, the White House sex scandal, Election 2000, and the 2003 U.S. war on Iraq are immediately translated into protracted media carnivals and spectacles. Less obvious, however, is the growing intrusion of hyperreal "events" into both filmmaking and film viewing, which turns out to be another way of conceptualizing the postmodern shift. A number of critically acclaimed films since the 1970s have appropriated the power of spectacle as one expression of all-consuming images: *Being There*, *The Player*, *Network*, *Zelig*, *Bob Roberts*, *The Truman Show*, and *Wag the Dog*, among others. Less transparent representations of the hyperreal can be found in films such as *Taxi Driver*, *Chinatown*, *Apocalypse Now*, and *Bulworth*.

This spectacular element of postmodern cinema becomes all the more intelligible when considering the industry's perpetual drive to capture larger, more specialized, more culturally diverse audiences. The interests and proclivities of film producers and audiences alike have changed dramatically in the wake of altered historical circumstances; we need only compare the decades of the 1930s, 1970s, and 1990s, stylistically and thematically, to capture something of this immense cultural transformation. Of course, film *viewing* has become more and more integral to the individual socialization process, testifying to the vast influence of media culture as it competes with and sometimes overtakes familiar vehicles of socialization: family, peer groups, educational context, work, government institutions, and the legal system. Starting with early childhood, people assimilate norms of patriotic loyalty, heroism, violence, sexuality, and everyday language through the seemingly omnipresent world of cinema, ambiguous or conflicted as such norms might be. Within the postmodern shift, as we have seen, film images are often murky or disjointed because styles, themes, and social roles now lack the coherence that had previously characterized modernism.

As media culture reproduces and extends the hyperreal, individuals can be expected to form attachments to big-screen images, indicating that the cinematic experience can have a unique socializing power that, unfortunately, is not yet fully understood. Jacques Lacan's famous "mirror stage" of personal development—according to which children learn to differentiate character development by viewing the self as if reflected through a mirror, with the self in effect contemplating the "self"—is suggestive here. Lacan's focus was mainly on early childhood socialization, but his "reflection" metaphor has relevance to later development stages, applicable to the molding of consciousness that occurs largely *outside* family and kinship systems. From this standpoint, media culture can be seen as providing a kind of mirror of the self, constituting an assemblage of "mirrors" where audiences reflect back on their purportedly "real" selves and experiences while vicariously identifying with any number of fictional or imagined "selves." The (potential) result is a complex process of psychological transformation that today, in many cases, can be traced to influences within postmodern cinema, as conventional formulas, narratives, motifs, and roles give way to a more diffuse, fragmented, and rapid flow of images. If famous "action heroes" like Arnold Schwarzenegger, Chuck Norris, Sylvester Stallone, Bruce Willis, and Jackie Chan represent an up-to-date incarnation of John Wayne or Errol Flynn (in classic Western and combat roles), the postmodern embrace of dispersed, atomized selves with its profound confusion of social roles and narrative themes takes on new meaning in postmodern cinema.

THE COMMODITY MEETS THE SPECTACLE

The past few decades have witnessed stupendous growth in what Ritzer calls the "new means of consumption"—mass consumerism, advertising, credit purchasing, and leisure pursuits—much of it defined through and shaped by the culture industry.[50] The expanded realm of consumption includes shopping malls, Disneyland-style theme parks, casinos, cruise ships, special tourist attractions including glitzy museums, and giant entertainment meccas like Las Vegas, Atlantic City, Disneyworld, and Universal City. Ritzer argues that such hyperconsumption, available to broadening sectors of the population, works to soften the cold, bureaucratic, rationalizing features of advanced capitalist production and work, "reenchanting" an economic system that people otherwise experience as harsh, boring, and alienating. Post-Fordist capitalism becomes more comfortable for people who have the resources to consume, who have means to enter the gratifying cathedrals of consumption. Ritzer's analysis, however, should be augmented by recognition of the role of media culture in which the commodity and the spectacle converge with seeming fluidity: Consumerism and the hyperreal reinforce each other in a society where simulations and visual images transmitted through television, music, the Internet, and film increasingly shape and reshape the cultural terrain. Postmodern cinema has built a dynamic relationship with the new modes of consumption, where it contributes to reenchantment of a mass public longing for identity, purpose, and engagement—a reenchantment that, however, turns out to be illusory in many ways.

The "softening" of post-Fordist capitalism is accompanied through a powerful shift in the system linking economics and culture, production and everyday life, and material relations and the hyperreal that is now framed mainly by and within popular media and the culture industry. Ronald Inglehart understands this shift as one favoring "postmaterialist" concerns of lifestyle, leisure, and entertainment, that is, favoring quality-of-life over economic priorities connected to work, income levels, and the mere circumstances of survival.[51] While the familiar "modern" syndrome of growth, productivity, efficiency, and technological innovation continues into the present, it is complemented—in some cases superseded—by "postmodern" themes of diversity, creativity, and autonomy that Inglehart sees, correctly we believe, as the logical outgrowth of mature industrialism. Viewed from this angle, postmodern values gained momentum with the development of 1960s radicalism, the counterculture, and later new social movements like feminism and ecology—values that were also central to the New Hollywood ferment of the 1970s.[52]

Media culture rides the crest of large-scale transformations within capitalist industrialism that have no doubt reached their most mature expression in the United States. At this historical juncture, the commodified spectacle, as Debord well knew, has come to represent a major focal point of social and institutional change, helping to reproduce and strengthen hegemonic forms of cultural and political life.[53] The spectacle merges with postmodern cinema as it celebrates the visual, ephemeral, and illusionary, carried forward at the level of surface images through "its very monopolization of the realm of appearances."[54] In Debord's view, the spectacle becomes overpowering because of its organic linkage to mass consumption: "The spectacle corresponds to the historical moment at which the commodity completes its colonization of social life."[55] Yet if media culture reflects a universe of apparent integration, it is nonetheless grounded in an economic system fostering social dislocation and personal alienation, with everyday life colonized by the omnipresent commodity. Thus, "the spectacle's function in society is the concrete manifestation of isolation."[56] Media culture erases the ostensible dividing line between self and society, between self and the spectacle in a world where, as we have seen, stark opposition between true and false, real and unreal, and fact and illusion vanishes into the night.[57]

Following Debord, Baudrillard locates the spheres of media and mass consumption as generalized sources of identity and "engagement" within the public realm; the proliferation of strong but elusive images and symbols typical of postmodern culture helps undermine citizen participation as media-driven images end up confused with real-life experiences. The expansion of media culture and consumerism turns back on itself as it engulfs new realms of social life. The marriage of technology, media, and commodity amounts to the ultimate triumph of form over content, style over substance, deepening and even transcending what McLuhan anticipated in his groundbreaking media theorizing of the 1950s. If Debord and Baudrillard exaggerate this historic trend, the attention they devote to the fusion of media culture with commodity production does help us unlock the origins and consequences of postmodern cinema beginning in the 1970s. With our gaze focused on the simulated environment, we can begin to grasp some of the powerfully hegemonic, yet in many ways destabilizing, forces within the popular culture. Here it is possible to see how the information revolution unfolds on two levels, de-differentiating or dissolving old boundaries while at the same time colonizing society as a whole.

It is here that Ritzer's emphasis on new cathedrals of consumption makes sense, for the postmodernity of simulations, images, and commodified culture runs against the rationalizing thrust of modernity outlined by such theorists as Comte, J. S. Mill, Marx, Durkheim, and Weber—a trend most visible in the realm of popular culture. Industrial, managerial, and political structures are the locus of comprehensive rationalizing processes that show no signs of diminishing any time soon. The commodified spectacle performs new hegemonic functions as its reenchanting features soften the impact of alienation and powerlessness, taking people into a magical, mysterious, dreamy, fantastic zone—the very stuff of Las Vegas, Disneyworld, the Super Bowl, and *Star Wars* blockbusters—where everyday "reality" loses its mundane clarity and harshness. In Ritzer's words, "If in the modern world everything seems pretty clear-cut, on the cusp of the postmodern world many things seem quite hazy. This is especially true in the realm of consumption. . . . Virtually every means of consumption is a simulated setting, or has simulated elements, or simulated people, or simulated products. Even those things that still seem real have an increasing number of unreal elements. As a result, it is no longer so clear what is real and what is unreal."[58]

As corporate power reconfigures popular culture through the media spectacle, social life and the public sphere are further weakened. Of course, postmodern culture does allow for limited autonomy insofar as conditions favoring aesthetic creativity and audience diversity are built into its very logic. Thus, while media culture surely helps reproduce a wide array of dominant structures and values, the familiar total-manipulation or one-dimensional model first introduced by Frankfurt School theorists is much too exaggerated for our purposes. Far from being monolithic, the cultural sphere (fully commodified as it is) must be understood as a contested terrain where corporate agendas and simulated messages can be, and frequently are, questioned, diverted, refracted, and sometimes even subverted. And postmodern cinema is today one of the best examples of such a contested terrain.

If boundaries separating the real and the illusory, fact and fiction, have been dissolved because of the enormous influence of media culture, then efforts to identify specific manifestations of "truth" and "knowledge" in the increasingly complex and shifting visual field become increasingly elusive. Postmodern cinema is part of an epistemological tendency holding that fundamental "reality" is difficult to locate independent of those discourses and symbols associated with media culture.[59] Tied to the all-consuming images of postmodernism, cinematic experience reinforces the phenomenon of the "voyeur," allowing for the popular mood of anxiety and impotence to be "overcome" by means of identification with particular images, icons, and figures. Cinematic realism associated with the capacity of filmmakers to unravel "essential structures of meaning" is undermined with the assistance of new technologies that nourish an opaque, simulated universe where, in Denzin's words, "the everyday is now defined by the cinematic. The two can no longer be separated. A single epistemological regime governs both fields. The hegemony of the camera's eye, with its fine-grained realism, elevates to new heights the visual gaze and the narrative text that contains and explains what is seen. Cinema not only created the spectator in its own eye; it created what the eye of the spectator would see. It then subjected that eye and its vision to the unrelenting criteria of realism and the realistic image of reality given in the camera's eye."[60] Here again, "knowing" is fully equated with a range of perceptions, generally arbitrary and tenuous, of visual representations within a highly articulated, variegated media culture.

Collapsing distinctions between simulated images and everyday realities are equated with dramatically changing forms of social interaction and civic participation that in themselves become increasingly refracted and illusory. What media culture can readily provide, of course, is a definite *sense* of individuals and collectivities being part of something larger: Social identities and consumer preferences pass through larger-than-life images that dominate the simulated environment. Much the same holds for perceptions of work, family, sexuality, politics, and violence as well as foreign or military policy. Feeling rather cut off and insignificant in a society obeisant to corporate and market priorities, sense of meaning and empowerment can often be obtained through a variety of fantasies and romanticized images like those reproduced through film and television. For better or worse, individuals may carve out "selves" framed by representations of media images of events, issues, and personalities—through exposure to the rich and famous, superstar athletes, rock personalities, television sit-com celebrities, and film stars who sometimes dwarf their cinematic vehicles.

These trends seem to be accelerating just as old Hollywood institutional patterns began to erode, solidifying the artistic and intellectual foundations of postmodern cinema. Through the byzantine structures of the culture industry, an emergent cinematic elite has been able to mobilize power and build status, carving out an embryonic legacy of narratives, images, and themes that are the hallmark of an experimental and original cinema, often inspired by deeply rebellious impulses. With cinematic influence on popular consciousness now outreaching anything previously imagined, and as every day becomes more saturated with media images and spectacles, filmmakers working in the loosely defined postmodern idiom hold views that are often sharply critical of both the Hollywood establishment and the larger structures of power. The common belief that Hollywood has in recent decades been a bastion of establishment or corporate ideology cannot be sustained in the face of so much evidence to the contrary, especially when we look at the (liberal or progressive) political orientation of most film directors today.[61] Since the 1970s, movie audiences have become younger, more affluent, better educated, more cinematically sophisticated, more attuned to new ideas and techniques, and more accustomed to a generation of actors famous for their nonconformist, "outlaw" roles (including Brando, Pacino, DeNiro, Beatty, Penn, Nicholson, Hoffman, and Jane and Peter Fonda). The vast majority of viewers have become familiar with a large body of films containing such themes as corruption, family breakdown, alienated sexuality, random violence, and social chaos, much of it informed by a hostility to corporations, government, law enforcement, the military, patriotism, family values, and religion. Yet such visceral antagonisms could go only so far: The bulk of innovation, change, and diversity inevitably wound up confined to the (always shifting) parameters of media culture and the commodity.

2

THE RISE AND DECLINE OF MODERNISM

Viewed along its broadest panorama, Hollywood filmmaking has evolved gradually from modernism to postmodernism, from a "national consensus" in support of definite social and aesthetic values to more dispersed, plural, and ambiguous modes of cultural expression. It is sometimes forgotten that American cinema, like other forms of popular culture, grew out of a largely pragmatic, business-oriented, instrumental tradition befitting the general contours of U.S. history.[1] Modernism was always grounded in optimistic, even somewhat messianic visions of human progress inspired by Enlightenment rationality that, in the United States more than elsewhere, has equated with economic growth, technological innovation, and strivings toward national grandeur. Norms of individualism, competition, hard work, material self-interest, and upward mobility (the Horatio Alger myth) were deeply embedded in modernity, which helped define the hegemonic artistic patterns of the time. While modernism readily affirmed a world of flux and transformation bound up with the "age of democratic revolution," this flux and transformation was generally thought to be part of a stable, orderly universe of social and political institutions. Attached to virtues of democracy, justice, and equality, modernism took shape within a process of capitalist rationalization that swept across the industrialized world. Through all this, the uneasy quest for truth and knowledge could follow different paths—left and right, socialist and liberal, progressive and conservative, secular and religious— depending of course on the ideological sensibilities brought to the enterprise. Yet a vital (national) commitment to particular ideals and interests remained firmly in place well into the 1960s.

THE TRADITIONAL HOLLYWOOD "CONSENSUS"

The guiding motif of American cinema from the 1920s through the 1960s (with some important exceptions) was typically modernist, reflected not only in the work of great auteurs but also in the legacy of the studio system built at the turn of the century. In the realm of film, modernism has developed according to a powerful narrative and thematic logic invoking its own distinct elements of style and technique. It upholds a "realism" embedded in a highly optimistic understanding of U.S. history with its attachment to ideals rooted in capitalist industrialism, liberal democracy, national identity, a pragmatic business culture, and fascination with strong heroes (usually white and male) struggling against overwhelming odds. Such heroes, depicted in films like *Stagecoach, Mr. Smith Goes to Washington, The Grapes of Wrath*, and *It's a Wonderful Life*, often carried forward values of individual redemption and social renewal. The product of dominant strains in American history but still influenced by European traditions and sensibilities, modernist filmmakers of the Hollywood golden age created works that resonated with mass audiences wanting to identify with protagonists who embodied virtues of hard work, resilient individualism, honesty, romance, and perhaps an abiding sense of personal and/or historical destiny. Overriding emphasis on the *self*—a hard-toiling, triumphant, redemptive self—loomed large among modernist producers and directors who, more often than not, were able to adapt to the confining parameters of the studio system.

While the ideological thrust of Hollywood cinema was on the whole conservative and conformist—confined to the liberal-capitalist paradigm—modernism as such cut across political boundaries; in fact, it could be readily adapted to Marxist, mainstream liberal, or indeed conservative discourses. Thus, the cinematic/social realism of such classic filmmakers as Eisenstein, Lang, Pudovkin, Renoir, Griffith, and even Chaplin can be viewed as "modernist" insofar as it sought to capture actual, living history on celluloid, hoping to grasp the social world in its totality. At its best, therefore, modernism gave visual and narrative expression to particular events, situations, and conflicts with an eye to influencing popular consciousness. We know that cinematic projects were not always informed by sharply defined ideological messages, especially in the United States, where oppositional politics and culture were for the most part weak, marginal, and delegitimated. In contrast to the rather conservative ethos of the studio system, European modernism was more uniformly leftist and Marxist, most strikingly visible in the classic Russian directors, the Italian neorealists (Visconti, De Sica, Rosselini, and Pasolini), and the later French New Wave (Godard, Truffaut, and Resnais).

Inspired by Enlightenment thinking, modernism in all its ideological incarnations advanced a cultural pursuit of truth, knowledge, reason, and progress that gave definition to images of historical transformation. Here the legacy of cinema verité would leave an enduring imprint on the work of later American filmmakers like Martin Ritt, Mike Nichols, Steven Spielberg, Oliver Stone, and John Sayles. If Hollywood modernism—associated mostly with Westerns, combat pictures, and historical dramas—adhered consistently to mainstream conventions, it did embrace an aesthetics that could be (indeed often was) appropriated by later progressive filmmakers highly critical of the studio system. If *Stagecoach*, *She Wore a Yellow Ribbon*, and similar Ford classics romanticized the westward push and frontier life among white settlers, then films like *Matewan* (Sayles), *Silkwood* (Nichols), *Norma Rae* (Ritt), *Salvador* (Stone), and *Milagro Beanfield War* (Redford) offered yet other, darker, and more critical images of American history—although ones that still held out prospects for individual heroism and redemption.

An enormous conduit of cinematic realism, the studio system produced hundreds of (usually low-budget) films yearly from the 1920s through the 1960s under what can only be described as the most bureaucratic, assembly-line conditions. As is well known, the network of major studios rapidly developed into a well-regulated oligopolistic structure: Paramount, MGM, Warner Brothers, Columbia, Universal, RKO, and Twentieth Century Fox. It was a rationalized system that evolved into a closed fortress of film production with rigid managerial structures, a quasi-factory system, the rationalization of most filmmaking operations, and the familiar obsession with market shares and profits. Studio chieftains wanted to bring the public formulaic, predictable, and socially conventional kinds of films: Westerns, thrillers, combat movies, comedies, musicals, and so forth. With few exceptions, these films were modernist in style, replete with linear narratives, standard photographic techniques, a tightly woven mise-en-scène, and social themes consistent with positive, often mythical views of the American experience. Even where the main characters did inhabit a corrupt environment and suffered grievous setbacks of one sort or another, the more overarching film motif celebrated a spirit of optimism and progress, looked to a hopeful (if nonetheless ill-defined) future, and assumed a stable but continuously evolving world. Whatever the genre or director, movie production veered toward what was safe and comfortable, what seemed most popular and marketable. Yet the system, always deeply embedded in the larger mainstream culture, relied on interesting scripts, innovative photography and other techniques, and of course directing (and editing) skillful enough to attract a critical mass of viewers in the United States and abroad. Everything came to fruition within an institutionalized studio empire that left filmmakers subservient to the dictates of managerial power; the very idea of European-style auteurs making independent "art films" within the American film industry seemed rather contradictory, at least through the 1960s. Creative autonomy would be hard to win at a time when the movie enterprise had become so integrated, so nearly monolithic—all in the service of a marketable commodity. Yet even at the height of the studio system, one could speak of innovative, experimental directors the likes of Ford, Hitchcock, Welles, Hawks, Lang, and Wilder, and these directors would surely leave their mark on the Hollywood legacy and beyond. As Schatz writes, the most ambitious and creative directors were able to work effectively (if sometimes tenuously) within the system,[2] but they had to battle for whatever independence they achieved, and of course it was these same directors who were among the first to break with modernist conventions.

Modernism and the studio system turned out to be a perfect fit: The authoritarian, tightfisted producers and executives preferred streamlined, economical scripts with linear narratives, straightforward photographic techniques, a well-regulated set, and a sense of managerial prudence. Studio chieftains, most of them Europeans, bought into the liberal-capitalist national consensus and mobilized their resources behind pictures that somehow embellished this consensus or at least did little to challenge it. Producers, always obsessed with market priorities, were naturally deeply involved in every aspect of the process—locating scripts, writing, directing, cinematography, editing, and even casting and acting. And their interests and sensibilities easily carried the day, with only rare exceptions. The stupendous growth of the American film industry through the 1930s and 1940s seemed to validate those formulaic principles laid down by the studio heads. By 1946, movie audiences reached a total of more than 100 million, there were 17,000 theaters across the nation, and the major film company profits soared (the bulk of it from successful low-budget B movies). The studios on the whole scarcely entertained the notion of making "artistic," "significant," or thematically cutting-edge pictures—despite such achievements as *Stagecoach*, *The Grapes of Wrath*, *Casablanca*, *Gone with the Wind*, *Citizen Kane*, and *Rebecca* just before or immediately after the start of World War II. Production units invested little creative energy in assembly-line items, and while directors, writers, and actors usually chafed under this structure, the larger viewing public seemed happy enough with the routine fare of low-grade Westerns, horror films, comedies, war pictures, and so forth. Through all this, the studios found little time or resources for offbeat scripts, novel techniques, or socially incisive themes.

The large Hollywood studios were founded by European Jewish immigrants who, excluded from the main avenues of economic and political power, looked to build a cultural empire that for many decades so deeply influenced American public consciousness that the population, over time, came to identify with the universe carved out by Hollywood mythmakers. As Neal Gabler writes in *An Empire of Their Own*, the studio heads—Adolph Zukor at Paramount, Carl Laemmle at Universal, Harry Cohn at Columbia, Louie B. Mayer at MGM, Harry and Jack Warner at Warner Brothers, and William Fox at Twentieth Century Fox—created a new magical place (Hollywood) that became the heart of the American Dream, forging and disseminating its values, myths, visions, and personal archetypes. Marginal in their social origins, Hollywood Jewish entrepreneurs were fiercely assimilationist, hoping to reinvent themselves consistent with the prevailing liberal-capitalist ideology while viewing the nascent film industry as a perfect mechanism of cultural integration and upward social mobility.[3] The studio oligarchs were joined by a whole generation of directors, writers, producers, executives, and exhibitors who, themselves also largely Jewish immigrants, contributed mightily to this dynamic of artistic and corporate architectonics.

Turning their back on a past filled with poverty, marginality, and oppression, they wound up with a "ferocious, even pathological embrace of America."[4] They sought a new language, new culture, and sometimes even a new religion along with a new country—part of their crusade to "cleanse and renew," which indeed came to pass in the several decades following the birth of Hollywood filmmaking around the turn of the century. Gabler writes, "While the Hollywood Jews were being assailed by know-nothings for conspiracy against traditional American values and the power structure that maintained them, they were in fact desperately embracing those values and working to enter the power structure."[5] In promulgating a cluster of engaging (but partially fictitious) images of American life that colonized the imagination of tens of millions of people, the studio chieftains "would fabricate their empire in the image of Americans as they would fabricate themselves in the image of prosperous Americans."[6]

As Gabler illustrates, the film industry offered relatively easy financial access to European Jews otherwise denied entry into the world of Wall Street banking and other regions of big business. Further, they seemed to be in touch with the popular mood and tastes of the time insofar as the vast (potential) moviegoing audiences were made up of workers and immigrants, most of whom also wanted to participate in the unfolding American Dream; in certain respects, the studio heads *were* the audience for this new medium of entertainment. Thus, it was relatively easy for these entrepreneurs to both understand public tastes *and* fashion cinematic representations of status and success appealing to that very same public. The result was a cultural modernism quite powerful in its national impact—a modernism that celebrated an often virulent patriotism, strong patriarchal family values, an ethos of cultural integration, and strivings for upward social mobility. Zukor, who had unwavering faith in the movies as a vehicle for reshaping popular consciousness, stated as early as 1908 his aspiration to make American film a legitimate form of art that could draw from literature, theater, graphic arts, and even the humanities. The better the quality of pictures, the more successful they would be in bringing dynamism to popular culture and meaning to public life in general. In the end, Zukor of course turned out to be decades ahead of his time, even if the pattern of cinematic modernism born in the early studio system was already set in motion. The fact that moviegoing was relatively inexpensive virtually guaranteed a widespread and deep national response that, predictably enough, became more intense at a time of patriotic mobilization during both world wars. The mythology of Hollywood eventually tapped into the diffuse American *Zeitgeist* that spanned nearly seven decades after 1900.

Yet the structure of Hollywood filmmaking was hardly monolithic: Cracks in the modernist edifice could be detected as early as World War II with the birth of film noir and then widened during the 1950s as the studio system began to enter into crisis. The infamous Hayes Code gradually lost its censorial hold, the big theater chains were broken up, and a new generation of directors flexed their independence vis-à-vis the old-line producers who wanted to hold on to the mainstream genres and formulas. Decline of the studio system was hastened by the growing popularity of television in the 1950s. The first stirrings of creative autonomy, though veiled and indirect, were visible in the huge output of suspenseful urban detective thrillers (later dubbed "film noir") of the 1940s and later. While these pictures were usually low-budget, quickly produced B-style fare, they did enlist the creative energies of directors, writers, and actors known for their independent or rebellious cast of mind. Their films addressed themes of dark intrigue, urban despair, and moral ambiguity, emphatically nonmodernist in aesthetic and social definition.

The first American director to gain (modernist) auteur status was D. W. Griffith, whose innovative and bold feature-length epics like *Birth of a Nation* (1915) and *Intolerance* (1916) set elevated artistic standards for the silent era. Griffith even today remains a cinematic icon despite the fact *Birth of a Nation* was an overtly racist film, since he laid down a good many rules and standards for directors toiling many decades later. Hitchcock, among others, was greatly impressed by Griffith's work, admitting that "like all directors, I was influenced by Griffith."[7] Yet Griffith inspired filmmakers as much through his own personal accomplishments in Hollywood as through his work itself: A self-made success, he rose from failed dramatic actor never really wanting to perform in cinema to the status of internationally acclaimed director and producer. In 1907, Griffith—out of work and desperate—found a low-paid job as a screen actor with pioneer director Edwin S. Porter. Later, he undertook a directing career with Biograph Studios, where he made several one-reel films weekly, paving the way toward later successes that included *Way Down East* (1920) along with the two previously mentioned films. Griffith's movies displayed a fresh inventiveness as well as some familiar elements of modernism: linear narrative, celebration of dominant American values, and a vibrant sense of historical progress. Even at this early juncture, modernity in popular culture could be seen as a powerful impulse toward human self-actualization, secured (if tenuously) in the face of all-pervasive mechanisms of social control and repression.

Another early modernist director was Ford, who, like Griffith, Hitchcock, Lang, and Chaplin, learned the art of filmmaking during the silent era. And like Griffith, he was able to present narratives with a highly visual flare since that was the only possible way to reach truly mass audiences. Ford came to Hollywood in 1913 and by 1917 was directing his first feature picture, *Straight Shooting*, followed in 1924 by *The Iron Horse*, a silent Western classic chronicling the long saga of the building of the transcontinental railroad. *The Iron Horse* constructs its narrative through a series of compelling visual images that depict harsh conditions of construction work, the constant presence of threatening Indian tribes, and epic scenes of steam engines threading the continent that became part of the historic westward push—a theme familiar to later Ford classics emphasizing freedom, spontaneity, and adventure within the frontier ethic. In classical modernist style, Ford re-created the historic period of the 1860s with unswerving devotion and painstaking accuracy. Shooting on location in the West, Ford worked tirelessly to control the activity of hundreds of actors and technicians—though predictably with mixed results.[8] The cast of *The Iron Horse* suffered frequent and extreme hardships, enduring harsh cold, biting insects, and wrenching demands of shooting on location. Railroad towns were built and then dismantled, only to be rebuilt at a new location down the line. Ford's well-known dedication to historical realism endowed this epic with an elaborate documentary feel not unlike later works of European cinema verité. Like Ford's later Westerns, this movie glorifies the frontier ethos that accompanied conquest of the West by white settlers.

In *Stagecoach*, the first truly classic Western, Ford broke cinematic precedent through his casting of a fascinating, slightly offbeat mix of characters aboard a stagecoach moving through hostile Indian territory. The personalities included a banker fleeing with $50,000 in stolen money, a gentlemanly card shark, a married pregnant woman, a prostitute, a drunken doctor, a traveling liquor salesman, and a young cattleman recently escaped from prison (played by John Wayne in his breakthrough role)—their bonding reinforced by the stagecoach's engagement with a band of Apache warriors led by Geronimo. As the wagon moves across Indian territory on a journey framed against Monument Valley's sandstone cliffs and pinnacles, the travelers quarrel, betray one another, and finally bond together as they confront a series of life-and-death situations. They ford deep rivers and traverse menacing terrain while managing, somehow, to sustain feelings of community. Their perpetual struggle with the elements and hostile Indians serves to temper their character, much in the fashion of past mythological characters. Along lines of *The Iron Horse*, Ford's *Stagecoach* upholds the ideal of a great "civilizing" mission that is to be carried out by Anglo-Saxon settlers in the name of freedom, progress, and adventure.

Yet while *Stagecoach* embraces a militantly colonialist stance toward the West, it nonetheless conveys a downbeat, ironic tone in its complex (but none-too-subtle) portrayal of the motley gathering of travelers. Like most other Ford movies, this work is a tribute to social realism with its meticulous devotion to historical detail. To an extent even more pronounced than *Stagecoach*, *The Grapes of Wrath* (1940) ranks as a leading modernist American film—an epic depiction of Dust Bowl migrants fighting starvation in California that still dazzles viewers with its endearing simplicity and realism. To give a heightened mood of social authenticity, Ford used actors without makeup, genuine migrant jalopies, real Dust Bowl settings, and original blues and folk music; with this backdrop, depiction of the Joad family's herculean struggle surely amounts to a landmark of cinematic realism. The Dust Bowl migration was shot from the vantage point of famous Route 66, the original pathway west conveying dynamic movement away from harsh material circumstances of the "East" toward an open-ended future of the "West," expected to bring a promise of new beginnings. In many ways, *Grapes* can be viewed as a distinctly American narrative grounded in the historical values of democracy and equality, though in social realist fashion the message that emerges is eminently *universal*. It contains a populist though hardly oppositional motif. Andrew Sinclair writes that "Ford and his colleagues took most of the radical politics out of [Steinbeck's] *The Grapes of Wrath* and made a universal film about how a poor family may yet survive through its qualities of courage and decency and love. Ford's new cameraman, Gregg Toland, used the documentary techniques of a Pare Lorentz or a Flaherty to capture the shabby eroded look of the land and its threadbare people, blown off the soil by dusters and drained by mortgages."[9]

Ford continued to produce one classic after another, including *Young Mr. Lincoln* (1939), *Tobacco Road* (1941), *How Green Was My Valley* (1941), *Fort Apache* (1948), *She Wore a Yellow Ribbon* (1950), *The Searchers* (1956), and *The Man Who Shot Liberty Valance* (1962). The bulk of Ford's impressive work, like that of contemporaries Capra, Hawks, and Kazan, for example, bore a uniquely American stamp of optimism linked to ideals of democratic citizenship, industrial development, and individual achievement. As Sam Girgus observes, such cinematic modernism was often motivated by sentiments of hope, renewal, and transformation that came to form the (dominant) national consensus of a populace oriented toward perpetual change, mirrored in part by the historic westward migration.[10] Modernist filmmakers captured a universalist outlook in which the main protagonists had an all-consuming mission: Wayne's epic Ringo Kid and Captain Nathan Britles, Stewart's Mr. Smith, Fonda's Abraham Lincoln and Tom Joad, William Holden's Golden Boy, and Spencer Tracy's Clarence Darrow. In the classic moviemaking of Ford, ideological "consensus" encompassed virtues of adventure, spontaneity, freedom, mobility, and the triumphant power of masculine heroes epitomized by the commanding persona of Wayne. Themes of religious devotion, patriotism, family values, hard work, and rugged individualism were frequently woven into a cinematic whole that, in the case of films like *Stagecoach*, *Fort Apache*, and *The Searchers*, succeeded for critics and mass audiences alike. More than other genres, the Western evoked romantic images of hope and renewal, of optimism and search for meaning in a world filled with dangers and obstacles. For Capra, this same modernism achieved its expression through what might be called cinematic populism—celebration of the ordinary person, hostility to powerful elites, and affirmation of the Alger myth of endless upward mobility. Much like Ford, Capra held firmly to the notion of democratic citizenship, which, though honored mainly in the abstract, had become so integral to the American Dream, visible in such pictures as *Mr. Smith Goes to Washington*, *It's a Wonderful Life*, and *A Hole in the Head*. For Kazan, this aesthetic took the form of modernist realism in which the heroic efforts of the dispossessed (working people) could transform the world, as in *A Streetcar Named Desire* (1951) and *On the Waterfront* (1954), where protagonists could become an agency of both individual and social rebirth, vital to what Girgus calls the "civic religion of democracy."[11] A dynamic component of the prevailing culture, film at the hand of such directors held out prospects for a dialectic of "renewal and consensus" where the forces of historical destiny were expected to triumph over corruption, evil, and any number of fearsome external circumstances; life turned out to be much like the boundless landscape of the Western where ultimately everything seemed possible. Commenting on *The Searchers*, Girgus writes that the protagonist "Ethan [Wayne] epitomizes modern man in his search for a vision of values and beliefs to give life direction and his world meaning."[12]

In the case of Ford, this mythology involved nothing less than the epic colonization of the West; for Capra, it was a populism rooted in faith that the common person would prevail over evil and corruption; and for Kazan, it was a more explicit identification with oppressed groups struggling to achieve the historic goals of freedom, democracy, and justice. What all shared in common was dedication to a cinema of modernist optimism with its euphoric view of America as the site of destiny and progress. Such white male heroes as Wayne, Cooper, Stewart, Fonda, and Brando emerged as perfect vehicles for this difficult cultural journey toward collective national redemption.

Many films of the studio era were produced and directed by (generally conservative) patriarchs deeply attached to mainstream American values of the sort reflected in findings of the famous Middletown sociological study conducted by Helen and Robert Lynd in 1938. The setting for this research project (and others like it) was a bedrock midwestern community carved out of the images of Norman Rockwell's America, replete with stable nuclear families, a strong work (or business) ethic, surface racial and social homogeneity, and a willingness to adopt the ethos of possessive individualism. Change, innovation, and dissent were always possible within such a provincial order, but only within parameters of a well-established national "consensus"; real deviation from this norm (political radicalism, atheism, homosexuality, and so forth) was incomprehensible.[13] Capra's time-honored film *It's a Wonderful Life*, set in the small New England village of Bedford Falls, simultaneously affirms and challenges this version of cinematic realism. Middletown values were, of course, accepted as a kind of benchmark for the American experience. Capra's hero George Bailey (James Stewart) devotes his childhood to figuring out just how to escape this parochial social life, hoping at some point to travel and experience a world beyond the boredom and conformity of Bedford Falls. Bailey challenges the very idea of normalcy driven into him while growing up, and for this he is quickly labeled a misfit and outsider. As a young boy, he boasts to Mary Hatch (Donna Reed) of his exotic travel plans, announcing that "I'm going out exploring some day, you watch, and I'm gonna have a couple of harems, maybe three or four wives.

Wait and see." As an adult, he later states, "Mary, I know what I'm gonna do tomorrow and the next day and next year and the year after that. I'm shaking the dust of this crummy little town off my feet and I'm gonna see the world. Italy, Greece, the Parthenon, the Coliseum." While Bailey is obviously a product of the American mainstream, these and similar utterances conflict with important parts of the dominant ideology while extending it in potentially subversive directions. Here, Capra begins to articulate two identifiable elements of modernism—belief in the status quo and its reconstruction in the form of populist critique.

Despite Bailey's restlessness and critical outlook, his persona ultimately meshes perfectly with the mainstream values and attitudes of Bedford Falls. In one scenario, he affirms a vital component of the American Dream—home ownership—as he opposes villain Henry Potter's attempt to block bank loans to working and poor people. Potter is shown as a familiar captain of industry, a rich and mean person who prefers ostentatious spending and conducts himself in the most imperious manner. Potter scorns the working class and belittles their jobs and lifestyle. Bailey responds that "this rabble you're talking about, they do most of the working and paying and living and dying in this community. Well, is it too much to have them work and pay and live and die in a couple of decent rooms and a bath?" A classic modernist film, *It's a Wonderful Life* reveals extreme differentiation and conflict within small-town America—calling into question facile definitions of national "consensus"—but the conflict is inevitably played out within the framework of prevailing liberal-capitalist values. When the movie opened in 1947, military personnel had just returned home from a protracted, devastating world war; millions of people had delayed getting married and raising a family, but once the war ended, they could hope to pursue these rewards of the American promise. In historical terms, home ownership had surely become both more desirable (and more feasible) for the average citizen. Lending institutions such as the Federal Housing Authority and the Veterans Administration were created to facilitate expanded housing demand. In Bedford Falls, it was none other than Bailey Building and Loan that was set up to provide loans for middle- and working-class families so they could build their own homes in accordance with the time-honored American ethic of property ownership. For all this to happen, however, Bailey would need to discard his nonconformist ways and become a model citizen. Though hindered by a bumbling yet sympathetic uncle, he finally succeeds, thanks to the massive assistance he receives from his large working-class following. He forgoes dreams of travel and adventure, remaining instead in Bedford Falls to get married, buy a house, and build a family.

Yet Bailey's scenario runs up against its own contradictions: He still harbors aspirations for a carefree, adventurous lifestyle and eventually has to confront the dreaded reality of business failure. With the impending loss of his savings and loan company, a desperate Bailey is shown getting ready to commit suicide by jumping off a bridge into a raging, frigid river. He is rescued by Clarence, an angel who throws himself into the river, forcing Baily to rescue him. When the two finally emerge from the water, Bailey discovers that Bedford Falls has been transformed into "Pottersville," a sleazy town filled with unhappy, cynical people—a world out of balance, now cut off from cherished Middletown-style values and lifestyles. Next we see Bailey's childhood friend Violet, now a prostitute, being dragged into a squad car. Working people in the town are no longer friendly but seem deeply alienated, having adopted a mean and harsh attitude. In the end, Bailey returns to the safe haven of conventional American values—a move that rescues him from a terrible nightmare. During this process of psychological conversion, he learns how to conform, realizing he would have to abandon his visions of carefree adventure in exchange for status and comfort within small-town America. In *It's a Wonderful Life*, Capra upholds the national ideal of both individual and social rebirth—a theme coinciding with Girgus's reference to a "civic religion of democracy"—but he simultaneously reveals some of the flaws and contradictions of that ideal. These same conflicted sensibilities, deeply rooted in American traditions, have indeed permeated other Hollywood genres, including a representative sampling of Western, gangster, combat, and thriller films.

The 1940s naturally witnessed a rise in popularity of combat pictures that included a variety of films with war-zone backdrops. The most notable of these was *Casablanca* (Curtiz, 1942), with its legendary cast (Bogart, Ingrid Bergman, Claude Rains, and Paul Henreid) whose turbulent lives centered around the now famous Rick's Café. This movie (surely a classic among classics) inaugurated a legacy of World War II films including *Thirty Seconds over Tokyo* (Mervyn LeRoy, 1944), *The Purple Heart* (1944), *Sands of Iwo Jima* (Allan Dwan, 1949), *From Here to Eternity* (Fred Zinnemann, 1953), *Paths of Glory* (Stanley Kubrick, 1957), and *The Longest Day* (Ken Anniken, 1962). Strongly modernist, celebratory fare of this sort extended to explicitly propagandistic films that received both financial and logistical support from the U.S. War Department—a practice that continues to this day. The department's "Why We Fight" series included seven "information films" about World War II cranked out by directors the caliber of Hawks, Ford, and Capra, whose contribution (*Prelude to War*) began with the declaration that "this film, the first of a series, has been prepared by the War Department to acquaint members of the Army with factual information as to the causes of the events leading up to our entry into the war and the principles for which we are fighting." Scored with martial music, the film opens with a close-up of the American flag and a quotation from Chief of Staff General George C. Marshall, followed by a group of soldiers marching to the tune of the Marine Corps hymn. A narrator asks the audience, "What are the causes [of the war]? Why are we fighting?" The answer soon follows with a list of nations invaded by Germany and a montage of footage from several war-torn countries, at which point the narrator asks, "Just what was it that made us change our way of living overnight? What turned our resources, our machines, our whole nation into one vast arsenal? What put us into uniform ready to engage the enemy on every continent, on every ocean?" To answer such leading questions, the film constructs elaborate imagery of a "free world." As for enemy forces, they are readily identified with the horrors of slavery and barbarism along with the seduction of demagogues like Mussolini, Hitler, and the war makers of Japan. Hitler's undeniable charismatic appeal to the German people, according to the narrator, had a certain powerful logic insofar as Germans have supposedly always had an "inborn natural love of regimentation and harsh discipline." Military enemies are associated with a stratum of wealthy and powerful industrialists. The narrator intones, "Yes, in these lands the people surrendered their liberties and threw away their human dignity." Worse, "they gave up their rights as individual human beings and became part of a mass, a human herd."

The Hollywood combat film—plentiful indeed over the years—stressed the familiar American dedication to patriotism, religion, family values, and the populist celebration of the ordinary citizen. As might be expected, the outlook was clearly Manichaeistic in its rigid demarcation between "allies" and "enemies," friends and scoundrels, and right and wrong, tied inexorably to a belief in American moral supremacy; some pictures (*Sands of Iwo Jima* and *Pork Chop Hill*) were outright xenophobic and racist in their projection of a demonized Other—a refrain commonly found in the Western. The vision of military heroism was strongly patriarchal, expressive of a culture that depicted women as either nurturing mothers or vulnerable sex objects, supportive wives and girlfriends or slutty prostitutes. Interestingly, however, while such virulent nationalism (and cultural modernism) infused combat movies about the two world wars and Korea, the portrait is dramatically altered once we come to the Vietnam War: With just a few exceptions, like *The Green Berets*, we find a far more critical, skeptical, pained, and in some ways "postmodern" perspective prevailed as the familiar demonizing images began to crumble.

Although war movies continued in popularity during the 1950s and later, they were soon matched and then superseded by sci-fi pictures that, while projected into a wildly imaginary future, echoed social themes familiar to both Western and combat genres. In the sci-fi canon, there emerged a similar bipolar thinking around obsession with foreign or "alien" demons bent on attacking a peaceful, ordinary, stable community—in this case, typically menacing invaders from another planet. Here we generally find one protagonist (a scientist or a doctor) who moves to alert authorities about impending danger, and of course those authorities are exceedingly skeptical at first. Thus, Jack Arnold's *It Came from Outer Space* (1953), Don Siegel's *Invasion of the Body Snatchers* (1956), and Steve Sekely's *Day of the Triffids* (1962)—all seemingly Cold War parables—serve to exemplify the pattern of alien menace met with cool establishment indifference. In Siegel's film, the invaders bear a striking resemblance to human beings, actually replicas of California small-town inhabitants. Dr. Miles Benell, the hero–physician (Kevin McCarthy), discovers a strange illness among his patients after returning from a medical convention. In the film's prologue, Dr. Benell warns, "Make them listen before it's too late." He then relates, via flashback, that he has unfortunately discovered that "something evil has taken possession of the town." An omnipresent evil manifests itself in the strange behavior of an increasingly large number of the town's citizens. A young boy, Jimmy Grimaldi, runs away from his mother in fear and horror, swearing the woman is not his mother and pleading with Dr. Bennell, "Don't let her get me!" A woman swears that her uncle, Ira, is not really the uncle but rather an imposter disguised as her uncle. When the doctor investigates, he winds up convinced that the man is the real Uncle Ira. Eventually, however, he learns that huge vegetable "pods" have been replacing nearly the entire city with aliens from a distant planet, but the aliens display no emotion except when pretending to be human. Uncle Ira's niece says, "But Miles, there ain't no emotion. None. Just the pretense of it. The words, gestures, tone of voice, everything else is the same, but not the feeling. Memories or not, he isn't my Uncle Ira."

As *The Invasion of the Body Snatchers* progresses, we discover that Dr. Bennell and his girlfriend are the only humans left in town, everyone else having been supplanted by alien replicants while they were sleeping. The replicants appeal to Dr. Bennell to join them, but he refuses. His instincts for self-preservation keep him from falling asleep and being replaced by a replicant, although Jack, the doctor's best friend and a holdout, finally falls victim to the aliens. Jack tells Dr. Bennell that "once you understand [being taken over by an alien] you'll be grateful." A psychologist (alien variety) explains that seeds drifting through space once took hold on Earth, creating pods with the power to reproduce any life form. He holds out the promise that, some time after falling asleep, the doctor will be "born into an untroubled world." In the end, Dr. Bennell rejects this frighteningly vacuous, emotionless world where inhabitants lack individuality and freedom, hoping to transform human life into a soulless, diabolical existence with machine-like features such as one might find in a mural by Jose Oroszco. It is this mission that renders the aliens a dire mortal threat.

During the Cold War, communism and Soviet power were viewed precisely in such alien, mechanistic, fearsome terms—the machinations of an omnipresent, diabolical enemy that would have to be fought and conquered if the virtues of freedom, democracy, and individuality were to be preserved. McCarthyism during the 1950s became simply the most extreme domestic incarnation of this bipolar, paranoid outlook, which ultimately did great harm to the filmmaking community. In the 1960s and later, a variety of other "alien" forces appeared as a threat to the national "consensus": beats, atheists, hippies, New Left radicals, gays, terrorists, drug traffickers, and so forth. These ostensibly subversive groups were castigated by many as godless, soulless, manipulative, un-American, and devoid of patriotic or even human loyalties. Relegated to a zone outside the established social order, they were viewed as innately treacherous and barbaric—in other words, fair game for all manner of political intimidation, investigation, blacklisting, and repression. Not only sci-fi movies but also detective pictures (including many in the classic noir vein) often presented villains as thinly disguised ideological enemies bent on ruthless, endless cycles of military violence and conquest. In many films, science itself was depicted as the villain, particularly if the science or technology dealt with nuclear power or space travel. In *Day of the Triffids*, the fearsome intrusion comes once again from outer space, as weird meteor showers blind millions of people while experimental plants mutate to become giant walking killers. The plants function like massive Venus's-flytraps, sucking their human victims dry. Popular insecurity over science and technology came from a number of sources: doomsday weapons, innovations of the period, the Cold War and the arms race, mounting environmental problems, and the unfathomably rapid pace of technological change itself. In any case, the appeal of sci-fi pictures evoking Soviet-style villains and scientific experiments gone berserk attests to the power of such concerns in the minds of both filmmakers and viewers.

As can be seen in the case of Western, combat, sci-fi, and a good many dramatic films, when Hollywood cinematic heroes embark on their fictional journeys, they sooner or later find themselves engaged in epic struggles over particular beliefs and values—even where such beliefs and values may be disguised or only peripherally implied. As we explore narratives, motifs, and themes of popular films, we find that beliefs and values in question usually pertain to significant historical forces at work within the public sphere; political content can be deflected or suppressed but cannot easily be avoided. This is true whether protagonists are depicted as romantic heroes seeking to reunite with their true loves, melodrama heroes attempting to rid the world of some pernicious threat, military saviors (*Patton*) fighting desperately to conquer a hated enemy, or frontier settlers moving west in their conquest of rugged terrain, horrible weather, and a stubborn, righteous native population. What was true of the Hollywood film industry through the 1950s and 1960s (with some noteworthy exceptions) was a complex, multifaceted modernism associated with a studio system rooted in mass production and mass consumption—a system where the commodity was interwoven with the obeisance to liberal-capitalist ideology as understood by studio chieftains at the time. Viewed from this perspective, modernism in filmmaking was shaped from the outset by Enlightenment rationality, an outlook that, with all its problems and challenges, remains seductive up to the present.

MODERNISM REVISITED

The gulf between the modern and postmodern, in cinema as elsewhere, has rarely been so total and systemic as to fully obscure what is often a considerable overlap between two points on a continuum; even the most radical New Hollywood ventures have roots in, and often go out of their way to pay respects to, film classics. The flourishing of postmodern styles since the 1970s has been far from monolithic despite its constantly growing influence. Moreover, new cultural trends often give rise to their very antithesis—in this case a more or less self-conscious return to modernism—visible even among those directors (Stone, Lee, Altman, and the Coen brothers) most frequently identified with the postmodern shift. So far we have focused on discrete aesthetic and social elements of modernism: a strong, usually victorious protagonist; a sense of historical progress; a coherent narrative structure with rather fixed definitions of work, politics, gender relations, nation, and so forth. Early modernist directors like Griffith, Ford, Capra, and Hawks generally valorized, to one degree or another, such historical ideals as individual freedom, democratic participation, community, patriotism, hard work, and upward social mobility. In some ways, these virtues transcended familiar left–right divisions, adhering as they did to one or another variant of Enlightenment rationality. The neomodernist filmmakers of the 1970s and beyond, including Spielberg, Nichols, Ritt, Stone, and Sayles, often returned to such themes but embellished them within a more technologically refined and cinematically ambitious framework.

It follows that, despite the cinematic postmodern upsurge, modernism persists as a seductive force in Hollywood filmmaking, grounded as before in the actual social experiences of human beings in this and previous eras. It embraces the force of historical mythology, offering a range of moral choices, real-life characters, resilient heroes, and enlightened social narratives. Films like *Silkwood* (1982), *Norma Rae* (1979), *Milagro Beanfield War* (1990), and *Matewan* (1990) furnish concrete representations of historical dramas, building on the sense of realism and citizen participation brought to the screen long ago by classic modernist auteurs. Yet significant differences are worth noting: In the present-day world, certain traditional beliefs and assumptions (tied to rugged individualism, romantic love, upward mobility, extreme patriotism, and so forth) have become increasingly difficult to sustain—in movies as in real life. This mounting crisis of national values, of the famous American "consensus," has generated a pervasive mood of cynicism calling into question Capra's simple faith in the ordinary person to take on adversity and create a better world. Such differences go to the very heart of the postmodern ethos. It might be argued that the American Dream, celebrated for so many decades within the Hollywood studio system, has been transformed into a nightmare that now seems an inescapable part of everyday life in the United States. Hence, the particular modernism that gets refashioned today has in fact been reshaped to engage vastly new psychological sensibilities as well as the incredible power of the media spectacle. An early injunction of cinematic modernism—resist unnecessary stylistic flourishes and artifices—has become impossibly difficult to follow at the turn of the twenty-first century.

Neomodernist films developed along three fundamental lines: blockbuster epics of Spielberg, such as *Jaws* (1975), *Close Encounters of the Third Kind* (1981), *E.T.* (1982), and *Jurassic Park* (1996); the Reagan-era tribute to masculine-hero dramas, such as the *Rocky* series, the *Rambo* series, and *Top Gun* (1986); and progressive change-oriented realist cinema, such as *Norma Rae* (1979), *Silkwood* (1983), *The Front* (1976), *Eight Men Out* (1987), and *Born on the Fourth of July* (1989). The epics were spectacles fueled by simple action narratives involving old-fashioned modes of heroism and redemption, a glittering cinematography filled with bright images and positive messages, glorification of patriotism, and traditional "family values"—not to mention obligatory happy endings. Politically, these films set out to recapture a (presumably lost) sense of national purpose by means of heroic action, while cinematically they amounted to formulaic spectacles described by what Biskind calls "big screen infantilism."[14] The seductive popularity of films by Lucas and Spielberg, including above all Lucas's enormously successful *Star Wars* episodes (to be analyzed in chapter 4), shows that even in the post-modern era what can be labeled modernist filmmaking remains just as vital as during the heyday of the studio system. The main difference today, of course, is that Hollywood modernism no longer enjoys the same hegemonic, taken-for-granted status it enjoyed earlier.

If the epic blockbusters turned out to be commercial windfalls, the masculine-hero action films were more ideologically self-conscious, usually more inspired by right-wing values. These pictures followed rather predictable lines: a tight narrative formula, abundant technical flourishes, hyperviolent images, and romanticized macho protagonists (Sylvester Stallone, Arnold Schwarzenegger, and Chuck Norris) facing herculean obstacles and challenges. The original Rambo film, *First Blood* (1982), exemplifies the warrior hero (Stallone) who must battle enemies depicted as ideologically evil and militarily almost invincible—a task made even more difficult by the nagging presence of doubters and stragglers within his own ranks, in this case a political (and military) bureaucracy that we have come to know as spineless, inept, and corrupt. Interestingly enough, the *Rambo* series portrayed an individual hero, rebellious and nonconformist to the core, who stands resolutely opposed to stifling authoritarian power, a theme familiar to the 1960s counterculture.[15] Military heroism is depicted as the highest form of life, well beyond the prosaic, hedonistic, selfish exploits of ordinary men. As in the case of earlier Western, gangster, and combat genres, crisis is resolved by the nearly superhuman energies of male warriors dedicated to cultural renewal and national rebirth, a vision anticipating the later proliferation of local militia groups and ideological cults in the 1980s and 1990s. As a mythical warrior, Rambo provides moral strength through violent redemption, towering above all the loathsome bureaucrats, naysayers, terrorists, and faceless "others." As Kellner suggests, the *Rambo* series is best understood as a cinematic project designed to facilitate U.S. military recovery from its post-Vietnam decline and, ultimately, to ideologically bolster American struggle for global hegemony.[16]

As with blockbusters, modern action films evoke menacing hyperimages of a Hobbesian world in which evil can be found everywhere, often surfacing in the most unexpected places. But it is a world where order and stability are restored sooner or later—in contrast with noir and postmodern films, where social turbulence typically veers out of control. There are other parallels: Action sequences enable the male hero to recover a sense of untram-

Do the Right Thing **(Spike Lee, 1989)**   *Lee as Mookey and Danny Aiello as a pizzeria owner in Brooklyn on the edge of a mounting civic explosion destined to engulf Aiello's establishment in a cauldron of urban social and racial violence.*

meled self, and he is able to achieve this—indeed, he *must* achieve it—by using extraordinarily violent, draconian methods. Nothing less would suffice to tame a chaotic universe that, despite the waning of the Cold War and weakening of the communist "threat," is still populated by evil forces (terrorists, drug traffickers, and rogue states) that must be pacified or extirpated. Action movies like *First Blood* set in motion a new cycle of modernist films that transmitted markedly conservative, patriarchal, jingoistic messages often more virulent than those of the McCarthy period.

In contrast, the films of semi-independent, post–studio era auteurs like Stone, Ritt, Sayles, Nichols, and Lee (*Malcolm X*) expressed an entirely different type of neomodernism: a mostly subversive, bold, hard-hitting, quasi-documentary realism consistent with the tradition of cinema verité. Like film noir and some currents of postmodernism, this cinematic departure—much indebted to Italian neorealists of the 1950s and 1960s—turned toward the dark underside of American life and its extension around the world. Leftist modernism was committed to the unveiling of some version of historical truth, which meant debunking certain official proclamations and myths along with a graphic representation of social forces historically associated with struggles for freedom, democracy, justice, and equality. In many ways, it was a film culture of *conscience*. In such a world, there is ample room for heroes who can help transform society, who stand by a vision of human betterment and progress: Malcolm X; JFK/Jim Garrison; Norma Rae; Karen Silkwood; Ron Kovic; Michael Collins; the citizens of Milagro, New Mexico; and even the embattled and ill-fated Frances Farmer in *Frances* (1981). As a larger canon of works spanning two decades, Stone's films deserve special mention within this tradition—not only *Born on the Fourth of July* (1989) but also *Platoon* (1986), *Salvador* (1984), *Wall Street* (1991), and *Nixon* (1997) fit the neomodernist approach shaped, in this case, by a hard-edged realism and passion for calling attention to stubborn but highly elusive social and psychological truths. Stone's often frenetic documentary-style technique is starkly enhanced by a general cinematic approach rooted in dynamic action, quick flow of images, rapid and sometimes chaotic camera movement, and powerful images of pain, anger, and despair that reinforce his gripping emotional narratives. No doubt Stone's work alone did much to stimulate the rebirth of cinematic realism, although several of his films (*Talk Radio*, *The Doors*, *JFK*, and *Natural Born Killers*) offer a view of history and social life that is distinctly postmodern.[17]

In *Salvador*, which follows the bizarre escapades of maverick journalist Richard Boyle (James Woods), Stone subjects U.S. foreign policy in Central America to a withering critique. In the manically paced *Wall Street*, he gives viewers something of a morality tale about the unscrupulous exploits of a ruthless, wheeling-dealing Gordon Gekko (Michael Douglas), a character loosely based on the real-life stock market schemes of Ivan Boesky. In *Born on the Fourth of July*, he chronicles the agonizing personal struggles and transformations of Ron Kovic (Tom Cruise), who, wounded in the Vietnam War, returns to a world where old patriotic values and loyalties evaporate in the midst of growing antiwar sentiment and, for Kovic, disillusionment with not only the war but also his family, friends, and the military establishment itself. In *JFK*, Stone brilliantly depicts the long, arduous campaign waged by New Orleans District Attorney Jim Garrison (Kevin Costner) to discover the real truth about the 1963 John F. Kennedy assassination, hoping to show (by means of logic and painstaking investigation) that the murder was an outgrowth of a conspiracy involving the CIA, anti-Castro Cubans, the Mafia, and even plotters within the military–industrial complex. Stone's contributions to a neomodernist progressive realism surely occupy a place of their own despite a pervasive surrealism that has come to define so much of his work.

What emerges within this third pattern of neomodernism is a keen sense of social and political *conflict* that becomes an endemic feature of late industrial capitalism, in contrast to familiar notions of consensus, stability, and civic participation characteristic of earlier modernist films by directors like Ford and Capra. This "new" modernism is distinctly more cynical about established American institutions and practices and more skeptical of their very ideological foundations in eighteenth-century liberalism. Thematic attachment to ideals of justice, equality, and democracy remains, as does the critique of wealth, privilege, concentrated power, and corruption; so too does an emphasis on the role of ordinary people struggling to better their working and living conditions. The prospects for an emancipatory outcome are now more obscure, indeed, seemingly out of reach—and this outlook begins to merge with the shifting postmodern sensibilities of the 1980s and 1990s. Through all this, the classic influence of modernist directors like Griffith, Eisenstein, Renoir, Visconti, and Ford—tied to a cinematic realism where personal, moral, and political choices are an integral part of the total experience—is creatively sustained and renewed.

CRACKS IN THE EDIFICE: HITCHCOCK, WELLES, AND LANG

The Hollywood studio system projected, for the most part, a mythological image of American history and society coinciding with a profoundly conservative (even if occasionally "liberal") ideology and lifestyle. By the 1930s and the onset of the Depression, such affirmative views served distinctly escapist functions, helping distract tens of millions of people otherwise burdened with a collapsing material and social life. As the dominant studio of the 1930s, MGM fit this pattern exquisitely; its head, Louie B. Mayer, was committed to flashy dramas, comedies, and musicals offering reassurance to a population beset with social miseries and personal anxieties. MGM pictures were decidedly assimilationist in the spirit of Mayer, who, as Gabler writes, was "desperate to be connected—to a family, a community, a studio, a country. It was one of the motives behind his almost pathological possessiveness and his unbridled paternalism."[18] Mayer's studio was able to establish a powerful hold over the popular consciousness "by fashioning a vast, compelling national fantasy out of his dreams and out of the basic tenets of his own dogmatic faith—a belief in virtue, in the bulwark of the family, in the merits of loyalty, in the soundness of tradition, in America itself."[19] One of the guiding aims of studio production was to portray good women, saintly mothers, and honorable men. This idealization of America provided an all-embracing vision, or fantasy, that could be shared by many groups, urban and rural, rich and poor, men and women, conservative and liberal alike.

Yet modernist hegemony did not go unchallenged: Rival views of American society surfaced throughout this period, and they gradually entered the cinematic idioms, especially after the 1930s. A rebellion against modernism became manifest in the work of Hitchcock, Welles, and Lang, film noir, and even the later work of Ford. Cracks in the conformist paradigm were visible well before the onset of postmodernism and could be detected even at the peak of the studio era.

If, as Gabler suggests, MGM "would go to any lengths to fabricate America as a sanctuary, safe and secure, and then promulgate this idealization to other Americans,"[20] then Warner Brothers managed to convey through its ambitious film output quite a contrasting image—a tough, blunt, contested world that scarcely lived up to standard Hollywood ideas of glamour and romance. Warner Brothers was, after all, a studio fashioned after the no-nonsense pugnaciousness and strong liberalism of Harry and Jack Warner, whose major director was the noirish Michael Curtiz and whose main actors included James Cagney, George Raft, Edward G. Robinson, Paul Muni, Humphrey Bogart, and Bette Davis. They championed films set in explosive urban, lower-class, immigrant environments replete with cynical, rebellious, hard-bitten protagonists who had little respect for the proprieties of conventional social and political life. In Gabler's words, Warner Brothers built a cinema revolving around "dark shades of despair" (195–96), exemplified by cheaply made dramas and gangster movies populated by all manner of outsiders, loners, losers, and racketeers. Immersed in the popular anxiety of the times, these pictures anticipated the later noir cycle in much the same way as 1920s German expressionism: In contrast to the escapist fare of Paramount and MGM, they acknowledged deep class, ethnic, and regional divisions within American society and brought the notion of "outlaw hero" to the fore in Hollywood filmmaking. It was this milieu that contributed so much to the rise of directors like Hitchcock, Welles, Lang, and Wilder, who, in the 1940s and 1950s, would make films anticipating the more mature development of postmodern cinema in the decades that followed.

Perhaps more than anyone else, it was Hitchcock who adopted a filmmaking style closest to later postmodern aesthetics, even as he relished certain modernist virtues. Hitchcock's dualism runs throughout his films, but it can been seen most clearly in his later films: *Rear Window*, *North by Northwest*, *Vertigo*, and *Psycho*. In *North by Northwest*, he pits his hero, advertising executive Roger O. Thornhill (Cary Grant), against omnipresent, faceless, treacherous forces over which he can exercise little control—forces, moreover, that he can scarcely identify much less comprehend and defeat. The film depicts a shifting universe of chaos, manipulation, confusion, and violence where rules are unceremoniously overturned and nothing makes sense beyond tactical maneuvers of the moment. Like much later postmodern cinema, this film is propelled by rapid action, movement, and conflict—a style further enhancing the viewer's sense of enclosure within a vast conspiratorial power apparatus. At one point, Thornhill asks the government agent, "Are you from the FBI?" The agent replies, "FBI, CIA, it's all the same alphabet soup." This cynicism about who and what really controls society was a defining feature of many noir classics and would be central to the later postmodern outlook in which movies depict a venal, corrupt system manipulated by impersonal spin doctors, advertisers, lobbyists, and just ordinary sleazy politicians, exemplified by Stone's *JFK*.

Few Hollywood directors were more obsessive about the art of filmmaking than Hitchcock, whose unmistakable imprint can be detected in virtually every frame of his movies. It was this stylistic uniqueness that gave his films their strongly enduring quality; for this and other reasons, they occupy a special niche in American popular culture. His long and prolific career brought together elements of classical European cinema, noirish features within the studio system, and sensibilities of an experimental, semi-independent auteur—making him a vital transitional figure in the evolution of twentieth-century film. If Hitchcock's painstaking concern for the mise-en-scène is the mark of a realist, his realism was nonetheless tenuous, essentially a surface phenomenon that barely concealed yet another range of experiences grounded in the dark side of the American experience: fear, violence, criminality, the interconnection of villains and victims, and a specter of chaos. His "reality" was ultimately subverted by deeper, more powerful elements of deceit, treachery, psychopathology, and, of course, death in a world where evil is so often unavoidable—witness *Rebecca* (1940), *Shadow of a Doubt* (1943), *Strangers on a Train* (1951), and *Rear Window* (1954) as prime examples of this suspenseful duality. Whether in a small town or a large city, Hitchcock imagines a universe of inescapable tension, uncertainty, and angst festering beneath the tranquil normalcy of everyday life, where villains and victims are bound together in a social web trapping everyone involved.[21] In *Shadow of a Doubt*, set in sleepy 1940s Santa Rosa, California, the suave and attractive uncle Charlie (Joseph Cotten) turns out to be a sinister monster wanted by law enforcement as a serial killer. The "normal" here becomes illusory, while "crime" ends up not as some kind of pathological deviation but as a natural extension of daily life. Much the same could be said of *Rear Window*, *Rope* (1948), *Strangers on a Train*, and *Psycho* (1962).

In *Rear Window*, Hitchcock evokes images of ordinary, routine life in a New York apartment complex where the central character (James Stewart) is confined to his residence after having broken his leg. As Stewart quickly finds himself indulging a passion for voyeurism—closely scanning the claustrophobic environs of his neighbors with a telescope—he uncovers an everyday urban life that is anything but ordinary and routine. What he finds is a crowded, expansive sphere of alienation, loneliness, fragmentation, paranoia, and (inevitably) murder: One of Stewart's neighbors, Lars Thorwald (Raymond Burr), kills his invalid wife and stuffs her body into a trunk, a horror Stewart is finally able to unravel owing to the fruits of his obsessive voyeurism. The film shows that, once the surface of daily life is penetrated by the viewer's gaze through blatant entry into the private worlds of scattered individuals, urban social existence is reduced to mordant decadence and criminality.[22] *Rear Window* investigates an otherwise uneventful milieu in which danger lurks about but one where the camera (both Hitchcock's and Stewart's) manages to transform everything into a coherent, intelligible whole, extending modernism while simultaneously subverting it. As Denzin writes, "This disturbing, reflexive pivotal film closes the modernist period even as it begins."[23]

Hitchcock's later works continued this trend away from rational, ends-oriented modernism. *Marnie* (1964) pits Mark Ruttland (Sean Connery), a brilliant business executive, against Marnie (Tippi Hedren), a ruthless swindler of business executives. Marnie sheds her identities like last year's fashions, becoming a blond, a redhead, and a brunette, and working under aliases in order to keep her nefarious objectives from her bosses. Ruttland falls heavily in love with this protean character who exhibits all the symptoms of childhood sexual trauma. In this film, Hitchcock seemed to warn audiences that no one really knows another person and that no one can protect him- or herself from duplicity and deceit. Marnie's world of psychological traumas and severe personality disorders makes Melanie Daniels's attention-getting stunts seem harmless and juvenile. Eventually, in *Frenzy* (1972), Hitchcock would unleash one of his most dangerous villains, Rusk (Barry Foster), a full-fledged psychopath who covers his serial rape/murders with a sweet, sympathetic, friendly neighborhood fruit seller act. In order to satisfy his appetite for sado-sexuality and murder, Rusk strikes again and again, eventually putting even Norman Bates to shame with his psychopathic mayhem.

Yet Hitchcock's "postmodernism" was always partial, uneven, and contained within the parameters of modernist Hollywood. If his films anticipated a more deeply pessimistic critique of American culture—if they focused on anomie, hovering demons, impending disaster, and the collapse of selfhood—they still reflected an auteur's drive toward obsessive control over production, tightly structured narratives, and thoroughly planned scene development. Like Ford, Hitchcock left practically nothing to chance or to outside intervention. Above all, there is a certain truth-seeking process involved in most of Hitchcock's movies, an attempt to penetrate the illusions and distortions of a murky social (and psychological) reality, reflected, for instance, in *Shadow of a Doubt, Rope, Rear Window,* and *The Wrong Man* (1956). One might argue, therefore, that what one finds in these suspenseful dramas is a deliberately complex interplay between order and chaos, reality and illusion, and truth and fiction.

While few classic directors could match Ford or Hitchcock for overall cinematic power, Hitchcock himself voiced supreme admiration for only one other filmmaker of the period—Orson Welles. François Truffaut once observed that Welles was "probably the one that has started the largest number of directors on their careers."[24] In fact, Welles influenced aspiring filmmakers, writers, and actors as much for his flamboyant, maverick, innovative "boy wonder" persona, ever eager to astound viewers with his bold projects, as for his unparalleled mastery of the directing craft. He was partly an iconoclastic genius battling studio executives for the right to produce artistic films and the director who, through his great ingenuity, emerged as the quintessential Hollywood auteur. An unrivaled blend of talents (producing, directing, writing, and acting) along with a radical, daredevil image made Welles into something of an "outlaw hero," able to cajole studio heads and producers into giving him resources needed for experimental projects that even the most outlandish directors wanted to avoid. In the end, as is well known, Welles's career turned into Hollywood tragedy—a youthful, creative genius stifled by conservative, bureaucratic, profit-driven studio hierarchies unwilling to produce anything but formulaic genre pictures for mass audiences. Like his cohorts among auteurs, Welles was above all a modernist filmmaker whose work, however, was steeped in the noir style and seemed to anticipate later postmodern themes. His canon, to be sure, was relatively small—the most enduring being *Citizen Kane* (1942), *The Magnificent Ambersons* (1942), *The Lady from Shanghai* (1948), *Touch of Evil* (1958), and *The Trial* (1962)—but one destined to leave a lasting mark on filmmaking in the United States and around the world.

Starting with *Citizen Kane,* which appeared about the same time as Hitchcock's *Rebecca* and just before Curtiz's *Casablanca,* the young and audacious Welles challenged viewers to appreciate the craftsmanship, innovation, and sheer genius of cinematic storytelling. Instead of the handsome, all-American-hero-who-saves-the-day type of scenario characteristic of modernist drama, Western, and combat films—or even the romantic hero who dies violently for a good cause—Welles depicts a powerful, charismatic hero who gradually degenerates into a hardened, ugly, tragic old man. The first scene of *Citizen Kane* shows a protagonist's death and his famous dying word, "Rosebud," from which point until the end of the movie John Foster Kane continues his ill-fated downward slide into the abyss of loneliness and despair. When Kane's youthful enthusiasm for creating a respected newspaper evaporates into a bitter attempt by the arrogant and egocentric publisher to make the public think "what I tell them to think," the audience realizes it is in for a classic human tragedy. Viewers accustomed to standard Hollywood endings where the victorious heroes are shown enjoying the fruits of their exploits or perhaps saving the world from evil must have regarded the complex but villainous Kane (played superbly by Welles himself) as a creature from another world. To bring such psychological depth to the screen, Welles collaborated with cinematographer Gregg Toland to create a series of striking montages, extreme close-ups, birdlike crane shots, and images distorted through glass and mirrors.

As a breakthrough film, *Citizen Kane* was a compendium of thematically interwoven scenes that dazzled audiences with multilayered levels of meaning of the sort that would be found in later postmodern works. In the famous "breakfast montage," for example, Welles compresses the history of an entire marriage into a brief but emotionally powerful scene of Kane and his first wife at their morning ritual: In the first shot, we see the two soon after their marriage, still in the throes of romance, followed by a scene in which a slightly older Mrs. Kane begins to quarrel about being abandoned by her husband in favor of his cherished newspaper office. "What do you do at a newspaper in the middle of the night?" she demands. "My dear, your only correspondent is *The Inquirer*," Kane replies. In subsequent shots, we see the gradually aging couple sitting farther and farther apart, increasingly detached and alienated. Finally, the husband and wife sit in embarrassing silence across the distance of an elongated dining table as he reads *The Inquirer* while she reads a rival newspaper. The whole scene flashes by in a few minutes yet depicts, critically and graphically, the sad trajectory of a fading marriage.

Citizen Kane still resonates among filmgoing audiences not only for its innovative techniques but also for its poignant images of a tragic hero seen disintegrating morally and psychologically frame by frame. The film compels viewers to reflect on issues of success and failure, hubris and denial—indeed, mortality itself—through the lenses of a deteriorating Kane. No doubt the fear of descending into Kane-like tragedy is rather universal—a fear grounded in the insecurities of aging and the prospect of individual transgressions coming back to haunt. In one important sense, therefore, Kane emerged as the quintessential modern hero self-obsessed to the point where he cannot sustain intimate relationships; like Willy Loman in *Death of a Salesman* and Captain Queeg in *The Caine Mutiny*, he becomes immersed in some of the deepest contradictions of modern life. At the same time, Kane veers toward postmodern motifs insofar as he captures the pervasive mood of chaos and decay in the downward slide of a hero who on the surface is dedicated to wonderfully high-sounding principles. Welles's achievement in *Citizen Kane* was the mark of creative auteurial independence won through protracted battles with studio executives at RKO. In fact, Welles produced the film, coauthored the script, chose the entire cast and crew, starred in the leading role, and directed the filmmaking process without major obstructions. He set up the major shots, determining the narrative and photographic flow, which captured the mood of tragedy through powerful images of darkness, confusion, loneliness, and (in the end) chaos. Viewed thusly, the film leaves a legacy comprising both modern and postmodern elements that, as in subsequent films like *Touch of Evil* and *The Trial*, helped pave the way toward the New Hollywood explosion of the 1970s.

Fritz Lang's Hollywood films also displayed an ironic, noirish perspective that anticipated the later postmodern turn. Lang achieved some renown in earlier decades while working in Berlin with such German expressionist classics as *Metropolis* (1927) and *M* (1931). After Hitler came to power, Lang emigrated to Hollywood, where he became an influential figure in the nascent film noir movement, bringing the German expressionists' darkly ironic aesthetic to his films. *Fury* (1936), a bitter portrayal of a western lynch mob gone berserk, represents a major work of biting social criticism at a time when Hollywood was more known for Westerns, musicals, and screwball comedies. In 1944, Lang released *Ministry of Fear* and *Woman in the Window*, two early films noir that helped set the tone for many to follow: *Scarlet Street* (1945), *Rancho Notorious* (1952), *Clash By Night* (1952), and *The Big Heat* (1953). Lang brought to Hollywood a deep sensitivity regarding social injustice and capitalist greed, not to mention an expressionistic, almost surrealistic aesthetic that strongly influenced many later filmmakers. Along with Hitchcock and Welles, Lang brought to the screen a sardonic, dark, and at times almost nihilistic sensibility, lending cinematic power to his critique of modern industrial society. Yet Lang, much like Hitchcock, ultimately encountered limits imposed by the Hollywood studio system; their critical outlook could carry them only so far. Thus, Robert Kapsis writes that Lang's later films (once he emigrated to the United States in 1934) never fulfilled the promise embraced by earlier movie critics of a culturally radical cinema.

He observes that "many were thrillers and, like Hitchcock's, were attacked for their subject matter—pulpy crime stories, implausible plots, sketchy character delineations, and overall oppressiveness and rejection of the idea of social betterment and progress. The principal charge against both film-makers was that their works lacked verisimilitude."[25] Hence, the break with modernism was at best only partial and ineffectual.

Mainly because of the creative departures of Hitchcock, Welles, and Lang—along with the work of noir directors like Wilder, Curtiz, and Edward Dmytryk—the modernist ethic associated with the studio system faced new challenges throughout the 1940s and 1950s. Even Ford, whose Western epics did much to define the classic Hollywood style, joined this trend with the making of *The Man Who Shot Liberty Valance* (1962), which many crit-ics regard as his best film. Here, Ford cast John Wayne and James Stewart as contrasting outlaw/official heroes, standing a number of familiar Western clichés on their head just as Hitchcock did with the thriller genre. Ford re-versed the classic Western iconography that viewers had come to expect, rather like elements of a Christian religious ceremony being subverted for purposes of satanic worship. In one moment of this reversal, the final gun battle in *Liberty Valance* takes place not at high noon but at *midnight*, con-trary to the standard Western formula. Moreover, the rugged frontiersman Tom Doniphan (Wayne) does not defeat the villain (Lee Marvin) during what might be considered a "fair" gunfight; instead, Wayne shoots Marvin (Liberty Valance) from behind as Marvin's attention is drawn toward killing the Stewart character (Ransom Stoddard). Wayne then gets Ranse to think that he, not Doniphan, was responsible for disposing of the villain. In a script clearly anticipating later postmodern themes, Ranse is soon plagued by hav-ing to experience the psychological torment of knowing that he was not "the man who shot Liberty Valance," that he cannot lay claim to the status of con-ventional hero.

The emotional tone of *Liberty Valance* is one of depression and, ulti-mately, cynical resignation over the tyranny of deception and ambiguity per-vading life on the frontier. It is a tone more akin to the sensibilities of film noir, with the embittered hero (Ranse) being forced into a life dominated by falsehood and inner chaos where his ego progressively implodes. A variety of noir icons abound in this film, including night-for-night shots and flash-backs, and these icons convey an atmosphere of psychological ambiguity and moral confusion. Like many noir classics, this Western seems to indict society as a decadent whole—not merely one sector or dimension of it. At the same time, Ford's classic permits no easy solutions, no simple or finished or enclosed endings. Inevitably, Ranse is forced to live with a monstrous deception even as he appears to be obsessed with finding the truth. Even the stark modern characters of Shinbone, the film's setting, are forced to accept one set of imposing compromises after another. Hence, the editor of the Shinbone newspaper tells one of his reporters, when the authentic tale of Valance's death becomes known, "This is the West, son. When the legend becomes fact, print the legend." From this angle, any concept of justice (or truth) winds up obscured in a cloud of historical mythology. With such strong hints of postmodernism, *Liberty Valance* stands out as a surprisingly radical departure from Ford's generally modernist body of work; it marked the end of an epoch. Commenting on *Liberty Valance*, Sinclair writes, "If it could never become a popular film, because Ford's rigor had cut all the flesh and amiable detail out of his work, he had ordered the cemetery of his career, laid out the burial plots, and prepared the funeral speeches on the legends of the West."[26] Of course, the idea of a multiperspectival approach to social reality is a postmodern theme that would later dominate the films of directors like Allen, Scorsese, Lynch, Altman, the Coen brothers, and Tarantino. Not only does Ford's movie call forth an undeniable ambience of confusion and cynicism, but it also offers an insightful critique of mass media that would later infuse such films as *Network*, *Wag the Dog*, and *The Truman Show*.

THE CRACKS WIDEN: FILM NOIR

The success of Welles and Hitchcock in creating antiheroes like Charles Foster Kane and Uncle Charlie (in *Shadow of a Doubt*) gave rise to a new cinematic discourse during the 1940s and 1950s characterized by what would later be called film noir. A term brought into general usage by French writers in the mid-1950s, the noir concept was invented to describe cinematic adaptations of novels by writers like Raymond Chandler, Dashiell Hammett, and James M. Cain, whose hard-boiled detective thrillers fit broadly within the larger tradition of "roman noir," a style that goes back to the nineteenth century and notably refers to a body of Gothic novels by such authors as the Brontë sisters and Edgar Allan Poe. Like Gothic novels in general, roman noir dwelled on a bleak, menacing world of crime, mayhem, and evil—a world of antiheroes like Sam Spade and Philip Marlowe, tough guys out for themselves and indifferent to social causes or political ideologies. When strict Hollywood production codes enforcing conventional motifs and norms were relaxed during and just after World War II, the most risk-oriented film executives and producers were ready to test film versions of these popular but offbeat novels. But the decision makers expected that such films would be made relatively cheaply and without much artistic pretension.

The first "official" film noir was John Huston's adaptation of Hammett's *The Maltese Falcon* (1941). Huston cast Humphrey Bogart as Sam Spade, a sleazy private eye who must confront an even sleazier bunch of criminals, including Bridgit O'Shaugnessy (Mary Astor). After having an affair with his partner's scheming wife, Spade decides to dump her after her husband is mysteriously murdered. Throughout most of the film, in fact, Spade seems to be preoccupied with little more than his own daily ordeals. Later, when his client O'Shaugnessy hints at offering him a bribe, he complains that she has tried to bribe him with money alone. "What else do I have to bribe you with?" she asks. "This," he replies, taking her in his arms and kissing her. Still later, Spade demands and receives a $1,000 bill from a gang of criminals trying to steal a rare, valuable gold-and-jewel-encrusted statuette. When he hands over the bill to police at the end, he remarks, "Don't be so sure I'm as crooked as I'm supposed to be. That sort of reputation might be good for business, bringing high-priced jobs and making it easier to deal with the enemy."

Huston's Sam Spade, like Hitchcock's Roger O. Thornhill and the Bogart character Rick in *Casablanca*, is shown to be a likable but severely flawed protagonist who must continuously struggle for survival in a dangerous, angst-filled world. Spade is a modernist hero surrounded by venal enemies in a world where survival depends on adopting modes of duplicity and coercion that have become predominant throughout society as a whole. Although Spade manages to fight off a series of threats in *The Maltese Falcon*, he ends up little better off than Charles Foster Kane, who dies in the first scene of the picture. For all intents and purposes, neither hero is alive, although Spade's physical life lingers on even as his emotional and spiritual being progressively deteriorates. His partner is dead (even if avenged), his recent girlfriend is on her way to prison, and he is in the process of leaving yet another girlfriend (his dead partner's widow). While Spade is keenly aware that the police have little use for him, for his own part he makes no secret of his hatred and disgust for them. Having defeated the would-be falcon thieves, every indication is that he will have to face a good many other unsavory characters in the future. Viewed accordingly, Spade must be judged quite differently from conventional Griffith- or Ford-style heroes who are destined to prevail while achieving some form of redemption by the end of the film. There is, of course, no hope for Spade since he inhabits a world in which the very possibility of redemption and change (either personal or social) has essentially vanished.

Huston gave visual articulation to *The Maltese Falcon*'s alienated subject matter with a variety of lighting and camera techniques emphasizing night shots, blighted city streets, and omnipresent shadows. Over time, the concept "film noir" applied to movies resembling the dark mood and pessimistic view of the human condition found throughout *The Maltese Falcon*. (Hitchcock's *Rebecca*, produced at roughly the same time, evoked an even darker imagery.) While these pictures fit the modernist pattern in terms of their narrative flow, overall structure, and fascination with a central protagonist/hero, their darkly etched cinematography, along with a Hobbesian portrait of the world as fearsome jungle, amounted to a departure from modernism. While many noir classics were nothing more than simple detective stories or B-grade thrillers—or, in many cases, Cold War–driven anticommunist pulp narratives—the best of this style (*Double Indemnity*, *Mildred Pierce*, *Out of the Past*, *The Kiss of Death*, and *Sunset Boulevard*) gave superbly innovative, often surreal or at least unsettling depictions of urban life that dramatized the actual harshness, corruption, and violence that had become a hallmark of American society. The noir canon anticipated a postmodern cinema that would make splendid use of noir icons (fog, rain, broken glass, dark alleys, concealed guns, and so forth), technical style, and bitterly harsh narratives about the human condition. Nicholas Christopher refers to "the labyrinth of the hero's inner workings—mental and physiological—subjected to brutal stresses and strains that mercilessly reveal his flaws. His anatomy is a kind of corollary to, and reflection of, the city's inner workings, in all their rich complexity."[27]

During the 1950s, noir-style films reached their height of popularity—at first with critics and later with a legion of writers and directors. Edward Dmytryk, whose noir legacy included the classics *Murder My Sweet* (1944) and *Cornered* (1945), was once asked by members of a university audience during a film festival to "tell us about film noir." In a somewhat puzzled tone, Dmytryk replied by simply asking, "What is film noir?" The audience replied, "You're one of the founders of film noir." In what might later be defined as a "postmodern" response, Dmytryk then blurted out, "I don't know what the hell it is."[28]

Dmytryk's *Murder My Sweet* in fact contains a typical noir story, with its own markedly individualized style and technique. Chandler's private eye, Philip Marlowe (Dick Powell), becomes embroiled in a dark trail of blackmail and murder with a deep sexual undercurrent. He is lured into a sleazy, nightmarish urban underworld where he is twice knocked unconscious, strangled, and imprisoned in a mental hospital where he is forced to take mind-altering drugs. Escaping his captors, he hides out at his client's daughter's apartment. She tells him, "You know, I think you're nuts. You go barging around without a very clear idea of what you're doing, everybody bats you down, smacks you over the head, fills you full of stuff, and you keep right on hitting between tackle and end. I don't even know which side you're on." Marlowe replies, again suggesting the postmodern motif of ambiguity and confusion, "I don't know which side anybody's on. I don't even know who's playing today."

The relentlessly downcast, ironic tone of Marlowe's monologue would be echoed in the later work of beat poets and novelists like Jack Kerouac, Allen Ginsberg, and Lawrence Ferlinghetti along with such writers as Ken Kesey and Hunter Thompson. Marlowe's mysterious persona symbolized an individual in transition from war-driven world to peacetime society in which old ways of thought and action were crumbling, with the routines of social reality no longer to be taken for granted. Referring to World War II and after, RKO producer William Fadiman remembers this era as "a period of great awakening, of great consternation, of great regret over what had been accomplished, if anything had been accomplished, by that particular war." People's lives had of course changed dramatically—in the family, the workplace, and the community at large. Women had entered the workforce in larger numbers than at any time in American history. Minorities were further displaced or marginalized in the workforce, a phenomenon later serving as a catalyst behind the civil rights movement. In Fadiman's words, such factors led to "a kind of social unrest, and the revealing and opening up and exploring many problems that had been either brushed under the rug or at least revealed to a large number of human beings."[29]

The noir style gave relatively unknown "B" directors like Dmytryk, Edward G. Ulmer (*Detour*, 1945), and Delmer Daves (*Dark Passage*, 1947) the chance to experiment with new cinematic techniques, sometimes with little oversight from Hollywood censors. With the passage of time, a number of more established directors—such as Wilder (*Double Indemnity*, *Lost Weekend*, and *Sunset Boulevard*), Fritz Lang (*Scarlet Street* and *The Big Heat*), Curtiz (*Casablanca*, *Mildred Pierce*, and *Johnny Guitar*), Hitchcock (*The Wrong Man* and *Vertigo*), and Welles (*Journey into Fear*, *Lady from Shanghai*, and *Touch of Evil*)—all took turns at directing what might be loosely regarded as noir films. Hitchcock, Lang, and Wilder were already well versed in German expressionism along with 1920s and 1930s surrealism that, in tandem with Gothic literature and the detective thriller, served as a powerful current behind the emerging noir canon. Film noir worked as well in low-budget pictures as it did in higher-budget pictures because it offered prospects of stylish camera angles, plot twists, creative lighting techniques, and unique cinematic icons, mostly available at bargain prices. To achieve a sense of foreboding darkness, noir directors employed a variety of night-for-night shots, or footage taken at night but without special "night" filters used in standard Hollywood sets. Low-level lighting enabled directors to make creative use of shadows, terse dialogue, simple camera shots, and natural lighting—technical modes compatible with downbeat, surreal, even radical motifs at a time when leftist ideas and themes were essentially forbidden. As Christopher writes, "The oblique lighting and camera-angling referred to, in both studio and location scenes . . . reinforce our implicit understanding that the characters' motives are furtive, ambiguous, and psychologically charged; that their innermost conflicts and desires are rooted in urban claustrophobia and stasis; and that they tread a shadowy borderline between repressed violence and outright vulnerability."[30] Much of this, of course, anticipates the postmodern condition of later social life and cultural creation.

It is easy enough to see now that noir films often expressed social ferment and criticism insofar as they depicted modern industrial society as rife with alienation, powerlessness, and corruption—quite at odds with the Hollywood "consensus" typical of cinematic modernism. In this world, heroes are besieged with awesome challenges but rarely triumph at the end, their losses usually adding up to more than their gains. Sam Spade endured pain, indignities, and humiliation, and was knocked unconscious at least once in *The Maltese Falcon*. They seem incapable of experiencing genuine love and intimacy or even companionship: In this vein, Spade coldly sends O'Shaughnessy to prison with his tell-all testimony to the police. Curtiz's *Casablanca* features the cynical (one might say nihilistic) Rick, who, in the final scene, gives up Ilsa, the love of his life. Rick concludes that "the problems of two little people don't amount to a hill of beans in this crazy world," while Ilsa affirms that "it's a crazy world and anything can happen."

Through dozens of cheaply made but often well-crafted Hollywood thrillers of the 1940s and 1950s, the audience is brought into the orbit of various existential themes, complex and frequently twisted narratives, mordant views of the human condition, and an infinite variety of flawed and severely compromised protagonists best described as antiheroes. In noir classics, men routinely turn out to be cowards, drunkards, liars, killers, sex maniacs, and outlaws, while women often fit the femme fatale persona, using their sexuality and charm to seduce and exploit men for their own selfish ends. Defenders of law and order (politicians, cops, and judges) are typically portrayed as corrupt, bungling, and more often than not part of the criminal underground themselves. Thus, *The Asphalt Jungle* (1950) portrays an outlaw subculture where every actor seems to wind up sucked into a world of insatiable greed, desire, and scheming. In *The Big Clock* (1948), viewers encounter a web of dark intrigue that gradually but inexorably works its way through a machine-like, cynical, soulless corporate system. Set in the midst of postwar angst and confusion, *The Blue Dahlia* (1946) depicts a society where established moral and social rules have largely broken down, where nothing any longer makes sense, where all characters are caught up in the same web of intrigue. In *Force of Evil* (1948), a veiled anticapitalist thriller, the main characters exhibit both heroism and villainy in a bleak world overrun by corruption and greed. In *Gun Crazy* (1949), two young lovers (Peggy Cummins and John Dall) are united in their all-consuming passion to strike out in a series of violent escapades where, with predictable futility, they seek to purge the demons of the world. In yet another existential landmark starring Bogart, *In a Lonely Place* (1950) features a protagonist who, like nearly everyone else in the film, winds up trapped in a harsh, unforgiving milieu veering out of control. And Stanley Kubrick's first major film, *The Killing* (1956), constructs a tightly enclosed universe in which processes of social and psychological implosion (helped along by a deadly femme fatale played by Marie Windsor) seem all but guaranteed by the end of an engrossing but dark narrative.

The sense of ironic detachment resonating through noir classics later took on new meaning with a run of powerfully neo-noir pictures in the late 1960s and early 1970s, including John Boorman's *Point Blank* (1967), John Huston's *The Kremlin Letter* (1970), Don Siegel's *Dirty Harry* (1971), Roman Polanski's *Chinatown* (1974), Arthur Penn's *Night Moves* (1975), and Martin Scorsese's *Taxi Driver* (1976). Jake Gittis, the hero of *Chinatown*, fails to save his client from a police bullet or her young daughter from a lecherous villain with a history of child molestation. Gittis (played by Jack Nicholson) cries out in anguish as the police threaten immediate arrest if he utters another word about the case. "Come on, Jake, it's Chinatown," his partner tells him as he leads him away. The high idealism permeating films like *The Maltese Falcon*, where Sam Spade gives up O'Shaugnessy to justice, and *Casablanca*, where Rick gives up Ilsa to the Resistance leader so she can continue her fight against Nazism, here turns into outright disgust and suffering as the wealthy, murderous, child-molesting villain is left to attack yet another victim—this time his own granddaughter/daughter—to further his own boundless lust. During this later period, a new generation of auteurs (along with some older directors like Huston) made a number of bleak, pessimistic films, clearly influenced by noir classics (as Scorsese, for one, always likes to emphasize). These films inhabited a grotesque, menacing kind of universe—an urban jungle where brutality and violence dominate everyday life, where hopelessness and despair seem bound up with the human condition.

Neo-noirs like *Chinatown*, *Taxi Driver*, and *Dirty Harry* feature heroes that, in postmodern fashion, are well along the road to becoming *anti-heroes*—tough characters who wind up utterly defeated and powerless. As in *Chinatown*, such protagonists are often caught up in a web of lies, infidelities, and acts of violence—all part of a voyeuristic (and thus extremely insecure, frightful) world.[31] Nonconformist heroes of this sort, resilient but incapable of changing themselves or the world, symbolize a mood of social ferment, although the ferment would seem to run much deeper than in the earlier postwar years. Situated within a protracted Cold War era, neo-noir evokes images of the Vietnam War and its aftermath, the civil rights movement, feminism, the counterculture, and the many popular upheavals growing out of the 1960s. These films mirrored a new consciousness with echoes in a turbulent decade just as the earlier noirs were deeply influenced by World War II and its aftermath. Glimpsing a more fully mature postmodern aesthetics, both the original and the later noir cycles tapped strong elements of alienation and conflict in American society without, however, offering much hope for human redemption or social change—or for old-fashioned heroism. By integrating some central features of the classical noir syndrome, the new generation of filmmakers not only followed their precursors but even appeared to turn self-consciously toward nostalgia—a shift characteristic not only of neo-noir but of such "realist" works as Kazan's *The Last Tycoon* (1976) and Coppola's *The Godfather*, parts 1 and 2 (1973, 1974). In their cinematic nostalgia, the new directors revealed a certain disgust with the status quo, both in Hollywood and in society as a whole.[32]

Converging with postmodernism, neo-noir was shaped in part by a surrealism that helped determine choice of set locations, acting styles, dialogue, and lighting techniques. Take, for example, the character of Travis Bickle (Robert De Niro) in *Taxi Driver*. At one point in the movie, Bickle, sporting a Mohawk haircut and war paint, has a shootout with pimps in a rundown bordello depicted through a variety of dark underground motifs and symbols. Or consider the *Chinatown* scene where Jake Gittis is washed down a dam's overflow, then has his nose slit open by a knife-wielding Roman Polanski. In both cases, the fast-moving, slightly off-center screen images challenge a modernist understanding of narrative, action, and coherent shot sequences, calling forth a kind of surrealism that, like the nostalgia it so often implies, seems to coincide with a *rejection* of established institutions and values. Surely this tradition anticipated a more full-blown hostility to the dominant social norms that would enter into the cinematic discourses of postmodern film.[33]

In his brilliant study of the noir tradition, Christopher shows that perhaps 400 Hollywood films have been strongly influenced by noirish themes and techniques—films that, moreover, span several decades from the early 1940s into the present rather than the more enclosed time capsule (1940s and 1950s) conventionally assigned to the tradition. As we have seen, Christopher views noir as a kind of cultural "labyrinth" or dark urban life that extends—indeed, often deepens—throughout a postwar period characterized by the threat of nuclear holocaust and a cityscape that envelopes people in its corruption, violence, and environmental degradation. Those settings historically portrayed in film noir—buildings, cafés, bars, alleys, offices, shops, streets, cars, and so on—graphically reflect this labyrinth, with its Hobbesian specter of fear, doom, and annihilation. In Christopher's words, "Every film noir is the shadow land of a lost paradise, a fallen state."[34] Viewed from this perspective, noir evokes far more than simply a technical or stylistic approach to filmmaking, conveying instead an ethos, a state of mind, a social thematic, and indeed a philosophical stance that also encompasses style. It captures (and sometimes exaggerates) the raw underside of American life, visible in the crime, poverty, alienation, powerlessness, and, above all, sense of dread permeating the modern industrial landscape. Christopher writes that "every American city is always a tale of two cities: the surface city, orderly and functional, imbued with customs and routine, and its shadow, the nether city, rife with darker impulses and forbidden currents, a world of violence and chaos."[35]

The quintessential noir city, as Christopher defines it, is a "place ruled by the dizzying calculus of the jungle, whose prime functions emanate from sex, violence, and death."[36] This is clearly a world in which money, power, and sexuality—shorn of their mystification—stand at the heart of corruption and evil, with a bizarre mixture of grifters, thieves, gangsters, bribed cops, and femmes fatales vying for power. Viewed in their most progressive sense, the noir classics gave expression to a profound sense of alienation from—and rebellion against—the decay and conformism of an industrially mature, technologically advanced order. In the noir subculture, where such alienation and rebellion become manifest, it is the nightclub that emerges as the strange but exciting center of everyday life where, as Christopher points out, the city's undercurrents merge, allowing for a nighttime life-world of fun, eroticism, game-playing, spontaneity, and, of course, criminality.[37]

This same brooding existential commentary, postmodern to the core, infused Woody Allen's film *Manhattan* (1978), where the glitter and efficiency of a great city are barely masked an underlying everyday life of gloom, paranoia, depression, and harsh conflict. To the degree a strong noir legacy persists as a vital cultural force at the beginning of the twenty-first century, those sensibilities shared by it and postmodernism alike resonate with those dystopic, paranoid, nightmarish, even apocalyptic images that increasingly dominate the American landscape—the sort of images explored by Mike Davis in *Ecology of Fear*, going beyond the "Blade Runner" culture.[38] Further, as Pratt stresses, the noir tradition embraced "dark, complex, often hidden forces and conspiracies—revealing depths of corruption most of the audience would probably rather deny."[39] Such anarchic images (they hardly correspond to Marxian notions of class warfare) pervade other neo-noir films like *Dressed to Kill* (1980); *L.A. Confidential* (1998); *The Grifters* (1994); *Seven* (1995); and *The Usual Suspects* (1998); remakes of earlier noirs like *Cape Fear* (1994), *The Kiss of Death* (1996), and *A Perfect Murder* (1997); and such quasi-noir pictures as *Blade Runner* (1982), *Unforgiven* (1993), and *The Last Seduction* (1994).

3

THE POSTMODERN REVOLT: A NEW ERA?

Neo-noir filmmakers were joined by a small group of avant-garde directors who came of age in the late 1960s and 1970s, producing movies
that resonated with a dark, pessimistic, often dystopic view of social life and
were, for the most part, sharply critical of the established order both in the
film industry and in American society as a whole. It might be argued that the
New Hollywood auteurs in effect simply extended and refined the classical
noir ethic, but this was hardly the entire story. Mike Nichols's *The Graduate*
(1967), George Ray Hill's *Butch Cassidy and the Sundance Kid* (1969), and
especially Dennis Hopper's *Easy Rider* (1969) were among the first pictures
articulating countercultural themes of alienation and rebellion, sexual freedom, and sense of community, at times incorporating and at times departing
from prevailing elements of classical noir cinema.[1] A mood of psychological
escapism often permeated these films, evoking images of degradation, violence, and impending chaos. Following along the path of Hitchcock, Lang,
and Welles, this new generation of filmmakers worked on the premise that
evil or danger is likely to be found in the most unexpected places—not only
in the city as historical locus of noir motifs but also in the suburbs and coun-
tryside, where hatred and conflict are rampant even as this darker side of existence is covered with a veneer of civility. The neo-noir and New Hollywood
directors took their freewheeling, irreverent, rebellious impulses far beyond
the more conservative styles of earlier directors. The reality was that Hollywood movies dealing with rebellion (especially *youth* rebellion) had been in
vogue for many years, going back to László Benedek's *The Wild One* (1953),
Nicholas Ray's *Rebel without a Cause* (1955), and later Arthur Penn's *Bonnie and Clyde* (1967). These were followed by such popular movies as *The*

Graduate and *Easy Rider*, along with Haskell Wexler's *Medium Cool* (1969), Stanley Kubrick's *2001: A Space Odyssey* (1969), George Lucas's *American Graffiti* (1973), Coppola's *Rumble Fish* (1983), and Scorsese's *Mean Streets* (1973)—films that laid the groundwork for a New Hollywood "revolution" made possible by the crumbling of the old studio system with its authoritarian modes of production. Other pictures with a less direct relationship to youth alienation—but still part of this historic cinematic shift— were Bob Rafelson's *Five Easy Pieces* (1970), Peter Bogdanovich's *The Last Picture Show* (1971), and Milos Forman's *One Flew over the Cuckoo's Nest* (1975).

THE NEW HOLLYWOOD AUTEURS

Many critics suggest that *Easy Rider* was the film most pivotal to the counterculture, exemplified by two outlaw heroes (played by Dennis Hopper and Peter Fonda) who embark on an epic cross-country motorcycle venture beginning with a drug deal and ending with the death of these two along with a third character (Jack Nicholson) who dies at the hands of redneck vigilantes. The narrative frames the heroes as flawed and doomed from the very outset. Their demise, along with the sad fate of other rebel-heroes of the period like Bonnie and Clyde, Butch Cassidy and the Sundance Kid, and the entire grouping of actors in *The Wild Bunch* (Sam Peckinpah, 1969), signified a gradual darkening, to some extent growing apocalyptic mood that infused so much of postwar Hollywood cinema.

While darkness and pessimism were hardly new to American cinema, these motifs now entered the popular culture as part of a deeper, more pervasive Hobbesian outlook—a shift that came as a visceral reaction against the dominant strands of modernism and the studio system. David Ashley conceives of modernist art as an "attempt to impose a temporary and highly abstracted pattern onto a mosaic of sensation and feeling." He views the modernist hero as a person struggling to constitute the inner, self-reflective subject, foregrounded by the painful and terrible modern condition.[2] The hero, faced with a harsh and dangerous world, typically overcomes his or her frailties on the road to ultimate triumph and happiness. Both *It's a Wonderful Life* and *Mr. Smith Goes to Washington*, as we have seen, exemplify this cinematic representation of the modern hero. In the former picture, Capra's hero George Bailey, concluding that his life and career as a small-town businessman are a failure, attempts to commit suicide but is saved by Clarence, a guardian angel who allows him to experience what life would be like if he

(Bailey) had never been born; Bailey now realizes his life made a difference, that it is possible for him to go on. Modernist directors like Capra and Ford made films exuding optimism and a visionary sense of the future where heroes were attractive, charismatic, and resourceful. The message was that life, though fraught with dangers and uncertainties, can be a source of triumph and regeneration so long as enough human willpower is mobilized. Such facile belief in psychological and social progress, grounded in a romanticized view of American history, had already been interrogated by directors like Hitchcock, Lang, Welles, and others situated in the noir tradition. Following in the tracks of surrealism and existentialism and in some cases German expressionism, their films instilled doubt as to whether people can ever hope to achieve meaning and purpose in a world of chaos and uncertainty, where individuals often seem so insignificant and powerless. They raised troublesome questions about distinctly modern, liberal notions of justice, equality, and freedom—notions that were of course central to the French and American Revolutions and to the unfolding of the U.S. Constitution. On the worldly stage, filled with intractable complexity and ambiguity, villains are just as likely to triumph as are the ostensibly more well-intentioned heroes, if indeed a clear distinction between villains and heroes could any longer make sense.

The precise moment when identifiably "postmodern" films initially appeared remains a matter of debate; but we do know that the seeds of a novel cinematic style were sown as early as the 1960s and perhaps as far back as the noir heyday of the 1940s. We suggest that the noir tradition actually combined elements of both modern and postmodern, although in the 1940s and 1950s the very concept "postmodern" (as well as "noir") was hardly part of the intellectual or cultural (much less cinematic) lexicon. Precursors can be found even well outside the noir legacy—for example, in Kubrick's *Dr. Strangelove* (1964), Nichols's *Catch-22* (1970) and *Who's Afraid of Virginia Woolf?* (1966), and Richard Brooks's adaptation of Tennessee Williams's play *Cat on a Hot Tin Roof* (1958), all of which depict greedy, malevolent, and dissolute worlds. These films were galvanized by a social dynamic far removed from earlier modernist fare stressing redemption, heroism, and progress against even the most daunting obstacles. The poststudio generation of directors that included De Palma, Scorsese, Coppola, Allen, Altman, and Schrader, most of whom achieved preeminent stature during the 1970s, can now be understood as the cultural foundation of what might later be labeled postmodern cinema. New Hollywood auteurs departed significantly from earlier filmmaking traditions, embellishing a more openly insurgent stance along with a penchant for narratives that require metaphoric, self-conscious interpretation, that are critical and self-reflective even in their sometimes overwhelming darkness and pessimism.[3] This is not to say that films produced by these directors were impervious to established cinematic practices and codes; on the contrary, the new cinema sometimes embraced a romantic nostalgia for the past, including the classical Hollywood period.[4] The postmodern shift that began to take shape in the 1970s built on the legacies of Hitchcock, Lang, Welles, and other noir directors but went beyond them, bringing to filmmaking a world of social crisis and moral ambiguity that coincided with a growing national mood of alienation, cynicism, and powerlessness.

The birth of New Hollywood filmmaking in the late 1960s and early 1970s has been entertainingly chronicled by Peter Biskind in *Easy Riders, Raging Bulls*, an account describing how the counterculture helped spawn a cohort of directors who would forever alter the trajectory of the film industry. Young filmmakers like Schrader, Coppola, Scorsese, Altman, Allen, Spielberg, and Lucas—along with more established figures like Nichols, Penn, and Ashby—brought a wide range of new sensibilities to the cinema, energized by a culture of rebellion, sexual freedom, antimilitarism, rock music, and drugs.[5] What is sometimes referred to as the "revolutionary decade" of Hollywood cinema was made possible by the long-term decline of the studio empire, although the new auteurs—motivated by a surprisingly wide range of political ideologies—made their mark both within and outside the corporate film structure.[6] If they were largely dependent on what the major studios could provide in terms of material and institutional resources, they were generally culturally if not ideologically repulsed by the conformism and predictability of traditional Hollywood fare. In boldly and systematically challenging the old hierarchical system, they endowed the concept "auteur" with an entirely new meaning since for them, as Biskind writes, "film was no less than a secular religion."[7] Biskind nowhere refers to a specifically postmodern shift corresponding to the influence of New Hollywood directors, but the concept surely applies to that quite large body of films that departed radically in many ways from cinematic modernism: Coppola's *The Godfather* (parts 1 and 2), Scorsese's *Mean Streets* and *Taxi Driver*, Altman's *McCabe and Mrs. Miller* and *Nashville*, Ashby's *Coming Home*, Nichols's *Carnal Knowledge*, Lucas's *American Graffiti*, Allen's *Annie Hall* and *Manhattan*, and Schrader's *Blue Collar*, to mention only some.

The postmodern shift gave rise to a series of powerful films that subverted the very idea of structured narratives, questioned the emphasis on conventional heroes, thematically criticized the simple Enlightenment view of progress, offered a mainly unflattering view of American society, and experimented with new technical and stylistic approaches that brought novelty to the cinema. The appropriation of discourses and symbols from the counterculture, if only for cosmetic effect, brought to the screen postmodern attitudes that typically dwelled on the underside of everyday life as rife with psychological and social dislocation, consistent with the postmodern concern (already visible in film noir) with social fragmentation and decentered subjects. The new cinema simultaneously challenged visions of progress grounded in modernity and in the grand heroic narratives generated within European high culture.[8] What emerged was a universe of alienated social relations, moral ambiguity, and elusive representations that gave old-fashioned protagonists little hope of carving out spheres of autonomy or winning the day. The distance between *Grapes of Wrath* (late 1930s) and *Nashville* (mid-1970s) could not have been wider.

The New Hollywood cinema appeared willing to overturn established stylistic and thematic conventions, reshaping the enterprise of filmmaking in accordance with deeply personal visions, experiences, and idiosyncrasies— even where it meant sacrificing commercial viability. More oriented to the youth market than the studio system, these films typically crossed genre boundaries, celebrated a narrative amorphousness, dwelled on fast-moving images of violence and sexuality, and celebrated the kinds of renegades, outsiders, and low-life characters that populated the noir classics. They rejected and mocked the assemblage of myths that comprised the national "consensus" or American Dream. And they upheld the director's craft as a kind of ideology of auteurism endowing the filmmaker with the status of historical agent[9] that, in turn, transformed some of them (Coppola, for example) into celebrities who could compete with actors for star recognition.

Biskind argues that the New Hollywood creative explosion came to a grinding halt with recuperation of studio power in the early 1980s, when the 1970s generation of auteurs seemed to have exhausted its creative energies.[10] But this was not quite the reality: In fact, independent filmmaking, carrying forward many of the earlier motifs, actually expanded and in some ways deepened in the 1980s and 1990s. Some of the 1970s innovators, of course, continued to make first-rate movies even if their output was spotty or inconsistent: De Palma, Coppola, Altman, Scorsese, Allen, Nichols, Lucas, Kubrick, and even Schrader and Ashby kept laboring within or on the fringes of the established film industry well past the end of the "revolutionary decade." Meanwhile, newer directors (some with an even fiercer dedication to creative autonomy) would make important contributions: the Coen brothers, Oliver Stone, Spike Lee, John Waters, John Sayles, David Mamet, Amy Heckerling, David Lynch, and Barry Levinson, among others.

Bugsy **(Barry Levinson, 1991)** *Warren Beatty as the charismatic but ill-fated gangster who, inspired by starlet Virginia Hill (Annette Bening), sets out to create a Las Vegas gambling kingdom but is ultimately destroyed by a combination of his fellow gangsters' retribution, Hill's financial shenanigans, and his own limitless hubris.*

BENEATH THE SURFACE

Among the auteurs coming of age in the 1980s, Mamet emerged as one of the most representative figures of a more developed postmodern sensibility. Mamet's fascinating and experimental *House of Games* (1987), for example, involves a twisted plot in which best-selling author Margaret Ford (Lindsay Crouse) is pitted against a slick confidence man named Mike (Joe Mantegna) and his "team." The hero quickly finds herself ensnared in a surrealistic world where things are never what they appear on the surface. Dr. Ford at first attempts to study this demimonde of crime and seediness, complete with nostalgic bar and pool hall from the 1930s, but eventually succumbs to the allure of crime. In the end, she discovers that she is capable of just about any nefarious deed: Thus, she learns that stealing can be routinely fun and then finds that even killing and maiming can be done with little remorse. She turns into a character whose entire persona gives expression to the darkest side of human nature, a motif informing the bulk of postmodern cinema. Like De Palma, Mamet uses a multiplicity of visual techniques introduced by Hitchcock and various noir directors, all galvanized by a visual script and shot list rather than a conventional written script.

In his reflective book *On Directing Film* (1994), Mamet warns, "If you find that a point cannot be made without narration, it is virtually certain that the point is unimportant to the story."[11] No doubt this statement could have been made by such directors as Scorsese, Altman, and Coppola as it was by earlier filmmakers like Hitchcock and Wilder. In the manner of Hitchcock and Wilder, Mamet crafts his films visually, in part by the use of meticulously planned storyboards, and he strenuously avoids resorting to narrative clichés and formulas. *House of Games* works brilliantly as a visual enterprise mainly because the shots are so tightly framed and noirish elements (including surrealism and different noir icons) are used so deftly. The film asks, at least indirectly, the ultimate postmodern question, "What is reality?" and answers, "Reality is, at bottom, evil"—a philosophical stance partly inherited from Hitchcock, Joseph Lewis, and the entire noir tradition. Mamet expands on this theme in a more recent film, *The Spanish Prisoner* (1997), which explores the familiar idea of a ubiquitous though largely unseen layer of evil persisting beneath the surface of ordinary human activity. Here the villain, Jimmy (played by Steve Martin), in a typical postmodern reversal of type, dupes an ingenious software engineer named Ross (Campbell Scott) out of a computer program worth millions of dollars in revenue. Jimmy employs a slick adaptation of the age-old "Spanish prisoner" confidence game to deceive Ross, then coolly attempts to kill him on a ferry boat. Jimmy and his confederates create the typical postmodern confusion where things are never what they appear and people are never what they seem to be on the surface. In the end, Mamet strips away the last remaining layer of the apparently normal reality to unveil still another layer of conspiracy where characters are not what they appear to be, this time created by police in pursuit of Jimmy.

Still another dimension of postmodern cinema can be filtered through Jean Baudrillard's concept of the "hyperreal" (discussed in chapter 1), one of the defining features of contemporary media culture. For Baudrillard, what can be described as postmodern events are best viewed as a manifestation of the "unreal," as media-generated "models of a real without origin or reality."[12] The hyperreal constitutes essentially "non-events" mediated through a commodified popular culture and communications system that dwells on images, surface appearances, and spectacles. In Baudrillard's terms, simulation involves substitution of "virtual" for "real" moments, as when media-constructed images and spectacles replace actual objects in the real world; the process can be so omnipresent as to obliterate the distinction between what is real and what is its (distorted) representation.[13] An example of the hyperreal was the 1996 television special devoted to the spectacle of unlocking and revealing the contents of Al Capone's safe. Host Geraldo Rivera presided over this pseudoevent, which turned out to be anticlimactic when the safe proved to be empty, but the media "event" of opening the safe received vastly exaggerated media attention related to the prospects of uncovering hitherto unknown Capone "secrets"—before the whole escapade fizzled. Similar contrived events and spectacles, given force by an image-driven mass media, seem to take place with almost daily frequency: celebrity trials, car chases, sex scandals, and so forth. Recent examples of such hyperreal phenomena were the O. J. Simpson murders and trials, the Unabomber saga, the media obsession with often manufactured foreign demons like Manuel Noriega, Muammar Gadhafi, Saddam Hussein, and Slobodan Milosevic, and the sensationalized White House sex scandal of 1998–1999.

Baudrillard's theories, while sometimes taken to absurd proportions, apply equally to the world of cinema, which both reproduces and artistically reflects on the hyperreal. Barry Levinson's *Wag the Dog* (1998), for example, depicts a scheme by White House operatives to deflect public attention away from charges than an American president has had sex with an underage girl "firefly" troop member inside the Oval Office. The president's staff hires a "spin doctor" to refocus media attention away from potential disaster. The spin doctor (Robert De Niro) harnesses support of a Hollywood movie producer (Dustin Hoffman), and the two conspire to manufacture a threat of war between the United States and tiny Albania over a supposed terrorist bomb threat. The Hoffman character, using state-of-the-art computer equipment inside a studio, creates newsreel footage of a young Albanian girl fleeing with a baby—footage that would only too soon be duplicated in the hyperreal fixation on internal conflicts within Yugoslavia followed by the massive NATO bombing campaign in the spring of 1999.[14] In the Levinson film, technicians later dub in a combat scene: The United States invades Albania, though apparently with little resolve, in order to make the "event" seem authentic. Meanwhile, the sex scandal/child molestation story gets bumped to the inside pages, while the hyperreal "war" with Albania is naturally splashed all over the front pages, day after day. The movie ends by suggesting that the president receive a Nobel Peace Prize for his efforts to fight a "war" against an "enemy" deemed a threat to world peace and U.S. national security. In this case, the hyperreal becomes source material for a rather intricate and, unfortunately, not so far-fetched film plot. *Wag the Dog* is just one example of 1990s-style postmodern cinema—not only because it depicts a bogus military conflict or dramatizes the larger-than-life role of mainstream media and popular culture (done even more effectively in Peter Weir's 1998 movie *The Truman Show*). What is further evident in Levinson's picture is that even the most nostalgic moments turn out to be hyperreal, including a faked 1930s folk song written and performed by Willie Nelson. (Of course, the paramount example of such contrived historical nostalgia is the 1997 blockbuster *Titanic*, which is analyzed in chapter 4.) Levinson's plot makes use of a phony record in the National Archives designed to accompany the Albanian war story involving the heroism of a young soldier named Shoemacher. The song, about an old "shoe," is "revived" and played over and over on the radio as part of a carefully orchestrated campaign to mobilize widespread war hysteria.

Wag the Dog, much like Warren Beatty's *Bulworth* (1998) and Nichols's *Primary Colors* (1998), is deeply pessimistic and cynical in tone, especially regarding the efficacy of American politics in the age of corporate control and media manipulation. (Indeed, there is a certain undertone of *antipolitics* that informs postmodern culture in general—a theme explored more fully in this book's conclusion.) Herculean efforts to distract the public from the White House scandal in *Wag the Dog* become successful even if ludicrous in their reliance on sleazy, illegal tactics. One presidential staff member has sex with a television reporter so that he can persuade her to plant the idea of a bogus "shoe" recording. The president manages to come down with a serious case of the "flu," enabling him to remain out of the limelight just long enough to let the whole episode blow over. The "heroic" soldier Shoemacher turns out to be an incorrigible rapist who attacks a young woman at the very time he is being groomed for the part of war hero. Finally, the producer is murdered by the Secret Service after threatening to reveal the truth about phony Albanian war footage. In the end, the only winners in this film are the president and his shrewd but unscrupulous spin doctor—both of whom seem capable of any deed in the service of power. The big losers are, of course, the American people, not to mention the many victims in Albania (a fact that goes unmentioned in the film). In contrast to such classics as *Mr. Smith Goes to Washington* and *Grapes of Wrath* or even *All the President's Men*, this pathetic story is far removed from the familiar narratives of valiant heroism overcoming great odds; rather, it is a lurid tale of seduction, deception, and murder—a walk on the darkest side of American politics.

Like *Bulworth* and Tim Robbins's earlier political satire *Bob Roberts* (1993), *Wag the Dog* often moves in the direction of surrealism, a sensibility it shares with film noir. There is also the familiar postmodern mood of cynical detachment, especially when it comes to "politics."[15] Levinson's attempt to show how media overdramatizations can influence not only popular consciousness but also government policy may seem preposterous, yet the hyperreal has become just as integral to American society as a whole as to the more instrumentalized realm of Hollywood filmmaking and Madison Avenue advertising. No doubt this manufacture of "reality" can have disastrous consequences such as those presented in *Wag the Dog;* it can help mobilize citizens behind virtually any military adventure, as Kellner shows at length in *The Persian Gulf TV War.*[16] Here the only victories that postmodern "heroes" could hope to win were essentially pyrrhic victories—a tragic outcome seemingly endemic to a world where human subjectivity has been so thoroughly neutralized. Change often turns out to be illusory, with "heroes" trapped in an evil labyrinthine web of relations not far removed from the noir syndrome. Hence, directors working within a postmodern motif appear, whether self-consciously or not, to embrace an image of society torn from the veneer of civilization: raw, greedy, banal, violent, and even barbaric. Their films tap deep psychological anxiety, raising a number of hard questions about the role of government, the media, family, and personal relationships in a society viewed as teetering on anarchy. A close reading of such films leaves us with a trenchant critique of a corrupt, decaying social order without any sense of possible alternatives to it; there is a mood of entrapment. Films like Altman's *The Player*, Mamet's *House of Games*, Ridley Scott's *Blade Runner*, Scorsese's *Casino*, and Sam Mendes's *American Beauty* lay bare the elements of a repressive, dark, violent society, but we mostly are left with the specter of return to a supposedly idyllic past, rendered all the more inescapable by the absence of identifiable self-activating heroes, that is, historical subjects. If postmodern cinema suggests nostalgia for a more livable past, its romanticism ultimately denies any far-reaching social or political vision.[17]

URBAN CHAOS AND DYSTOPIC FUTURES

The early postmodern films of Allen, Scorsese, De Palma, Altman, and a few others led to more intensely pessimistic and cynical films of the 1980s and 1990s by (then) less well-known directors like Stephen Frears, Tim Burton, Paul Verhoeven, John Dahl, and Joel and Ethan Coen. Motifs of the 1970s soon gave way to cinematic revisionism and further refinement of postmodern themes and styles. The 1980s and 1990s produced a series of evocative postmodern films containing nightmarish and dystopic visions of both present and future, characterized by the appearance of compelling antiheroes like Lily in *The Grifters*, Griffin Mill in *The Player*, Wendy in *The Last Seduction*, and Verbal in *The Usual Suspects*—personae we encounter later in this

The Usual Suspects **(Bryan Singer, 1995)** *With Kevin Spacey, Stephen Baldwin, Gabriel Byrne, Kevin Pollak, and Benicio Del Toro, it paints an amazingly graphic picture of duplicity, scheming, and murder surrounding the robbery of a ship docked at a pier.*

chapter. Congruent with their seductive qualities, these are actors who lie, cheat, steal, and murder, but they do generally manage to come out in one piece by the end. *Batman*'s Joker might be the first postmodern villain to dominate a film, but directors with a distinctly postmodern outlook, such as Altman, Verhoeven, Tarantino, Burton, and Allen, made films dispensing with anything like a conventional hero in favor of an emphasis on multidimensional, tortured, often tragic protagonists. Social themes darkened over time. The postmodern setting, moreover, gradually went beyond its early focus on the urban milieu and youth culture to incorporate the Old West, science fiction, suburban high schools, suburbia in general, and even the film industry itself. The pervasive mood of alienation, powerlessness, and cynicism within American society as a whole during the 1980s and 1990s was bound to deeply influence Hollywood filmmaking.[18]

***Blade Runner* (Ridley Scott, 1982)** *A seminal sci-fi thriller depicting Los Angeles in the year 2019 with its chaotic, menacing setting, a zone of crowded, rain-soaked, violent streets teeming with desperate humans and androids struggling for survival— the ultimate dystopic narrative, and one of the early ventures in postmodern cinema.*

Ridley Scott's surrealistic *Blade Runner* (1982), set in a fearsome Los Angeles of the future, paved the way for other films that followed by presenting a shockingly dystopic world in which human beings merge into robots and the nightmarish features of city life have veered totally out of control, a state of nature unchecked by any viable system of rules or laws. Scott's highly stylized sci-fi techno-noir thriller revolves around the persistent efforts of a reluctant hero named Deckard (Harrison Ford) to track down and destroy dangerous "replicants": lifelike robots endowed with superhuman qualities. Deckard tracks his prey through the streets of Los Angeles, which represent a diabolical underworld full of treachery and deceit. The city becomes a polyglot jungle filled with a haphazard collection of policemen, small shopkeepers, exotic dancers, computer technicians, inventors, and, of course, replicants. The filthy, cluttered streets teem with glitzy neon signs written in foreign languages, exotic animals (mostly artificial replicants), huge floating billboards advertising "off-world colonies," and flying cars. This setting, like that of so many later postmodern films, consists of a pastiche of curiously retro buildings and menacing products of high technology—for example, slowly rotating ceiling fans that cool office buildings reminiscent of a 1940s and 1950s noir locale, along with flying police cars and floating billboards that furnish a unique sci-fi touch. Matters have gotten so bad that Deckard is forced to spit out some unsavory debris from his beer. After barely surviving against three superhuman replicant adversaries, the protagonist finally confronts Roy, leader of the replicants. Roy proves to be virtually immortal until the climax, when, in a tribute to Hitchcock, Scott has him saving Deckard from a skyscraper roof because he (Roy) has reached the end of his preprogrammed life and does not want to die alone. In the controversial final act, Deckard flies off with a beautiful female replicant who is also doomed to be terminated at the end of her preprogrammed existence. "I didn't know how long we'd have together," says Deckard. "Who does?" This is doubly ironic considering Deckard's own ambiguous status: Is he a replicant or not? This ending, though ironic, falls short of apocalyptic endings typical of many later postmodern works. As the postmodern style matured over time, the images and messages became somewhat darker and bleaker, reflecting an increasingly anarchic universe of mayhem, conflict, and violence.

Joel and Ethan Coen's *Blood Simple* (1984) depicts a similarly bleak and threatening world but one set in the present—in contrast to the distant future of *Blade Runner*. The Coen brothers (Joel directed, Ethan produced, and the two cowrote the script) turn the noir formula inside out by transforming all the males into weak but nonetheless evil villains. The central female character, Abby (Frances McDormand), far from being the standard femme noir, is, in the words of her former psychiatrist, "the healthiest person he had ever met!" Marty (Dan Hedaya) is Abby's churlish husband, a villain seemingly devoid of compassion and everyday intelligence but who does possess one strong personality trait: He is, as he himself puts it, "anal." Marty is obsessed enough to hire a private detective (Emmett Walsh) first to uncover an affair between Abby and Ray (John Getz)—a bartender at Marty's seedy, crowded bar—and then to order the detective to kill both of them. Like a good many postmodern antiheroes, Ray lacks the wisdom and insight to realize he is being manipulated into covering up a crime he believes Abby committed after the detective kills Marty with Abby's gun. In the end, not only Ray but all the other "weak" male characters die, leaving Abby as the sole survivor—the only person with enough strength to survive Marty and his hired killer (by shooting the detective who was trying to kill her). Abby, having committed adultery with Ray in the first act, fills the role of postmodern hero in a film where conventional morality seems totally ruled out. In this film, true to its postmodern ethos, most of the characters are feeble, unintelligent, doomed victims capable of pulling off virtually any crime as long as they are provided with an incentive.

In *Dead Ringers* (1988), David Cronenberg goes so far as to divide the postmodern hero into two identical twins, both of them brilliant gynecologists named Beverly and Elliott Mantle (played in a dual role by Jeremy Irons). The Drs. Mantle are so close that their lives intertwine to the degree that they share not only their innermost feelings but their girlfriends as well. Elliott, the dominant character of the two, seduces famous actress Claire Niveau (Genevieve Bujold), then turns her over to Bev without her knowledge. After Claire discovers she has been sleeping with both brothers, she angrily confronts them and decides to leave. Over time, the twins become intricately (and dangerously) entangled in each other's lives: Thus, when Bev acquires a drug habit from Claire, Elliott becomes addicted to the medications. The twins begin a long downward slide as their careers slowly but surely disintegrate, and they ultimately lose everything. Unable to cope with life's unbearable stresses—and unwilling to differentiate into separate personalities—the twins finally opt for joint suicide. As in many of his other films, Cronenberg delivers a message of profound hopelessness and despair in *Dead Ringers*. Much like his even darker films, such as *Videodrome* (1983) and *Crash* (1996), this picture is designed to shock audiences into an awareness of the bizarre, sometimes disempowering ironies and contradictions of postmodern social and personal life. Cronenberg states, "Dramatically, of course, something that goes wrong is always more interesting than something that goes right. I have to confess to being part of that structure. It's Shavian: conflict is the essence of drama."[19]

Tim Burton's *Batman* (1989), a blockbuster moneymaker based on the popular cartoon character, takes shape within a setting that owes a huge debt to Scott's *Blade Runner:* a retro-noir city complete with surrealistic buildings, a futuristic car (the Batmobile), and even a personal aircraft with scalloped bat-shaped wings (the Batwing). The familiar Batman character (Michael Keaton) lives as mild-mannered multimillionaire Bruce Wayne by day and becomes transformed into Batman, a crime fighter extraordinaire, by night. Both personalities run across Vicki Vale (Kim Basinger), a prize-winning photojournalist. The real hero of Burton's film is neither of these characters but rather the Joker (Jack Nicholson), who turns out to be the story's unofficial villain. (Nicholson in fact receives top billing in the publicity for this film.) The Joker's character overpowers Batman's in much the same way Satan's character overpowers God in John Milton's *Paradise Lost*, although Nicholson's Joker turns out to be more bizarre, surreal, and fascinating than Keaton's Batman. When Batman, equipped with his aircraft, tries to defeat the Joker's plan to murder everyone in the city with poison gas, the Joker calmly pulls out a long gun and shoots the Batwing down. Even the Joker's lines are funnier, resembling a sort of Hitchcockian gallows humor. After one of the underworld goons the Joker has just killed falls out of his chair during a party, he calmly announces, "Look at that, folks, we've got 'em rolling in the aisles." Batman finds himself merely reacting to the Joker's latest criminal escapade and is forced, accordingly, to play a more serious (and less interesting) role, his most memorable line being "I'm Batman." Burton's film goes a long way toward reversing the traditional roles and expectations of hero and villain, a trend given new definition with *Blade Runner*, *Blood Simple*, and kindred movies of the 1980s.

In *The Grifters* (1990), Stephen Frears exposes the tension between slickly manipulated appearances and a sinister reality lurking just beneath the surface. The film combines familiar postmodern themes of alienated, tormented sexuality with deceitful, scheming characters who prey on not-so-innocent victims. All the characters turn out to be some variant of con artists ("grifters") who make their living by duping their victims out of large or small amounts of money. Angelica Huston plays Lily, a mob underling who steals a huge sum of illegal gambling money from her gangster boss. John Cusack plays her grifter son Roy, while Annette Bening plays Myra, Roy's girlfriend. Like Lily, Myra is a devotee of the "long con," an elaborate bunco game involving weeks or months of careful planning. Myra wants to enlist Roy, a "short con" artist, as her accomplice in a scheme to rob Texas oilmen, but he shies away for two reasons: He believes that criminal partnerships are extremely dangerous, and he prefers a short con modus operandi that would allow him to dupe unsuspecting barmen and patrons out of small increments of money. Myra sets out to seduce Roy with the idea of persuading him to join her in the long con, but he demurs, saying, "Forget the long con, cause I'm the one being conned." When Myra asks why, Roy responds, in what turns out to be an apt commentary on the femme noir persona, "The best reason I can think of is that you scare me to death. I have seen you, women like you before. You're double-tough, and you're sharp as a razor, and you get what you want or else." Roy's own mother, Lily, is no different. Roy adds that "sooner or later the lightning hits, and I don't wanna be around when it hits you." Myra stares at Roy incredulously, then realizes, "It's your mother, isn't it? Your own mother! And you don't even know it." Not long after, Myra, in classical femme noir style, attempts to murder Lily in her sleep, hoping to eliminate what she believes is the only obstacle to winning Roy's assistance, but Myra proves no match for the more experienced Lily, who turns the tables and kills her. Lily then acts to obtain Roy's stashed money so she can start life over again and warns Roy that "you don't know what I'll do. You have no idea! To live!" Desperate, she finally tries to seduce her own son, who is confused and distracted by her sexual advances just long enough for her to overpower and kill him and steal his money. In the ultimate scene, with both Roy and Myra dead, Lily absconds with Roy's money and Myra's identity, a frenzied person willing (and clearly able) to carry out any nefarious deed in order to survive. Frears's movie denies the idea of any bond between human beings—including that between mother and son—strong enough to prevail over an individual's greed, lust, and instinct for self-preservation—a theme central to the noirish urban labyrinth. Thanks to Huston's performance, Lily (the film's villain) earns viewers' grudging respect for her sheer determination and resourcefulness to survive; at the same time, one recoils viscerally from such utter displays of ruthlessness. *The Grifters*, like most of postmodern fare, leaves its audience with deep feelings of cynicism and paranoia about social relations in American society and indeed about the very frailty and vulnerability of the self in everyday life.

DEATH OF THE HERO

Film heroes (or main protagonists) continue to fascinate audiences today just as they have since the invention of motion pictures. Viewers never seem to tire of vicariously identifying with heroic individuals (less often groups) struggling to pursue some goal, usually in the most difficult circumstances and against terrible, seemingly impossible odds. This preoccupation with heroes, of course, dates back to ancient times, when audiences flocked to Egyptian, Greek, and Roman theaters (sometimes amphitheaters) to attend plays about the fate of dramatic, tragic, or comic protagonists, marveling at the deeds of such figures as Osiris, Perseus, Theseus, Heracles, and Odysseus. In most cases, these early heroes managed to emerge triumphant in one way or another, often by virtue of slaying dragons and other monsters. A variety of conquering hero types still evokes reverence and adulation today, spanning the fields of politics, sports, the military, business, and, of course, entertainment. In 1748, Thomas Morell wrote the now famous lines "See, the conquering hero comes! Sound the trumpet, beat the drums!" thereby echoing a common form of hero worship for his period. Many contemporary heroes, by contrast, display frail, idiosyncratic, compromised, all-too-human qualities corresponding to an entirely different category of protagonists we have come to expect in present-day film culture.

The familiar hero's journey has long been mapped and plotted as well as deconstructed and psychoanalyzed; heroes and their deeds have an undeniably seductive appeal within an infinite variety of personal and historical contexts. The complex trajectory of the hero figure in classic modernist cinema can be understood as following a roughly three-act structure that begins with depiction of the "normal" environment inhabited by the main protagonist: riding across the plains on horseback (Westerns), cruising through urban streets (gangsters), living a staid existence on a vaguely remote planet (science fiction), and so forth. It is here the audience comes to identify with the hero, who is sure to exude a powerful charisma on screen. The second act is marked by some profound challenge to the hero, who accepts what Joseph Campbell refers to as a "call to adventure"—a point at which the saga's ordeals and obstacles can be expected to intensify or take new twists. (One way directors may choose to dramatize this epic conflict is through a drastic change in setting, for example, by transferring the action from plains to town, from urban streets to office or apartment building.) It is in this "second act" that the protagonist faces trials and challenges that provide a severe test of the hero's mettle and resolve; if the cinematic journey demands *successful* heroes, then the characters in question must be able to rise to the occasion, negotiating a journey Campbell defines as the "road of trials."[20]

Moving along this "road of trials," the hero figure often encounters a series of crises putting his or her resources, fortitude, and self-esteem to the test while exposing weaknesses or flaws that must somehow be acknowledged and then conquered. This transformative moment normally constitutes the "turning point" of a plot, which occurs in the middle or toward the end of the second act. Once this midpoint has been reached, the hero will begin to assert the upper hand by means of resolving problems and transcending roadblocks—predictably with the assistance of good fortune or help from others. As this climactic stage is reached, the modernist scenario allows the hero a platform (either metaphorical or real) for the purpose of justifying ultimate goals and the stratagems employed to achieve them. Here, in the "third act," matters conventionally return to "normal" as the protagonist is shown reentering the world of the first act, although this trajectory does have its nuanced differences.

One clear deviation from this pattern is the tragedy, where the hero eventually fails to pass the midpoint challenge and reverts back into something of a weak, flawed, self-centered existence that could never be represented, for example, in the classic Western, combat genre, or historical drama. As we have seen, Charles Foster Kane in *Citizen Kane* represents the quintessential ideal type for such a tragic pattern: He faces a personal crisis when his opponent in the New York governor's race threatens to reveal that Kane—married to a well-connected woman—is having an affair with another woman, news that will surely lead to his political defeat. Confronted by the choice of retiring from the race for "health reasons" or facing certain scandal and defeat, Kane stubbornly holds fast to his course despite its consequences for family, friends, and the public, not to mention his own mental sanity. "Don't worry about me," he says. "I'm Charles Foster Kane. I'm no cheap, crooked politician trying to save himself from the consequences of his crimes." Kane's friend Leland (Joseph Cotten) then responds, "The truth is, Charlie, you just don't care about anything except you. You just want to convince people that you love them so much that they should love you back. Only you want love on your own terms. It's something to be played your way, according to your rules." Unfortunately, Kane never wins much empathy from people in his social milieu, a fact that immediately sets up this film as a classic tragedy. Like film noir (which in many ways *Citizen Kane* exemplifies), tragedies depart from standard melodramas in that the hero never changes or else changes only when it is too late. *Hamlet* exemplifies the tragic hero who finally takes the proper action (at least according to custom) in dealing with his murderous uncle, but his action comes too late and he (Hamlet) dies at the hands of his uncle's treachery. By contrast, Kane never changes despite obvious pressures to reconsider his course of action—the irony being that the hero dies bereft of the love he so desperately sought.

In the realm of tragedy, as the hero dauntlessly resists change in the face of strong, sometimes unbearable external pressures, it becomes increasingly difficult to alter those character flaws that contributed so much to the predicament in the first place. Thus, Rod Steiger plays a New York pawnbroker who, though deeply compromised, decides to change but does so much too late in Sidney Lumet's drama *The Pawnbroker* (1964). Sol Nazerman, the pawnbroker, struggles with his suppressed memories of Nazi concentration camp horrors and must confront a number of personal challenges along his "road of trials." The main problem for Nazerman lies in the fact that he has allowed his regard for humanity (not to mention *himself*) to dissipate because of his repression of the past. After decades of calloused demeanor that has been rather functional to his inner-city business, Nazerman finds himself unable to either give or receive friendship much less love. In the end, he does in fact strive to peel away layers of repression—but not before his young pawnshop assistant is killed trying to protect him. In this film, Nazerman joins a long list of tragic heroes, including Hamlet, King Lear, Othello, Oedipus, Willy Loman, Charles Foster Kane, Captain Queeg, and

Bonnie and Clyde. He would be joined by an even larger assemblage of failed, miserable, tragic protagonists in later postmodern films.

In a movie like *Thelma and Louise*, on the other hand, the two heroines do in fact rise to meet their excruciating predicament: Fed up with the horrors of their domestic situation, the two women rebel and set out on their own journey together before they quickly encounter a major crisis—Thelma having to fight off a rapist in a tavern parking lot—that is quickly "resolved" when Louise shoots and kills the man, leading to their desperate "road of trials" as they confront a world of unyielding patriarchal and law enforcement nightmares. Endlessly resourceful but unable to turn the tide against mounting pressures for their capture, Thelma and Louise decide to commit suicide by driving their surrounded car into the Grand Canyon. Because the heroines die, *Thelma and Louise* might properly be labeled a tragedy, yet the characters have been transformed and in fact redeemed insofar as they wind up better off than they were during the "normalcy" of act 1. Thus, Thelma tells Louise that she feels "wide awake" for the first time as they both contemplate their ultimate journey while trapped by pursuing cops. "I don't remember ever feelin' this awake. Everything looks different."

E. M. Forster's distinction between "flat" and "round" characters within a narrative seems appropriate here, the former being typical of modernist works in which the hero is able to maintain a morally strong, socially distinct persona from beginning to end. Such protagonists include John Wayne in most of his classic Western roles, James Stewart in *Mr. Smith Goes to Washington*, James Bond in his multiple incarnations, and Preston Tucker (Jeff Bridges) in Coppola's *Tucker* (1988). While "flat" heroes of this sort will struggle against powerful external forces and (possibly) against some inner demons, the character modality is generally one-dimensional, which, though perhaps "real" in some sense, ultimately takes on the veneer of cinematic familiarity and predictability. "Round" characters, on the other hand, are those who simultaneously possess strong and weak qualities: Bugsy Siegel in Levinson's *Bugsy* (1991), Godfather Don Corleone in *The Godfather*, Jake Giddis in *Chinatown*, and, of course, Thelma and Louise. The heroes and heroines of film noir exemplify "round" characters in the fullest sense of the term. It is hard to imagine Philip Marlowe, Sam Spade, Mildred Pierce, or Guy Haines (Farley Granger) in *Strangers on a Train* as anything but complex and multidimensional—sympathetic yet vulnerable, psychologically compelling but flawed, and visionary while trapped in their own social immediacy.

Modernist heroes fit within the theoretical framework of Max Weber, notably, the concept of charisma or charismatic leadership according to which the strong leader makes history by powerfully influencing, sometimes transforming society in the capacity of particular roles: shaman, prophet, warrior, magician, or revolutionary.[21] In the realm of Hollywood film, the Weberian-style hero often takes on the warrior form, though the protagonist occasionally emerges as prophet (*The Day the Earth Stood Still*), shaman (*Star Wars*), or magician (*Batman*). In any case, to Weber the hero/leader is conceived as a figure who stands apart, endowed with the vital element of charisma and under some circumstances superhuman powers, akin to Freud's description of psychologically imposing individuals capable of exercising enormous personal and intellectual power over others in their orbit. Great men, Freud argued, typically receive the veneration of their contemporaries, even if their greatness rests on qualities and achievements completely foreign to the culture of the majority of people.[22] Whether we define them as great men, gods, mystics, or supermen, modernist narrative heroes embody this more exalted view of the heroic ideal. The Weberian hero appears in modernist films like classical Westerns and combat movies depicting protagonists with rare skills and abilities to perform virtual feats of magic as they cleave a hangman's noose from 200 yards while riding a galloping horse, shoot holes in silver dollars thrown high into the air, or storm enemy barricades against impossible odds. Modernist heroes embody a kind of Promethean ideal that can apply to virtually any historical or social context. No matter how many guns were arrayed against him, the classic Western hero as portrayed by John Wayne, Gary Cooper, and Alan Ladd triumphed over the most ruthless, skillful villains, and, of course, they were usually forced to use the most coercive methods.

Weber observed that modernist heroes tend to emerge during tumultuous and crisis-ridden times—moments calling forth the intervention of a strong, creative leader who becomes a vehicle for salvation or some type of social change. Taken to extremes, this idea evokes Nietzsche's theme of an "Ubermensch" who has the capacity to transform society through the will to power. Modernist heroes may not exactly possess such Nietzschean capabilities, but fierce tenacity in the face of overwhelming obstacles seems to be a nearly universal feature of such protagonists, scattered throughout the history of literature as well as film. In contrast, the postmodern actor is more likely to be shaped by an existential ethos involving perpetual struggle with and against the *limits* and *contextual restraints* of action: The life-world is dominated by conditions that generate moods of anxiety, chaos, ambiguity, confusion, and indeterminacy. The stress here is placed on individuals trapped in a precariously (though not necessarily *hopelessly*) difficult existence, with few prospects for escape or redemption; they are more likely to be trapped within, than to be shapers of, the flow of history. Hobbes's familiar pessimism regarding the human condition, stated in his famous passage about life being "nasty, brutish, and short," in many ways coincides with the spirit of postmodern culture. Hobbes wrote that in a state of nature, people are constantly at war with each other—that is, unless a powerful government emerges to impose a binding system of rules and procedures. The fate of individuals here is to live out a miserable, dangerous life in the midst of conflict and insecurity.[23] In postmodern films, the viewer comes to expect characters who fear and distrust each other, much as they would in the kind of unbridled state of nature assumed by Hobbes. Postmodern actors will frequently embellish states of cynicism, pessimism, fear, and confusion, unless or until they are already resigned to their imminent death—as in the case of Lester Burnham in *American Beauty*.

The eclipse of the modernist hero takes on new meaning with the evolution of postmodern cinema, as we have already seen with *The Grifters*. In contrast to *The Grifters*, Altman's *The Player* (1992) features a slick, ethically detached Hollywood producer named Griffin Mill (Tim Robbins), described by Burt Reynolds (sitting at a café in a cameo role) as a classic (Hollywood) "asshole." Reynolds's luncheon companion, the film critic Charles Champlin, then mutters, "One of a breed," but Reynolds immediately corrects him with, "No, actually not one of a breed, there's a whole breed of them, they're breeding them, actually." That statement, in effect, sums up Altman's message in what might be his best film. Mill shows his dark, treacherous side early when he kills a young, down-on-his-luck would-be scriptwriter (Vincent D'Onofrio) during a struggle in a dark parking lot, then calmly steals the victim's wallet and smashes the car window to make the crime look like robbery. Mill then proceeds to seduce the dead man's girlfriend (Greta Scacchi), to whom he has become fatally attracted. Robbins delivers a superb portrayal of an ambitious, unprincipled, heartless, and ultimately murderous character who in the end not only avoids jail but instead receives a fat promotion to head the studio. Altman embellishes his version of the postmodern antihero by showing that crime *can* pay (a traditional film noir motif), that the consequences of pulling off even the most serious of crimes amount to nothing as long as one has money and clout. *The Player*, like *The Grifters*, suggests that people willing to lie, steal, and murder can be found walking the streets of every American city—charming but dangerous people who are able to turn their vices into great success and privilege.

Paul Verhoeven's *Basic Instinct* (1992) evokes similar images of vast, incomprehensible threats closing in on the individual in a world where it seems absolutely no one can be trusted. The film costars Sharon Stone

(Catherine Trammell) as a rich, emotionally cold, and manipulative novelist who enjoys hot lovemaking with both sexes and surrounds herself with killers she uses as case studies for her crime fiction and Michael Douglas as Nick "Shooter" Currin, a tough San Francisco police detective with a reputation as a maverick with the propensity for using his gun in the line of duty. Nick becomes powerfully attracted to Catherine during his investigation of her boyfriend's murder. Jeanne Tripplehorn plays Dr. Beth Garner, a police psychologist and Nick's former girlfriend—yet another femme fatale and the film's central villain. *Basic Instinct* opens with refracted, upside-down images of a couple making love: As they reach the moment of climax, the woman calmly ties her partner's hands to the bedstead with a white silk handkerchief. Then, sitting astride him, she bends over, grabs an ice pick, and, as the two reach orgasm, suddenly stabs him repeatedly, winding up covered with his spurting blood. Although the murderer has the appearance of Catherine, we never actually see her face, allowing for the surprise ending where it is revealed that Beth, the psychologist, is the real murderer. Catherine, however, turns out to be Beth's psychological twin who, only after a powerful internal struggle, is able to refrain from murdering Nick in exactly the same way—as the two reach orgasm. Both women are highly manipulative, sexually dangerous, and (potentially in the case of Catherine) murderous. Nick, for his part, is hardly a saint, exhibiting an addictive personality, an uncontrollable temper, and a quickness to fire his gun. Indeed, every character in the Verhoeven film happens to be weak, corrupt, and even criminally psychotic, which is likely to generate among viewers not only feelings of revulsion against these specific characters but also feelings of contempt for the human condition.

Clint Eastwood, once a Western icon, directed *Unforgiven* (1992), perhaps the first Western to be made in what might be called a neo-noir postmodern style, overlaid with elements of nostalgia tempered by cynicism.[24] A retired gunfighter turned pig farmer, William Munny (Eastwood) is tempted to emerge from his poverty-stricken retirement in 1880 by the irresistible lure of reward money. Munny is joined on the killing trip by two accomplices, the Scofield Kid (Richard Harris), a young wanna-be gunfighter, and Ned (Morgan Freeman), Munny's former outlaw sidekick. The three arrive in Big Whiskey, Wyoming, hoping to earn their reward by killing two cowboys, only to run afoul of a tough and sadistic sheriff named Little Bill (Gene Hackman). Little Bill beats Munny to a pulp, but Munny is able to escape and is nursed back to health by several prostitutes. He and the Scofield Kid then complete the task of killing the two cowboys, but instead of becoming a heroic act, the fatal shootings, as might be the case in classic Westerns, come to appear as little more than unadulterated murder. In contrast to the familiar modernist heroic gunfight on Main Street or at the OK Corral, the Kid shoots one of the cowboys while he is relieving himself in the outhouse. Modernist Westerns like *Stagecoach*, *High Noon*, and *Shane* portray the killing of villains as a glorious, courageous, and necessary act, whereas Eastwood demonstrates the banal and primitive nature of killing by stripping it of all its traditional glory and heroism. Unlike modernist narratives in which order evolves out of chaos at a point when the villains die, there can be order (and no redemption) in *Unforgiven*. Eastwood's portrait of the Western experience is too sordid, harsh, and foreboding to provide any solace to its protagonists or indeed to its audience. It turns out to be a Western shorn of the romantic patina it had acquired throughout the modernist period. Commenting on this film, Eastwood remarks, "What was so fun in playing [William Munny] is that he's sort of forced by lack of prosperity into doing the only thing he really knows how to do well. And he has bad feelings about that, and he keeps bringing up his own demons—people he has killed. . . . I've read it in a way, have been able to interpret it in a way, that death is not a fun thing. Somebody, somebody is in deep pain afterward—the loss of a friend, or even the person who perpetrates it."[25]

John Dahl's *The Last Seduction* (1994) offers yet another example of a neo-noir thriller in which the human condition appears nothing short of wretched. This film centers on the exploits of femme noir Wendy (Linda Fiorentino), an aggressive young woman working as a telemarketer by day who starts a murder-for-hire business at night. From the moment Wendy appears on screen, there is no doubt about her role as a scheming femme fatale capable of destructive acts. Although she is seen arriving at a small town in upstate New York, it is clear she is really "city trash"—a persona she expresses in multiple ways, such as inserting her finger into a pie she finds in her boyfriend's refrigerator labeled "Love, Grandma." Cold and sadistic, she uses sex and violence in the time-honored manner of the femme fatale, what Nicholas Christopher calls "a sort of low-end parody of a Manhattan yuppie."[26] She gets immediate attention in a bar when she complains, "Who's a girl have to suck to get a drink around here?" When Mike tries to build a romantic relationship with Wendy, she coolly pleads that "fucking doesn't have to be more than fucking, o.k.?" Mike attempts to pull back from Wendy as she tries to convince him to join her murder-for-hire operation, declaring, "I just realized that I don't want to be with you enough to be like you." Yet like Roy in *The Grifters* and so many other socially compromised men in neo-noir films, Mike finds he is not strong enough to stand up to Wendy; in the end, he becomes her willing accomplice, even trying (unwittingly) to kill her husband. Wendy in fact eventually kills her husband, then calmly burns the only shred of evidence that could link her to the murder, saving Mike for taking the blame in the process. She goes off by herself, probably to find another victim/accomplice to help with her terrible business. In the fashion of postmodern cinema, Dahl's thriller leaves audiences feeling deeply pessimistic not only because all characters in the film are base and weak but also because any of them can easily turn out to be deadly killers.

Oliver Stone, possibly the most politically (if not culturally) radical of postmodern filmmakers, constructed several films on a foundation of perished heroes, including most notably *Wall Street* (1987), *Talk Radio* (1988), *The Doors* (1991), and *JFK* (1991). In *The Doors*, of course, it is rock icon Jim Morrison (Val Kilmer) who serves as the idealized dead postmodern hero. A tragic victim of his own commercial success in the highly charged rock world of the 1960s, Morrison wastes his brilliant talents by becoming hooked on both alcohol and drugs, dying at the age of twenty-seven (the same age as Janis Joplin and Jimi Hendrix) after reaching unparalleled cult status. *JFK*, of course, features what must be considered the ultimate dead hero, President John F. Kennedy, who in the film shares center stage with maverick New Orleans District Attorney Jim Garrison (Kevin Costner), who reopened the JFK assassination case only to run aground after years of the most herculean efforts. Garrison sets out to uncover a shadowy conspiracy said to consist of elements within the CIA, FBI, Mafia, and anti-Castro Cubans—a conspiracy covered up by the infamous Warren Report. In Stone's view, these groups conspired to murder Kennedy because he supposedly refused to escalate the Vietnam War fast enough and because he decided against committing U.S. military forces during and after the ill-fated 1961 Bay of Pigs invasion of Cuba. In the end Garrison fails to convict anyone of Kennedy's assassination. Garrison, Kennedy, and Morrison all fit the paradigm of dead or powerless heroes, although Kennedy and Morrison go on to achieve larger-than-life heroic status well after their untimely deaths. The difficult and tragic sagas of Wall Street manipulator Gordon Gekko (*Wall Street*), talk radio host Alan Berg (*Talk Radio*), journalist Richard Boyle (*Salvador*), and Vietnam veteran Ron Kovic (*Born on the Fourth of July*) all fit this pattern to one degree or another, although Kovic at least was able to transform himself into an antiwar activist. In the case of *JFK*, however, Stone places blame for catastrophic personal and political events on the bloated power of the military–industrial complex (and its strange mixture of allies), enabling him to situate the death of the hero within specific structural and historical circumstances.

Postmodern cinema offers an image of failed, confused, or simply inept protagonists within the comedy genre as well—drawing on the legacies of such influential cinematic figures as the Marx Brothers and Charlie Chaplin. Thus, Woody Allen's main protagonists typically exhibit what might be defined as "postmodern" flaws in the form of neuroses, insecurity, indecisiveness, and abject failure in personal relations. In *Annie Hall* (1977), Alvy Singer (played by Allen) experiences overwhelming difficulties in his relationship with Annie (Diane Keaton) and can only observe ironically that his involvements with women remind him of a story about a man whose brother thought he was a chicken. After explaining that he did not turn in his brother for being a chicken because they needed the eggs, Singer muses, "Well, I guess that's pretty much how I feel about relationships. You know, they're totally irrational and crazy and absurd, but I guess you keep going through it because most of us need the eggs." At another point, Alvy confesses that he has a rather pessimistic view of life, saying, "Life is divided into the horrible and the miserable. Those two categories." Allen comments, "That's a reflection of my own feelings. Be happy that you're just miserable."[27]

Allen's *Zelig* (1983), featuring a chameleon-like figure played by Allen, manages to survive in a media-saturated, celebrity-crazed world only by becoming the ultimate conformist, able to spontaneously and effectively alter roles, shapes, and even hair and skin color in order to fit in with the dominant feature of his surroundings. He becomes a jazz musician, a Chinese man, an extremely obese character, and even a member of Adolf Hitler's entourage, among his other personae. *Zelig* appears as the quintessential postmodern mock hero who embodies virtually every known disorder and insecurity of a world shaped by the fleeting images and spectacles of media culture. Allen himself maintains that Zelig must be regarded as the true embodiment of social conformity—a notion supported in the film by such intellectual luminaries as Irving Howe. Allen explains, "Well, I think it's a personality trait in everybody's life. It began in Zelig's life when he said that he had read *Moby Dick*. And you can often find this with many people. Somebody asks, 'Have you read this or that?' and the other one says 'Yeah, yes, of course,' even if he hasn't. Because they want to be liked and be part of the group." In *Zelig*, Allen depicts a world in which a mechanistic regime of technology, conformity, and artificiality works against human individuality at every turn.[28] It is hard to imagine any construct farther removed from the Weberian ideals of charisma and heroic action than Allen's *Zelig*.

Tim Burton's *Ed Wood* (1994), like *The Player*, critically explores the Hollywood movie industry, but Burton's film goes to further extremes than Altman's by virtue of documenting the strange career of Edward D. Wood Jr., posthumously named "Worst Director of All Time" in 1980 by the Motion Picture Society of America. Wood's notoriety arose after he directed two horrific bombs: *Glen or Glenda* (1953), a film loosely depicting the life of Christine Jorgenson (the first man to undergo a sex change operation), and *Plan 9 from Outer Space* (1959), a poorly crafted sci-fi thriller dramatizing an alien plot to conquer the Earth by resurrecting corpses. Both low-budget films could lay claim to being the worst ever made, but they continue to enjoy loyal cult followings because they are hilariously (though unintentionally) funny. Bela Lugosi stars in *Glen or Glenda*, and he has one scene in *Plan 9 from Outer Space* that was shot just before his death. In Burton's excellent film, Johnny Depp stars as Ed Wood, and Martin Landau portrays an old, drug-addicted Lugosi, with both giving outstanding performances and both winning Academy Awards (in 1995). Burton keeps the audience laughing at Wood's clueless demeanor as a producer/director, especially during reenactments of the shooting of Wood's films. In *Plan 9 from Outer Space*, for example, Wood uses spray-painted paper plates hanging upside down from fishing poles as flying saucers, igniting one of the plates to simulate a burning saucer. In another scene Wood, dressed as a woman for *Glen or Glenda*, runs into Orson Welles at a Hollywood bar. Wood asks Welles's advice about shooting the film, and Welles advises, "Visions are worth fighting for. Why spend your life making someone else's dream?" Armed with this inspiration, Wood returns to the studio to insist that the picture follow his ill-conceived schema. In contrast to most postmodern melodramas, Burton's fast-paced comedy does not leave the viewer with feelings of pessimism or despair but rather elicits a cathartic response filled with pity toward Wood and his tribulations with the film industry (and his own demons). Injecting large portions of satire and irony, Burton manages to soften the emotional blow that often accompanies postmodern cinematic narratives. By exposing the worst aspects of Hollywood filmmaking, however, he manages to turn the postmodern gaze inward toward the industry itself, much like Altman in *The Player*.

In a rather different postmodern-style comedy, Amy Heckerling's *Clueless* (1995) focuses its lenses on Beverly Hills high school kids (and parents) with their materialistic, provincial, culturally insular lives. Like several other Beverly Hills–themed films of the same period, including *Down and Out in Beverly Hills* (1986), *Beverly Hills Cop* (1984) and its successors, *Beverly Hills Brats* (1989) and *Beverly Hills Vamp* (1990), along with Heckerling's earlier *Fast Times at Ridgemont High* (1982), *Clueless* adopts a harshly critical stance toward the wealthy and their pampered, selfish, hedonistic lifestyles. Heckerling's hero in *Clueless* is Cher (Alicia Silverstone), a spoiled "valley girl" who divides her time between shopping at the mall with her upscale friends and setting up her best friend (Stacy Dash) and even her teachers in relationships. Cher's philosophy is inherited from her father, a suc-

cessful litigation lawyer who believes that clever argumentation and manipulation will always prevail, social ethics and other proprieties be damned.
"Tell me the problem," he explains to Cher, "and I'll tell you how to argue
it." On learning that Cher had used specious arguments and manipulation to
raise her report card grades from C pluses to A minuses, her father erupts
with praise, telling her, "Honey, I couldn't be happier than if they were real
grades." But Cher soon becomes trapped in situations that cannot be resolved through even the most shrewd forms of argumentation and scheming.
First, having failed her driver's test, she fails to manipulate the motor vehicle
examiner into giving her a passing grade. She then discovers that the boy she
covets is gay, a reality further distancing her from the "I can manipulate anything" approach to life she is so fond of utilizing. Finally, she falls in love with
her stepbrother, an older, more intellectual college student who somehow is
able to make her ashamed of her clueless ways. In the end, Cher decides to
give herself a spiritual makeover, turning into something of an activist with a
budding interest in world affairs. In the manner of *Ed Wood*, Heckerling's
film does not leave the audience with strong feelings of depression about human existence since, after all, it is a comedy. But it does point a cynically ac-
cusing finger at what might be called the cream of American youth by portraying them as mindless, materialistic schemers totally unaware of the
universe outside their self-contained, privileged suburban world.

Bryan Singer's *The Usual Suspects* (1995), structured along neo-noir
lines, takes the audience back to a familiar hopeless and dystopic outlook
characteristic of the postmodern drama. The title seems borrowed from the
famous line near the end of *Casablanca*, spoken by Claude Rains: "Round
up the usual suspects." Singer's film revolves around five hardened felons apprehended by the New York Police Department for a "voice lineup." Kevin
Spacey plays Roger Kint, a crippled criminal so quiet that he was mockingly
nicknamed "Verbal," who provides voice-over narrative that, along with
abundant rain, regular flashback scenes, and night-for-night cinematography,
imparts a Gothic style appropriate to film noir. Following the lineup, police
grill the men thoroughly, but not one of them shows signs of breaking down.
Verbal says, "What the cops never figured out, and what I know, is that these
men would never break, never lie down, never bend over for anyone, anyone." In reality, however, one of the men decides to leave the group after it
becomes involved in a string of armed robberies—but, sadly, he turns up
dead. In retaliation, the (now four) men attack a lawyer supposedly working
for "Keyser Soze," a shadowy, legendary criminal whose vast business empire
seems to reach into every corner of the nation and beyond. As the film progresses, we become aware that the narrative, related by Verbal and presented

in visual form by Singer, departs significantly from the course of events we observed in the first scenes; we gradually come to realize that Verbal has not been telling the whole truth to the police. In the final scene, as Verbal walks out of the police station a free man, we see him straighten his crippled gait and relax his twisted arm, and when he swings briskly into a waiting car, we finally realize that Verbal is actually Keyser Soze. Further reflection enables the viewer to conclude that the entire series of crimes was manufactured by Verbal so that he could murder the only man who could have identified him as Soze. It finally becomes clear that everything in the film, aside from the first and last scenes, is entangled with lies told to the police to draw suspicion away from Verbal. In the end, Verbal/Soze gets away with the crime, absconding with a vast sum of money and the knowledge that no one can identify him for his crimes since he has become, in effect, a completely different person, a sort of "nonperson."

American Beauty's Lester Burnham suffered one of the most curious fates in Hollywood film history, that of being dead before the film even begins— following the path of *Sunset Boulevard*'s Joe Gillis. Both heroes begin their narratives with foreknowledge of their demise—the main difference being that Burnham seems happily reconciled with his fate, crying again and again just before he is shot that "I'm great! I'm great!" Gillis's doom-laden confession at the outset of Wilder's classic strikes an inevitably fatalistic chord, while Burnham's spiritual philosophizing moves closer to the shallow optimism and anti-intellectualism of post-1960s New Age thinking. Contemporary postmodern heroes may die in the fashion of Burnham, but an undercurrent of narrative redemption and psychological renewal can often be found to permeate the whole scenario. Earlier film noirs, as we have seen, consistently lack this element of redemption, exhibiting a one-dimensionality that is transcended in movies like *Pulp Fiction*, *Dream Lover*, and *American Beauty*. On the other hand, postmodern films like *Thelma and Louise*, *The Grifters*, and *The Last Seduction* offer a more relentlessly bleak, cynical account of contemporary American life—an account virtually without the possibility of redemption. These two quite disparate yet intersecting currents of postmodern cinema reflect a parallel divergence of trends across the social terrain in general. The more labyrinthine, ambiguous tone of films like *American Beauty* may be symptomatic of a culture of material affluence—but that culture too is riddled with its own sharp contradictions that indeed become readily visible in the film's narrative. In any event, it seems clear that postmodern heroes of whatever psychological or ideological stripe illuminate in some fashion the dominant popular mood of anxiety, despair, and cynicism in post-Fordist capitalist society.

Critics like Michael Medved bemoan the emergence of such postmodern antiheroes, arguing instead for a return to less controversial, less complex, more positive heroes of the past. "In years past, in the heyday of Gary Cooper and Greta Garbo, Jimmy Stewart and Katharine Hepburn, the movie business drew considerable criticism for manufacturing personalities who were larger than life," he writes. In comparison, more present-day Hollywood protagonists are shown as "smaller than life, less decent, less intelligent, and less likeable than our own friends and neighbors." He decries the fact that "Hollywood increasingly invests its most artistic aspirations in loathsome losers, disturbed and irresponsible misfits who give us little to care about and nothing to admire."[29] Here Medved makes the familiar error of confusing the thematic intentions of a writer or filmmaker with the particular mode of character development filling out the narrative. Thus, we know that Captain Ahab may be the egomaniacal, tormented protagonist of *Moby Dick*, but the notion that Herman Melville somehow hoped his readers would become just as insanely obsessed as Ahab is, of course, preposterous, totally irrelevant to the narrative structure at hand. The same point could be made regarding Arthur Miller's Willy Loman in *Death of a Salesman*. Authors and directors establish characters who may or may not be intended as positive role models: Many cinematic portraits of heroes are in fact designed to shock or anger viewers into emotionally reacting to certain scenes, motifs, and characters that might have little resonance with the filmmaker's actual values. In this vein, Medved fails to grasp that harsh, dissonant, even pessimistic images can serve to make a poignant statement about the contemporary human condition in general or American society in particular. Such images, as we have seen, are at the core of filmmaking for postmodern directors like Allen, the Coen brothers, Tarantino, and Stone.

Just as postmodern heroes often reflect a brooding pessimism or cynicism about everyday life, they also seem obsessively self-absorbed and introspective, ready to provide viewers with sophisticated analyses of just what went wrong and why they were doomed to ineptness and failure. They seem to be aware of the frailty not only of the human condition but also of nature; life is filled with circumstances of tragedy that entrap the self, and this can be cause of self-reflection.[30] Gillis in *Sunset Boulevard* refers to himself as a "poor dope," while Bickle in *Taxi Driver* complains that "loneliness has followed me my whole life. Everywhere. In bars, in cars, sidewalks, stores, everywhere. There is no escape. I'm God's lonely man." This kind of gut-wrenching, self-effacing narration, of course, would rarely be found in modernist cinema or, if found, would be quickly ameliorated in some way. It is difficult to imagine characters played by John Wayne or Gary Cooper somehow fitting into the category of postmodern hero as we have conceptualized it here—possibly Humphrey Bogart and Spencer Tracy, but even then within limited parameters. Modernist figures would not typically be seen baring their souls on screen—yet this is precisely what postmodern heroes do as a matter of course in film after film. Deckard in *Blade Runner* casually informs the audience, "Sushi, that's what my ex-wife called me. Cold fish." Protagonists in Woody Allen and Oliver Stone films routinely confess to the audience their sometimes disabling feelings of anxiety, insecurity, fear—and failure. Such characters not only wind up mired in failure but are further inclined to blame themselves for the generally miserable state of their existence.

Some more recent modernist heroes have in fact assimilated certain elements of the postmodern ethos, drawing in some cases from the noir and neo-noir sensibilities. Thus, action pictures like *The Patriot* and *Gladiator* celebrate admirable modernist figures who give expression to more than a patina of critical, even pacifistic views about war, violence, and patriotism. Mel Gibson plays Benjamin Martin, a revolutionary war hero in *The Patriot* who starts out as a strong opponent of war. The film's trailer chronicles the crimes committed against him: "They threatened his family. They destroyed his home. They killed his child." After such brutal attacks by the British, Benjamin sheds his pacifism and assumes the normal attitude of a modernist action hero: He kills effectively and enthusiastically. Similarly, Maximus (Russell Crowe) in *Gladiator* pledges his life to ancient Rome, only to be forced into killing for his emperor. Both of these conventional protagonists are ultimately able to carry out their mission, but to do so they must overcome deeply ingrained antiwar sentiments on the road to heroic action destined to change the world.

Viewed within its larger panorama, postmodern cinema offers a harsh critique of present-day social existence, culture, and politics that places it alongside existentialism, chaos theory, surrealism, anarchism, and Marxism in its multiple twentieth-century variants. It explodes a good many powerful myths of contemporary American society, including above all the notion that any individual can, with just the right mixture of work ethic, motivation, and fortune, create his or her own personal destiny. By establishing heroes as extraordinarily complex beings with a mixed ensemble of "good" and "bad" qualities, postmodern narratives depict characters with greater depth and realism than in the case of mainstream Hollywood filmmaking. Heroes like Jake Gittes, Travis Bickle, Deckard, and Lester Burnham are held back by deep, sometimes fatal personality flaws—Gittes being too powerless to overcome the greed and lust of antagonist Noah Cross, Bickle being too overcome by life on the streets, Deckard being too emotionally cold and detached to fully engage himself in public life, and Burnham being so taken with his sudden discovery of life's great beauties that he cannot save himself from the clutches of homophobic Colonel Fitts. Each protagonist illustrates in different ways the utter hopelessness and frailty of the human condition. What we observe in postmodern settings is anything but the stability and order infusing modernist film culture, but rather corruption, brutality, lust, greed, violence, and destruction that is usually far more visible and graphic than in the noir tradition.[31]

THE TORMENTED FAMILY

No discussion of American cinema—postmodern or otherwise—would be complete without an attempt to engage the realm of the family, gender relations, and sexuality, probably the most emotionally charged of all spheres of social life. The vast majority of film plots relate in some fashion to this sphere, even where (as in combat and sci-fi movies) they would seem to be rather peripheral to the larger narrative structure. If modernist filmmaking has not always romanticized the conventional nuclear family, with all its patriarchal features, it has, to one degree or another, upheld this basic social unit of American society as the standard repository of established values, intimate personal relationships, and effective childhood socialization. Hollywood studio heads typically venerated patriarchal family values even where reality was shown as radically departing from the ideal—as in the familiar noir cycle where children were usually nowhere to be seen and treachery, deceit, and violence were frequently the norm in relationships between husbands and wives. Postmodern cinema, on the other hand, offers a far more jaundiced view of the family as an institution wracked by conflict, disillusionment, and mayhem in a rapidly changing labyrinth of chaos and violence.

Few things in American culture evoke more intense feelings than family life—or at least those *symbols* of family life that permeate the general culture. Politicians regularly build their election campaigns around the theme of "family values," although both the meaning and the policy implications of such "values" have remained at best remote or opaque. By the nineteenth century, the family had been established as a core economic and social institution, furnishing labor for such activities as clearing land, barn raising, house raising, and, of course, harvests; it was surely the central agency of childhood socialization and became (in Christopher Lasch's reference) a kind of "haven in a heartless world" where both men and women could find solace away from the stresses and tribulations of everyday social life.[32] Large extended families prevailed during the first generations of colonization and the push westward, a period when the vast majority of Americans made their living off the land. In his book *The Third Wave*, Alvin Toffler refers to this largely agrarian period as the "first wave" of social transformation that eventually gave way to smaller "second wave" nuclear families that would be characteristic of a modern order shaped by industrialization and urbanization. Rapid and extensive transformations throughout the twentieth century placed enormous burdens and strains on the American family. As Toffler observes, the extended family unit—always inhabited by elderly relatives—was not sufficiently adaptive or mobile, so it was eventually torn apart by migration to the cities, battered by the inevitable economic storms that came with modernity. The old family structures were increasingly streamlined, stripping themselves of unwanted dependents as they grew smaller, more flexible, and more detached from the economic sphere, that is, as they evolved to meet the pressures of industrial society.[33] It is these smaller, more adaptive nuclear families that have become synonymous with the concept of family life in contemporary society—and it is this definition of family that resonated throughout the popular culture (including filmmaking) in most decades of the twentieth century.

The American nuclear family was reaching perhaps its most mature expression just when American cinema was taking off as a dynamic cultural form, and indeed depictions of seemingly stable family life entered into the romanticized cinematic world erected by the first Hollywood studio chieftains, whose conventional audience was drawn largely from the working class.[34] Of course, mass media always celebrated smaller nuclear families over extended traditional structures—a phenomenon rarely depicted except as a target of ridicule, as in modern-day television comedies like *The Beverly Hillbillies* and *The Real McCoys*. In general cultural terms, the nuclear family is still understood as a pillar of social order and economic stability, vital to reproduction of the existing state of affairs at least where gender relations and personal lives become well established, routinized, predictable. The family here guarantees a smooth, harmonious transition from one generation to another, ensuring a more or less fixed connection with the larger social order. The comfortable nuclear family of modernist fare was nowhere more vividly depicted than in Capra's *It's a Wonderful Life* (1946), a film perhaps even better known for its highly romanticized version of family life than for its uplifting portrayal of the Christmas spirit. The protagonist George Bailey, as we have seen, takes it upon himself as local savings and loan president to assist the working-class people of Bedford Falls toward financing their modest homes. Married with three children, Bailey winds up pitted against a wealthy Scrooge-like banker who, lacking any discernible family bonds, is driven by greed to acquire the town's whole expanse of real estate. The tear-jerking climax, in which the entire community rises to support the Baileys with hundreds of small donations, powerfully reaffirms the values of family life in small-town America while also vilifying the rich businessman because of his lust for power and wealth—a familiar Capraesque theme. Capra's film set the standard for postwar family melodramas, even as it embellishes a cloying sentimentality destined to be seen as maudlin by later audiences. At the same time, as Girgus observes, *It's a Wonderful Life* also anticipated the coming crisis of the American family insofar as it revealed a growing sense of insecurity within the structure; indeed, Bailey himself winds up abandoning the family in a social context beset with dramatic change.[35]

John Ford's *The Grapes of Wrath* (1941) depicts a first-wave extended family, the by-now famous Joads, that through its protracted, difficult odyssey winds up transformed into a second-wave nuclear family in reaction to powerful social forces—Dust Bowl migration, agricultural centralization, and the rise of union solidarity—depicted in John Steinbeck's book. Galvanized by Ma Joad (Jane Darwell), a strongly maternal figure who struggles valiantly to keep the family together, the central protagonists of *Grapes* face a series of daunting obstacles along their journey to California. Once removed from their Oklahoma roots, however, the family begins to disintegrate—the first casualty being Grandpa Joad, who initially refuses the invitation to move west and then dies shortly after the journey starts. Grandma Joad dies soon thereafter. Noah, the oldest child, later drops out as the family reaches California. Others within what was earlier a solidly extended family follow suit. What finally emerges for the Joads is a smaller reconstituted family unit that, in its compressed evolution here, bears a striking resemblance to the larger transition from first- to second-wave families representative of historical trends in American society at this juncture. Thus, from its initial composition of nine people spanning three generations, the Joads as portrayed in *Grapes of Wrath* develop into a modern nuclear family comprising married parents and their two children.

Reflecting on the thematic evolution of postwar cinema, one could argue that a vital strain within the modernist hero has been embellishment of the nuclear family—often against harshly difficult intrusions and obstacles—as in the case of *It's a Wonderful Life*. Thus, the protagonist of George Stevens's classic Western *Shane* (1953), played by Alan Ladd, winds up saving the Starrett family along with other local homesteaders by outgunning the villains in a protracted, action-packed shootout. As Shane prepares to ride into the sunset, little Joey Starrett (Brandon de Wilde) begs him to stay so that he can continue to help the family, but Shane recognizes that his role as protector is no longer needed since the family is now strong enough to survive after the villains are dispatched. Yet the unstated premise of this film, like the majority of Westerns, is that a Shane-like savior will surface whenever needed to defeat the omnipresent forces of evil and mayhem. A similar case is J. Lee Thompson's 1962 noirish thriller *Cape Fear*, where respectable small-town attorney Sam Bowden (Gregory Peck) is forced to use every device at his disposal to protect his family from vengeful psychopathic villain Max Cady (Robert Mitchum). Early in the film, Cady tells Bowden that he will avenge himself against Bowden's family for Bowden's part in sending Cady to jail for eight years on rape charges. Says Cady, "I like to put values on things, like the value of eight years, the value of a family. Interesting calculations, wouldn't you say, Counselor?" When, after seemingly endless days of terror, Bowden finally prevails over the desperate and wily Cady, Bowden has the last word: "You're strong, Cady. You're going to live a long life. In a cage. That's where you belong and that's where you're going. And this time for life. Bang your head against the walls. Count the years, the months, the hours—until the day you rot." Anticipating future postmodern fare, *Cape Fear* focused on psychopathic behavior and the theme that beneath the harmonious veneer of suburban society lie horrors waiting to be revealed. As Meyer observes, the film asks the basic question, "Would the *Leave It to Beaver* lifestyle be safe from dark forces within and without?" He adds, "Intended or not, the clear message of *Cape Fear* is that in the heart of every suburban daddy burns a vicious, bloodthirsty demon." The two main characters, while ostensibly separated by good and evil, "prove to have much in common. Each will murder, each is capable of brutality, each is driven to dominate."[36] Thompson's picture suggests a prelude to such later films as Lynch's *Blue Velvet* and Mendes's *American Beauty*, showing a definite continuum from earlier noir classics through neo-noir and, later, more embellished postmodern cinema.

During the 1950s and 1960s, Americans gathered around their television sets to view modernist serials of family life such as *Leave It to Beaver*, *Ozzie and Harriett*, *Father Knows Best*, *Dobie Gillis*, *The Dick Van Dyke Show*, and *I Love Lucy*—all shows steeped in family values and depicted an essentially conservative, romanticized image of daily life with its patriarchal "normalcy." Through literally thousands of episodes, the family appeared as the unquestioned bastion of all meaningful social interaction: dating, getting married, having children, sitting together at family meals, meeting with neighbors, sharing household chores, going out to restaurants, and so forth. As with television, most popular films of the period embraced this idealized vision of family life, where stability was the norm, all problems were manageable, and men were the breadwinners while women stayed home raising children and tending to household chores. The nuclear family was first and foremost the center of everyday life, the pillar of traditional gender relations and social order, and the main source of childhood socialization.[37]

Since the 1960s, however, this image of the nuclear family has come under sustained challenge, to the point where it may now be possible to speak of a postmodern shift in which the old model more or less collapsed and has given way to fundamentally new social realities. Toffler's work pointed toward the onset of a "third wave" characterized by new levels of diversity and fragmentation of social life in general, reflecting changes even more profound than those associated with the earlier industrial revolution.[38] With the emergence of post-Fordist society defined by heightened geographical mobility, social dispersion, and deep cultural transformations, the nuclear family appears as simply *one* of several possible living arrangements: people living alone or in groups, gay/lesbian couples, single-parent families, and couples living without children. The "Ozzie and Harriett/Father Knows Best" pattern stands today as quite exceptional both in its composition and in its romanticized stability. Where the American family is concerned, the prevailing experience today is that of fragmentation, alienation, and conflict—a trend unfolding over several decades even where the popular culture ignored or deflected it.[39] In the United States, as in other advanced industrial societies, divorce rates have skyrocketed (now at nearly 60 percent for the United States), while the average length of marriages has plummeted to just twenty-six months. Children are influenced more by the mass media, schools, and peer groups than by parents.[40] Family bonds have eroded in the face of far-reaching changes in the workforce, suburbanization, the pervasive role of media and popular culture, cultural trends spawned by the 1960s including the sexual revolution and feminism, and the broad consequences of material affluence. While the third-wave family structure described by Toffler and others was expected to be emancipatory, the historical reality has turned into something far more harsh and disillusioning: The turbulence and insecurity that now seems endemic to civil society as a whole has infiltrated the most intimate arenas of daily life, including the inner sanctum of the nuclear family. And this has become a defining feature of postmodern cinema, which, here as elsewhere, has built on the established legacy of noir culture.

Conventional marital and familial arrangements have become an intensely vilified social arena in postmodern cinema, as they were for film noir, insofar as sexuality is depicted less as a pleasurable, loving activity than as something alienating and tormented, indeed, a source of conflict and violence. Where the family does not vanish altogether within such cinematic narratives, it is depicted as a realm of deceit, conflict, disorder, and violence—not much different from the familiar turbulence and harsh urban existence of film noir and clearly resonant with the actual historical situation. This is a great remove from the modernist worldview, articulated in its classic form by Hegel, who understood the family as a divinely ordained union established on "love, trust, and common sharing" built around the sacred purpose of conceiving and nurturing children. Postmodern cinema depicts the family as bereft of love and romance; rife with jealousy, betrayal, and violence; and grounded in little more than a crude, scheming instrumentalism.[41]

Of course, terrible personal conflict involving duplicity, treachery, and murder has long been a staple of film narratives, going back to the early crime thrillers as well as such classics as *Gone with the Wind*, *A Streetcar Named Desire*, *Cat on a Hot Tin Roof*, *Who's Afraid of Virginia Woolf?*, *Mildred Pierce*, and *The Graduate*. Indeed, manipulation, deceit, and triangular affairs can be found in such literature as the Bible and of course enters into a good deal of ancient mythology: We know that Eve tempted Adam in the Garden of Eden (first chapter of Genesis) and that Delilah betrayed Samson. In dramatic fashion, classic noir movies dwelled on duplicitous relationships that, more often than not, led to murder, and, of course, the same could be said of neo-noir films set in the 1970s and later. What sets postmodern cinema apart from its antecedents, however, is the relentlessly harsh cynicism (and fatalism) it expresses regarding what has long been considered—at least on the surface—the most sacred institution of American society. We argue that the extremes to which Hollywood filmmaking has presented an anguished, tormented, hopeless image of the contemporary family reflects the ways in which family and personal relationships have so deteriorated over the past three decades or so. Films like Woody Allen's *Interiors* (1987), Robert Benton's *Kramer vs. Kramer* (1979), Paul Mazursky's *An Unmarried Woman* (1978), Lewis John Carlino's *The Great Santini* (1979), and Graeme Clifford's *Frances* (1982) all, in quite different modes, exposed the deep and often paralyzing contradictions of family life in the modern, rationalized, urban or suburban setting. Perhaps more to the point, as Medved argues, the observer is at pains to find *any* positive representations of the family in even the most conventional movies made after the 1960s.[42] However bleak this picture, it merely served to lay the groundwork for darkening images of the family constructed by filmmakers, both mainstream and indie, during the 1980s and 1990s.

One of Allen's few "serious" films, *Interiors*, draws on the acting skills of Diane Keaton, Kristin Griffith, Marybeth Hurt, E. G. Marshall, Geraldine Page, Maureen Stapleton, and Sam Waterston, all part of an extended family of talented, upper-middle-class folks who experience the gradual, wrenching breakup of parents and its devastating emotional impact on three daughters and their husbands. We witness the entire family reeling from the shock of a disintegrating relationship that hits the mother Eve (Page) hardest. Having designed the interiors of their fashionable apartment tastefully if also very precisely, earning her the epithet "Ice Queen," Eve is so domineering that her husband Arthur (Marshall) decides he has no recourse but to leave the marriage. Anticipating one of the opening scenes of *Husbands and Wives*, the film shows the husband announcing his idea of a "trial separation" at the start, throwing the others into a state of anguish and disorientation—although this scarcely deters him from remarrying a woman just the opposite of Eve, someone more lively and socially outgoing. Harboring an interest in reconciliation with Arthur, Eve becomes more depressed over time and winds up committing suicide. In the wake of such trauma, the family is able to pull together enough to furnish its members with an element of stability and normalcy, suggesting that at least *some* harmonious family life can be attained even in the midst of tragedy and chaos. While *Interiors* departs from Allen's typically jaundiced view of relationships, the mood it conveys is nonetheless that of inescapable depression. Referring to the tragic theme of the picture, Allen comments, "*Interiors* was not the usual kind of affair. So not only were people annoyed at me—their lovable comic figure—for having the pretension to try something like this, but giving them *this kind of drama* as well. They felt there was a solemnity to it, which I like in films."[43] It is probably accurate to say that such "solemnity" fits Allen's general view of the family.

In *The Great Santini*, Robert Duvall plays Lieutenant Colonel Bull Meacham, a skilled Marine fighter pilot obsessed with his macho image and with the idea of going to a war at a time (1962) when there was no war to fight. Meacham's modus operandi is to confront the world head-on, neither giving nor taking quarter, starting with his treatment of young pilots assigned to him and carrying into his apparently picture-perfect family over which he strives to create a benevolent, tutelary dictatorship. Family members set out to mediate his dictatorial rule in small ways, but with minimal results at best. Meacham's oldest son Ben (Michael O'Keefe) experiences the greatest difficulties as he struggles to achieve manhood under the commanding eye of "The Great Santini," as his father is nicknamed. Ben is initially unable to confront his father, who repeatedly insults and humiliates him over the most trivial failings. For example, when Ben plays for his high school basketball team against a heated rival, his father demands that he "deck" an opposing player—an action that breaks the player's arm and gets Ben thrown off the team for the rest of the season. Over time, as family members rebel one after the other, Meacham's goal of converting his family into a hierarchical, disciplined military unit fails; the whole structure falls apart, generating more chaos than order. Much like Eve in *Interiors*, Bull Meacham has an obsessive lifestyle and dictatorial tendencies that in the end do not, and probably cannot, succeed, although Meacham winds up partially redeemed when, at the end, he steers his crippled plane away from a populated area rather than choosing to save himself by bailing out. One possible conclusion here is that the breakup of such families signals the emergence of new, freer, but more disorderly social units that are the hallmark of the postmodern era. The newer units, insofar as they can achieve cohesion, more fully resonate with the fragmented social conditions surrounding the family in a post-Fordist world.

Throughout the 1980s and 1990s, cinematic depictions of family life turned increasingly mordant and violent, filled with characters (including children in many cases) who exhibit cold, selfish, hateful, and even murderous traits; gender relations have come to embody little that is positive or redeeming, much less inspiring or romantic. In the view of conservative critics like Medved, harsh, dystopic images of the family must be understood as part of a broader ideological onslaught on "family values": "It's the wildly disproportionate emphasis on the darkest, most downbeat aspects of marriage that betrays Hollywood's anti-family agenda."[44] Medved refers to such films as *Thelma and Louise*, *Reversal of Fortune*, *Mortal Thoughts*, *Sleeping with the Enemy*, *War of the Roses*, and Scorsese's remake of *Cape Fear*—all produced after the late 1980s—as strong indictments of monogamy, romance, marriage, and the nuclear family. Other kindred observers like William Bennett echo this sentiment, identifying Hollywood filmmaking as a major source of moral breakdown. One of the most frightening depictions in this vein is *Fatal Attraction* (Adrian Lyne, 1987), which by the late 1990s had become a sort of mainstream cult classic, reportedly the most written-about film in recent history. No doubt *Fatal Attraction* has had an enormous influence on the flourishing of low-budget "erotic thrillers" beginning in the 1990s—films that rarely portray the family as anything but a hornet's nest of trouble.

Lyne's film revolves around the infamous extramarital affair between Dan Gallagher (Michael Douglas), a highly charged business executive, and Alex Forrest (Glenn Close), an editor for a publishing house. The two meet at an office Christmas party and become immediately attracted to each other, and, with Dan's wife out of town, they decide to have dinner. Dan quickly becomes vulnerable to Alex's seductive charms. After initial physical contact in an elevator, their encounter explodes in a bout of lovemaking at Alex's apartment: The sex is pursued with great passion as well as humorous ineptness, reflecting Lyne's desire to belittle a relationship destined to be nothing more than a brief fling. Indeed, for Dan, still committed to his wife (Anne Archer), this was to be nothing more than a casual encounter. For Alex, however, a romantic interlude with Dan means that she has found a true mate; she quickly becomes cloying and possessive. After Dan returns home, she phones him and demands, "What happened? I woke up and you weren't there. I hate that!" Psychological turmoil for both of them is the inevitable result, giving rise to all manifestations of scheming, counterscheming, and mayhem within a narrative that immediately became familiar to most Americans. Feeling rejected and humiliated, Alex threatens to tell Dan's wife about the sexual encounter, a move that would naturally place the marriage in jeopardy. In the end, Alex, frustrated and desperate, tries to murder Dan's wife, but, after a harrowing struggle, it is Alex who ends up killed by her intended victim. Not only does Alex's menacing behavior violate the unspoken rules of extramarital affairs, but she is forced to pay the ultimate price (her life) for nothing beyond a few moments of sexual indiscretion. *Fatal Attraction* evokes deepseated fears of intimacy and sexuality—not to mention the fearsome risks (psychological and physical) that accompany sexual desire—that go back to the beginning of human societies, yet rarely have these fears and risks been depicted with such frightening power. The film demonstrates, moreover, just how easily familial arrangements can be challenged, subverted, and subjected to nightmarish outcomes; the family structure, like society in general, is highly vulnerable to any number of (internal and external) forces.

Much the same point was established, with equal force, in Scorsese's 1991 remake of *Cape Fear*, a film that takes on a more postmodern veneer than the original. The basic motif of the earlier narrative has been aptly described by Meyer as "Leave It to Beaver Goes to Hell," but the new version departs significantly from the original even as the plot line changes little. The lawyer in Scorsese's adaptation (Nick Nolte) contrasts with Peck's earlier representation insofar as he runs a sleazy legal practice that even his wife (Jessica Lange) attacks for its excessive reliance on "dirty tricks." (Peck's lawyerly status in the original *Cape Fear*, on the other hand, was nothing if not blandly respectable.) Further, in keeping with the postmodern ethos, Scorsese's Bowden is shown cheating on his wife and is even caught at it, provoking a series of violent rows—whereas Thompson's Bowden lived a

***Cape Fear* (Martin Scorsese, 1991)** *A distinctly postmodern remake of J. Lee Thompson's 1962 film noir classic, it chronicles attorney Sam Bowden's (Nick Nolte) harrowing encounter with psychotic ex-con Max Cady (Robert De Niro), graphically depicting a suburban middle-class family's descent into hell, with villainy extending to both sides.*

very traditional, midwestern family existence not too far removed from the 1950s television sitcoms. More tellingly, the free-spirited young woman involved with Bowden is later raped by Cady (Robert De Niro) in the kind of brutal scene that would never have found its way into the original script. Scorsese's Bowden is also revealed to have actually withheld crucial evidence at Cady's trial, whereas the earlier Bowden had apparently conducted himself with ethical propriety—the emphasis thereby shifting from a noble defense attorney (Peck) to a crooked lawyer whose social standing and professional respect were sharply called into question. In the end, Scorsese's remake of *Cape Fear*, shown almost thirty years after the original, represents a darker, more relentlessly cynical vision of both the family and its menacing environs.

In a similar vein, Andrew Davis's 1998 remake of Hitchcock's classic *Dial M for Murder* (1954), retitled *A Perfect Murder*, was given a distinctly postmodern motif. Based on Frederick Knot's play, Hitchcock's version has the husband (Ray Milland) arranging to murder his beautiful wife (Grace Kelly), involved in a romantic affair with a character played by Robert Cummings. Both Kelly and Cummings are portrayed as virtual saints, with the husband emerging as a natural villain. In the Davis film, however, the heroine Emily Taylor (Gwyneth Paltrow) is married to wealthy investor Steven

Taylor (Michael Douglas) but decides to carry on a romantic dalliance with con artist David Shaw (Viggo Mortensen). Rather quickly, Shaw discovers that he is helplessly in love with Emily. As in the case of *Fatal Attraction*, the extramarital affair inexorably leads to a downward spiral of deception, scheming, threats, and murder. In the case of Emily, she must fend off a killer hired by her cuckolded husband, who does everything possible to make the murder appear like an attempted robbery—a killer hired by her lover David, who was paid handsomely by the husband. As in *Dial M for Murder*, the wife physically resists and then kills her assailant. But in *A Perfect Murder*, there is a further plot twist as the husband winds up killing the hired lover in order to retrieve the money and also get revenge. After Emily confronts Steven with her suspicions about his role in the botched murder attempt, she sets out to flee what had become a tormented marriage but in the process winds up getting sucked into a deadly cycle of violence and counterviolence. She finally kills Steven in self-defense, freeing herself from the pernicious web of conspiracy, murder, and corrupt personal relations established at the outset of the movie. As the quintessential neo-noir thriller, *A Perfect Murder* spins a tale of treacherous entanglements leading to destruction and death. In depicting all characters as fully embroiled in this harrowing journey, Davis's remake turns out to be a far darker, more jarring film than its predecessor, where scheming and mayhem are given a more isolated, idiosyncratic definition. In the postmodern world, scheming and violence appear more natural and pervasive, more endemic to those corrosive social conditions engulfing the whole terrain of family and gender relations.

Curtis Hanson's *The Hand That Rocks the Cradle* (1992) similarly chronicles a ruthless assault on and in some ways disintegration of contemporary family life. A young doctor's widow named Peyton Flanders (Rebecca de Mornay) seeks revenge against the Bartel family for the parents' alleged role in her husband's suicide. The saga commences when Claire Bartel (Annabella Sciorra) undergoes a routine physical exam by Peyton's gynecologist husband and is fondled, prompting her to file sexual abuse charges with the support of her husband Michael. Devastated by the charges, Dr. Flanders commits suicide, at which point Peyton goes into a bout of hysteria and loses the baby she was carrying. Flanders blames the Bartels for her husband's death and decides to seek revenge by getting hired as a nanny for the Bartels' infant child. Unaware of Peyton's sinister motives, the Bartels welcome her to the household—but the welcome is soon worn thin as the family is put in a state of siege by a series of calamities resulting from the diabolical schemes of the new nanny. Emotional discord quickly takes over the previously tranquil Bartel home, in much the same way it consumed the

Bowdens' happy family life in *Cape Fear*. Hanson shows the extreme vulnerability of the family to unpredictable incursions coming from both within and outside the household. Here the tension is finally resolved only with Peyton's death, a fate that befalls her only after her plots against child and husband go awry. Although the Bartels family somehow managed to survive these catastrophes, it was forced into a state of siege requiring it to adopt aggressive, manipulative, and street-smart modes of coping, much as in *Cape Fear*. This film, like *Fatal Attraction*, which probably served as its inspiration, resurrects the kind of bleak portrait of nuclear family life that permeated classical noir cinema: Threats to personal and social stability can appear at any time, often without reason or logic. *The Hand That Rocks the Cradle* suggests that everyday American life has become so venal and corrupt that even the "safe haven" of the family provides no secure place to hide; a menacing social milieu permeates even the most intimate of personal realms. The film graphically warns that people can no longer trust their doctors, nannies or baby-sitters, or indeed members of their own family, for it becomes apparent that evil is to be found lurking everywhere, to be discovered at the most confounding times and places—a familiar theme in Hitchcock and noir cinema.

An even bleaker view of personal life is depicted in Nicholas Kazan's *Dream Lover* (1994), which pairs wealthy, divorced architect Ray (James Spader) with the beautiful but enigmatic Lena (Madchen Amick). The two happen to meet at a supermarket, initiate a torrid romance, and then rather impulsively decide to get married. But Ray soon becomes suspicious of Lena, whom he believes is hiding dark secrets about her background—an awareness partly inspired through recurring dreams that take place at a carnival where clowns mock his capricious and hasty choice of partner. He soon learns that Lena has been spending one day each week at the Hotel Chanticleer and is convinced she is having an affair. As suspicions pile up, Ray investigates Lena's life history (and finds a good deal of deceit) and then questions her about her activities at the hotel. Overcome by a rush of honesty, Lena speaks glowingly of her sexual encounters, provoking such intense anger in him that he attacks her—a moment she brilliantly seizes on to have her husband committed to a mental asylum. In the asylum, with plenty of time to reflect, Ray comes to believe that his wife has been scheming from the outset to have him institutionalized so that she could get his money. The whole concept of "dream lover" on which the relationship is built turns out to be bogus, with Lena surfacing as the quintessential femme noir. Ray, for his part, becomes yet another victim of the marriage trap—an arrangement presented here as intrinsically duplicitous, corrupt, and violent. He finally

Dream Lover (**Nicholas Kazan, 1994**)   *With Madchen Amick and James Spader, it exudes a strongly postmodern undercurrent of dark turbulence lurking beneath a seemingly harmonious "dream" relationship, as both partners deploy ruthless methods to get what they want, leading to the husband's murder of his wife while he is incarcerated at a mental hospital.*

achieves the ultimate revenge when he lures his wife to the asylum with the intent of strangling her to death, knowing that as a certified lunatic he cannot be held legally accountable for his deed. He winds up quickly transformed from naive, helpless victim into a scheming, ruthless murderer, all in defense of his dignity and possessions. In postmodern fashion, *Dream Lover* illustrates that redemptive violence can be an efficacious response for individuals faced with a threatening universe of thieves, con artists, character assassins, and murderers, replicating familiar motifs of pictures like *Fatal Attraction*, *The Grifters*, *Basic Instinct*, and *A Perfect Murder*.

Sam Mendes's Oscar-winning *American Beauty* (1999) depicts one of the most visibly dysfunctional families in the history of American cinema. Kevin Spacey plays Lester Burnham, an advertising executive who hates his job and who is married to Caroline (Annette Bening), a real estate agent on the verge of having an affair with Buddy (Peter Gallagher), the self-styled "king of real estate." Thora Birch plays the couple's teenage daughter. The middle-aged Lester becomes infatuated with his daughter's high school friend (Mena Suvari), precipitating a severe midlife crisis: Lester quits his job, starts jogging and pumping iron, and smokes marijuana with teenage neighbor

Ricky, who has a crush on his daughter. In fast motion, the Burnham family begins to unravel as Lester and Caroline declare war on each other, just after Lester decides to take a job at a local hamburger stand. All three family members wind up despising each other at one time or another. Then Ricky's homophobic (but latently gay) father murders Lester—he imagines Ricky and Lester are having an affair—at which point Caroline is convinced that she has been deeply in love with Lester all along and feels guilty for not making amends. By the end of the film, the Burnhams seem to have actually regained a sense of normalcy, but this is reached only after Caroline's affair with Buddy, Lester's obsessive infatuation with a teenager, and then Lester's tragic murder. The notion of "beauty" contained in the film's title refers ironically to the love that family members share for each other but also to the enormous pressures of a conflicted, individualistic, materialistic world that have effectively driven love out of their consciousness.

Don Roos's comedy *The Opposite of Sex* (1998), made more than fifty years after *It's a Wonderful Life*, presents an image of American family life that could not possibly be further removed from Capra's romantic vision. The film's star (and narrator) is Christina Ricci, who plays Deedee Truitt, a precocious, scheming, sexually active seventeen-year-old who comes from what is now ritually defined as a dysfunctional home. The Truitt family includes Deedee's shrewish, self-centered mother; a gay half brother; and the latest of her several stepfathers. Deedee nonchalantly informs the audience that the Truitts "started out as a typical American family, and you know how that ends up—they typically went to shit pretty quick." After her stepfather dies early in the film, Deedee decides to run away from her suffocating Louisiana home to live with stepbrother Bill (Martin Donovan), a gay high school teacher who lives in a small Indiana town. Arriving on Bill's doorstep, she meets Matt (Ivan Sergei), Bill's youthful live-in lover, whom she proceeds to seduce because she finds gays "clean" and "attractive." Deedee announces that she is pregnant, presumably the result of her liaison with Matt. Pleased that she is going to have his baby, Matt opts to escape with Deedee and set up housekeeping in Los Angeles. Devastated by this turn of events, Bill does everything he can to track down the couple in hopes of being reunited with Matt. Meanwhile, Bill's friend and fellow English teacher Lucia (Lisa Kudrow) decides to make a play for the now available Bill. The two track Deedee and Matt to Los Angeles with the help of their sheriff friend Carl (Lyle Lovett), who turns out to have a crush on Lucia. This byzantine plot becomes even more complex with the appearance of Jason (John Galecky), Deedee's teenage lover who, we learn, is the real father of the baby she is carrying. During a heated argument, Deedee accidentally shoots and kills Jason, at which point she and Matt flee to Canada, where they encounter first Bill and Lucia, who have been following them, and then Carl, who has been following Lucia. Eventually, Deedee gives birth to a boy, Lucia informs Carl she is pregnant with his child, and Matt links up with a young gay man. In the end, Bill somehow becomes involved with Deedee's male probation officer, Lucia and Carl marry and have a child, and everyone in the melodrama seems reconciled to their situation except Deedee, who by the end of the film decides yet again to flee. In the final scene, she cynically tells the audience that "sex always ends up in kids or disease or, like, you know, relationships. That's just what I don't want—I want the opposite of all that, because it's not worth it."

The Opposite of Sex epitomizes postmodern sensibilities toward family life and personal relationships, celebrating a wide variety of phenomena that never would have been associated with earlier Hollywood versions of the harmonious nuclear family: abject personal irresponsibility, flight from familial obligations, divorce, remarriage, homosexuality, bisexuality, unwed pregnancies, infidelity, and general mayhem. In place of the established pattern of "boy meets girl, boy loses girl, boy gets girl back," this film refashions that narrative structure into "girl meets boy, who is bisexual, loses boy to another boy, has child out of wedlock, leaves it with her gay half brother, and then abandons them all." Despite its radical departure from conventional norms and the collapse of anything resembling familial stability, the film still manages to end on a strikingly positive note, as Deedee grudgingly admits she has matured while the other characters seem to have achieved loving relationships in the most difficult of circumstances. Here *The Opposite of Sex* echoes sentiments contained in *American Beauty* with its tongue-in-cheek cynicism about family—at the same time conceding the possibility of a reconstituted (i.e., postmodern) family. Still, this and other pictures of its genre portray a vision of families and relationships rife with sexual tensions and infidelities, fear of commitment, moral breakdown, and selfish behavior. Problems such as teenage sexuality, homosexuality, AIDS, drug use, personal duplicity, emotional callousness, and stealing form the backdrop against which the multitude of individual characters enter into inevitably difficult relationships.

Following this trend, Neil LaBute's *Your Friends and Neighbors* (1998) explores the intricate personal lives of two couples and two friends trapped in a series of complicated, painful love triangles. Building on his 1997 film debut *In the Company of Men*, LaBute focuses his narrative mainly around the psychological dynamics of three male characters. He whimsically gives all his characters rhyming names, such as Mary, Barry, Cheri, Terri, Cary, and

Jerry—played by Amy Brenneman, Aaron Eckhart, Nastassja Kinski, Catherine Keener, Jason Patric, and Ben Stiller, respectively. As the scenes unfold, however, we see the characters referring to each other simply as "him," "her," "that guy," "wife," "husband," and "best friend," all of them possessing a variety of sexual hang-ups, neuroses, anxieties, and fetishes we have come to expect from the postmodern setting. The crosscutting personal interactions charted in *Your Friends and Neighbors* begin to unravel after Cary (Patric), who lives with Cheri (Kinski), seduces Mary (Brenneman), who in turn is married to Cary's best friend (Eckhart). Of course, Cheri and Barry soon discover the infidelity, which spurs Cheri toward a covert homosexual relationship with Terri (Keener); other relationships begin to disintegrate as new ones appear. Thus, Mary ends up with Jerry (Stiller), and Cheri winds up with Terri. This offbeat film can be interpreted as a powerful statement about the increasing fragility of contemporary gender relations and sexuality that, it would appear, remain trapped within the larger world of fragmentation and alienation endemic to contemporary American society.

Steven Soderbergh's *Erin Brockovich* (2000) provides a different view of the postmodern condition, one grounded in (historically modernist) popular struggles against corporate power. A prime example of cinematic realism, this film contains a nuanced mixture of modern and postmodern set against Promethean legal battles waged by Brockovich (Julia Roberts) and her attorney boss Ed Masry (Albert Finney) on behalf of hundreds of victims of toxic chemicals that California utility giant PG&E allowed to seep into the groundwater over several decades. In the vein of Mike Nichols's *Norma Rae* (1982), Brockovich, a twice-divorced mother of three young children, represents the divorced-woman-with-children committed to the social justice side of the family trajectory. Soderbergh's film chronicles Brockovich's difficult but inspiring emergence from abject poverty to millionaire legal researcher—a true account that seems stranger than fiction. In between, Brockovich connects with an unemployed biker (Aaron Eckhart), but she is able to build her most genuine relationships with working-class residents of the desert town of Hinckley, for whom she becomes a heroine because of her tireless, selfless fight to expose the horrors that PG&E has visited on hundreds of residents. While Brockovich forges rather close bonds with Masry, she has trouble maintaining intimacy with her children while (as in the case of Norma Rae) her personal relationship deteriorates because she lacks time and energy—presumably one of the terrible (inevitable?) conditions resulting from the decision of a mother/girlfriend/wife to participate in a social movement. There is the usual postmodern cynicism regarding what had been previously regarded as standard familial arrangements. Viewed in a positive light, *Erin*

Brockovich emerges as the portrait of (postmodern) social interactions extending to the workplace and other zones of everyday life far beyond the nuclear family; it offers hope for a *reconstituted* sense of community appropriate to the dispersed, pluralistic life-world of advanced industrial society.

Yet another dystopic view of nuclear family life passes through the vehicle of what might be called the postmodern black comedy, an early example being the Coen brothers' *Blood Simple*. Peter Berg's *Very Bad Things* (2000) stands as a more recent illustration of this cinematic trend. The film chronicles a series of bloody events during and just after an out-of-control bachelor party in Las Vegas: Five young men embark on a wild night of celebrating the long-anticipated marriage of one of them, Robert, to the beautiful but domineering Laura (Cameron Diaz). The party begins over drinks at a few Vegas casinos and then takes off in earnest as the men imbibe prodigious amounts of alcohol, marijuana, and cocaine, reaching a peak when Kyle (Christian Slater) hires a prostitute to visit their hotel room. Once the prostitute arrives, the men seem to go absolutely crazy, falling down and breaking furniture—but the real mayhem occurs when Michael accidentally kills the prostitute as he impales her head against a light fixture while having frenetic sex. Faced with a dead, naked woman bleeding all over the bathroom floor, the group sobers up, and, with Kyle acting as leader, the men decide to spirit the body out of the hotel and bury it in the desert. However, before they can pull this off, the hotel security officer visits the suite and discovers the prostitute's body. Kyle stabs and kills him to keep things quiet. United in their resolve to conceal their murderous deeds, the men clean up the hotel room (no small task) before dismembering the two corpses and stuffing them into two suitcases that they take to the desert in the middle of the night. Later, having returned to the surface calm of their suburban homes without being discovered, the men become frightened when they see a newspaper photo of the security guard, now listed as a "missing person." Here the plot degenerates into further murder and mayhem as the various characters become totally unglued and start attacking each other. In outlandish comedic fashion, this brutal action unfolds against the ceremonious backdrop of the wedding. At Kyle's insistence, the men manage to act calmly during the wedding rehearsal dinner, but two of them (brothers) wind up fighting in the parking lot until one fatally rams the other with a sport-utility vehicle. Although they avoid suspicion, telling police the death was accidental, by this point Kyle emerges as a full-fledged psychopath: He dispatches the now suspicious wife of the dead brother (Jeanne Tripplehorn), then shoots and kills the surviving brother in order to give the new crimes the semblance of a love triangle among family members.

As the wedding day arrives, best man Kyle realizes he must murder the groom out of fear he will talk to authorities about the grisly events. Discovering Kyle in the act of murdering her future husband, Laura nearly beats the assailant to death with a floor lamp. Though badly beaten and bloodied, Kyle intends to climb the stairs and burst into the wedding, but one of the men flings a door open and accidentally pushes him down the stairs—finishing off the killing job Laura had begun. After the wedding Laura, having shown her own psychopathic side, orders Robert to murder his one remaining friend—along with their dog—and bury both of them in the desert. At the last moment, Robert refuses to go along with this scheme, but as the two men drive home, they run head-on into another vehicle. In the final scene, Robert has both legs amputated at the knees, while his friend is turned into a paraplegic; even the dog now limps along on three legs. At this point, Robert and Laura gain custody of two handicapped young boys belonging to the dead couple. Watching the two men and two boys—along with the dog—trying to play in her backyard, Laura sees Robert's wheelchair overturn, dumping the double amputee ingloriously on the lawn. Witnessing all this, she runs into the street screaming in agony and is nearly run over by a car. When we last see Laura, who alone among this macabre group remains physically intact, she suffers a mental breakdown: Lying in the middle of the street, we see her furiously pounding her fists into the pavement. *Very Bad Things* no doubt stands alone as an improbably dark representation of contemporary family and personal existence where intimacy quickly and irrationally turns into deadly violence. By comparison, such films as *Interiors* and *The Last Seduction*, forerunners of the full-blown postmodern narrative of familial demise, seem rather tepid if not old-fashioned. In *Very Bad Things*, we wind up with endless mayhem and destruction where norms of deceit and violence penetrate the deepest consciousness of seemingly every character in the film. We know that Laura and her new family have somehow emerged intact from the chaos, but they are so disabled, physically and mentally, that we are left with nothing less than a deadening process that immobilizes this incarnation of the postmodern family.

Those "families" we have explored here are generally composed of middle-class Anglos, providing us with only a partial view of the multicultural terrain that is contemporary American society. More recent films that have been labeled "postmodern" reflect social and demographic changes that have resulted in a vastly different family structure, one closely resembling Toffler's third-wave stage. It is no wonder, then, that recent filmmakers have begun to explore a few of the nuances and implications of these new family structures. In its own halting and limited fashion, Hollywood cinema has begun to engage a more culturally diverse family structure—a phenomenon that might loosely be associated with the postmodern turn.

Chris Eyre and Sherman Alexie's *Smoke Signals* (1998) is the first film depicting Native American families made by native filmmakers. Based on Alexie's novel *Lone Ranger and Tonto Fistfight in Heaven*, *Smoke Signals* ventures beyond previous Hollywood films in its frank depiction of native families battling what Alexie calls "our dysfunctions," above all child abandonment and alcoholism. The film features Thomas Builds-the-Fire (Adam Beach) and Victor (Evan Adams), two Coeur d'Alene, Idaho, men. On July 4, 1976, Thomas's alcoholic father (Gary Farmer) and his mother (Tantoo Cardinal) decide to celebrate the American bicentennial, but the party rapidly turns into tragedy. A fire starts and gets out of control, incinerating them and their trailer. A local resident manages to throw the infant Thomas out of a window just as the trailer turns to ashes. Thomas is caught by a local man who proceeds to raise him alongside his natural son Victor. In 1988, now grown, Vincent accompanies Thomas to Phoenix to settle his late father's affairs and return his ashes to the reservation. This movie depicts what might be understood as "dysfunctional" nontraditional families with an unprecedented frank realism. It premiered at the 1998 Sundance Film Festival, where it won the Audience Award and Filmmakers Trophy. Alexie's film, which grossed $7 million, created an opening for other Native American filmmakers. As a result, "Every dusty Indian screenplay that's been sitting on a shelf for fifteen years is offered to us for development. Every loincloth movie in Hollywood has been resurrected."[45]

Wayne Wang's *Joy Luck Club* (1993) traces a Chinese family's journey from China in the 1940s to California in the 1990s. It is a long and difficult odyssey during which the family experiences any number of hardships, deprivations, adultery, abduction, and even murder. Along the way, one Chinese mother is forced to abandon her infant children during the brutal Japanese invasion. The story begins when June (Ming-na Wen), a young Californian, receives a letter from her long-lost cousins, abandoned infants who remained in China. June decides to visit China in order to be reunited with this hitherto unknown (to her) branch of the family. Using Amy Tan's narrative as a foundation, Wang interweaves poignant stories of family life in China during the 1940s, most of it narrated through flashbacks involving her aunts. This film can be broadly understood as part of a category of family "weepies" that evoke powerful emotional responses to ongoing personal dramas. The older generation depicted in this film represents Toffler's first wave of extended families, while the younger members have entered into the realm of third-wave families where divorce

Blood Simple (Joel and Ethan Coen, 1984)   *An offbeat, satirical thriller oozing with sleazy atmosphere and gloomy, noirish settings filled with postmodern cynicism— elements of a highly ironic, mordant black comedy. Pictured: the Coen brothers on the set.*

and remarriage have thoroughly eroded the second wave of nuclear family structures. Comparable films established along the extended versus post-modern family opposition include Peter Wang's *A Great Wall* (1986), which chronicles a Chinese American family's journey to China in search of long-lost relatives, and Steven Okazaki's *Living on Tokyo Time* (1987), which replays with some variations essentially the same drama from a Japanese point of view.

Mira Nair's *Mississippi Masala* (1992) casts Sarita Choudhury as Mina, a young East Indian/Kenyan/American woman who irrevocably crosses racial barriers by falling in love with a black man, Demetrius (played by Denzel Washington). Mina's family is characterized as a first-wave extended clan that is clearly out of step with the various African American families shown in the film. This is not a simple East/West story, though, insofar as both char-acters have deep African roots. Despite pressures from both families to call off a relationship that is both intercultural *and* interracial, the two young people elope to aspirations for carving out a life for themselves, much like millions of people in contemporary American society who have elected to marry outside their particular ethnic groups—one manifestation of the third-wave postmodern family conceptualized by Toffler.

Prominent African American directors of recent years have depicted postmodern families in equally poignant if less sentimental tones. In many of these films, the family is represented as a form subjected to precisely those social and cultural pressures at work in society as a whole. Thus, Spike Lee's *Mo' Better Blues* (1990) derives its psychological tension from the sexual and aesthetic drives of its hero, Bleek Gilliam (Denzel Washington), a jazz trumpeter who cannot decide between the love of two beautiful women and thereby winds up losing both of them. *Mo' Better Blues* involves Gilliam's attempts to save Giant (Lee), his gambling-addicted manager and best friend, from a beating by gangsters that results in his own severe injuries requiring several months of recovery. Gilliam realizes he has lost his trumpet-playing skills and, in desperation, turns to one of the ex-girlfriends (Joie Lee) for help. He then returns to the more conventional sexual and familial world by marrying Lee and raising a child, but not before he experiences terrible depression, alienation, and defeat. In this case, filmmaker Lee retreats into the more traditional nuclear family, which seems to be his way of resolving the film's initial dalliance with postmodern departures.

Widely diverse images of family life seen in these films revolve around a cynical understanding of gender relations, intimacy, and sexuality where familiar references to "dysfunctional" families may come to appear rather archaic; these families are nothing if not moribund, useless relics of the past. Postmodern cinema embraces images of family life that seethe with conflict, infidelity, and corruption, more often than not leading to violence and domestic terror and going well beyond any theme contained in film noir, neo-noir, or Woody Allen. The romantic discourses typical of mainstream classics like *It's a Wonderful Life*, John Ford Westerns, and combat features must appear today like bizarre representations from another planet. Of course, such postmodern representations turn out to be much closer to the truth than anything we are likely to see in these older classics—and surely closer to the truth than most Americans may be willing to concede, as Stephanie Coontz reminds us.[46] In actuality, the nuclear family, born during early phases of industrialism and sustained by preindustrial social relations, has for better or worse become a casualty of the times—a victim of post-Fordist social fragmentation, heightened mobility, massive technological and cultural changes, and, more recently, globalization. Postmodern filmmakers like the Coen brothers, Peter Berg, Ridley Scott, Woody Allen, and Mike Figgis have been criticized for exaggerating the chaos, duplicity, and harshness of what remains of the family structure, but their narrative renditions can hardly be said to be removed from social reality. American families at the beginning of the twenty-first century are rife with insecurity, fear, hatred, and violence—reflections indeed of a larger society veering toward uncontrollable levels of civic (and, yes, domestic) violence—even as media pundits and politicians continue to celebrate "family values." The intimate relationship here between art and reality seems clear: Themes common-place in postmodern cinema of the 1980s and 1990s were not long ago taboo in Hollywood filmmaking as in American popular culture as a whole. Thus, in contemporary cinema we see fathers molesting their children and sometimes even their grandchildren, mothers seducing their sons, fathers lusting after young girlfriends of their daughters, wives and husbands cheat-ing with their partners' best friends, wives and husbands plotting to kill each other, teenagers having sex with multiple partners, relationships falling apart at the slightest provocation, and so on. Moreover, homosexuality and bisexuality regularly appear in these films as subplots and usually with no stigma attached. This is hardly the stuff of "family values" that seems so thoroughly to captivate politicians, but it is increasingly closer to the daily lives of ordinary Americans forced to listen to such rhetoric (no doubt one of many reasons why citizens vote much less often). If postmodern cinema is bleak, it is probably not much bleaker than the lived social relations it has come to encapsulate, however unevenly or melodramatically.

As postmodern cinema reveals a world of urban nightmares, antiheroes, and dystopic futures, its dark images of the family, marriage, gender rela-tions, and sexuality appear no less oppressive and frightening—trends long ago set in motion by the classic noir cycle of the 1940s and 1950s. This is a universe of isolated, alienated human beings devoid of authentic rela-tionships, swept up like hapless creatures in deadly webs of intrigue, strug-gles for survival, domestic violence, and murder. There are no assurances that seemingly gentle, charming, attractive characters—much like Joseph Cotten's Uncle Charlie in *Shadow of a Doubt*—will turn out to be anything other than psychotic killers. There is little to guarantee that familial rela-tions will be consonant with "havens in a heartless world" that is the stuff of romantic mythology. Characters engulfed by the postmodern condition can rarely hope to escape the lethal power and impact of that condition—any more than they can escape the social Darwinian ethos pervasive throughout capitalist society.

THE MANY FACES OF
POSTMODERNISM

The postmodern turn reflected in the work of social theorists like Foucault, Derrida, Baudrillard, Jameson, and others marks a profound shift in popular culture just as it has in the general intellectual, aesthetic, and political arenas within advanced industrial society. Despite its enormous and potentially epochal impact on contemporary life, however, we have yet to arrive at anything resembling a unified understanding or "theory" of postmodernism—much less any coherent view of the "postmodern condition."[1] The major ideas and concepts surrounding this nascent discourse remain diffuse, fragmented, and often contradictory and conflicted, nowhere more so than in their application to the production, viewing, and interpretation of the cinematic enterprise after more than a century of its history. While postmodern film culture is thus remarkably variable and hard to define, its diverse currents do share a particular set of themes and styles of representation and make sense as a response to specific historical trends: post-Fordist economic development, globalization, media culture, social atomization, the high-tech revolution, and worldwide decline of Marxist or socialist politics.

If postmodernism by definition involves plural meanings and lines of development, it entails just as much *continuity* as rupture with its modernist antecedents. The gulf between modern and postmodern has never been so clear or so total as to obscure the considerable overlap between the two, nor has the recent explosion of postmodern techniques and styles turned out to be monolithic or even dominant. We know that earlier modernist directors like Ford, Capra, and Hawks (as well as marginal cases like Hitchcock and Welles) typically valorized historically resonant themes, such as individual freedom, democracy, community, patriotism, hard work, and family values.[2]

The films they produced celebrated strong protagonists, clear demarcations between good and evil, a sense of historical progress, coherent narrative structures, and rather fixed understandings of politics, religion, work, nation, and law enforcement. Such time-honored motifs went far beyond long-standing left-versus-right ideological divisions, adhering as they did to Enlightenment rationality in one its multiple forms. More significantly, such themes were never simply tossed aside by postmodern auteurs but were in

Body Heat **(Lawrence Kasdan, 1981)** *With Kathleen Turner and William Hurt, it inspired a long cycle of neo-noir films depicting the hero's fall and terrible demise, surrounded by a general scene of chaos, violence, and dystopia.*

fact reappropriated in different ways, given new definition, and often more fully interrogated within the new historical context. This is precisely why so many filmmakers—Lucas, Spielberg, Coppola, Stone, Altman, and the Coen brothers, for example—cannot be easily labeled as either "modern" or "post-modern"; their work represents a sometimes uneasy mixture of the two.

With this in mind, we can proceed to identify five basic modalities within postmodern cinema as it has evolved over the past two or three decades, representing the many faces of what has become the most creative and innovative trend in filmmaking, outlined as follows: 1) the blockbuster spectacle, combining distinctly modern with postmodern elements, as exemplified by the *Star Wars* episodes, the *Batman* films, and such epics as *Jurassic Park* and *Titanic;* 2) the "existential" film, stressing the social and psychological trends toward anxiety, loneliness, and dispersion of life in the modern urban setting, perhaps best reflected in the work of Woody Allen; 3) depiction of recent American history as a deep quagmire, a moment of decline characterized by political loss of innocence, social chaos, and eclipse of universal values, as found in the films of Oliver Stone; 4) what might be called the "cinema of mayhem" rooted in the growing social turbulence, psychological dislocation, and civic violence of postwar urban America, as seen most graphically in the neo-noir tradition and the work of Quentin Tarantino; and 5) ludic, or playful, postmodern filmmaking, probably best illustrated in the biting, irreverent, satirical comedies of John Waters. Of course, these five categories are hardly airtight: When viewed across the cinematic landscape of the 1980s and 1990s, the many films that fit *predominantly* one of these ideal types will often overlap or intersect with others. Whatever their divergent thematic and aesthetic flourishes, however, the scores of movies falling under the postmodern heading generally share a deep skepticism of or revolt against modernity with its optimistic, linear, and conformist views of social life and cultural representations. Yet while postmodern cinema frequently subjects elements of the status quo to withering critical scrutiny, it shrinks from adopting any coherent progressive or visionary approach to the future; more often than not, its artistic representations embrace cynical, fatalistic, and emphatically dystopic images of history.

THE BLOCKBUSTER AS SPECTACLE

On the surface, the familiar blockbuster epics can be seen as distinctly and powerfully modernist, focusing on spectacular, sweeping visual images of far-fetched scenarios with simple action narratives tied to old-fashioned heroism, redemption, idealistic goals, a glittering cinematography filled with a Manichaeistic struggle between good and evil, along with the obligatory deference to patriotism, celebration of traditional values, and happy outcomes. The blockbuster indeed embellishes all manner of formulaic spectacles that seem ready-made for the big screen.[3] The enormous popularity of films by Lucas, Spielberg, and Cameron—from the first *Star Wars* episode and *Jaws* to more recent fare such as *Schindler's List* (1993), *Titanic* (1997), and *Saving Private Ryan* (1998) and the more recent *Star Wars* epics (1999 and 2002)—shows that, even in a supposedly postmodern era, modernist cinema (especially when done with great technical flare) retains as much appeal as it did during the height of the studio system. The main difference today, of course, is that Hollywood modernism no longer enjoys the same hegemonic, taken-for-granted status it enjoyed earlier. But the differences do not end here. While modernist in narrative content and social themes, the blockbuster has emerged as a central feature of those "cathedrals of consumption" analyzed by Ritzer as part of the post-Fordist economy: Their larger-than-life, hypercommodified visual panorama transforms them into a postmodern-style commercialized spectacle of the sort Debord and Baudrillard viewed as constitutive of hyperreal media culture.[4] The convergence of spectacle, the commodity, and technology within an evolving film industry endows the blockbuster with mixed dimensions of the modern and postmodern. This result is reconstruction of typically modernist narratives, characters, situations, and motifs within what would become postmodern cinema.

The term "blockbuster" normally refers to films grossing at least $100 million in box office receipts, a phenomenon first appearing in the mid-1970s, when audiences flocked to highly stylized, often romantic adventure pictures with young heroes and heroines ready to overcome insurmountable odds in order to save the world from demons, monsters, tyrants, or aliens. Such films presented a clear opposition between good and evil, as in the *Star Wars* episodes, the *Batman* series, and the *Terminator* films, all among the highest-grossing films in motion picture history. Their immense popularity among mainstream viewers of all ages helped lay the foundations of the New Hollywood in which directors like Lucas and Spielberg initially came to the forefront.

To fully understand this development, one must step back in time a few years to Lucas's second feature film, *American Graffiti* (1973), produced by Coppola and immediately successful in both financial and critical terms. In a period that witnessed four political assassinations, the Vietnam War, and the turbulent 1960s, Lucas's film evokes nostalgia for a more orderly and conformist time devoid of later social and political conflicts. *American Graffiti* features recent high school graduates and their high school–age friends, played by Richard Dreyfus, Ron Howard, Harrison Ford, and Cindy Williams, all struggling for personal identity and a break with strong family and personal ties linking them to conservative middle-class lifestyles in Modesto, California. The film became an instant sensation, grossing $55 million on a budget of just $1.4 million, making directors like Lucas, Spielberg, and Lawrence Kasdan aware that immense audiences awaited youthful, romantic, adventurous films with rather conventional plots and glamorous, victorious, modernist heroes—an awareness that led directly to the blockbuster projects that soon followed. To capitalize on his success, Lucas decided to produce a film based on the *Flash Gordon* and *Buck Rogers* series of the studio era, one designed to appeal to the same audiences lining up to see *American Graffiti*. He gambled on a film evoking ancient myths of simple, courageous heroes defeating cartoonish evil villains amid magical, romantic settings: The result was *Star Wars* (1977), and this became the first actual blockbuster. Costing only $9.5 million and grossing over $100 million within three months of its release, Lucas's ambitious project ultimately earned $193 million in rentals and inspired dozens of souvenir products, theme parks, stores, and, of course, four notable sequels: *The Empire Strikes Back* (1980), *Return of the Jedi* (1983), *Phantom Menace* (1999), and *Star Wars: Episode II—Attack of the Clones* (2002). By the 1990s, *Star Wars* had become an entertainment empire and film genre by itself, making Lucas one of the richest men in the world.

Phantom Menace earned for Lucas more than $2 billion, including $500 million for video, $150 million for television, more than $1 billion for merchandising, and $800 million in box office receipts. Movie production has enabled Lucas to amass huge profits from video games, action figurines, toys, books, magazines, lamps, toothbrushes, cereal, shampoos, and other goods that have become part of a gigantic entertainment complex that seems destined to reproduce itself almost endlessly. *Phantom Menace* relies even more heavily than the earlier trilogy on elaborate, computer-generated images and sequences, making it perhaps the most ambitious cinematic undertaking ever. It was reputed to have been covered financially through a variety of franchises and merchandising deals well before it was released—an incredible breakthrough testifying to the laser accuracy of Lucas's intuition that American (and worldwide) audiences would continue to be drawn to comic book–style blockbusters with their larger-than-life representations of characters, settings, events, and plot trajectories. In *Phantom Menace*, we have an array of powerful, mythological figures in Jason, Rama, King Arthur, Robin

Hood, and Ivanhoe—all capable of Promethean deeds. As with the earlier stories, Lucas turned to philosopher Joseph Campbell for inspiration in constructing updated *Star Wars* narratives and themes; a basic plot pattern took shape in a way that could take the viewer to both the distant past and distant future. With a simple change of props, *Star Wars* could easily be transported to medieval Europe, ancient Greece, Rome, Japan, India, and even the American West. Quite unlike anything produced in cinematic history, *Phantom Menace* conjures up a fairy-tale narrative familiar to most children, tapping legendary myths in which brave heroes face impossible odds in their struggle to conquer evil. The film is an astonishing visual and technical achievement, propelled by a kind of space opera filled with colorful figures, extraordinary feats, and mind-bending special effects. And it appeals to young boys' fascination with space exploits, electronic toys, gadgets, uniforms, simple plots, and, of course, technological wizardry.

For Lucas, it seems clear that Luke Skywalker and Han Solo define the *Star Wars* heroic pattern based on two ancient hero prototypes, with Solo (Harrison Ford) representing the older type of hero along the lines of Odysseus, King Arthur, and King Richard the Lion-Hearted and Skywalker exemplifying the younger hero initiate forced to make peace with a stern father figure along the lines of Theseus, Robin Hood, and Billy the Kid. As the *Star Wars* episodes unfold, we see Skywalker moving from initiate hero to full-fledged classical hero bearing the stamp of other Promethean figures in the annals of mythology. In the initial *Star Wars* film, Skywalker—a thinly disguised Lucas—evolves from a weak orphan into a seasoned space fighter pilot who learns to harness the mysterious "Force" emanating from all life-forms, which Campbell defines as the interface between what can be known and what is, the mystery going beyond all human knowledge. Lucas himself refers to it as a combination of "talent" and "self-awareness." After he learns to master the Force, Skywalker gains control over his actions and, to a lesser degree, is able to manage the larger course of events.

Skywalker belongs to a class of heroes, including Han Solo, Princess Leia, and Chewbacca, who appear to symbolize the American postwar generation's rejection of authority, conformity, and privilege, with its rebellion against an oppressive government (the Empire) and all it represents—notably, its military power and its neocolonial interests. We can see the Empire as the embodiment of virtually any government: Not surprisingly, it is often understood as the embodiment of the U.S. military-industrial complex with its recurrent aggressive wars against weaker nations. Ronald Reagan labeled the Soviet Union an "Evil Empire," perhaps referring to the *Star Wars* incarnation of Empire, while Campbell himself associated the Empire with a huge machine, a vast hierarchical system capable of crushing the human spirit and its strivings for freedom and self-activity. In this scheme of things, Darth Vader exemplifies the "older" generation, molded by the Great Depression and World War II, that values discipline, conformity, and patriotism and is often associated with less flattering expressions of fanaticism, violence, and megalomania. Vader symbolizes the archetypal father figure, consumed with violence, arrogance, and control; he commands the Storm Troopers, modeled after the Nazi SS, and even wears a Nazi-like helmet. According to Vader, this "Dark Side" of the universe surpasses the power of the Force, but viewers will know that the Dark Side is a menace to be overcome, as Skywalker does when he refuses Vader's urgent plea to join him in the quest. "With our combined strength we can end this destructive conflict and bring order to the galaxy," he reasons, but Skywalker adamantly refuses to go along.

Eventually, Skywalker, Han, Princess Leia, Chewbacca, and Lando forge the elements of a "counterculture" in opposition to the sinister, machine-like Empire; they create a stratum of outlaw heroes for whom the Empire means nothing more than violence, corruption, authoritarianism, and megalomania—manifestations of the Dark Side of human existence that Lucas depicts brilliantly throughout the episodes. Yet there is something peculiarly seductive about the Dark Side in these pictures. For example, Vader turns out to be more dynamic, indeed a far more vividly remembered character than Skywalker, who emerges as a rather tedious figure in the end as he takes on the role of conventional hero much like the sheriffs of classical Western films who don white hats and defend their territory against outlaw gangs. There is something almost *too* noble about Skywalker. Were it not for his forgivable inexperience at the outset, he would have to be seen as yet another flat, one-dimensional figure; as it is, his character lacks the depth of Solo's, who at least displays some amount of anger, lust, and petulancy. Skywalker's persona suffers from what Oscar Wilde described as a "lack of redeeming social vices"—he is, for example, devoid of any romantic interest, evident once it becomes clear that Princess Leia is his sister. *Star Wars* embraces the classic paradox faced by writers from John Milton to the present, namely, how to make a powerfully evil villain less compelling or seductive than a strong, virtuous, attractive hero. Exactly the same problem surfaces in Tim Burton's *Batman*, where the Joker (Jack Nicholson) gains top billing over the title character, Batman (Michael Keaton). Possibly reflecting the influence of postmodern values, Lucas succeeds no better than Burton or Milton in creating heroes who turn out to be more charismatic than the energetic yet somehow attractive villains opposing them.

The great rebels of *Star Wars* (and kindred blockbuster spectacles) represent classic virtues of courage, independence, and heroic individualism. It is the rebels, after all, who are shown to have personal relationships, while rebel technology, with its fascinating druids and patched-together yet lightning-fast starships and star fighters, appears friendlier than the Empire's Death Stars and Earth Walkers. Moreover, the rebels affirm personal *loyalty* toward each other, while Vader is depicted as summarily executing anyone failing to carry out his orders. The rebels ally themselves with useful, friendly aliens, while the Empire aligns itself with monsters like Jabba the Hutt and sleazy bounty hunters, and it is these modernist rebels who prevail in the end. They defeat Vader and the Empire time after time without suffering greater pain and sacrifice than that encountered by mythological heroes, enabling them to live out a comfortable existence. Still the most profitable blockbusters, the *Star Wars* episodes contrast sharply with other sci-fi films of the period like Kubrick's *2001: A Space Odyssey* and Ridley Scott's *Blade Runner*. Although Kubrick's hero Dave manages to triumph in the end, he does so only after having perished and been reborn as an entirely different being. Like Vader, Kubrick's villain (Hal the Computer) is actually more interesting than his hero insofar as he emerges as a symbol of repressive technology gone out of control. *Blade Runner*'s neo-noir protagonist Deckard (Harrison Ford) triumphs at least for the moment but is condemned to live in a repulsive utopia that has no greater moral or political integrity than the Empire; we can imagine that the Empire has won the war, with Los Angeles becoming its capital. Deckard, seen as deeply flawed through his extreme coldness and his falling in love with a replicant, is more attractive than the replicants who serve as Scott's fearsome villains. In both *2001* and *Blade Runner*, as in the majority of sci-fi pictures, the ironies are too great, the environment is too degraded, and the heroes are far too compromised to generate truly benevolent outcomes. In contrast, Lucas's films seem almost sunny in tone: Thus, in *Star Wars* we encounter clearly defined and culturally sanctioned forces of good that vanquish cartoonish though strangely attractive villains.

A series of other blockbusters appeared just before and after the first *Star Wars* breakthrough—Spielberg's *Jaws* (1975), *Raiders of the Lost Ark* (1981), and *Indiana Jones and the Temple of Doom* (1984), among others. These latter two films are situated not in the future but in remote, exotic countries at the time of World War II, while the villains remain Nazis (real historical Nazis rather than futuristic ones as in *Star Wars*.) As larger-than-life spectacles, these projects exhibit the same exaggerated conflict between good and evil involving a range of conventionally simplistic characters and situations that, despite narrative limitations, have the power (in Lawrence Kasdan's words) to "reach deep into . . . our mythic closet." A key element of all blockbuster films is construction of overdrawn figures who nonetheless fit into ancient mythological patterns and thereby manage to appeal to wide audiences. Interestingly, many of these films are derived from comic book characters like Batman, Superman, Teenage Mutant Ninja Turtles, and Dick Tracy. Their gross distortions of anything resembling social reality—assisted by computer-generated images and sequences—happen to coincide with their emergence as a powerful new medium for ancient mythological storytelling that, despite its surface modernist conventions, is sure to have far-reaching postmodern implications.

The only film to rival, perhaps even surpass, the blockbuster status of the *Star Wars* movies has been *Titanic* (1997), James Cameron's $200 million superproject based on the kind of epic disaster guaranteed to furnish a cinematic spectacle. By any standards, this picture became a remarkable technological achievement that mesmerized audiences in the United States and around the world, receiving no fewer than fourteen Academy Award nominations and winning an astounding eleven in all (matching the previous record set by *Ben-Hur*). *Titanic* opened nationally in December 1997, at which time Todd McCarthy in *Variety* enthused, "This *Titanic* arrives at its destination. A spectacular demonstration of what modern technology can contribute to dramatic storytelling, James Cameron's romantic epic, which represents the biggest roll of the dice in cinematic history, will send viewers in search of synonyms for the title to describe the film's size and scope."[5]

Of course, the producers as well as the director believed they had brought to life the most ambitious and powerful spectacle in film history, toward which they spent nearly $300,000 a day to finish what turned out to be a nightmarishly long and difficult production ordeal. When the film was first released, it was met with huge mob scenes composed mainly of teenage girls anxious to get a glimpse of the film's main star, Leonardo DiCaprio. The unbelievable box office success of *Titanic* can be explained by virtue of its enormous star mythology, its unparalleled special effects, its compelling disaster narrative, the romance between the DiCaprio and Kate Winslett characters that emerged as the centerpiece of the film, and its larger-than-life status as commodified extravaganza not too different from *Star Wars* and *Batman*. By February 1998, *Titanic* had reached $300 million in gross box office receipts faster than any film ever; with immense popularity in Europe, Japan, and elsewhere, by March 6, 1998, it became the first picture to earn more than $1 billion in worldwide theatrical box office sales. Including a nearly full-scale mock-up of the ill-fated ocean liner and awesome display of ornate costumes, the scope of just about everything connected with *Titanic* was indeed gargantuan, seemingly without limits. By the time of the Oscars in 1998, *Titanic* had been number one at the box office for fourteen consecutive weeks, while the film's soundtrack had remained first on the Billboard Hot 200 albums chart for ten weeks in a row. With the exception of *Phantom Menace*, *Titanic* dwarfed the marketing success of all previous blockbusters.

The film begins with black-and-white documentary images of the *Titanic*'s maiden voyage from Southampton, England, framing the impending catastrophe as realistic historical narrative that would finally end with the excruciatingly slow sinking of the ship in the icy Atlantic waters where more than 1,500 people perished. The cinematic detail fashioned by Cameron is overpowering, lending a sense of awesome (even if distorted) realism to the whole epic. Embedded in the liner's ill-fated voyage were many interwoven motifs: the supposed invulnerability of the largest and fastest (not to mention most luxurious) ocean liner ever built; the inflated claims of the new oceanic technology; the smug certainties of Edwardian elites about the efficiency of British industry; the frenetic, ill-advised quest for a new transatlantic speed record through a heavy ice field; the fearlessness (and fatal mistakes) of those in command; the highly visible class differences on board that so heavily influenced the fate of both crew and passengers; and the unbelievable series of fortuitous events that made the disaster inevitable. There are a good many folkloric myths tied to the legend of the *Titanic* and even richer historical narratives connected to the sinking itself. The discourses of power, novelty, and indestructibility surrounding the *Titanic* episode were in full force at the beginning of the 1912 voyage—yet all these discourses, modernist to the core, would soon be undermined by events. Enlightenment views of reason and progress through technological development would be contradicted by a single disaster, a single iceberg looming as the metaphor of historical crisis.[6]

In the end, however, few of these ingredients found their way into Cameron's grandiose cinematic undertaking: Romance takes center stage, with disaster appearing as backdrop—one reason the film was able to attract such huge mainstream audiences. The familiar and powerfully dramatic tale of the ship's encounter with fate, moreover, was essentially ignored. Many episodes were left out or given rather short shrift: the delay of the maiden trip by three weeks, the failure of the crew to heed any of six major ice warnings, the speed of the *Titanic* set at just a knot too fast, the inability of a nearby ship (the Californian) to accurately interpret distress flares or otherwise respond to the *Titanic*'s plight, the absence of a normally choppy sea that would have illuminated the iceberg, the crew's sighting of the iceberg just ten seconds too late, the lack of a double hull, the failure to build water-tight compartments only one deck higher, and the decision of White Star Lines to provide lifeboats for less than half of what was needed—a scandal that would haunt this calamity forever. But viewers of the film were not drawn by such historical details; they could not have been, in fact, since the details were largely absent from Cameron's account or were distorted beyond recognition.[7] Hence, the real meaning of the *Titanic* was lost in a blurry spectacle promising unprecedented cinematic realism but ultimately delivering a form of postmodern baroqueness with all its bizarre simulations.

Despite all this, the film, dwelling as it does on a catastrophic historical moment, cannot fully avoid the consequences—social or aesthetic—of that catastrophe. The sinking of the *Titanic* represents an undeniably dramatic event in revealing the limits of modernity, a vast undermining of the optimism, stability, and arrogance of pre–World War I British capitalism. As Daniel Allen Butler writes in his account of the *Titanic*, the sinking of the superliner "was one of those rare finite events that history on occasion does afford humanity. It illuminated with stark, sometimes harsh clarity the strengths and weaknesses, virtues and flaws of the society that gave impetus to her existence. In those nine hours, the men and women aboard the *Titanic* demonstrated almost every derogatory characteristic of Edwardian society: arrogance, pride, snobbery, prejudice, racism, chauvinism, and maudlin sentimentality. . . . In many ways, what makes the *Titanic* disaster as compelling is that it catches that society at its pinnacle—before the decade was out it would have vanished forever."[8] More profoundly, the catastrophe would deal a powerful blow to the nearly mystical reverence people had for technology after the turn of the century. Thus, "After the loss of the *Titanic*, engineers would no longer be hailed as modern-day saviors, their works greeted as panaceas for the assorted ills of mankind, or their efforts the repository of humanity's confidence. . . . What had appeared to be the ultimate accomplishment of science and progress was shown to be helplessly flawed and deadly fragile."[9] The seeming power and invulnerability of the *Titanic* is confounded by crisis and terror lurking beneath the surface of the ocean, indicating that appearances are not nearly as permanent as they might seem.[10] Disaster turned out to be the ultimate postmodern event, if such an event can indeed be identified through a particular discourse. The irony is that Cameron's film—itself a tribute to the virtues of modern *cinematic* technology—confronts this historical message at best only peripherally. Yet as both disaster movie and perhaps the greatest blockbuster epic of all time, the film could not entirely avoid such implications, which in the final analysis makes it *doubly* postmodern.

Rob Cohen's *XXX* (2002) is one of the most chilling depictions of postmodern uncertainty, angst, and paranoia. The film retells the standard blockbuster action melodrama but with a decidedly postmodern twist. Vin Diesel stars as Xandar Cage, an elusive underground sports figure who has mastered everything from motorcycles and cars to skateboards to snowboards. Cage comes to the attention of the CIA after he steals and wrecks a state legislator's Corvette to protest the senator's anti–rock and roll rhetoric. He becomes targeted as a special agent, one who can infiltrate groups by deploying the kind of tough counterculture persona he cultivated so assiduously through similar legal exploits. Once selected for special training, Cage encounters spymaster Augustus Gibbon (Samuel L. Jackson), who promptly engineers a series of seemingly realistic tests of Cage's special-ops potential. Cage passes the tests with flying colors, even shooting and apparently wounding a policeman at one point, though not (he learns later) with real bullets. Eventually, he infiltrates the headquarters of a terrorist organization calling itself Anarchy 99, which is planning to ignite wars between the major powers through the release of massive doses of a deadly biological microbe.

Once he has gained the members' confidence, Cage begins collecting information on Anarchy 99, risking his life time after time through superhuman feats of motorcycle maneuvering and snowboarding. The final battle with terrorists involves even more dazzling athletic feats, such as boarding a speeding boat from a parachute. He has prevailed over his foes even though vastly outnumbered and outgunned. While he has developed professional acumen as undercover agent, nothing prepared him for the ultimate realization, communicated by Gibbon in the final scene, that everything he encountered in his struggle with Anarchy 99 was just an illusion. The entire conflict had been a staged event in order to test and hone his skills to their maximum.

XXX furnishes solid evidence that blockbuster action adventures can cover and indeed embellish postmodern themes. This film deftly constructs illusion after illusion in hyperreal fashion until there is essentially no reality left or at least until there is nothing left to believe in; absolutely nothing is as it appears in this picture. The government, presented here in the form of the CIA, seems at first to be largely rational and believable, but soon enough it turns out to be completely absurd and destructive, wasting huge sums of money and even lives on elaborate games designed to train and manage undercover agents. If everything here is nothing but a game, what business remains for the CIA to actually carry out? How can U.S. intelligence agencies effectively spy on foreign enemies when they have become so preoccupied with manipulating reality and indeed falsifying enemies? How can people trust a government in which events such as these take place under its auspices? The answer—that no trust is ultimately possible—takes the audience in an emphatically postmodern direction.

While the blockbuster phenomenon has enthralled *general* audiences in the United States and around the world since the first appearance of *Jaws* and *Star Wars*, its special appeal to young viewers is guaranteed by virtue of high-tech action sequences, overblown figures with emphasis on male heroes, and dialogue ranging from vulgar to clichéd. As sci-fi pictures, the huge, expensive, fast-paced epics evoke simple values of individual heroism, good versus evil, and a sense of conventional morality, endowing them with a distinctive modernist quality further enhanced by a return to forceful, direct, linear narratives. As Biskind observes, the Hollywood blockbusters were set up in such a manner that the stories would essentially tell themselves while appealing (in Lucas's words) to "the kids in all of us."[11] Indeed, these films hope to essentially reconstitute the audience as children, tapping into the innocence and simplicity of childhood—a trend toward infantilization of film culture that undercuts elements of critical thinking so vital to more complex dramas. At the same time, standard conformist narratives, motifs, and symbols within the blockbuster syndrome were inevitably assimilated into the commodified spectacle, lending them a postmodern character in the form of media simulations. Referring to Lucas and Spielberg, Biskind writes that "their attempt to restore traditional narration had an unintended effect—the creation of spectacle that annihilated story"[12]—indeed, that seemed to annihilate all historical and social content much as postmodern culture would lead us to anticipate.

On the surface at least, the blockbuster films celebrate distinctly modernist characters and heroes—in contrast with the postmodern fixation on doomed or failed heroes trapped in a social or psychological morass. Postmodern leading figures, from Charles Foster Kane through Travis Bickle in *Taxi Driver*, Alvie Singer in *Annie Hall*, Deckard in *Blade Runner*, and Jim Garrison in *JFK*, are typically presented as alienated, powerless, and tortured people incapable of altering the course of events, a motif never likely to inspire praise and hope among viewers looking for positive images in their filmgoing. The mass audiences that flock to blockbuster movies like *Star Wars*, *Batman*, *Jurassic Park*, and *Titanic*, with their Manichaeistic vision, straightforward narratives, and simply drawn characters, attest to the enduring popularity of films that fit neatly within the commodified spectacle and its supporting youth market. Not only are such blockbusters huge extravaganzas, but their immense visual sweep now renders them very special products of the digital age; they both reflect and shape advanced technology, for computers are needed to re-create the fantastic, exotic, and futuristic sets demanded by such expensive projects. In this sense, they are the cultural and material expressions of the postmodern age.

EXISTENTIAL MORASS: THE FILMS OF WOODY ALLEN

In many ways, Woody Allen can be considered the ultimate postmodern auteur, a filmmaker virtually unique in his capacity to master so many dimensions of the cinematic enterprise—directing, writing, producing, acting, editing, and music—while at the same time articulating some of the most powerful cultural trends of the late twentieth century. From the early 1970s to the present, Allen's work has challenged long-established modes of storytelling, revealing a mosaic or pastiche of rapidly flowing images, symbols, and motifs that endow his films with an unmistakable style. His narratives reflect a cinema of unpredictable breaks and disruptions, a celebration of chaos, that stylistically coincides with his mordant, existential approach to life in an urban scene rife with anxiety, insecurity, and collapse of identity. As a body, the films amount to a particular tribute to a contemporary (largely postmodern) state of psychological upheaval, to a darkness and pessimism that surfaces even amid the endless, absurdly humorous scenarios and witty one-liners. He emerges as probably the most compelling narrator of human relationships today, a director willing to confront issues endemic to the dreadful state of family life, romance, and sexuality in one picture after another, from *Love and Death* (1975) through *Deconstructing Harry* (1998), *Small Time Crooks* (2000), and *Hollywood Ending* (2002). As Girgus writes of Allen, "His films reveal a decentered world of displaced, dislocated characters who question their ability to find meaning in their lives."[13] Often in characters written for and played by himself, he depicts a complex variety of antiheroes resigned to a life of sexual misery, failed personal relationships, dysfunctional families, and intense, unrelenting personal angst. In the tradition of film noir, he constructs an enclosed universe of urban pathos, turbulence, and tragedy, a subterranean reality that runs counter to the surface appearances of even his beloved Manhattan, an urban setting aesthetically and socially fascinating at first glance until the deeper, everyday miseries and struggles of people trapped in their unhappy lives are cinematically revealed. Allen does a masterful job of uncovering this deeper, underlying psychological chaos on screen, representative of his hard-edged but nonetheless laughable caricatures.

Allen's work suggests a good many intellectual and cinematic influences, as he frequently acknowledges in interviews: the work of European auteurs like Federico Fellini and Ingmar Bergman, surrealism, existentialism, film noir, and earlier comedy fare like the Marx Brothers, who brought to filmmaking (in Girgus's words) a certain "unmotivated craziness." No major American director better epitomizes the style and output of the independent auteur than Allen, who, for more than thirty years, has managed to exercise control over financing, script, performance, editing, and music—in reality the overall creative project—while still operating within the broad confines of the Hollywood production and distribution system. Allen's remarkable genius lies in his consistent ability to capture on film the rich psychological complexities of everyday urban life without at the same time sacrificing any of his famous witty humor, sense of irony, and wry detachment. He depicts a world in which ordered relationships and meanings have essentially collapsed, where stable definitions of sexuality, gender, family, and even friendship have eroded in the midst of a bleak, decadent social existence that seems to resist any coherent understanding. Such a milieu is, of course, quite hospitable to the familiar antihero struggling to combat inner demons of angst and futility—a character established by Alvie Singer (Allen) in *Annie Hall* (1977) and later pushed to its zenith in the person of the "chameleon" Leonard Zelig (also Allen) in *Zelig* (1983), where biting humor barely masks the riveting psychological turmoil of modern life.

Allen's harsh critiques of the contemporary human condition and the impoverished relationships it spawns revolve around a complex dualism opposing appearance and essence, illusion and reality, perception and fact, consistent with the postmodern outlook: "Reality" for Allen, in fact, can no longer be identified or presented. Thus, in his analysis of *Manhattan*, Girgus writes, "The great paradox of *Manhattan* is that beneath the wonderful structures of the skyline and complex, sophisticated lives of the characters we see the rather banal but cruel forms of unfulfilled desire seeking expression in generally twisted, distorted, and destructive ways."[14] Of course, Allen overdoes the skyline in the opening sequence, as it suddenly explodes with a dazzling display of fireworks just as George Gershwin's *Rhapsody in Blue* reaches a dramatic climax. The seductive beauty of this film, as with other Allen pictures, scarcely conceals an underlying reality of human beings trapped in a distorted urban space of alienation, dislocation, and violence—a milieu teeming with action and excitement yet inhabited by an assortment of empty, lonely, disempowered souls. *Manhattan* opens at Elaine's, a popular Upper East side café, where four people converse earnestly about whether luck or courage is more important in human success. The assembled characters are Isaac (Allen), a forty-two-year-old writer, his seventeen-year-old girlfriend Tracy (Mariel Hemingway), a professor named Yale

(Michael Murphy), and his wife Emily (Ann Byrne). Yale privately confides to Isaac that he has gotten involved with a young journalist named Mary (Diane Keaton), to which Isaac replies, "Listen, you shouldn't ask me for advice. When it comes to relationships with women, I'm the winner of the August Strindberg Award"—a reference to the Swedish dramatist's three failed marriages. The irony of the situation is that only Tracy, the seventeen-year-old, appears to have enough maturity to maintain her sense of balance in a relationship. Yale becomes more deeply involved with Mary, while Isaac and Tracy soon drift apart because Isaac feels they can never have a serious romance owing to the huge age difference. Frustrated by Yale's refusal to leave his wife, Mary flirts with Isaac, while Tracy decides to spend six months in London to study acting. After saying good-bye to Tracy, Isaac decides at the last minute that he cannot live without her, at which point she reassures him, "Look, six months isn't so long. Not everybody gets corrupted. Tsch. Look, you have to have a little faith in people." Her words are somewhat negated, however, because of her supposed youthful immaturity—meaning we can expect her to be naively optimistic; Isaac, Mary, and Yale are older, more experienced, more jaded, and far less likely to subscribe to the belief that "not everybody gets corrupted."

At this juncture Allen's cynicism about "reality" becomes all the more transparent, a theme he would refine later in movies like *Stardust Memories*, *The Purple Rose of Cairo*, and *Zelig*. He is very candid about his cinematic methodology, stating in one interview (conducted in 1993) as follows: "It has been said that if I have any one big theme in my movies, it's got to do with the difference between reality and fantasy. It comes up very frequently in my films. I think that what it boils down to, really, is that I hate reality."[15] Later in the same interview, he adds, "Here also comes my view of nature, that when you look closely at nature you find that nature is not your friend. It's marked by murderous and cannibalistic competition."[16] This Hobbesian ethos of perpetual human turmoil, associated with a menacing state of nature, that enters into so many of Allen's films could hardly be set forth more directly.

In *Zelig*, one of Allen's most original yet most underappreciated films, we find the portrait of a human chameleon set in the 1920s with a narrative developed along mock documentary lines, starring Allen as Leonard Zelig and Mia Farrow as his psychiatrist, Dr. Isadora Fletcher. With his apparently superhuman capacity to fit into any situation, Zelig emerges as an archetypal character of media culture; his obsessive need to conform, to assimilate into the dominant culture, drives him to take on precisely those characteristics of the most visible personae around him—intellectuals, politicians, athletes, movie stars, and so forth. Prefiguring the enormous growth of technology and mass media in modern industrial society, Allen's *Zelig* represents an image not only of intensifying angst and loss of identity but also of the power of the media spectacle to absorb and reconfigure social relations in a fragmented, dispersed urban world. Taken to extremes, the chameleon figure suggests a distinctly postmodern theme: The spectacle becomes so all-consuming, so difficult to resist, that it readily leads to the submission of individuals to some form of higher authority, a motif familiar to readers of Erich Fromm's *Escape from Freedom*.[17] With *Zelig*, Allen constructs a film motif that, in different ways, has shaped a variety of Hollywood pictures over the past two decades, including *Bob Roberts* (1992), *Forrest Gump* (1994), *The Truman Show* (1998), and *Pleasantville* (1998).

In *Hannah and Her Sisters* (1986), Allen presents an intricate, crosscutting mosaic of relationships involving three sisters (Farrow, Dianne Wiest, and Barbara Hershey) who are shown coping with recurrent bouts of anxiety and despair over their frustrating relationships with men—a situation in which the family turns out to be no less crisis ridden than the urban milieu surrounding it (where in fact the two realms intersect with and reinforce each other at every turn). Every character is involved in some form of deceit and manipulation, none of them capable of emotional giving except for the long-suffering Farrow (Hannah), who plays the wife of Michael Caine. The complex interplay of individuals in relationships unfolds on a terrain of psychological and sexual combat where pain and guilt seem inescapable. Descending into the clearly forbidden, the Caine character decides, in the midst of some perfunctory soul-searching, to initiate an affair with Farrow's beautiful sister Lee (Hershey), whose boyfriend (Max von Sydow) is so curmudgeonly as to drive her away, making her available to Caine's seductive entreaties. The soap-operaish nature of *Hannah and Her Sisters* barely conceals a more serious underlying motif reflecting Allen's familiar cynical view of both relationships and sexuality. While the same motif was visible in earlier pictures like *Annie Hall* and *Manhattan*, it would receive even fuller articulation in subsequent films: *A Midsummer Night's Sex Comedy*, *Crimes and Misdemeanors*, *Husbands and Wives*, and *Mighty Aphrodite*.

In *Hannah and Her Sisters*, Allen weaves an intricate narrative told from the multiple perspectives of family members—mainly the three sisters—immersed in their upper-middle-class Manhattan culture. The film opens with a shot of Lee juxtaposed against one of Elliot (Caine), who fantasizes, "She's got the prettiest eyes, and she looks so sexy in that sweater," but, suddenly feeling guilty, he tells himself, "Stop it, you idiot! She's your wife's sister!" He then quickly adds, "But I can't help it." Of course, Elliot is unable to help it because he is going through a midlife crisis, one aspect of which is a fixation on his young, fascinating, seemingly vulnerable sister-in-law. His anxiety and obsession become ever more powerful as he muses, "I'm consumed by her. It's been months now. I think about her at the office!" Elliot appears ready to act out his passion for Lee, pursuing her with a variety of pretexts, such as loaning her books or offering to help her crusty, difficult boyfriend. Soon Elliot sets out to capitalize on every opportunity to entice Lee, phoning her, telling her of his feelings, and finally opening up to her more than he had ever done with Hannah. Mickey (Allen), Hannah's hypochondriac, infertile ex-husband, provides additional narration. An independent television producer, Mickey bears a striking resemblance to Allen himself, perhaps something of an autobiographical takeoff refracted through the lens of comic exaggeration. At one point, Mickey fears that he has cancer because a doctor has noted a spot on his X ray. "I'm dying! I'm dying!" he screams to himself. "There's a spot on my lungs! Take it easy, would you?" he reasons. "It's not on your lungs, it's on your ear." He asks himself, "It's the same thing, isn't it?" All this naturally makes for high humor, and *Hannah*, though not strictly a comedy, abounds in similarly humorous scenes, such as Elliot's dogged pursuit of Lee on the street, the decision of Mickey and Hannah to ask a friend (played by Tony Roberts) to act as a surrogate father for their child, and Mickey's repeated bouts of hypochondria along with his erratic pursuit of Holly. One result of these multiple narratives is a lively plural viewpoint that Allen says is inspired by "ensemble" novels like *Anna Karenina*. Thus, "I like the format of an ensemble, and I wanted to experiment with it. And I've done it a few times since then."[18] Allen seems comfortable with narratives in which no single protagonist or hero emerges around whose goals, deeds, and exploits the plot inexorably advances; the story unfolds through the combined experiences and viewpoints of different characters who are frequently in conflict, an approach creating additional space between actors and viewers, between subject and object. It is no longer possible for the audience—by means of cinematic illusion—to become the lead character since the role changes drastically from one moment to another. In the end, much of the ambiguity is removed, and a measure of stability is restored: Elliot, finally realizing that his fling with Lee is mainly an immature response to midlife crisis, is drawn closer to Hannah, while Mickey, for his part, finds romance with Holly. Previously married to Hannah, Mickey is now able to rejoin the family through his marriage to Holly. The result is that *Hannah* ends on a somewhat upbeat note—perhaps *too* upbeat. Allen himself complained that "I tied [the movie] together at the end a little bit too neatly. I should have been a little less happy at the end than I was."[19] By gravitating toward a more conventional Hollywood happy ending, Allen winds up negating—no doubt intentionally—much of the cynicism and despair pervading the film. Still, given its overall stylistic and thematic trajectory, *Hannah* can be described as one of Allen's most distinctly postmodern films.

Perhaps more than any other Allen film, *The Purple Rose of Cairo* (1985) reflects his conviction about the role of movies as escapist forms of entertainment that serve to distract viewers from the mundane, boring, often painful experiences of daily life. Cecilia (Mia Farrow) personifies the dedicated, even obsessed, filmgoer of the Great Depression, a time when mass audiences were enthralled by cultural products that appeared during the golden age of cinema. Cecilia's life revolves around going to the movies, even those she has seen again and again, resulting in an addiction that functions as a kind of opiate dulling her unhappy existence, that has become a parody of 1930s misery. Cecilia slaves as a waitress in a small town and is married to an aggressive, philandering loafer named Monk (Danny Aiello), who appropriates her meager income so he can spend it on liquor and women; he routinely beats her, further alienating her and giving his own character a more brutal definition. Monk's strong, actually overbearing, presence allows him to steal practically every scene, even as his behavior obviously stereotypes him as yet another selfish, patriarchal husband willing to use violence to get his way. "Look, I hit you when you get out of line," he rationalizes when Cecilia makes plans to leave him, "and I never just hit you, I always warn you first and then if you don't shape up you get whacked."

Cecilia's obsession with romantic pictures as a means of escape leads to the improbable situation of having a film image—in this case the actor Tom Baxter (Jeff Daniels)—walk directly out of a movie screen and into the audience. What enables Baxter to make such a startling appearance in real life is Cecilia's rapt devotion to a new romantic comedy in which he is performing, titled *The Purple Rose of Cairo*. Cecilia's fascination with the film compels Baxter to suddenly come to life, walk off the screen, and head straight toward her. Once Baxter thusly materializes, the audience senses his ardent desire to become "real" and empathizes with Cecilia's own bizarre fixation. At one point, she asks about his belief in God, but Baxter has no concept of a deity outside his reverence for the two authors of *The Purple Rose*. Baxter (also played by Gil Shepard) is shocked to learn that his screen persona has materialized inside a movie theater, commenting to a studio executive, "You know, I worked so hard to make him real," at which point the executive replies, "Yeah, well maybe you overdid it." Daniels searches for and ultimately confronts Baxter, his errant screen double, explaining, "You can't learn to be real. It's like learning to be a midget. It's not a thing you can learn." But Baxter gives it a try anyway, and in keeping with a familiar Allen motif, the lines between fantasy and reality blur and then disappear altogether.

The idea that images and story lines constructed in films can somehow materialize and cross the boundary to become actual events—or at least influence events in the immediate social world—is, of course, a distinctly postmodern one, invoking the theory of cinema as simulacrum where the gulf separating art and temporal reality breaks down. Allen's film breaches the nebulous barrier between films and their subjects in portraying a movie character who plays another film character in a different movie who selects life in the "real" world of the movie against life in the celluloid world inside the motion picture. It depicts a world in which cinema and "reality" blend into a third reality, the hyperreal, a phenomenon that, in effect, makes "reality" all the more elusive. *The Purple Rose of Cairo* not only contains a film within a film but also presents a film character coming to life and falling in love with a member of the film audience inside another film (Allen's) in which he (Baxter) plays a substantially different role. Such a radical cinematic departure distorts and rearranges reality to such a degree that, as Girgus observes, "everything turns to chaos."[20] Of course, such chaos is completely disorienting to the audience, in part because it breaks with the "Hollywood standard" of seamless editing and linear plots. With its aura of the hyperreal, Allen's work here invokes a range of ambiguities and nuances: As he moves to establish a film inside a film, while also bridging those two cinematic worlds by means of Baxter's maneuvers, we encounter an ironic sense of distancing from the actors. While attempting to make sense of Cecilia's and Tom's social turmoil, the willing suspension of disbelief that modernist films require falters and then vanishes entirely.

The interior film of *The Purple Rose of Cairo* can in fact be seen as a parody of the 1940s-style romance genre, but the audience is not supposed to like this film because Baxter, we are led to understand, is to be united with a "society woman" who is obviously wrong for him. It is only through his willful act of materializing out of his on-screen image that the Baxter figure takes on life since he clearly has none to speak of within the interior film—a situation that raises questions about the nature of film and reality, about what constitutes the essence of a character in real life. Baxter's naively rebellious persona, involving a refusal to accept his assigned on-screen role despite its allure, endows the film with a mood of subversion as it taps into a common rejection of an individual's boring, mundane existence. The idea that characters must depart from their prescribed on-screen images in order to find self-actualization has its parallel in theories of intergenerational conflict whereby children rebel against oppressive parental authority to discover and unlock their "true selves." *The Purple Rose of Cairo* poses fundamental questions about the relationship between media and reality, about complex mediations involving actors and the characters they depict, hinting at Freud's concept of repressed desire struggling to achieve expression within the unconscious mind. If Allen's film raises more issues about the interplay of film and reality than it seems to answer, the film nonetheless leads us into some important, rarely explored cinematic terrain. By calling forth this perennial struggle between the id and the ego, between the supposed inner child and the harsh paternalistic adult, between rebel and establishment, Allen builds a scenario filled with emotional tension and intellectual excitement—one overlaid with a multiperspectival focus that remains central to postmodern culture. Moreover, the film represents one of the great statements of what has been called the "cinematization of American society."[21]

In *Crimes and Misdemeanors* (1989), Allen builds on a similar postmodern sensibility but here steadfastly avoids anything resembling the (tentatively) neat resolutions or happy outcomes found in *Hannah and Her Sisters*. The film is easily one of Allen's gloomiest and most cynical about the fate of personal relationships, seemingly filled with anguish, bitterness, and guilt. At the very outset, Allen introduces the theme of guilt by means of a frightening image—the "eyes of God" that seem to be riveted on us—and this becomes a guiding symbol for the entire movie. Dr. Judah Rosenthal (Martin Landau) is involved in a turbulent affair with a young flight attendant named Dolores (Angelica Huston), but as we encounter this wounded couple, Dolores threatens to tell Rosenthal's wife unless Judah resolves to get a divorce. Despite the doctor's fervent pleas, Dolores starts calling his home with the aim of speaking with Rosenthal's wife and revealing the whole messy situation. Traumatized by all this, the doctor turns to his criminal brother Jack (Jerry Nichols) for advice. At this point, *Crimes and Misdemeanors* becomes part moral allegory, part sad love story, part complicated farce. The allegory is, of course, an old one about crime and punishment, except that now the one responsible for an evil deed (Rosenthal) is neither captured nor suffers personal remorse. By setting up Dolores's murder as the only way out of a seemingly irresolvable dilemma, Rosenthal has committed a heinous crime that, however, goes without any clear personal or legal consequences. Quite in contrast to the heroes of novels written by Tolstoy and Dostoyevsky, Allen's protagonist carries off a murder and gets away with it—quite typical of the besmirched hero we have come to expect in many postmodern films. Much like the villainous antiheroes of pictures like *The Player*, *The Usual Suspects*, *The Last Seduction*, *Body Heat*, *Pulp Fiction*, and

Dream Lover, Rosenthal apparently commits the "perfect murder": He not only gets away clean, but his life takes off to new levels after he gets rid of his bothersome, menacing girlfriend.

Eyes perform a major symbolic function in *Crimes and Misdemeanors*, serving as metaphors for clear or cloudy vision, depending on the character we want to describe. Rosenthal is an eye doctor, so for him eyes suggest irony and symbolize a lack of vision and moral sense—reflected, of course, in the murder of Dolores. Another character, Rabbi Ben (Sam Waterston), goes blind—a family member in whom Rosenthal has confided his deepest feelings and secrets. Allen explains that the film is about people who do not see, who never see themselves as others see them, and, above all, fail to see the right and wrong of urgent life-and-death situations. The rabbi may have excellent vision regarding spiritual matters, but he ultimately lacks vision about the complex realities of life.

As the film progresses, we see maverick television producer Clifford Stein (Allen) pursuing a romance with television executive Holly Reed (Mia Farrow), but his efforts are completely thwarted. Holly works for Lester (Alan Alda), a self-absorbed mainstream television producer who hires the more independent Cliff to make a documentary of his life. Cliff regards his brother-in-law Lester as a vain, superficial, self-deluded fool, so we should hardly be surprised to find Cliff turning the documentary into a farce that serves to expose Lester's embarrassing personal flaws. Lester predictably fires Cliff, then sets off for London, where (it turns out) he moves to win over Holly, who has secured a temporary job there. Cliff, desperately wanting Holly to fall in love with *him*, is devastated when he learns of the romance between Lester and Holly. As in *Hannah and Her Sisters*, personal relationships here turn into a sphere of endless machinations, duplicity, and, of course, hopelessness. In fact, Rabbi Ben is the only character in *Crimes and Misdemeanors* who emerges with any kind of positive standing: He goes blind but in the end remains a spiritual force. Allen fixes his camera on Ben in the final scene: By now totally without eyesight, Ben dances joyously with his daughter at the wedding for Lester and Holly. For Allen, the meaning of Rabbi Ben's character is that "unless you have a strong spiritual meaning, spiritual faith, it's tough to get through life." Thus, "Ben is the only character who gets through it, even if he doesn't really understand the reality of life." It follows that Rabbi Ben's blindness can be equated with his ability to use spiritual faith as a tool of survival, but it comes at a high price because his faith ultimately turns out to be blind as well. "It will work," says Allen, "but it requires closing your eyes to reality."[22] At the same time, with Cliff devastated by Holly's defection to Lester and Rosenthal turning himself into a murderer, simply going blind while maintaining a sense of emotional and moral balance might seem like a tolerable price to pay, which of course means that Rabbi Ben winds up as the only character in this blackest of all Allen films able to retain a shred of dignity.

Allen's *The Curse of the Jade Scorpion* (2001) continues a lifelong obsession with existential concerns of human destiny and the capricious role of fate and fantasy. For Allen, the ultimate fantasy (as always) involves a beautiful young woman who falls in love with him even as the physical changes wrought by age become more visible. Here he returns to the earlier world of older men falling in love with young women, as in *Manhattan*, *Hannah and Her Sisters*, and *Husbands and Wives*, where love and redemption can be found despite the corrupt nature of human beings and their social conventions. In this case, the "convention" that Allen savages is the insurance industry, specifically the North Coast Insurance Agency. There, C. W. Briggs (Allen) works as senior investigator with a long string of successful cases to his credit and finds himself confronted by an assertive "efficiency expert" named Betty Ann Fitzgerald (Helen Hunt), who threatens to recommend farming out the private investigation work to outside agencies, meaning that Briggs's position would be eliminated. After participating in a hypnotic trance for a magic show, Briggs and Fitzgerald find themselves falling in love despite their mutual loathing—thanks to the magical power of posthypnotic suggestion. Both have come under the influence of mysterious hypnotist Polgar, who makes them do the bidding of the "jade scorpion," a gemstone scorpion attached to a long chain. The magician programs them to respond to certain commands as they enter hypnotic states, during which he can order them to commit robberies and then retain no memory of what they have done.

Clues soon appear linking Briggs to two robberies, although he has no memory of anything; he earnestly swears his innocence. Gradually, after much confusion, it becomes clear how the real thief has used Briggs and Fitzgerald as unwitting agents of mayhem. With some help, however, the two begin to throw off their hypnotic spells, except that their "love" inculcated through hypnosis has now taken permanent root, and so they discover they are madly in love with each other after all. Was it entirely the magician's doing, or did he simply intensify feelings that were already present? Did their deep-seated mutual antagonism, as is so often the case in film and literature, simply mask an underlying mutual attraction? At what point did the loathing that they expressed for each other turn into something akin to genuine love?

Allen seems to be at his best when he sets out to deflate arrogance and stuffiness, which he does in this film by ridiculing Fitzgerald's "expert" investigators. He also satirizes the American insurance industry, with all its silly precautions against theft, dishonesty, and malfeasance. In fact, the jewelry heists occur precisely because of the company's obsession with overly elaborate security systems set up for wealthy clients that make it simple for anyone with access to the right information to carry out mayhem. Briggs and Fitzgerald, overcome by hypnotic trances, effortlessly steal a fortune in jewelry precisely *because* of the company's needlessly stringent security policies. Nothing is really secure, Allen seems to be saying, no matter how much effort and money are put into security.

If material possessions take on an ephemeral quality in *Curse of the Jade Scorpion*, so too do human relationships—yet another familiar Allen motif. McGruder (Dan Aykroyd) gets involved in a sleazy, manipulative love affair with Fitzgerald; later spurns his wife in favor of Fitzgerald; and then still later attempts to reconcile with his wife after Fitzgerald rejects him in favor of Briggs. It so happens that Briggs too finds relationships extremely precarious, and his workaholic approach to life as an investigator begins to alienate his wife, just as it does Fitzgerald (although the "spell" helps overcome this). Of course, Briggs is bound to wonder whether Fitzgerald will continue under the spell, but this kind of uncertainty is, in Allen's scheme of things, the price one is ultimately obligated to pay for intimacy. Indeed, everything associated with love and romance is, in the final analysis, ephemeral and tentative. In the words of one of his characters, "Love fades." That captures the essence of Allen's philosophy, so that even where "love" appears to be durable, as in the case of Fitzgerald and Briggs, it is sure to vanish altogether with the passing of time.

Allen's version of postmodern cinema depends on a unique convergence of social and individual, urban and family-situated elements of alienation, despair, and cynicism that is never diminished by his occasional flirtation with spiritual values. The bulk of his work takes up an existential discourse preoccupied with issues of life and death—or, more precisely, encounters with human mortality. Thus, in *Hannah and Her Sisters*, the character played by Allen faces an imagined health crisis and finds himself contemplating suicide before he stumbles across a Manhattan theater showing old Marx Brothers films, at which point he decides that in a world that could nurture such a creative life force, his own life must be worth living after all. Yet the larger chaos and meaninglessness of social existence, another existential theme, sooner or later renders the vision and power of the narrative "hero" fragile if not entirely bankrupt; one finds scarcely any space for assertive, empowered protagonists in Allen's work. All of this— images of chaos, preoccupation with matters of life and death, tortured sexuality, and absence of a hero—figures throughout the entire corpus of Allen's filmmaking.

Allen's career represents one of the greatest tributes to independent filmmaking ever—an independence he has fiercely preserved through more than thirty films, most produced on relatively modest budgets and infused with the same idiosyncratic sensibilities that make his work so easily identifiable. The scripts, directing style, performances, cinematography, music, and social motifs all reflect a distinctive Allen methodology that, for better or worse, has shaped his movies from the very outset. A central motif, visible from *Play It Again, Sam* (1972) through *Small Time Crooks* (2000) and *Hollywood Ending*, is that of neurotic urban angst best exemplified by those characters played by Allen himself. Having written and directed thirty-three films over a span of thirty-two years, he has kept intact elements of a creative team that naturally permits a strong aesthetic continuity, and his films have been a magnet for scores of first-rate actors and actresses. As part of his iconoclastic style, Allen has only once attended the Academy Awards, rarely does much to promote his movies, and steadfastly resists most temptations of media culture. Through all this, his audience in the United States has dwindled to something like a cult status: His movies of the late 1990s averaged less than $8 million in gross domestic revenue—although overseas earnings were much better. The documentary *Wild Man Blues* (2000), made by Barbara Kopple, revealed (in largely musical settings) Allen's enormous popularity across Europe.

From the outset, Allen has been fascinated with the subculture of rebels, outsiders, criminals, and misfits, a mixture of types present in virtually every one of his films. With all his comedic genius, *crime* is the subject matter that seems most to captivate him: "When I was a child I was always interested in crime," he relates. "Other kids could give you baseball players' batting averages. I could do that, but I knew all the gangsters and their jail sentences too. In crime, you've got suspicion, tension, and there's always something at stake, which is a very good atmosphere for a comedian."[23] It is this blend of comedy and the outsider culture that gives Allen's work one of its trademark signatures. For the movies to connect with audiences, however, they must contain elements of spontaneity and playfulness that border on the "ludic" dimension we explore later in this chapter. Beyond all the codes of urban angst and cynicism, the overriding goal of filmmaking is always to be entertaining. Thus, "I'm so pessimistic overall as a human being that I'm always surprised by success. . . . I think in the end people don't care about you, they care about being entertained." He adds, "If you watch a Marx Brothers movie made in the 1930s, it's still hilarious today, whether you show it to a bunch of truck drivers or a bunch of college kids."[24]

Yet another component of Allen's genius lies in his ability to weave together a set of visual, literary, and musical texts into a unique creative totality in a way that addresses the existential theme of social displacement and psychological anxiety, as we have seen in films like *Manhattan*, *Zelig*, *Hannah and Her Sisters*, and *Crimes and Misdemeanors*. Packed with an immense variety of distorted, refracted, and surreal images, his pictures add up to a subversive legacy fitting squarely within the postmodern mold; indeed, his work has done much to *define* that legacy. These images capture an era of social breakdown, confusion, ambiguity, powerlessness, and loss of identity—a reflection in part of modern angst, in part an outgrowth of media culture itself, in part Allen's own distance from mainstream society and its conventions. Responding to the alienation motif, Allen comments, "I hope I'm not in sync because I've never been in sync. I think the culture is one that deserves a lot of criticism. I don't respect it. I've always been an outsider. I've always felt like someone who didn't fit in."[25] As Girgus writes, the entire body of Allen's work offers an incisive view into the decentered world of contemporary urban life in particular and the fragility of the human condition in general. He adds, "On the cutting edge of contemporary critical and cultural consciousness, Allen challenges most of our traditional notions of authorship, narrative, perspective, character development, theme, ideology, gender construction, and sexuality."[26] And nothing could be more descriptive of the auteur's role within postmodern cinema.

OLIVER STONE AND THE END OF THE AMERICAN DREAM

Aside from the brilliantly innovative, prolific character of his filmmaking, what sets Oliver Stone apart is the unique mixture of modern and postmodern sensibilities that frames most of his pictures. They are "modern" precisely in their epic cinematic realism, their obsession with generally male protagonists, and their embrace of certain morality tales usually embedded in rich historical narratives. But the modern is simultaneously compromised and eclipsed by a cinematographical style that often incorporates the most frenetic and surreal images, by motifs that stress the tragic or fallen nature of contemporary heroism, and by narratives that subvert the very meaning of progress understood within the framework of modernity. In fact, Stone's impressive output, spanning from *Salvador* (1986) to *Any Given Sunday* (1999) and beyond, can be understood as a kind of historical mythmaking in which the world—at least that part of the world dominated by *American* interests and priorities—appears as morally, psychologically, and socially compromised, largely bereft of cohesion, purpose, and direction. It is a cynical, tormented, manipulative world in which old-fashioned heroes lose their capacity to make history or even to save their turf or themselves. Most of all, Stone's films are about the epochal collapse of the mythological American Dream that once captivated the popular consciousness.

Stone's cinematic portraits, with powerful, fast-moving, quixotic images that often move between reality and illusion, truth and myth, and repression and fantasy, surely embellish the dark side of American history: political–military debacles in Central America and Vietnam, the Kennedy assassination and its cover-up, the greed and corruption of Wall Street, the doomed personae of rock stars like Jim Morrison, and the horrors associated with a media culture steeped in narcissism and violence. The fast action, rapid pacing, and quick editing of Stone's films make them seem quite appropriate to a postmodern ethos attuned to chaos, surreal images, and social decay. Thus, while Stone's undoubtedly progressive instincts bring him into opposition against ruthless economic and political interests, his artistic style leaves the viewer in a mood of cynicism or confusion rather than outrage of the sort needed for empowerment. Such visual dynamics are nowhere more visible than in Stone's treatment of history that, as Susan Mackey-Kallis argues, brings the audience directly into contact with the plight of heroes forced to confront their own flawed morality as part of the "postmodern condition." Thus, "Stone's protagonists, with greater and lesser success, are willing to face their shadow, plumb the depths of the unconscious, and search for the next phase of teleological development. This requires them to slay the monsters of modern rationality, which often means slaying themselves in either an ego death or a messianic sacrifice."[27] Any number of Stone's heroes could be described in this fashion: Richard Boyle in *Salvador*, Gordon Gekko in *Wall Street*, Ron Kovic in *Born on the Fourth of July*, Barry Champlain in *Talk Radio*, Jim Morrison in *The Doors*, and Jim Garrison in *JFK*. Mackey-Kallis describes these characters as being "often like Greek gods, railing against human injustice, folly, and vice to provide mere mortals with lessons on how to live and work."[28] Many of the figures belong to clearly progressive texts with superlative depictions of icons, heroes, villains, and victims generally associated with leftist discourses. Yet these same characters, alas, proved incapable of changing the world as they were forced to run up against a series of internal and external obstacles, part of America's general descent into spiritual and political atrophy.

Stone's first full-length feature film, *Salvador*, revolves around key events in the bloody Salvadorean civil war of the early 1980s, a war that left 75,000 people dead while severely damaging the country's already feeble social and political infrastructure. Failing to secure U.S. funding for the project, Stone eventually shot the film with British financing during the incredibly brief period of fifty-six days in California, Nevada, and Mexico. The film offers a snapshot of the war as seen through the eyes of independent journalist Richard Boyle (James Woods), fighting for professional survival and artistic freedom against a repressive, U.S.-supported regime. The real-life Boyle, with help from Stone, wrote the script, which depicts a society on the edge: divided, violence ridden, turbulent, lacking in political cohesion, and totally under the thumb of American interests. Here Stone manages to interweave historical footage, graphics, and handheld camera work to re-create the feel of television journalism—a glimpse of what would characterize later Stone films. We see a remarkable, richly textured chronicle of repression, intrigue, gross mistakes, brutality, and heroism against the backdrop of mounting warfare conducted throughout a tiny nation. Following a minimally noteworthy career as a maverick journalist, Boyle returns to El Salvador hoping to make enough money to support his family, only to discover that the civil war has heated up since his last visit. He falls in love with a Salvadorean woman, and, after she demands that he take confession in the Catholic Church, Boyle stumbles across the assassination of Archbishop Romero by a government thug—an event that energizes him as he sets out to expose the corrupt, violent regime that enjoys U.S. support. In the process, he antagonizes both the local strongman and his U.S. military adjuncts, barely surviving efforts to murder him.

Much of the drama in *Salvador* revolves around Boyle's twisted, seemingly self-destructive persona mixed with his incredible courage in defying a brutal Salvadorean government, the U.S. military, and death squads that roam the landscape. Boyle's character departs radically from the classic protagonist able to triumph over all hardships; he winds up trapped in a matrix of chaos, fear, and doom he is powerless to overturn, a victim of historical forces he cannot begin to grasp. Yet an even more powerful image of the doomed hero in *Salvador* is the actual "villain" of the piece, which, of course, turns out to be the omnipresent U.S. political and military might. It is in this area—harshly critical of American intervention—that Stone breaks new ground: Prior to this film, no director managed to reach a wide audience based on such a thorough indictment of American foreign and military policies. This filmmaking terrain is laden with obstacles; Stone risked censorship, libel suits, and government harassment—not to mention future commercial success. Further, by setting up an amorphous, faceless, *structured* target of this sort, he could easily have failed to build significant resonance with the audience. *Salvador* lacks any conventional, modernist, larger-than-life villain whose terrible deeds can be easily personified insofar as the U.S. presence reveals an often covert, diffuse evil with many faces that is not always so obvious in its horrific consequences. Thus, Stone's object of derision is actually more of a generalized assault on the Salvadorean peasantry and left opposition, paving the way for right-wing oligarchical rule. (While the U.S. villain remains essentially faceless, the film does present glimpses of brutal action carried out by a government supported to the hilt by the newly elected Reagan administration.[29]) In the end, Stone does manage to construct a viable cinematic villain out of an imperial U.S. government bent on preserving its interests by every means at its disposal. The result is that, by identifying the villain with a broad clandestine intervention rather than the actions of specific individuals, Stone establishes a milieu of deepening cynicism, despair, and powerlessness regarding the operation of U.S. foreign policy—a theme that would later enter into such films as *Born on the Fourth of July* and *JFK*. In *Salvador*, the forces of evil appear much too powerful, too diffuse, and too out of control to be effectively confronted. About the most that can be expected of Stone's hero is that he survives—not an easy proposition in this foreboding (if nonetheless entertaining) movie.

Far removed from the increasing tumult of U.S. foreign policy, Stone's later film *The Doors* (1991) features rock idol Jim Morrison (played convincingly by Val Kilmer), who embarks on an odyssey even more hazardous than Boyle's as he reaches the pinnacle of counterculture icon in the late 1960s. Morrison's visionary song lyrics seem conflicted on the surface, at once embellishing "the end" linked to decay and dystopia and then celebrating the glories of hedonism and free sexuality ("come on baby, light my fire"). While Morrison is shown as relishing his first moments of stardom tied to the huge success of the Doors, he is soon depicted as following the well-worn path of extreme narcissism and self-destruction characterized by booze, drugs, psychological turmoil, legal troubles, and, ultimately, death in Paris at age twenty-seven. As with other 1960s icons like Janis Joplin, Jimi Hendrix, and Mama Cass Elliot, stardom proved to be Morrison's undoing despite his remarkable creative gifts and personal charisma. While Stone is clearly aware of these gifts, at one point even comparing the Doors' leader to William Blake, the film dwells mostly on Morrison the debauched, self-indulgent, doomed hero of the counterculture: Morrison's energies are increasingly drained by wild orgies of drinking, drugs, sex, and simple outlandish behavior. (When interviewed about Stone's film, Doors keyboard player Ray Manzarek said he detested the treatment of Morrison, whose musical and poetic creativity was downplayed in favor of his bizarre, surreal antics.) Unable to continue his life of tormented stardom, Morrison gave up

The Doors (Oliver Stone, 1991)   *A deconstruction of the quintessential postmodern (failed, tragic) hero, rock star Jim Morrison of the Doors (Val Kilmer) is a man pushed by social pressures of his time and inner demons to a downward trajectory leading to premature death at age twenty-seven.*

music and eventually moved to Paris, where in 1971 he died of heart failure. Nearly thirty years later, his grave site remains the locale of a constant international stream of admiring pilgrims.

Stone presents *The Doors* in rich, lurid reds and yellows, often giving it a dreamlike, subterranean quality appropriate to the 1960s-style, drug-infused psychedelic surrealism. He constructs the film through an assortment of poetic images of snakes and the ghost of an old, seemingly wise Native American, evoking Morrison's famed mysticism supposedly inspired by Blake and Nietzsche. No social taboos were safe from Morrison's lyrics, and *The Doors* brings forth music celebrating everything from wild sexual experimentation to incest and, of course, hallucinatory drugs. Ultimately, however, all expressions of beauty and poetry implode with the downward psychological trajectory of the fallen hero; what begins as a more or less innocent, spontaneous journey gives way to a doomed fate so common to 1960s icons—to the very Nietzschean philosophical morass that Morrison wanted to embrace for himself. In this, Morrison is shown by Stone (on the whole accurately) as the quintessential postmodern figure, a tragic protagonist who in the end was unable to combine the virtues of anarchic individualism with hedonistic self-indulgence. In the manner of earlier cultural heroes like James Dean, Marilyn Monroe, and Elvis Presley, Jim Morrison died as a victim of his own unimaginable success, symbolizing the best creative energies and the worst excesses of his generation. Stone's film brilliantly captures both the splendor and the pathos of this cultural moment. The poet Blake's view that "the road of excess leads to the palace of wisdom" was true neither of Morrison's short, tragic life nor of the film that chronicled it.

Stone's popularity and critical standing as a director grew during the 1990s in the aftermath of such well-received films as *Platoon* (1986), *Wall Street* (1987), *Born on the Fourth of July* (1989), and *The Doors*. Yet these films were dwarfed by the tumult and publicity greeting *JFK*, a three-hour-plus epic that can only be described as a surreal docudrama replete with camera work and editing of unprecedented sophistication. A film comprising a dizzying kaleidoscope of rapid-paced shots (2,800 in all), *JFK* represents not only a cinematographical breakthrough but also an ambitious effort to revisit the 1963 Kennedy assassination and events surrounding the cover-up, brought to the screen from the perspective of New Orleans District Attorney Jim Garrison (played by Kevin Costner). Stone's incredibly fast-paced camera work (thanks

The End of Violence (**Wim Wenders, 1997**)   *Bill Pullman and Andie MacDowell star in a neo-noir thriller revolving around an ultra-secret government project that places a vast network of high-powered cameras ready to photograph literally every inch of Los Angeles from a concealed base located in the Griffith Park Observatory.*

to Bob Richardson) embellishes the mounting sense of chaos, confusion, intrigue, and violence associated with Kennedy's murder, identified by Stone as a seminal event in modern American history. The assassination meant not only the death of a charismatic president but also the slow, inevitable spiritual slide—or "fall from grace"—of an entire nation that would soon be embroiled in a corrupt, deceitful, and barbaric war in Vietnam. The film begins with resonant images of hope and optimism growing out of Kennedy's 1960 election, the new president symbolizing a mood of youthful enthusiasm and great transformative potential. It ends with the fiercely maverick Garrison's ultimate failure to convince a jury of his conspiracy theory linked to the role of New Orleans businessman Clay Shaw (Tommy Lee Jones in the film).

Stone, roughly following Garrison's book, constructs his narrative around a government conspiracy to murder Kennedy, conceal evidence, manufacture a false report (by the Warren Commission), and frame Lee Harvey Oswald as the lone gunman—a conspiracy involving elements of the CIA, the Mafia, anti-Castro Cubans, and possibly even upper echelons of the "national security state." Most films depict villains who embody some particular conception of "evil"—who are cold, cruel, heartless, often psychotic stereotypes and frequently "flat" characters beset with inner demons or some variant of monsters from the id. They are outlaws, schemers, gangsters, killers, and other diabolical figures who can readily be identified and hated. Of course, some villains (Bonnie and Clyde, Bugsy Siegel, and even Batman and Darth Vader) have such a powerful cinematic presence that they can seduce the audience, winning it away from the officially designated narratives. In *JFK*, however, the villain turns out to be an amorphous, clandestine, shadowy network of agents, criminals, spies, government officials, and outsiders who manage to concentrate their energies in Dallas on a fateful November day in 1963. Stone "reconstructs" this unbelievable maze of characters, plots, and intrigues with the skill and sensibility of an investigating journalist possessing unlimited historical, technical, and photographic resources.

In depicting such a catastrophic event that would so profoundly alter history and subvert a number of myths about American democracy, Stone relies on a complex interplay of moving and still images, newsreel-style montages and dramatic reconstructions, and clear representations and blurred images—all expertly edited to convey a frenetic pace of action and a world in chaotic descent. In this, he deftly merges style and content so as to provide a compelling sense of the larger historical picture: the death of a hero at the hands of assorted shadowy villains acting in shrewd concert. The assassination becomes a political watershed that refused to disappear, either from the historical record or from the national psyche, and, of course, Stone made his film with precisely this deep understanding in mind. The historical legacy is one of murder, deceit, cover-ups, and perhaps even (as Stone implies) a loss of collective innocence. From this standpoint, the factual accuracies of either Garrison's or Stone's accounts matter less than the more sweeping, impressionistic view of the American experience since the early 1960s contained in *JFK*. Hence, the standpoint established in *JFK* that Kennedy was murdered because he refused deeper military involvement in Vietnam is difficult to uphold once the historical documents are analyzed, but the motives easily could have derived from the ill-fated Bay of Pigs invasion and the president's decision to pull back from military operations against Cuba.[30] Likewise, Stone's identification of a conspiracy involving many sectors of government itself (a sort of coup d'état) may be far-fetched, yet the assassination might well have been the work of a consortium made up of the CIA, Mafia, and anti-Castro Cubans. That it could have been carried out by a maniacal lone gunman, as the Warren Commission tried to sustain, seems preposterous, as *JFK*—with the help of a refurbished Zapruder film—illuminates with great cinematic power.[31] As in the case of films like *Salvador*, *Platoon*, and *Born on the Fourth of July*, Stone in fact pursues a larger agenda here: depiction of a society caught in the throes of a deep crisis of values, mired in historical impasse.

In *JFK*, of course, it is Garrison who takes on the unlikely role of lonely, embattled hero on the trail of assassins—a postmodern hero inevitably trapped within the political quagmire, a far remove from the populist scenario played out in *Mr. Smith Goes to Washington*. Garrison must indeed confront a powerful monster when he reopens the criminal investigation into Kennedy's murder three years after the event. A courageous but somewhat naive undertaking, the case is beset at every turn by formidable obstacles: disappearing witnesses, Jack Ruby's murder of Oswald, compromised or vanishing evidence, public fear and recalcitrance, and even the antagonism of his own wife (played by Sissy Spacek). The signs of intrigue and cover-up are ubiquitous. Garrison's stubborn determination to find the truth and expose a web of lies surrounding the cover-up gets him in trouble with his friends, associates, and family, who resent his obsession with a case that most feel should simply be put to rest. Finally, his wife leaves him to confront the actuality of his failure, although he does win some measure of redemption simply through the eventual release of Stone's film. If Kennedy represents a tragic hero cut down by an assassin's bullet at the height of his powers, then Garrison's legacy—humiliated prosecutor in search of historical truth—is only slightly less tragic.

JFK (Oliver Stone, 1991)   *With Kevin Costner as New Orleans District Attorney Jim Garrison, it contains every element of postmodern cinema—death of the hero, a society in a state of shocking paralysis, eclipse of the family, conspiracies, and a brooding, dystopic sense of the future.*

Despite the massive bombardment of criticism that met the appearance of this film—much of it coming even before the picture's release—*JFK* established Stone as an important public intellectual for the 1990s and beyond. The director emerged not only as a powerful critic of the political establishment but also as a creative figure in touch with cultural trends associated with the postmodern ethos. In Mackey-Kallis's words, "That a Hollywood filmmaker's interpretation of a historic event could cause such strong reactions among journalists and film critics alike points to film as a powerful cultural voice and to the filmmaker as the new bard of the mass-mediated campfire. The debate also highlights the problematic nature of historical interpretation and the realization that modernist definitions of historicity, like modernist definitions of reality, are quickly being challenged in a postmodern world."[32] Thus, while Stone appears on one level to be presenting a morality play in which villains must be slain, the entire body of *JFK* tells us something entirely different—that history is a blurred, multilayered process where clear definitions of truth and reality are difficult to locate.

In both style and content, *JFK* shares much in common with the traditional noir lexicon. As Chris Salewicz notes, "In essence the film uses a simple detective story structure; yet *JFK* doesn't offer an omniscient point of view; there is a much more subjective, lateral presentation of the plot, the rhythm of the editing carrying the story."[33] Rather than a straightforward modernist narrative, Stone offers a view of history filled with chaos, confusion, and multiple angles of perception—a view enhanced by the rapid-fire camera work and editing that indeed situate the viewer in the very midst of that chaos and confusion. *JFK* contains many noirish touches replete with dark images, brutish behavior, paranoia, and an atmosphere of nebulous conspiracies; like many noir classics, it reveals a world in which terrible deeds seem ubiquitous. From beginning to end, one finds a mordant universe of despair, fear, insecurity, and powerlessness even as Garrison doggedly pursues his righteous cause. Further, a central theme of traditional noir—pervasive corruption often extending to the highest levels of government and law enforcement—achieves perhaps its fullest representation in *JFK*. The highly charged scene where Garrison interviews Willie O'Keefe (Kevin Bacon) at a prison farm is revealing: O'Keefe speaks knowingly of demons lurking about the land—in and out of government—and of a country on the brink of mayhem and fascism. To capture all this on celluloid, Stone integrated roughly 200 speaking parts and 2,000 visual-effect opticals, along with massive amounts of real archival footage and restaged historical images. The result is a cinematic product that, in Salewicz's words, "revolutionized the form of film structure."[34] And part of this "revolution" was Stone's achievement in bringing postmodern cinematic sensibilities to an understanding of postwar American history.

In *Any Given Sunday* (1999), Stone focuses his probing, scorching gaze squarely onto professional sports, with its pantheon of quirky, unsavory, power-mad characters. His preference for tormented heroes comes across in Tony D'Amato (Al Pacino), the ill-starred coach of the Miami Sharks football team. D'Amato's team has just suffered four losses in a row, and he is accused of incompetence by his boss, Sharks owner Christine Pagniacci (Cameron Diaz). D'Amato's challenge in this film is to balance the urgent demand for team victories with his own professional ethics and individual coaching style. When veteran quarterback Jack "Cap" Rooney (Dennis Quaid) recovers from an injury, D'Amato starts him in a playoff game over third-string Willie "Screamin'" Beamin (Jamie Foxx). Gifted with tremendous athletic ability, Beamin refuses to go along with D'Amato's micromanagement and insists on creating new plays that are not in the official playbook. As a matter of habit that has solidified into a creed, D'Amato demands strict adherence to the playbook, a list of previously agreed-on plays, expecting his quarterbacks to memorize every one and call only those approved by him. Beamin, on the other hand, wants to substitute ad hoc plays of his own, looking to act on instinct and spontaneous reaction to changing conditions on the field. This treacherous habit naturally results in a confrontation with D'Amato, who demands that Beamin play by the book. Owner Pagniacci, for her part, insists on winning at any cost, whatever it might mean for team protocol or loyalty to individual players, while Beamin too upholds victory as the supreme virtue. "Winning is the only thing I respect," he says to D'Amato. For D'Amato, however, football represents far more than wins and losses; he says to Beamin that "the game has got to be about more than winning."

In the final playoff game, the Sharks find themselves behind by several points when D'Amato yanks Rooney, whose age and accumulated injuries appear to have taken a heavy toll, from the lineup. Setting aside his loyalty to Rooney, not to mention his obsession with the playbook, D'Amato sends in the younger Beamin. That move is quickly vindicated when Beamin scores the winning touchdown. By this time, Beamin seems to have matured as a football player. He is not the only character, however, to learn some tough lessons in this film: D'Amato has learned about the severe limits of micro-management and is able to regain his focus on winning. Pagniacci, the owner, also learns some useful lessons. Her audacity had permitted her to stride casually into the men's dressing room and address Sharks players personally, including men who were completely nude, which got her into trouble when her manager and star quarterback defected to a rival team.

What we find in *Any Given Sunday* is some typical Oliver Stone counsel: never trust anyone in business, and never become obsessed with control over the lives of other human beings. The business of professional football is visibly ruthless and competitive, while players emerge as spoiled, overpaid prima donnas. There are massive ego clashes involved in one of the most violent and aggressive of all sports. Romantic entanglements easily disintegrate in such a milieu. The very fragility of human relationships, a common postmodern theme, indeed provides a crucial backdrop for *Any Given Sunday*. Triumph in the form of beating an opponent into oblivion is marred by every conceivable moral and social compromise. As is usually the case in postmodern cinema, there are no true winners since even "victory" always comes at an enormous price. For Stone, it appears that professional football amounts to a symbolic representation of the larger economic and political system, and a savaging of one must be understood to extend to the other.

In *Any Given Sunday* and *JFK*, as in several other of his films (*Platoon, Born on the Fourth of July, Wall Street,* and *Talk Radio*), Stone weaves a dystopic image of American society where cynicism, greed, and destruction reign, much of it because of the very structure of American society and much of it because of the Vietnam debacle and its aftermath. Bereft of reason and purpose, alienated from institutional life, and denied genuine empowerment, people wind up absorbed into an atomized, disembodied postmodern universe that was depicted, in some ways even more graphically, in *Natural Born Killers*. Embellishing such postmodern cynicism, host Barry Champlain tells his audience in *Talk Radio*, "Yes, the world is a terrible place; yes, cancer and garbage disposals will get you; yes, a war's coming; yes, the world is shot to hell and you're a goner. Everything is screwed up and you like it that way."

THE CINEMA OF MAYHEM

Violence in its infinite expressions has long been a staple of Hollywood filmmaking, going back to the earliest combat, Western, gangster, horror, and thriller genres; intrigue, suspense, murder, and even the worst manifestations of barbarism have attracted viewers of all social backgrounds, ages, regions, aesthetic preferences, and political ideologies. Beginning with what Kellner and Ryan call the "slash and gash cycles" of the late 1970s, however, the depiction of violence took an increasingly dark, cynical, often nightmarish and dystopic turn where conventional historical and moral frames of reference broke down. As cinematic violence entered a world of social violence and moral collapse, it could be described as more or less postmodern—most often filled with meaningless narratives, nihilistic schemas, barbaric monsters, and a wide range of antiheroes. To be sure, there were plenty of movies that carried forward earlier sensibilities in which the violence and chaos were socially contextualized: neo-noir, historical dramas, the military genre, and a good many male-oriented action pictures. We are concerned here largely with films of the 1980s and 1990s that built on and then successfully commodified the Hobbesian aesthetic with its emphasis on glamorized but essentially random, nihilistic images of violence that in many ways correspond to personal and social relations in a culture that itself appears more crime ridden, anomic, and turbulent with each passing day. The films of Quentin Tarantino perhaps best illuminate this cinema of mayhem.

Cinematic representations of violence and crime as such are not as crucial here as is the particular *framework* within which such images are purveyed. One could not imagine combat films like *A Bridge Too Far*, *Patton*, or *Platoon* to be purged of explosive, sometimes epic scenes of brutal violence; this is the stuff of the combat genre, without which it would be largely meaningless. Yet the bulk of military pictures were informed by a distinctly *modernist* ethic calling attention to values of heroism, moral obligation, duty, camaraderie, and patriotism. The same is true of contemporary action pictures such as the *Rambo* series, *Top Gun*, *Terminator*, and *Robocop*, where social messages converge with abundant representations of violence and mayhem within a rather coherent narrative structure—where, indeed, the male hero willing to use any means at his disposal comes to the forefront and generally prevails. Other films like Coppola's *Godfather* trilogy, Scorsese's *Taxi Driver* and *Casino*, and Lyne's *Fatal Attraction* similarly link images of violence to a larger social (and ethical) picture, as did neo-noir ventures in the tradition of *Chinatown*, *Body Heat*, and *The Usual Suspects*.

The postmodern shift originates with the first "death-trip spectacles" that raised cinematic brutality to new levels, that in effect aestheticized violence by disconnecting it from any discrete historical or social point of reference. Films like *Halloween* and *Prom Night* (both 1978) fit this pattern, focusing on psychopathic characters who carry out random criminal acts in a world infested with danger, aggression, and brutality and dominated by the darkest manifestations of the human spirit. The director who took this motif to its greatest artistic heights was probably Brian De Palma, who, influenced by Hitchcock, crafted such films as *Obsession* (1976), *Blow Out* (1981), *Dressed to Kill* (1980), and *Casualties of War* (1989). With De Palma, violence was associated with male rage over sexually threatening women at a time of mounting backlash against feminism and the simultaneous decline of traditional social relations, but it could be seen as the mark of something larger: reaction against a world in decay and disorder. What began as a "slash and gash" motif linked to male sexual anxiety thus merged with a more general "baroque" cinematic departure that Kellner and Ryan have characterized as an unpredictable "world of anxiety projections, threats potentially coming from anywhere, because the secure presence of meaning has withdrawn from it." It follows that "the fantastic exaggerated baroque style is thus essential to the sexist vision of the films"[35] and, it should be added, a broader Hobbesian view of contemporary social life. The dreams, fantasies, illusions, and nightmarish visions of this understanding would come to shape the film aesthetics of directors like Tarantino in the 1990s, when the idea of random, nostalgic, pointless, and even romanticized depiction of violence would be pushed to its extreme.

To speak of a Hobbesian-infected cinema is to enter into a universe where an imagined "state of nature" prevails in which binding ethical principles of community life are largely absent; a condition of quasi-anarchy is defined by a reign of extreme individualism freed of constricting rules, norms, and traditions. As Thomas Hobbes argued, in such a state people are motivated by strong appetites, passions, desires, and self-interest as well as fears born of everyday chaos, disorder, and unpredictability, part of "a general inclination of all mankind, a perpetual and restless desire of power after power, that ceaseth only in death."[36] Reflecting on the seemingly endless civil strife of his own times (seventeenth-century England), Hobbes concluded that such strife was the inevitable product of a dark, evil human nature endemic to a situation where society was nothing other than a chaotic field of forces that, lacking a coercive intervening power, would veer inevitably out of control. This meant a condition of more or less perpetual civil warfare. Thus, "Hereby it is manifest that during the time men live without a common power to keep them all in awe, they are in that condition which is called war; and such a war, as is of every man against every man . . . where every man is enemy to every man."[37] Then Hobbes adds, in one of his most famous passages, "and the life of man, solitary, poor, nasty, brutish and short . . . [is a] war of every man against every man." In such a terrible life, "the notions of right and wrong, justice and injustice, have . . . no place."[38] Without protection or security and filled with distrust and fear, human beings will inevitably be free to vent their greed, lust, pride, and revenge essentially beyond the scope of any community or public interest. In the final analysis, "civilization" is guided by little more than death and the fear of death.

Here we have a guiding motif underlying the cinema of mayhem, perhaps nowhere better appropriated—even if obliquely—than in the work of Tarantino. While rarely articulated within a structured narrative, this motif suggests an ongoing brutal struggle for survival just beneath the veneer of a modern, complex, technologically advanced urban order. Aggression and violence, much of it random and even mundane, is the natural outgrowth of the atomized violence built into the very rhythm and pulse of everyday life, in part a function of male fantasies of power and revenge and in part the result of an economic system that engenders social inequality and injustice. In Hollywood, not only De Palma but also Sam Peckinpah, John Milius, and Paul Schrader can be seen as forerunners of this cinematic mayhem where life becomes a jungle with precious few social or moral counterweights.

Quentin Tarantino is known mainly for two films, *Reservoir Dogs* (1992) and *Pulp Fiction* (1994), although he directed *Jackie Brown* (1997) and wrote an original script for *Natural Born Killers* (1994), which was so thoroughly reworked by director Oliver Stone that Tarantino has since maintained his distance from the film. It was *Reservoir Dogs* that established Tarantino as an innovative, bold, up-and-coming filmmaker not far removed from his workaday life in a southern California video store. While extremely violent, this film won critical acclaim for its experimental cinematography, the sterling performances of a nearly all-male cast, and liberal use of flash-backs and other stylistic devices intended to create an ambience of impend-ing doom. Tarantino's script is essentially his tribute to *The Killing* (1957), Stanley Kubrick's noirish first feature film about a racetrack heist gone sour, although the classic femme fatale role (played then by Marie Windsor) is now missing. *Reservoir Dogs*, according to Tarantino, is "about a bunch of guys who pull a jewelry heist and go back to this garage. One guy's been shot, one guy's been killed, and there's an undercover cop in their midst." He went on to explain that "you never see the jewelry heist. It's a low-budget movie, so you don't have to worry about that."[39]

The bank robbers of *Reservoir Dogs* constitute a motley assemblage of drifters and outlaws for whom brutality readily becomes a way of life; theirs is a largely nihilistic outlook infected with a good deal of gallows humor—one of Tarantino's well-known trademarks. For security reasons, the rob-bers go by code names such as Mr. White, Mr. Brown, Mr. Blond, and Mr. Orange, but none of these characters is seen as the property of any specific actor since Tarantino believes that any good actor able to play a robber could easily fit any role. True to the mayhem of the picture, everything is ar-bitrary, unpredictable, and overstated. The characters do banter endlessly about their choice of coded names, with Mr. White eventually stating, "Who cares what your name is?" Harvey Keitel, who receives top billing and whom Tarantino hoped would play the mastermind Joe, ultimately de-cided to play Mr. White, who, like everyone but Mr. Pink, perishes in the fi-nal bloody shootout. Tim Roth, whom Tarantino believed would make a good Mr. Pink or Mr. Blond, opted instead for Mr. Orange—a character who spends the entire movie bleeding to death in the garage where the rob-bers congregate. Michael Madsen decided to play Mr. Blond, who presides over the controversial torture scene in which Mr. Blond slowly cuts off the ear of a captured policeman. True to the ethically callous nature of the film, Madsen remarks that "I don't really give a good fuck what you know or don't know, but I'm gonna torture you anyway. Not to get information. It's so amusing for me to torture a cop. All you can do is pray for a quick death, which you ain't gonna get."

The final scene of *Reservoir Dogs* turns into a classical Mexican standoff that lasts for several minutes as the remaining robbers, who still have no idea what went wrong with their diamond heist except that one of them is obvi-ously a police informant, draw their guns on each other. In the end, Joe shoots Mr. Orange (the real traitor), while Mr. White shoots Joe. Then Nice-Guy Eddie shoots Mr. White, who shoots him in return. Everyone involved in this bizarre saga now goes down in the brutal (and seemingly pointless) massacre as Mr. White discovers that Mr. Orange is the detested traitor. Mr. Pink escapes with the diamonds just as the police arrive, but he is given very little choice of escape, so the robbers go out in a hail of gunfire.

Reservoir Dogs reflects Tarantino's special attraction to pop and junk culture and, above all, to a merging of comedy and violence. While the film has been sharply criticized for its reliance on spurious, sadistic violence, the director shrugs off such objections, stressing that "I do look at everything as a comedy, and *Reservoir Dogs* is structured to get laughs. I like the idea that the audience is laughing and that, BOOM, the next moment there is blood on the walls. Then there are more laughs."[40] He adds, "As an artist, violence is part of my talent."[41] Yet Tarantino's total immersion in the culture of everyday life suggests a larger picture: the use of graphic, shocking brutality to say something about the way American society works, much the same way Coppola used the *Godfather* trilogy to make a statement about capitalism. While he disavows any political agenda, he does apparently want to depict violence as it really is or perhaps in some exaggerated form: slow, blood soaked, torturous, yet somehow almost impersonal as if *technique* and affectation were all that mattered. As he puts it, "Violence is part of this world and I am drawn to the outrageousness of real-life violence. . . . To me, violence is a totally aesthetic subject."[42] Indeed, *Reservoir Dogs* represents nothing less than a tribute to the discourse on murder, death, and mayhem, its dialogue filled with a constant torrent of verbal and physical abuse that easily degenerates into rantings filled with racism and sexism. Thus, even where brutality is frequently accompanied by touches of humor, its broader relevance to the Hobbesian condition cannot be dismissed.

With the 1994 release of *Pulp Fiction*, Tarantino had become established as a first-rank postmodern auteur. Featuring Tarantino as writer, director, and actor, the film won the Palm d'Or at Cannes and the Academy Award for best screenplay along with an array of other critical honors. (Leonard Maltin named it among the top 100 films of the twentieth century.) Whereas *Reservoir Dogs* achieved only modest success at the box office, *Pulp Fiction* grossed a phenomenal $120 million after costing only $8 million. It was an even more boldly experimental picture, offering a number of separate but crisscrossing and overlapping stories of low-life characters in Los Angeles swept up in much the same kind of brutality and mayhem that defined *Reservoir Dogs*. Tarantino got excellent performances out of a star-studded cast, including John Travolta, Samuel L. Jackson, Uma Thurman, Harvey Keitel, Bruce Willis, and Tim Roth. Travolta delivers one of his finest performances as Vincent Vega, a heroine-addicted hit man for a local mobster, as does Jackson as Vincent's partner, Jules.

Pulp Fiction opens with a definition of "pulp," which is a "magazine or book containing lurid subject matter"; to this could be added a treatment of intrigue, crime, and outlawry—all fashionable subject matter for the pulp tradition as for Tarantino. From the first scene onward, we view dramatic examples of lurid (and criminal) activity, beginning with the saga of two convenience-store robbers, Pumpkin (Roth) and Honey Bunny (Amanda Plummer), who are having a casual breakfast at a restaurant. The robbers decide to switch from holding up convenience stores to restaurants, where they can also rob patrons. The action then jumps to a scene that took place the day before when Vincent and Jules cold-bloodedly and sadistically murdered some young criminals who had withheld large amounts of money from the mobster Marcellus. During the killings, a gang member takes dead aim at the two hit men and fires a volley from close range that somehow misses them. This seeming miracle (interpreted by Jules as an "act of God") sets off a chain reaction in Jules that ultimately results in his decision to go straight and take up another line of work. Other vignettes cross the screen, including a surreal date between Vincent and his boss's wife Mia (Thurman) that ends up with Mia near death from a drug overdose and Vincent being forced to stab her in the heart with a huge shot of adrenaline, a scene in which Marcellus is raped by out-of-control rednecks, and a scene where Butch (Willis) catches Vincent in his apartment and shoots him without provocation. Vincent reappears in the final act—depicted earlier on the day of his eventual death—and a Mexican standoff occurs at the restaurant as Pumpkin and Honey Bunny tensely square off against Vincent and Jules. But contrary to the similar climax in *Reservoir Dogs*, this time no bloodbath takes place since everyone walks out of the restaurant after Jules arrives at a workable compromise.

Tarantino's characters in *Pulp Fiction*, like those in *Reservoir Dogs*, are essentially licensed to kill—and they do generally kill (or threaten to kill) without much feeling or apology. In a world saturated with violence, there is a sense in which even more violence appears quite rational. The influence of lurid crime fiction (or even true-crime episodes) is omnipresent, with few apologies or pretensions, as illustrated by Tarantino's response to an interviewer: "I fancied *Pulp Fiction* as a modern-day spaghetti Western."[43] And the director's use of so many cinematic styles and languages, with a wide variety of characters floating in and out of the picture along with extensive commentary on Hollywood film culture, all contributed to a postmodern mood of dispersion, nostalgia, and upheaval. As with *Reservoir Dogs*, an aura of terror permeates the film, mixed with a romantic yearning for the past and an image of sexuality that can only be described as tormented. Male rage is visible at every turn. At the same time, despite Vincent's death, *Pulp Fiction* embraces an element of optimism not present in either *Reservoir Dogs* or another Tarantino script, *Natural Born Killers*. There is some measure of redemption here, with Mia seemingly returning from the dead, Marcellus rescued by Butch during the rape scene, Marcellus forgiving Butch for double-crossing him over the boxing match, and, of course, Jules abandoning his life of crime. As Jackson later observed, "The voice of redemption flows through the whole film. I mean, Mia gets it when she comes back to life after overdosing. Butch gets it. Marcellus gets it, and I'm the person who actually voices it [as Jules]."[44] *Pulp Fiction* is violent, yet this redemptive aspect makes the violence seem less horrific than in *Reservoir Dogs* and less sensational than in *Natural Born Killers*. Still, the film remains noteworthy for its celebration of mayhem.

In the case of *Natural Born Killers*, Tarantino had actually written a script for this film before he wrote *Reservoir Dogs*—although he immediately detached himself from Stone's picture once he realized how thoroughly Stone had revised the original script. Yet much of Tarantino's narrative structure and mood remain with the new version, and he received screen-writing credit. He refused to even watch the movie when it went into theatrical release, proclaiming himself an enemy of Stone's film while saying, "I may catch it some day if I'm in a hotel and it's on pay-per-view." As matters stand, *Natural Born Killers* elicited a decidedly mixed reception: Many (including mostly young males) regarded it as something of a cult masterpiece, while critic Maltin dismissed it because "whatever points Stone wants to make are delivered early on, with a bludgeon, the rest being all sound and fury," and Emanuel Levy describes it as a "vicious, cold-hearted farce."[45] What Stone and cowriter Don Veloz hoped to achieve was to elevate Tarantino's script—elements of which are visible in both *Reservoir Dogs* and *Pulp Fiction*—into a powerful satire on the madness of media violence in American society. In its final version, *Natural Born Killers* bears a strong resemblance to such earlier gun-rampage pictures as *Gun Crazy* (Joe Lewis, 1949), *Bonnie and Clyde* (Arthur Penn, 1967), and *Badlands* (Terrence Malick, 1973), in which eroticism and violence merge to form an explosive and dramatically seductive combination.

As the heroes (or antiheroes) of the story, Mickey and Mallory Knox (Woody Harrelson and Juliette Lewis) come together with two overwhelming purposes in mind: to commit unprecedented mayhem and to love each other passionately. They meet when Mickey delivers an order of beef to Mallory's child-molesting father (Rodney Dangerfield), who makes no secret of his lust for his beautiful daughter. Mallory reacts by rebelling to the

Natural Born Killers (Oliver Stone, 1994) *Mickey (Woody Harrelson) and Mallory (Juliette Lewis) are a sex-and-blood-crazed young couple who embark on a crime spree in which they kill no less than fifty-two people after murdering Mallory's parents. A biting satire of violence in both film culture and society as a whole.*

maximum, explaining, "I was born naturally, born being bad." Soon Mickey coolly justifies his own homicidal impulses by affirming, "It's just murder, all God's creatures do it." The two fall in love immediately and quickly consummate their first brutal act of violence—the grisly murder of Mallory's parents, justified by the father's sexual abuse and the mother's failure to prevent it. Then, in the fashion of *Gun Crazy*, they embark on a honeymoon crime spree in which they calmly but efficiently murder over fifty people and carry out a number of armed robberies before they are arrested and imprisoned. The nihilistic and pointless violence of the film is captured by Stone's (and cinematographer Richardson's) frenetic pacing along with a kinetic assemblage of images. As critic Richard Corliss wrote in *Time* magazine after the picture's release, "*Natural Born Killers* plunders every visual trick of avant-garde and mainstream cinema . . . and for two delirious hours pushes them in your face like a Cagney grapefruit. The actors go hyper-hyper, the camera is ever on the bias, the garish colors converge and collide, and you're caught in this Excedrin vision of America in heat." The film is clearly a twisted, mind-bending journey into the surreal. As for Stone, he called attention to the *illusory* nature of the movie while claiming at the same time that it was made to help people "understand where we're at as a society, what's going on."[46] Where "we're at," judging from this movie, is in the midst of intensifying civil crisis. This anarchic motif could hardly be more graphic.

In contrast to most Stone films, *Natural Born Killers* is replete with flat, cartoonlike characters who fail to measure up to the cinematic agenda seemingly laid out by the filmmaker. One finds little of the complexity and roundness associated with antiheroes like Peggy Cummins and John Dall in *Gun Crazy* or Faye Dunaway and Warren Beatty in *Bonnie and Clyde* or even Don Corleone and the Joker. One reason is that Tarantino reportedly drew his characters not from life but from popular pulp fiction heroes of the 1940s and 1950s; Harrelson and Lewis were essentially trapped in simple formulaic representations. Egocentric television host Wayne Gale (Robert Downey Jr.) is another case in point: Patterned on Geraldo Rivera, he is obsessed with high ratings and will stop at nothing to achieve them. Completing an interview with the couple in prison, he exclaims, "Am I God or what?" He gloats that his exclusive interview with the murderous pair will make him one of the greatest television personalities ever. "This is Elton John confessing his bisexuality to *Rolling Stone*," he shouts. "This is Truffaut setting the record straight on Hitchcock." Bernard comments, with irony, that "of all the analogies in the script the Hindenberg was most apt"[47] because the apparently deliberate one-dimensionality of the characters renders audience identification with them extremely difficult. Among other things, Mickey and Mallory possess absolutely no redeeming features—not even wit or humor—and Gale winds up as nothing more than a simplistic antimedia foil. By the end of the film, Gale has become a totally self-indulgent rebel who even participates in the final prison break by shooting at prison guards. Mickey and Mallory, however, remain unimpressed, and when the three of them escape prison, the homicidal duo ends up shooting Gale, believing that, having filmed the prison break, he has now outlived his usefulness.

To an extent greater than either *Reservoir Dogs* or *Pulp Fiction*, *Natural Born Killers* resonates with the images, sounds, tones, and motifs of sheer brutal violence, part of a cultural milieu in which it seems, in Harrelson's words, as if "the world is now coming to an end." It is cinema where virtually everything appears to be connected to violence: the family, mass media, adventure, lust, and romance. What emerges is an environment devoid of reason, trust, accountability, and ethical bounds, where serial killers (one thinks of "Night Stalker" Richard Ramirez or Ted Bundy) readily achieve celebrity status. The picture, in its compelling simplicity, poses the question of how people can possibly bring themselves to kill so indiscriminately and with such sadistic barbarism and answers in Hobbesian fashion that evil is an endemic part of human nature—indeed, that it is the inevitable outgrowth of all nature. The cinema of mayhem embellished by Tarantino and Stone here reaches its fullest expression in Richardson's brilliant camera work, which (as in *The Doors* and *JFK*) locates itself in the very midst of chaos and violence, where decay, insanity, and aggression come to represent normalcy. As graphic shots of the pandemonium of jail riots imply a larger breakdown of social order, we achieve the ultimate merger of media culture, social decay, and capitalist commodification. This is postmodern cinema with an especially surreal, brutal twist.

Tarantino's films, though few in number, have elicited a rare mixture of critical acclaim, mass popularity, and industry worship—ideal for filmmaking in the information age, where technology, commercialism, and the all-consuming image converge to produce an ideology of passive spectatorship. In some ways, these films represent the ultimate triumph of form over content endemic to the postmodern ethos. Indeed, Tarantino has been anointed as the exemplary postmodern auteur, although by the late 1990s his star had already been dimmed in part because of his relative inactivity and in part because of the proliferation of films transcending Tarantino's motifs. Tarantino no doubt represents the final triumph of postmodernism, which is to empty artwork of all content, thus voiding its capacity to do anything except helplessly represent our agonies. As Dana Polan writes: "In postmodernism . . . the universe is not to be seen but is, to put it bluntly, simply to be seen. . . . . Hence we witness another important reason for the bits and set pieces in *Pulp Fiction*: they float up from the film as so many 'cool' moments, hip instances to be appreciated, ingested, obsessed about, but rarely to be interpreted, rarely to be made meaningful."[48] With no genuine social or moral backdrop to the graphically brutal violence, which is often accompanied by schoolboy humor, we are left with little human resonance, no characters that we can actually care about. Perhaps the cinema of mayhem requires this kind of disconnectedness for it to be so aesthetically viable. Lacking any structure of meaning, Tarantino's pictures depart from the conventional action genre, which (as in the case of John Woo) in fact did so much to inspire Tarantino's work. Although possibly even more violent from beginning to end, action pictures in their cinematic modernism did usually contain four elements lacking in Tarantino: strong, often charismatic heroes; coherent narratives; clear moral or value conflicts; and a cast of believable characters. This may be inevitable given the casual indifference to narratives, scenes, and characters that shapes so much of Tarantino's narrow cinematic world. Scenes, references, dialogues often take on an arbitrary cast; they're pieced together from twenty years of watching movies. Tarantino's characters—and Tarantino himself—inhabit a world where the entire landscape is composed of

Hollywood movies.[49] Yet these very same characters are the product of a larger society increasingly shaped by fragmentation, chaos, and violence.

The cinema of mayhem became even more fashionable by the late 1990s: Influenced by the work of Tarantino as well as the growing body of male-oriented action films and the continuation of eroticized, violent thrillers made popular not only by De Palma but also by the scripts of Joe Eszterhas (*Jagged Edge, Basic Instinct, Sliver*, and *Jade*), a new cycle of films appeared depicting brutal violence, detestable characters, black humor, and extreme cynicism, though the violence in these films is often more psychological than physical. These include Peter Berg's *Very Bad Things* (1998), featuring a Las Vegas bachelor party run amok in what would become a blood-soaked casino hotel room, along with Todd Solondz's ill-titled *Happiness* (1998), *Your Friends and Neighbors* (Neil LaBute, 2000), and the much heralded *American Beauty* (Sam Mendes, 1999). In some measure, these pictures are designed to shock audiences not only with graphic representations of brutal violence but also with portraits of a wide variety of selfish, cruel, nihilistic, psychologically detached characters that could well have been borrowed from the scripts of Tarantino's films.

Along these lines, David Lynch's *Mulholland Drive* (2001) suggests a powerful restatement of such motifs, with the director returning to his postmodern roots after a brief flirtation with modernism in the Disney production of *The Straight Story* (1999). *Mulholland Drive* is just about as postmodern as a film can be, replete with duplicitous characters, stories ensconced within stories, the usual Lynch penchant for mayhem and violence, and several experimental flourishes that seem designed to perplex as much as enlighten the audience. Viewers can easily get lost in the labyrinthine "plot" of this film, partly because of a series of blurred, refracted, and seemingly contradictory narrative constructs. The story unfolds as a young woman supposedly named Betty (Naomi Watts) arrives in Los Angeles determined to achieve success in the movies. She lives at her aunt's apartment, conveniently available because of the aunt's departure. Immediately on arrival, she meets someone who calls herself Rita (Laura Elena Harding), an amnesiac victim of a car accident. We learn that the accident apparently saved Rita's life, though, since her limousine drivers were actually on the verge of murdering her when they were run down by an out-of-control vehicle. Rita manages to escape relatively unscathed and takes refuge in Betty's apartment. From this point onward, the film revolves around discovering Rita's true identity, with some minor detours as Betty gets involved in reading for film roles. Events quicken after Betty and Rita become lovers.

The narrative takes yet another turn as we find that Betty's true identity is really someone named Diane, living not at her aunt's residence but in an apartment on Mulholland Drive. Adding to the confusion, we also learn Rita's true name, which is Carmella, who turns out to be a successful actress with many fine performances to her credit. After Carmella leaves Diane and takes up with a male film director, Diane becomes unglued and pays a hit man to murder the unfaithful Carmella. Diane then becomes overwhelmed by guilt-ridden fantasies and takes her own life—a familiar Lynch plot device—by shooting herself in the head. Rather than viewing Betty/Diane as a sympathetic figure, the audience comes to realize she is a woman insanely overcome with feelings of jealousy and anger and prepared to act out her feelings. By presenting Diane's fantasies as if they were real, Lynch once again plays with the distinction between appearance and reality—another customary postmodern theme. Hollywood provides the ideal setting for this exploration of blurred reality boundaries, of course, since one of its main preoccupations is to create illusions of this sort. A scene in an auditorium carried out by ostensibly live performers underscores Lynch's attention to the realm of illusions and fantasies, in this case with cinematic brilliance. A woman sings "Hay no Bandera," which means "there is no band," and she decides to demonstrate it by shutting off the band music, and later another woman is depicted as apparently singing a song—but the song continues along as she physically collapses.

When the audience finally learns the truth about Diane and Carmella, such knowledge provides them with little solace; on the contrary, the film is beset with a deepening sense of pessimism and confusion. Lynch is able to manipulate the viewer into sympathy for Betty until he reveals her true persona as the twisted, deceitful, hateful Diane. As in the case of *Pulp Fiction* or *Very Bad Things*, the film offers no truly sympathetic characters, no intelligible distinction between good and bad, no coherent view of moral or psychological boundaries, and, indeed, no obvious narrative structure—all ingredients of postmodern filmmaking that owes so much to the work of David Lynch. The cinema of mayhem has taken on new meaning.

LUDIC POSTMODERNISM AND BEYOND

A world filled with Hobbesian images and social relations is also one in which expressions of what we call "ludic" postmodern filmmaking can be expected to surface in one form or another. By "ludic" here we have in mind a cultural motif of playfulness and irreverence that might evade direct, serious engagement with worldly concerns but that, quite often obliquely, amounts to a novel type of cinematic subversion. Virtually by definition, the ludic sensibility questions and resists the universe of established meanings, whether in popular culture, mass media, politics, religion, or traditional family life; nothing remains taboo, and little escapes the domain of satirical assault. The ludic dimension celebrates a sense of virtually "anything goes" in its playful, ironic, eclectic style that can easily shade into an outright nihilism owing much to the traditions of surrealism, dadaism, and existentialism. The renunciation of "serious" (and often modernist) cinematic discourses coexists with a mood of experimentation, a freewheeling relativism, and creative autonomy. Viewed from this angle, the whacky and irreverent Marx Brothers films of the 1930s—notably *Duck Soup* and *A Night at the Opera*—seemed to approach this definition of cinema, as in fact did some of Woody Allen's films. For a current, more distinctly postmodern representation of the ludic, we have chosen to explore the films of John Waters.

Among established directors, Waters is perhaps the most articulate exponent of playful cinema—a cinema that resists any coherent interpretation, any conceptual framework within which to view cultural production or social life. On the surface, at least, every visual or narrative representation is turned into a something of a mockery, a joke, or some form of self-parody. In the work of Waters, nothing is too scandalous for a world already densely populated by trashy characters, outsiders, and neurotic misfits of all sorts. Beginning with *Multiple Maniacs* (1970), *Pink Flamingos* (1972), and *Female Trouble* (1974), Waters set out to establish himself as something of a perverse, warped auteur of Hollywood shock art that might be seen as a parallel to Andy Warhol's entry into the New York art scene. These films combined grisly humor and outrageous sex, not to mention portrayals of people whom Waters himself has called some of the "filthiest people alive." (True to his irreverence toward established norms and canons, Waters dedicated *Female Trouble* to notorious Manson family member Tex Watson.) In 1977, he made *Dangerous Living*, a movie filled with freakish scenes of decay, violence, gore, and bizarre sexuality best described as a darkly humorous fairy-tale horror film that, over time, has become a cult favorite of many Waters fans. The setting for *Dangerous Living*—a fantasy town called Mortville—exists as a haven for every conceivable low-life and seedy character, a locus of cruelty, cannibalism, and simply endless bad taste. But Mortville also reeks of phoniness, a contrived and twisted domain of trash art characteristic of so much of the American pop scene. Referring to this film, Waters commented, "I hate reality, and if I could have my own way everything I captured on screen would be fake—the buildings, the trees, the grass, even the horizon."[50]

With the release of *Polyester* (1981), Waters entered onto new terrain: a more solidly financed film that reached large audiences beyond the art-house venues where his films were typically shown. Although hardly mainstream,

Polyester became Waters's first widely received movie despite its unconventional casting that included the character actor Divine, a 310-pound man who performs in several of Waters's pictures as a cross-dresser. Here Divine plays Francine, the abused wife of a sleazy pornographic theater owner who has an affair with his secretary (Mink Stole). Francine's troubles just begin with her swinish husband, however, and are quickly aggravated when her two teenage children from hell enter the scene. Francine's daughter turns out to be a sex-crazed brat who flunks out of high school and then seeks out an abortion so she can maintain a torrid sex life with her repulsive idler boyfriend. The son, known as the "Baltimore Foot Stomper," sniffs glue and attacks helpless women by stomping on their feet. As if this does not provide enough misery, Francine must deal with a controlling, aggressive mother who is the object of disgust on the part of her daughter. Francine's best friend, "Cuddles," an older, portly woman lacking most of her teeth, ends up as her only ally in this borderline insane harassment story that makes the Torment of Job seem rather tepid in comparison. Meanwhile, a character played by an aging Tab Hunter preys on Francine's loneliness and vulnerability by seducing her while simultaneously (and secretly) carrying on an affair with her mother. Consistent with Waters's earlier and later films, *Polyester* relies on a disjointed, irreverent narrative that trades heavily on surreal motifs and images. That all this takes place in Waters's native Baltimore, a largely middling, nondescript city, only further embellishes this surreal mood.

The massive and bizarre Divine has a strong presence in *Polyester* from beginning to end, a reality that festers with his exaggerated mannerisms and facial expressions filled with elements of camp and slapstick—a hallmark of Waters's movies. Here as elsewhere, the viewer encounters few pretty images, few conventional settings, and few cherished values that are not pilloried or satirized. Divine's hulking, larger-than-life presence epitomizes a ludic, tongue-in-cheek quality the filmmaker (in control of virtually the entire production) appeared to prefer.

In 1988, Waters made *Hairspray*, a satirical treatment of 1960s teenage television rock-and-roll programs like Dick Clark's *American Bandstand*—though in fact modeled along lines of a local Baltimore show, *The Buddy Deane Show*, which Waters himself followed as a teenager. Still probably Waters's most widely known picture, *Hairspray* features a young and talented (but overweight) girl named Tracy Turnblad (Ricki Lake), who not only manages to get elected to the coveted Buddy Deane Committee but also gets named to serve as the Auto Show Queen. Waters researched the script by interviewing former Buddy Deaners, hoping to capture the popular essence of the teenage dance craze. Divine returns in form, here performing two roles (as a man and as Tracy's mother), while the inveterate Sonny Bono plays the father of another Committee member named Amber von Tussle. The film's subplot revolves around efforts by Tracy and her friends to participate in the *Corney Collins Show*—and later to help racially integrate the program, which (aside from "All-Negro Night" on Thursdays) has excluded blacks. These efforts wind up largely successful, aided by Corney's tacit approval, in much the same way *American Bandstand* was integrated at roughly the same time. In *Hairspray* as elsewhere, we see on view a parade of the unfashionable: ugly, fat, sick, trashy, and demented. As Waters argues: "My films are about people who take what society thinks is a disadvantage, exaggerating their supposed defect, and turning it into a winning style."[51] Herein lies a certain logic to Waters's incessantly offbeat style of casting.

Waters' fourth theatrically released picture was *Serial Mom* (1994), arguably his best work and surely the first to attain high-level Hollywood production values. The film stars Kathleen Turner as Beverly Sutphin, an outwardly saccharin-sweet, conformist suburban housewife and mother whose alter ego turns out to be a serial killer who delights in making obscene phone calls to prim neighbor ladies like Dottie Hinckle (Mink Stole). Sutphin upholds her rigid ethical precepts around such mundane issues as recycling, wearing seat belts, littering, and video rewinding by resorting to murder: Anyone who even slightly deviates from prescribed norms is deserving of the death penalty, carried out summarily by Sutphin herself. She and her dentist husband (Sam Waterston) live in suburban Baltimore with their children Misty (Ricki Lake) and Chip (Matthew Lillard), and we first see this apparently idyllic family at breakfast when the meal is rudely interrupted by intrusions of a large fly. Angrily grabbing a flyswatter, Beverly quickly provides a deeper insight into her persona when she smashes the fly on the breakfast table. The image of this dead fly—bloody, huge, and grisly—appears just as Waters's directorial credit comes on screen. The Sutphin breakfast is interrupted again by the visit of two police detectives seeking the identity of a person making obscene phone calls and writing threatening letters. The detectives show the Sutphins a note composed of past newspaper headlines that reads, "I'll get you, pussy face!" Beverly protests, saying, "Officers, I've never said the 'p' word out loud, let alone have written it down." One officer responds that "no woman would," while the other observes that "Mrs. Sutphin is about as normal and nice a lady as we're ever going to find." But as soon as the detectives leave, Beverly anonymously telephones her despised neighbor Dottie, asking, "Is this the cocksucker residence?" She even impersonates a

Serial Mom (John Waters, 1994)   *With Ricki Lake, Kathleen Turner, Sam Waterston, and Matthew Lillard, it portrays a seemingly normal suburban housewife's journey into the world of a serial killer, as she (Turner) decides to kill those guilty of minor personal infractions and then is transformed into a media celebrity as her trial unfolds.*

telephone company investigator in order to get the prim and proper Dottie to repeat the word "cocksucker."

Mrs. Sutphin now launches her career as "serial mom" by cold-bloodedly murdering her son's teacher, Mr. Stubbins, who has just given her son a bad report during a parent–teacher meeting, by running over him with her car. She feels so exhilarated after this act of violence that she cannot wait to make passionate love with her husband. This first adventure into murder propels her onto a wanton, brutal crime spree extending to the murder of six people she finds utterly detestable—the boy who spurns her daughter (bludgeoned to death by a fireplace poker in a men's restroom), a couple dining on chicken (she has a fondness for birds), a woman watching the video *Annie* (her skull crushed by a leg of lamb), and even a member of the jury (played by Patty Hearst) that finally tries her, killed with a telephone for her sin of wearing white shoes after Labor Day. All these acts of murder, exquisitely surreal in their depictions, serve as vehicles for articulating Waters's satirical impulses and outlandish tastes. "I feel like shooting four or five people every time I step out of the house," he confides. "Once, on a plane, I was deeply offended by a passenger seated near me who was guilty of the ultimate fashion violation—wearing summer white after Labor Day."[52]

As she becomes transformed with maniacal frenzy into a compulsive serial mom, Sutphin comes under suspicion of the authorities and eventually members of her own family, who are spellbound at the thought of her reported gory murders. Her notoriety spreads throughout Baltimore, instilling fear in some and hero worship in others. Once conclusive evidence is found linking her to the crimes, she is brought to trial amid the tumult of O. J. Simpson–like publicity. The district attorney describes her as a monster, not a woman, and recites the list of her brutal murder weapons: a speeding car, fire poker, pair of scissors, toppled air conditioner, aerosol-can flames, a leg of lamb. Mrs. Sutphin's defense attorney, ready to enter a not-guilty plea, decides his client is insane after she writes him a note complaining about juror number 8 (Hearst) wearing white shoes. Rejecting this move, Sutphin fires her lawyer and ends up serving as her own defense attorney. When Dottie Hinckle takes the stand to explain the obscene phone calls, she quickly wilts under Sutphin's shrewd attacks and breaks down right in the courtroom. Hopelessly obsessed with all the off-color language she has been bombarded with, Hinckle is led away screaming it at Mrs. Sutphin—in the process destroying her credibility as a witness. The next witness for the prosecution, a young pothead who saw the first murder, is too stoned to testify coherently. At this point, actress Suzanne Somers, chosen to play "serial mom" in a documentary of her life, creates a massive diversion simply by showing up at the trial. In the final phase of this offbeat courtroom drama, Sutphin is able to deflect the testimony of a middle-aged sex fiend who witnessed her men's-room killing by repeatedly opening and closing her legs under the table. Overwhelmed by this apparently seductive move, the man recants his previous testimony implicating Sutphin in the murder. With the case for the prosecution effectively destroyed, Sutphin triumphantly walks out of the courtroom a free woman to discover that she has now become a significant media celebrity. For Waters, it seems, the more bizarre the form of celebrity, the more cinematically noteworthy it becomes; spectacle constitutes its own reality.

With *Serial Mom*, virtually every scene revolves around some form of dark humor mixed with satirical portraits of everyday American suburban life: the family, mass media, sexuality, the court system, schools, and law enforcement. As with Tarantino, Waters's obsession is with images of violence (both physical and verbal), murder, and gore, all incorporated within spectacle. In contrast to *Reservoir Dogs* or *Pulp Fiction*, however, where attention is focused on brutal, sadistic violence with a twist of black humor, the more ludic quality of *Serial Mom* brings a sense of humor and playfulness to the forefront, with violence and gore serving more as a backdrop or cinematic device; the gore is not taken seriously. For Waters, all scenes and characters are built around a kind of playful detachment that allows the filmmaker to indulge his irreverent, mocking depiction of all that might be considered "normal" in contemporary American society. Though perhaps covertly, the very concept of "serial mom" gives expression to a wide range of fears, anxieties, and hypocrisies that permeate everyday middle-class existence—even if Waters disavows any effort to bring social messages or "serious" commentary into his special brand of ludic cinema. Thus, while a fascination with violence and mayhem remains central to his cinematic approach, it plays a fundamentally different role for Waters than for Tarantino or De Palma, for example, even if many of the same elements of Hobbesian chaos enter into their filmmaking. There is a subliminal, postmodern theme present in both—that the orderly, stable, conformist world of everyday life barely conceals deep manifestations of anger, conflict, and violence lurking just beneath its mundane, sanitized surface. As for *Serial Mom*, it would unquestionably be considered a horror film if not for the blatantly comic tone established throughout; as things stand, it emerges as more of a horror spoof in keeping with the ludic tradition. Viewed from another angle, the film can be seen as a highly cynical depiction of the way in which American mass media is so riveted on gory crime—a more cynical and satirical treatment than we find, for instance, in *Natural Born Killers*.

Waters's 1998 film *Pecker* stars the relatively unknown Edward Furlong in the title role of a young Baltimore photographer who rises from cook in a tiny sub-style restaurant to elevated status in the art world—another play on bizarre celebrity. Pecker lives with his "culturally challenged family," as one art critic describes it, including his dad, who owns a neighborhood bar named The Claw; his mom, proprietor of a thrift shop; his ventriloquist grandmother, known as Mi Mama; and his hyperactive younger sister, Crissy, with her insatiable hunger for candy. Pecker spends virtually every free moment of his life snapping photos of people and animals in the act of doing almost anything, from injecting themselves with heroin to nude dancing. He even shoots a photo of two rats having sex in a garbage can. Armed with a cheap but always handy camera, Pecker combs his Baltimore environs for photo opportunities in the streets, alleys, thrift shops, bars, and strip clubs, often "looking for art where nothing is there" (in the words of his sassy girlfriend, played by Christina Ricci). One club, the Pelt Room, features lesbian strippers who verbally abuse their straight middle-aged patrons; another is a gay club parading Chippendale-type strippers. The Pelt Room sequence in

Pecker was derived from Waters's memories of an exotic dancer named Zorro, a "very butch local girl" resembling Johnny Cash. According to Waters, Zorro would "stomp around the stage naked after removing her cape and mask, sneer at the audience, and then snarl, 'What are ya lookin' at?'" As always, Waters casts a fascinating assortment of local offbeat characters who make their way around and through various Baltimore landmarks and haunts. As in most of his other films, he treats each locale, each situation, and each character with nothing but comic irreverence.

Following *Serial Mom*, the equally ludic *Pecker* depicts the mass media as a shallow, disgusting wasteland, while the culture of "high art" comes across as snobbish, narrow, small-minded, and ultimately plain boring. Pecker's photos, with their campy technical defects and amateurish mountings, soon catch the eye of a visiting art dealer (Lily Taylor), who decides to help Pecker's career in New York art galleries. Of course, Pecker's art is so unusual and outrageous that it does indeed catch on within the art community: The Whitney Museum of Modern Art decides to celebrate it with a special exhibit. But Pecker firmly rejects the seductions of the commercial art world, opting instead to remain true to his folksy Baltimore roots—a decision that stuns all the art critics and aficionados. He appears on the cover of *Artform* magazine as the photographer who had the chutzpah to snub the venerable Whitney. At this juncture, Pecker's celebrity status has little to do with his ability (or desire) to win acceptance of the established galleries and museums; his rank indifference toward *haute culture* becomes itself an incredible source of fame and celebrity. The New York art dealer epitomizes the pretentious, cold, shrewd urban intellectual so often brutally satirized in Waters's films. (As Waters observes in his commentary on *Pecker*, "In the art world nobody gets laid. They're too cold to have sex.") In the end, Pecker's return to Baltimore parallels Waters's own history of returning to his native city after a series of frustrating ventures into the Hollywood film scene.

Cecil B. Demented (2000) represents one of Waters's most irreverent attacks on contemporary entertainment culture. Here he takes aim at Hollywood itself, a favorite target of postmodern cinema. Choosing his familiar Baltimore setting, Waters focuses on an insurgent guerrilla film company headed by Cecil B. Demented (Stephen Dorff), a self-styled director/prophet who leads a cast and crew of film lovers who just want their chance to break into the film business—but on their own terms. Demented rails against Hollywood and the infamous "studio system," at one point chanting "death to those who support mainstream cinema" and "power to the people and punish bad cinema." At one point, he announces, "I'm Cecil B.

Demented, the enemy of family films." Demented kidnaps a visiting movie star named Honey Whitlock (Melanie Griffith) after she arrives in Baltimore to help raise funds to assist paraplegic children. Whitlock has just completed a sappy tearjerker, titled *Some Kind of Happiness*, that was enjoying a popular run in the mall theaters. But Demented is against mall theaters and mall movies, just as he is against narcissistic stars like Whitlock.

At first, Whitlock struggles against her captors but then learns to cooperate after they start shooting their guerrilla movie, casting her as star. Under Demented's tutelage, Whitlock begins to assume the role of agitprop performer, especially after she leaps onto a deck from a height of two stories to confront a group of filmmakers attending an event promoting Baltimore as the "Hollywood of the East." Whitlock's metamorphosis from a cynical, narcissistic, over-the-hill actress to a vibrant, larger-than-life revolutionary is remarkably similar to Patty Hearst's odyssey during her captivity by the Symbionese Liberation Army—a similarity all the more striking because of Hearst's presence here in a bit part as Demented's mother.

During their encounter with filmmakers attending the Baltimore event, Demented's lieutenants confront two men and accuse them of selling out their artistic standards. One demands, "Didn't you produce that bad Hollywood remake of that beautiful foreign-language film?" Explains the guest, "I had to, you know American audiences won't watch subtitles." Waters uses this phony convention to highlight his biting criticisms of not only Hollywood studios but also the entire film business. He turns up the volume after Demented's cast and crew burst into a mall theater showing of *Some Kind of Happiness*. There they confront the audience, which had been crying profusely at the maudlin movie, demanding they stop patronizing such mediocre productions. Next they invade a screening of one of Whitlock's sexier scenes, during which virtually the entire audience is seen masturbating, when Demented complains, "Your Hollywood studio system stole our sex and coopted our violence."

What does Demented (and, of course, Waters) want to do with the studio system? The studios need to be replaced by vibrant, irreverent ones striving toward some form of realism. "The first take is the only real truth," lectures Demented. "Technique too is nothing more than failed style." What is needed, apparently, is a regime not unlike the recent "Dogma" movement (discussed in chapter 6) that prizes spontaneity over rehearsal or staged performances and handheld digital cameras over elaborate studio equipment. Waters's comic vision is to remake Hollywood studios into mirror images of his own regional film company, and he wants them to avoid overly maudlin or sexually exploitative material. In other words, he seems to be advocating that all filmmakers turn themselves into a replica of John Waters. The farcical character of this picture fits squarely within the ludic tradition.

If Pecker turns out to be probably Waters's most likable character—one of the few, in fact, with whom most viewers can readily identify—Cecil B. Demented's overblown persona seems to merit nothing but disgust. Beverly Sutphin is surely the most (subversively) noteworthy of his major characters, mainly because of Kathleen Turner's outstanding performance and Waters's own writing and directing. Both Francine in *Polyester* and Tracy in *Hairspray* convey the kind of playful, dismissive, offbeat features that define the bulk of Waters's films. Not only do his pictures cast very quixotic and entertaining "heroes," but they savage a good many cherished American beliefs and traditions, not least of all "family values." Waters depicts the family as toxic (*Polyester*), sick (*Hairspray*), psychotic (*Serial Mom*), and simply dysfunctional (*Pecker*). As for the mass media, it gets satirically attacked as sex theater (*Polyester*), television fantasy (*Hairspray* and *Cry-Baby*), out-of-control journalism (*Serial Mom*), silly high-brow ruminations (*Pecker*), and mall-theater cinematic kitsch (*Cecil B. Demented*). These films valorize outsiders and misfits: the obese, gay, elderly, homeless, ghetto dwellers, sluts, mad psychologists, drunks, addicts, strip-club habitués, and even murderers. All of this has merely ensured Waters's status as one of the more iconoclastic of contemporary filmmakers.

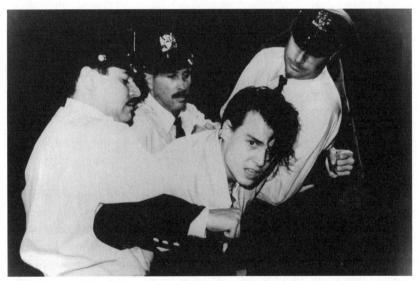

Cry-Baby **(John Waters, 1990)**   *Johnny Depp is arrested and jailed in this postmodern farce that satirizes "serious" cinema and popular culture by mocking the teenage-exploitation genre.*

What we have in Waters's films is essentially a cinema of the absurd that shares a cultural lineage with dadaism and surrealism, the Marx Brothers, the art of Salvador Dali, the theater of Antonin Arteau, and the aesthetics of Andy Warhol. This is precisely why William Burroughs could refer to Waters as the "Pope of Trash." During thirty years of filmmaking, Waters has dismissed works that are overly pretentious or serious, stating among other things that film school and learning "sophisticated" cinematic techniques are a waste of time. He prefers the horror movies of William Castle to the great Hollywood "masterpieces," which he views (with some justification) as mostly insufferably boring. One "serious" picture he finds valuable is Woody Allen's *Interiors*, predictably because it does so much to subvert the "normalcy" of family life: uncontrollable personal anguish, sibling rivalry, emotional breakdowns, divorce, suicide attempts, and so forth.

The ludic postmodern features of the Waters legacy are intertwined with moments of nostalgia, fantasy, melancholia, irreverence, and the eros–violence nexus. In many of his films—*Hairspray* being a good example—nostalgic references to the past (such as early rock and roll) seem calculated to keep that very past alive.[53] As Waters fully recognizes, the hyperreal element of media culture reappropriates and absorbs personal and social identities at the very same time it reproduces feelings of anxiety, self-doubt, and insecurity, and here his cinematic sensibilities parallel those of Allen (notably in *Zelig, Stardust Memories*, and *The Purple Rose of Cairo*). As in the case of Allen, moreover, Waters employs an ample stream of wit, fantasy, and illusory images that function as a mechanism of coping in a chaotic, often meaningless, predictably hostile world. In contrast to the modernist techniques of Bertolt Brecht, whose theater relied on comic satire for didactic ends, Waters disavows any such Enlightenment schema for his movies; there are no "messages" to be conveyed. Film is above all about entertainment, which, if done with sufficient creative flourish, can have a profound shock effect on the viewer. As Waters writes in his book *Shock Value*, "I hate message movies and pride myself on the fact that my work has no socially redeeming value. I like to think I make American comedies."[54]

Waters's peculiar cinema of the absurd shares much in common with the ludic surrealism of Dali's art. Much like Waters, Dali invoked an assemblage of wild images connected to his "paranoiac-critical method" to instill a sense of "visionary irritation" in the viewer.[55] In contrast to the more "serious," political surrealists like André Breton, Dali adopted a frivolous attitude toward society, often going out of his way to define his work as "apolitical." At the same time, his art would be subversive insofar as it challenged repressive constraints, rules, and formulas that usually governed modernist aesthetics.

There was a certain "purposelessness" to Dali's work that served to mock or negate ordinary discrete objects identifiable within the real world; the eye of the painter (or camera) distorts as much as it reveals. Interestingly, Dali was strongly attracted to the film world, having worked with Luis Buñuel on the surrealistic *Un Chien Andalou* (1930) and with Alfred Hitchcock on the equally surrealistic *Spellbound* (1944). He strongly preferred comedic movies displaying elements of mayhem, spontaneity, and irreverence—one reason he visited Hollywood during the 1930s to meet the Marx Brothers. (Dali drew Harpo Marx's portrait in 1937.) He worked with the Marx Brothers on a scenario for a picture titled *Giraffe on Horseback Salad*, although this bore little fruit. Until the end of his life, Dali saw an immense surrealist potential in what he called Hollywood's "hallucinatory cinema"—a cinema where boundaries separating the real from fantasy, normal from insane, and object from subject would be obliterated, much as it had in his paintings.[56] And much as in the later films of Waters, Dali had little but contempt for camera movements (or brush strokes) that were neatly focused, plodding, stable, and predictable— that were tied to relatively fixed objects or forms. The very idea of coherent plots and narratives in a world lacking stable, fixed identities seemed on its face rather preposterous. Waters's ludic cinema of the absurd thus carries forward much of the aesthetic formlessness and subversiveness, the profound feelings of cynicism and nihilism, and the comedic sense of irreverence that permeated the surrealist tradition, which turns out to be one of the great precursors to contemporary postmodern culture.

5

THE POSTMODERN VISUAL STYLE

The production of Hollywood films today is much less the work of a single creative auteur than it was at the height of the studio era, and roughly the same can be said about the role of stars and the star system. Cinema has become an increasingly technical, intricate, collaborative enterprise relying on the contributions of many: actors, directors, producers, cinematographers, writers, technical and sound people, set designers, and, perhaps most significantly, editors. One might even include marketers, advertisers, and critics in this process. Within what is now a labyrinthine series of activities, the role of film editors assumes ever more important functions, as they assume responsibility for assembling a finished product, the final cut, out of a vast array and disarray of film footage, technical effects, and sound materials. More than any other creative force, editors usually seek to achieve a grand synthesis of aesthetic and psychological/social effects that ultimately defines the completed motion picture. Editors labor meticulously over a grueling period of many weeks or months, their task one of integrating disparate shots, dialogue, lighting, music, computer imaging, and color visuals into what will ostensibly become a flowing, seamless totality of cinematic frames. A totalizing element of the ever broadening art and technique of filmmaking, editing achieved its classic definition in the early work of Edwin S. Porter, D. W. Griffith, Sergei Eisenstein, and others working in both the United States and Europe, emerging as what ultimately became known as the "syntax of cinema."[1]

The constituent elements of filmmaking depend in many ways on the multifaceted, sometimes convoluted art of editing—an art familiar to directors, producers, cinematographers, and even writers and actors, who may, on occasion, choose to exercise various creative editorial inputs. With dramatic recent improvements in film technology, the editing process has become more technical and demanding, more decisive than ever to what is eventually shown on screen. The electronic methods pioneered by such directors as George Lucas, Francis Coppola, Oliver Stone, and James Cameron have indeed revolutionized both the theory and the practice of filmmaking and with it, of course, the very character of the final product. The new digital technology, for example, makes it easier to traverse and comprehend hundreds of thousands of feet of film, allowing for at least a theoretically more rational and continuous integration of widely disparate components entering into the cinematic project. Editing is far more than a technical vocation, involving endless rounds of screenings of rough footage, intense discussions about that footage, ongoing negotiations, additional reviews, complex note taking, and multiple cuts designed to render the finished picture stylistically and emotionally coherent. To the degree that editors may be said to have the last word on film production, they are obligated to establish what Walter Murch calls "motion within a context."[2] From this standpoint, editing involves the painstaking construction of both time and space, made possible by continuous arranging and rearranging of shots within a larger conceptual framework. David Mamet writes that "our choice of shots is all you have. It's what the movie is going to be made up of."[3] In the purest, most absolute sense, this is still true, although in the contemporary period, when the postmodern ethos has become so widely accepted, the actual sequencing of "shots" amounts to just *one* specific dimension of the complex editing process, which, of course, varies enormously from one project to another, one style to another, one director and/or editor to another, one narrative structure to another, and even one time period to another.

FROM MODERN TO POSTMODERN

Like other aesthetic modes, film editing is just as subjective as the nearly infinite variety of preferences, techniques, styles, and outlooks associated with cinematic work in general. The "motion within a context" can assume multiple definitions and articulations, reflected in the various filmmaking styles that span the many decades of Hollywood filmmaking. Within the classical or "modern" paradigm of cinema, we know that editing usually followed certain well-established modalities: a linear sequencing of cuts and images, a coherent narrative structure with a strong protagonist, a finite understanding of time and space, and a trajectory grounded in particular cause-and-effect patterns. Such modalities shaped the editing process across diverse genres, including musicals, comedies, dramas, Westerns, combat movies, and (in more attenuated form) the noir detective thrillers. Against this paradigm there emerged an identifiable "postmodern" sensibility in which editing, expressed through the medium of thousands of "editorial" decisions, came to take on vital, even all-encompassing dimensions. In contrast to filmic modernism, postmodern cinema relies on a more mediated juxtaposition of cuts and images that counter the familiar emphasis on such elements as linearity, coherence, formula, and strict cause-and-effect relations. As with the surrealist tradition, this style functions more to obscure than to illuminate reality, its symbolic representations frequently more illusory than revelatory. As Murch puts it, "Although 'day-to-day' reality appears to be continuous, there is that other world in which we spend perhaps a third of our lives: the 'night-to-night' reality of dreams. And the images in dreams are much more fragmented, intersecting in much stranger and more abrupt ways than the images of waking reality—ways that approximate, at least, the interaction produced by [film] cutting."[4] From the earlier films of Welles, Hitchcock, and Lang to the later work of Altman, the Coen brothers, Tarantino, and Stone, this intersection between the postmodern filmmaking style and transformations in the art and technique of film editing is evident even if not always immediately apparent.

The growth of media culture lies in many ways at the heart of the film-editing enterprise. With the very beginnings of Hollywood, it was already possible to see how the development of photography and motion pictures hinted strongly at the force of spectacle, calling attention to the power of image reinforced by rapid movement of visual transmissions and the tremendous pull of commodity production in the media, popular culture, and the capitalist economy. From the outset, photography depicted a rather static world frozen over moments in time, captured on paper or a glass plate; it invited studious observation, worked in such a way as to slow the viewer's responses, while inviting a good deal of contemplation and self-reflection. Motion pictures, at the other end of the spectrum, expressed above all dynamic movement and depicted personal or social interactions in the midst of complex societal forces tied to a series of fleeting images less easy to grasp than the standard photographic or artistic representations. Film consists of literally thousands of photographic images speeding past the human vision so quickly that the eyes readily perceive *movement* and dynamism where, in fact, still pictures remain at the forefront. The "persistence of memory" that Salvador Dali, among others, represented on canvas is one vital feature endowing motion pictures with this peculiar illusion of movement, but this "illusion" requires a process of mediated structuring. The perpetual arrangement and rearrangement of individual shots and frames in motion pictures have come to be known simply as "editing," but the process is infinitely more complex than the carrying out of any single task.

To understand the increasingly prominent role of such editing, we need to understand two basic elements that create and sustain meaning in film: the shot and the montage. A film shot is simply the amount of film exposed while the camera is turned on—an interval ranging from a single frame to exposure of the entire stock in a film canister (up to ten minutes). When the camera is operating for an instant, the result is a "short take," whereas if the shooting continues for a minute or longer, we have what is called a "long take." A montage is nothing more than two or more shots spliced together to form a scene.

To analyze shots and montages, we begin with the conventional Hollywood process of "invisible" or "decoupage" editing. "Modernist" editing stresses the seamless "invisibility" of shots, focusing the camera on a particular actor or actors depicted as carrying out some kind of perilous or obstacle-laden activity. This modality has prevailed, in one form or another, since the earliest days of motion pictures, often harking back to ancient myths, and was further refined or standardized during the Hollywood studio era beginning in the 1920s. Its popularity waned little throughout the postwar years, even as the studio empires began to lose their creative power, but it was eventually modified at the hands of modern (and postmodern) directors and editors, inspired partly by the aim of removing cameras from the direct awareness of viewers. Such invisible editing tends to call attention to more dramatic, emotionally laden images while excluding the more ritual and mundane ones. Consider a scene in which a person enters a house and goes into a bedroom: The director might choose to open the scene with a shot of the person unlocking the front door, but instead of then showing the actor walking through the rest of the house, through the living room, and down the hallway, the director might simply depict the person walking into the bedroom. Here the boring, trivial shots have been left out, and once audiences become accustomed to such an editing style, they will probably notice neither the camera work nor the editing techniques. The audience simply follows the character and watches his or her actions without being made conscious of camera intervention.

During the studio era, such modernist editing, developed and refined by dozens of filmmakers and editors, reached the status of a veritable high-art form. Consider, for instance, the scene in Michael Curtiz's *Casablanca* (1942), where the legendary Rick's Café Americaine is first introduced to the audience. (Rick's winds up as the setting for so many crucial scenes in this movie that Curtiz and others originally thought of calling the film "Everybody Comes to Rick's.") The audience observes the café early in the movie when a shot of the exterior is taken from across the street, followed by a shot of a neon sign hanging just above the door, at which point a patron enters through the door. In the next shot, the camera slowly pans across the spacious café (actually nightclub) until it settles on Sam the piano player. None of the characters looks at the camera, generating the illusion of people observing without being observed. Here the film gracefully moves from depicting Casablanca the city to watching nonstop action inside Rick's, usually without revealing any dramatic cinematic shift. This is quintessential modernist editing, replete with linear development and coherent imagery.

Modernist editing follows routine procedures for both outdoor and indoor scenes, with the director usually starting from the perspective of an overall "establishing shot" enveloping the main characters even while a sense of distance is maintained. The next shot might encompass a full view of one or more characters followed by a close-up or series of close-ups. In Stanley Kubrick's 1968 classic *2001: A Space Odyssey*, for example, the opening credits flash on a shot of the moon precisely at the moment when the Earth and the sun come into full view. This constitutes a symbolic "establishing shot" or "master shot" insofar as it locates the film in space, but the real establishing shot comes in the first scene, titled "The Dawn of Man," depicting the powerful effects of sunrise flooding over a vast plain. The camera moves closer and closer to a large mound of rocks. Once the rocks are brought within closer view, Kubrick inserts the close-up of a primitive-looking skull with two tusks protruding, then follows with a close-up of two apes (the focus of the scene) in close-up. At this point, the viewer is emotionally drawn into a large, active, unpredictable milieu of strange creatures.

By responding to strategic moves of the camera, viewers are meant to be pulled into a world of cinematic magic—an essentially modernist world where so much is "invisible," removed from the sphere of conscious individual reaction. Where such editing works efficiently, few viewers will pause to consider exactly how a movie is composed of a series of images strung together and coherently assembled before their very eyes. Are we flying over the earthly landscape in an aircraft? Did we just land? Did we enter into an entirely new zone of existence? For the most part, of course, viewers rarely stop to reflect on what the cameras might be doing at specific locations or angles—that is, how the "motion within a context" is set up, how it encompasses a particular flow of images, how it is positioned relative to actors and setting, and how cuts are arranged and rearranged into some kind of seamless whole. Most viewers simply react more or less *automatically*, largely oblivious to the full range of vital but generally obscure technical factors associated with camera work, montage, and editing. The audience usually imagines that it has been magically placed within the scene as constructed on screen, as if it might be participating as hidden observer. Working through the realm of magical illusions, filmmakers can inculcate in viewers a certain "willing suspension of disbelief" where the audience is seduced into the notion it is observing a definite representation of reality, although such "reality" frequently winds up almost devoid of the tedious, mundane details of everyday life. Rarely do filmmakers employing this style invite audiences to observe characters in the *routine* activities of everyday life, such as sleeping, eating (except in brief shots), using the bathroom, walking, and driving to and from specific destinations. The creative anticipation here is that the audience will come to view the cinematic universe as something far more exciting, dangerous, and romantic than what it experiences in real life, and, of course, this phenomenon is clearly one of the more fascinating aspects of Hollywood film culture.

Hollywood directors have come to dwell on some variant of the invisible, modernist style of film editing, and this is precisely what the American film-going public has predictably come to expect; the presence of cameras, along with the rhythm of cutting sequences, is never supposed to intrude on or disrupt the consciousness of viewers. The main design of such editing is to force the audience to suspend awareness that it is in fact watching a movie, thereby allowing it to "participate" in the cinematic experience through identification with specific protagonists, narratives, symbols, and motifs. The last thing modernist directors want is for viewers to notice editing techniques, to respond thoughtfully and critically to the dizzying assortment of shots and montages. This is precisely why the invisible style perfected during the studio era remains the dominant "code" within the industry, even as the modality has come under challenge by a postmodern generation of directors whose writing, framing, and editing techniques are more flamboyant and self-conscious and therefore more readily "visible" to the movie observer.

The familiar cinematic mise-en-scène is perhaps best understood as the complex arrangement of foreground, background, set, props, and movement to establish the illusion of reality. While referring pointedly to "that which is on the stage," the more direct meaning of mise-en-scène is closer to "that which is shown on camera" as opposed to what is constructed from two or more camera shots. The mise-en-scène naturally calls attention to a vital component of filmmaking: the settings and background for multiple contrasting, supporting, and crosscutting shots. The aesthetic concept is to make the movie set and its myriad accoutrements appear visually compelling—and to some degree every film exhibits this quality. Of course, the mise-en-scène can incorporate virtually any physical totality: a Martian colony; the nineteenth-century town of Tombstone, Arizona; Peking during the Ming dynasty; a mental institution; bleak alleys; or literally any time/space dimension, real or imagined.

Those directors most inclined toward aesthetic realism—toward some approximation of cinema verité—rely heavily on this view of mise-en-scène to advance their narratives and social themes. The work of Alfred Hitchcock, John Ford, Orson Welles, Frank Capra, John Huston, Martin Ritt, Lucchino Visconti, and Jean Renoir generally fits this "modernist" style, even where generous use of formalistic or illusionary devices may be visible. These filmmakers are driven to capture "reality" as graphically as possible, devoting much of their resources to the detailed planning of virtually every scene, a process that in turn requires a sophisticated and time-consuming *editing* process. One aim here is to re-create the look and feel of a particular social or historical setting. Thus, in *The Grand Illusion* (1937), Renoir built a steel track for cameras to roll across an extensive set in which, for example, French war prisoners in Germany stage a mock Parisian variety show. As cameras roll across silent tracks, prisoners suddenly receive word of a French military victory, at which point they break out in wild cheers. German officers in the play find the cheers offensive; many of them abruptly leave the performance. The entire scene was shot realistically not in a montage of several shots, as would have been the method of most directors, but rather through one long take assisted by noiseless steel tracks. Such "tracking shots" would later become commonplace in Hollywood film production.

Cameras need not be mounted on steel tracks to permit such elongated takes. Hitchcock, among others, employed a variety of techniques to set up the mise-en-scène, as in his 1937 classic *Young and Innocent*, where he uses a huge boom and places the camera high above a ballroom. As the camera scans the crowd of dancers, it weaves its way closer and closer to a murderer who turns out to be a man with a pronounced twitch in his eye. He is a drummer in a swing band that just happens to be playing a tune called "The Drummer Man." The camera weaves in and out of the audience, following two characters as they dance around the room; it searches for a twitching man, finally resting on a man in blackface playing the drums and zeroing in for a close-up of his eyes with their unmistakable twitch. In Hitchcock's later films, including *Psycho*, we find bleak social spaces where protagonists confront demented serial murderers, ruthless schemers, and bumbling cops, where fearsome killers can suddenly appear from nowhere. Here the villains seem all the more menacing since they appear on the surface to be normal and harmless, perhaps even gentle and charming—as in the case of serial murderer Uncle Charlie (Joseph Cotten) in *Shadow of a Doubt*. At the same time, films like *Psycho* and *Frenzy* are composed of montages with great emotional intensity and technical brilliance, allowing the act of murder to be played out in all its grisly psychological detail. In these films, the editing cuts are crisp, rapid, and powerful, enhanced by Bernard Herrmann's jazzy, atonal scores. The point here is that emotionally powerful editing techniques, developed well before the computer age, help push these films already beyond modernism, providing a glimpse of the later "postmodern" style.

Orson Welles's *Touch of Evil* similarly anticipates the postmodern shift in at least one important respect: The film begins with a continuous take now legendary for its intensity and length, set in a Mexico/U.S. border town at night, where dark light and portentous music create a mood suggesting (quite rightly) that mayhem is just about to hit the screen. The opening image shows a shadowy figure planting a bomb in a car, at which juncture the camera pans along the sleazy border environment followed by a depiction of an older man driving a Cadillac, accompanied by a young woman. As the camera rolls, the woman is heard complaining that she hears a "ticking noise"; passing through the border checkpoint, the car blows up, and the camera turns to the burning, overturned car. The impact of this scene is startling, and Welles builds on the tension that persists throughout the picture. Arranged around a carefully framed mise-en-scène, the long take establishes one of the most dramatic opening scenes in cinematic history. It is hardly surprising, therefore, that *Touch of Evil* is today widely regarded as one of the finest examples of traditional film noir—indeed, it might be considered the last of "classic" noir films that go back to the early 1940s. Many film noirs begin with long takes, while the noir style revolves around a variety of night shots, tough urban settings, and various low-life activities, often borrowing montage devices from Hitchcock, Welles, and European directors like Lang and Eisenstein.

A more recent film that employs a long take to set up its guiding mise-en-scène is Robert Altman's *The Player*, which introduces this device to present humorous, self-reflecting commentary on the state of Hollywood film culture. Opening frames center around a Hollywood studio lot, with the cinematography taking the viewer mainly *inside* the studio, where it probes the details of people's workaday lives. A woman answers the phone and informs the caller that Joe Lasen has not yet arrived. She inquires, "May I take a message?" Another woman walks over briskly and informs the first one never to say that the boss is not in: "Say either in a conference or in a meeting. He's always here." The camera slowly pans across the lot and focuses on the arrival of someone in a four-wheeler, who turns out to be hotshot studio executive Griffin Mill (Tim Robbins). As Mill, the main protagonist, enters the studio, two other men walk out of the building and head toward the camera, which is still running. One man tells the other, "The pictures they make nowadays are all MTV. Cut, Cut. Cut. The opening shot of Welles's *Touch of Evil* was six and a half minutes long." "Six and a half minutes long!" exclaims the other man, who is pushing a bicycle along the cement walkway. "Well, three or four anyway. Why, he set up the whole picture with that one tracking shot." As the camera follows the two men along their minijourney, we begin to suspect that Altman is trying to surpass the great Welles in the elegance and duration of his own tracking shot. The camera moves along unceasingly and effortlessly to record the unfolding scenes, running all the while. Leaving the two men, it zooms into a window through which we can hear another conversation taking place and so on. By the time the shot ends (some eight minutes later), the audience has been introduced to the hero as well as the villain—not to mention several crosscutting elements of the plot.

Welles's film relied extensively on the long take to generate interest in overheated, nonstop action, while Altman introduces the same technique, only to arrive at completely different end results. In Altman's protracted scene, we see characters actually discussing *other* long takes, even speculating on their duration; surely the director wants them to realize that here too is yet another "long take" fashioned in the image of the great Welles. The audience is supposed to take notice that the film as an impressive work of art, the result of a series of lengthy, intricate shots. In *The Player*, viewers are manipulated into paying attention to the many contrived shots and the extraordinarily creative editing, whereas in *Touch of Evil*, the process is more seamless, limited to what is happening within the particular shot. From this standpoint, *The Player* can be appreciated as a quintessentially "postmodern" film crafted by a director committed to distinctive motifs—discontinuity, fragmentation, nonlinear narrative, sense of nostalgia, long takes, and dystopic images—many of which can be traced back at least to *Nashville* (1975) and perhaps even *McCabe and Mrs. Miller* (1971). A defining feature of postmodern cinema, clearly visible in films like *The Player*, is a profound self-consciousness on the part of the filmmaker; such pictures call attention to themselves as a matter of aesthetic flourishes or, as critics might argue, narcissistic self-indulgence. Audiences are encouraged to take notice—and to respond. Open-ended photographic and editing techniques, combined with a pronounced narrative or thematic cynicism, distinguish projects of this sort from classic Hollywood works of the studio era. Directors working within the postmodern visual style usually strive to seduce audiences by means of such formal aesthetic innovations rather than appeals to (realistic) drama of actual historical events.

As we have seen, postmodern culture blurs the dividing lines between fact and fiction, reality and illusion, and present and past—what is often connected to a nostalgic sensibility that enters into a good deal of filmmaking today. Abundant tributes to films of the 1930s, 1940s, and 1950s can stimulate imaginative editing techniques that the new forms help facilitate. Computer technology represents a driving force in the evolution of postmodern cinema; the simultaneous appearance of new technology and postmodernism in the 1970s was hardly coincidental. Computerized editing systems empower those involved with filmmaking to set up more intricate constructions of particular shots, a development integral to the postmodern style, although such technology may not be absolutely necessary to the desired outcome. We know that Altman's *The Player* contains many allusions to classic films along with cameo appearances by directors like Scorsese and Pollack; indeed, the film's plot in great measure hinges on actual footage of Vittorio Di Sica's seminal 1948 film *The Bicycle Thief*. The picture itself, moreover, revolves around a Hollywood movie studio, giving added dimension to its nostalgic motifs. Like disjointed narratives and strangely juxtaposed shots, nostalgia has become vital to the filmmaking of postmodern auteurs such as Allen, Tarantino, Stone, Lynch, Gilliam, Burton, and the Coen brothers, among others.[5]

This may not be the case, however, where directors rely heavily on filmed dialogue that moves along a relatively strict chronological progression with one scripted passage immediately following another. Thus, intercutting action scenes and script tends to produce a delicate balance between action and dialogue at the expense of cinematography and editing. A director preoccupied with action can make adventure, drama, and romance films more appealing to mass audiences that, in the present cultural milieu, prefer fast-paced images vital to the "entertainment" modality. Conversely, those fixated on dialogue run the risk of losing viewers, for they are more apt to violate the famous injunction of Billy Wilder, who once said that his philosophy of filmmaking was simply "never to bore." As Hitchcock noted in 1983, "In many of the films now being made, there is very little cinema; they are mostly what I call 'photographs of people talking'. When we tell a story in cinema, we should resort to dialogue only when it's impossible to do otherwise."[6] In his book *On Directing Film*, David Mamet goes even further: "If you find that a point cannot be made without narration, it is virtually certain that the point is unimportant to the story (which is to say, to the audience): the audience requires not information but *drama*. . . . Most movie scripts were written for an audience of studio executives. Studio executives do not know how to read movie scripts. Not one of them. Not one of them knows how to read a movie script. A movie script should be a juxtaposition of uninflected shots that tell the story."[7]

THE "MONTAGE OF MOVEMENT"

As Mamet aptly suggests, drama as movement and action is the crucial ingredient of good filmmaking. Editing functions to create a precarious balance between dialogue and action that for most cinema becomes the sine qua non of an emotionally charged drama. There are moments, however, where action alone may consume both filmmaker and audience. It is here that masters in the tradition of Lang, Hitchcock, Kurosawa, and Eisenstein have perfected the system of "parallel editing," a method that departs from the invisible editing of classic Hollywood insofar as it breaks with the illusion that one is quietly and unobtrusively observing long patterns of unfolding action. As the action shifts from one narrative line to another or even to a third line, calling attention to itself through its rhythmical motion, the audience has difficulty still believing it is observing ordinary reality since how can the viewer possibly be in two places at once? If the technique is carried out skillfully enough, viewers will be attracted to the flow of tension and energy built on the constant interplay of action and dialogue. Such parallel editing has its origins in the classic era, as revealed in films like Hitchcock's *Strangers on a Train*, where the technique is raised to new heights of dramatic intensity. The master of suspense cuts back and forth from a tennis match in which the hero is desperately competing against a murderer on his way to planting fake evidence that would convict the hero Guy (Farley Granger) of killing his wife. Hitchcock matches both lines of action perfectly, honing it down to the seemingly most trivial details. At one point, Bruno the villain (Robert Walker) accidentally drops fake evidence (a cigarette lighter) bearing Guy's initials into a manhole, but as the lighter rests on a trash-strewn ledge at the bottom of a storm drain, Bruno is shown straining every muscle in his body to reach the lighter. As Bruno reaches the planted evidence, Guy strains just as hard to win the tennis match so he can beat the villain to the murder scene and prevent him from planting the lighter. As Bruno finally reaches the lighter, Guy finally wins the tennis match.

Parallel editing was initially perfected by D. W. Griffith. By cutting back and forth between two or more action lines, directors can keep viewer interest at remarkably high levels: Just as tension created from seeing one action line grips the audience, experienced directors shift to another action line, thus relieving the pressure momentarily and giving the audience a certain respite. As noted previously, sequences of shots edited together and woven into one larger thematic unit constitute a "montage." The famous Odessa Steps scene in Eisenstein's *Battleship Potemkin* (1925) is considered one of the finest examples of montage in film history, exhibiting a series of complex, interwoven narrative lines. The Odessa Steps chronicles an event that took place in the midst of the 1905 Russian Revolution, when, as the title card indicates, "the city [of Odessa] lived one life with the rebellious battleship." In reality, no such events ever took place in Odessa; Eisenstein was simply inspired by the massive stone stairway leading to the harbor, so he decided to contrive the reality of a bloody massacre, no doubt inspired by what actually occurred in St. Petersburg. He has the citizens of Odessa reaching out to sailors on the battleship by means of launching a flotilla of small boats loaded with food and drink. To shoot this scene, Eisenstein employed several cameras placed at strategic locations to provide shots from multiple angles. He also strapped a handheld camera on the back of a circus acrobat whose job it was to run through the crowd, providing a cinematic sense of the crowd's energy. The end result of diverse cameras shooting the same scene must have initially been sheer chaos in the editing room, but the great Soviet director managed to splice the wild assemblage of individual shots into a coherent montage, allowing the bloody massacre to be filmed (and viewed) in an emotionally powerful fashion.

Film montage simply involves merging two or more shots together into a single, coherent scene, with the shots amounting to far more than a sum of the parts. Eisenstein recognized in the early 1920s that by joining shot A with shot B, the result was something more than simply A + B = A & B. He knew that the complex process of joining two shots could potentially give rise to entirely new levels of perception and meaning. Eisenstein's creative editing techniques made possible a series of dazzling scenes filled with visual inventiveness, achieved with minimal dialogue. His capacity to establish thematic linkages between shots was probably unmatched—a methodology that would later influence such directors as Charlie Chaplin and Jean Renoir. In his classic *Modern Times* (1935), Chaplin opens with a panoramic view of a flock of sheep hurrying somewhere. He follows this with shots juxtaposing a crowded sidewalk showing a group of human beings simply rushing around. Placed side by side in the film, the two shots take on qualitatively new meaning: By means of innovative editing, Chaplin demonstrates visually how persons isolated in a large crowd turn out to be much like aimless sheep milling around.

"Montage of movement" is the term applied to scenes created by joining together two or more shots depicting similar motion, a good example of which can be found in the 1948 British film *Saraband* (Basil Dearden). At a masked ball scene infused with chaos and confusion, the queen of England arrives to meet her secret lover, at which point we see a montage of masked faces but with no one emerging from the crowd. As the queen (Joan Greenwood) frantically intensifies her search, the edited cuts come faster and faster, coordinated in time with both the music and the dancing. The cutting is done exactly along lines of movement—in this case, that of dancers interacting at a costume ball.

Montages can be used as a device to either compress or expand time. For a classic example of time compression, consider the famous "breakfast montage" in *Citizen Kane*, depicting the gradual disintegration of Charles Foster Kane's marriage to Emily Monroe Norton, niece of the U.S. president. For the most part, the couple sits in silence at the breakfast table, engrossed in their respective newspapers, Kane (Welles) reading his *Inquirer* and Emily an edition of the competing *Chronicle*. A progressive widening gulf between the two takes place, revealed through a brilliant montage spanning roughly two and a half minutes of screen time, a period easily covering months or perhaps years of real time. What begins as a romantic "honeymoon brunch" graphically deteriorates as the years pass. Emily opens the montage with complaints about Kane's late-night parties, while in another shot she expresses her distaste for his late office hours. Kane, for his part, is shown to be a workaholic with little sympathy for his wife's complaints or feelings. Welles's use of the same set with minor changes in lighting and special effects was rather ingenuous, establishing a powerful yet economical montage over time. In every shot, he managed to dramatize the saga of a couple drifting apart because of the husband's increasing self-absorption, his obsession with work, and the ensuing breakdown in marital communication. The montage also reveals Kane's utter contempt for his reading public, at one point informing Emily smugly that readers of the *Inquirer* will think "what I tell them to think." In the final shot of the montage, the camera lingers on the now silent couple as they go about reading their (different) newspapers. Not only does Welles compress several years of marriage into a dramatic scene covering less than two and a half minutes of screen time, but he is also able to poignantly depict with great depth the sad implosion of a once-happy marriage. The lengthy narrative of an ill-fated relationship unfolds through a montage that is compelling mainly because it is so superbly edited. Although in many respects clearly a modernist film, *Citizen Kane*, because of its highly innovative editing flourishes and overall thematic darkness, anticipates elements of the later postmodern style.

Hitchcock's *Psycho* incorporates several montages of this sort, above all the famous shower episode that graphically and repeatedly depicts the stabbing of Marion Crane (Janet Leigh) shortly after she checks into the Bates Motel. This scene continues over a seemingly interminable forty-five seconds and is patiently constructed from a total of seventy-eight separate shots. Terrifying and tightly edited in the familiar Hitchcock manner, the scene conveys little actual violence: In fact, we never see the knife penetrate the naked woman in the shower. Within a few minutes, as the shower fills with blood, Crane slowly dies on camera as we see a close-up of the shower drain and then her expressionless eyes. For this montage, Hitchcock drew pictures of every one of the seventy-eight shots, planning exactly where the camera was to be positioned for each one. As he began shooting, Hitchcock, in his customary manner, was able to dispense with the script and more or less forget about the camera. (He claimed that he never looked through the lens of a camera since he already knew precisely what every frame was going to be, exactly how the mise-en-scène would emerge from a combination of planning, cinematography, and editing.) What Hitchcock hoped to achieve in the *Psycho* shower scene was not only powerful suspense but also a decidedly "subjective" point of view; he wanted the audience to fully identify with the character, and the superbly edited montage was his technique. Creative editing brought to *Psycho* a dramatic intensity rivaled by few films in Hollywood history.

Francis Coppola made comparably skillful use of time-compression montages, one example being his classic *The Godfather*, which derives much of its dramatic coherence from several creatively edited montages. This film, like its two sequels, inevitably calls into play some variant of the time-compression modality as it focuses on a series of events occurring over a span of several decades. In the original *Godfather* epic, as a way of constructing protracted sagas of two generations of gangsters, Coppola merges time-compression montages with standard decoupage and invisible editing for dialogue scenes. There are a number of defining scenes built around the wedding party of Don Corleone's daughter. Early in the film, Coppola uses standard invisible editing to frame Don Corleone's (Marlon Brando) conversation with an undertaker seeking retribution on behalf of his raped and beaten daughter: Dim, indoor lighting shrouds the characters looking for special favors from the Mafia boss. From a poorly lit room using decoupage editing, Coppola then shifts to a time-compression wedding montage, where we find people celebrating in a sunny, upbeat exterior setting:

Cut to: The Don meeting some guests outside.
Cut to: Mama dancing with Sonny's twin girls.
Cut to: Connie and Carlo laughing with guests at head table.
Cut to: Clemenza dancing with his wife.
Cut to: FBI arrive and take license plate numbers.
Cut to: Tessio sitting at a table peeling himself an orange.
Cut to: FBI continuing to take license numbers.
Cut to: Don Barzini (Don Corleone's rival) arrives.

This montage is quickly followed by several others conveying the narrative of a gala, sprawling wedding that is experienced from multiple points of view. Without going further into the plot, however, we can quickly detect FBI efforts to monitor the wedding—efforts interwoven with graphic features of the upbeat wedding celebration itself, which includes music, dancing, and infectious social conviviality. Coppola arranged his shots so as to demonstrate the great emotional power of Don Corleone as well as the imminent danger coming from both the feds and hated rival Don Barzini. In just a few minutes, the audience is able to assimilate vital historical information about the famous but still mysterious Corleone family.

Just as the montage style, in the hands of skilled film editors, can easily compress the passage of years into a few moments, in postmodern film, conversely, it can stretch time far beyond its temporal limits. One film (in the postmodern style) dramatizing this method is Robert Enrico's *An Occurrence at Owl Creek Bridge* (1962), the conversion of an Ambrose Bierce short story into a compelling film project. Enrico's fashionable black-and-white movie depicts the fractions of a second it takes for a man to be hanged after the trap is sprung. In gripping existential style, both Bierce's story and Enrico's film show the unbelievable amount of activity that can pass during that fraction of a moment when people are confronted with death. Here we see the cinematographer's art of manipulating time in a surrealistic atmosphere laced with unbelievable human anguish. From the very time the trap is sprung on the prisoner—a nameless individual who violated a local decree during the Civil War—time is arrested as history appears to be standing still. To establish these effects, Enrico cuts out the sound track for those intense moments preceding the hanging, staged on a scenic, wooded bridge. Time seems to float by like the sun's reflection on the quiet creek flowing beneath the gallows. The film cuts to a flashback scene involving the condemned man's wife and two children while the dreamlike action slows virtually to a standstill. At this point, we hear someone say, "Take his watch," while the executioners begin to strip the victim of his possessions.

An Occurrence at Owl Creek Bridge seems to unfold as if in slow motion. While the light of dawn begins to filter through the misty, peaceful forest and creek, the condemned man suddenly feels the trapdoor begin to open. We follow his fantasy as he plunges into the creek, his hangman's rope having broken during the excruciating fall; he struggles frenetically to free himself from his bonds, making his way slowly and painfully to the surface. At the end, we observe him swimming away freely, breaking the water with a tremendous gasp of breath. The sound track returns with the song "A livin' man, a livin' man, I wanna be a livin' man," at which point the screen is visited with a montage of water, spider webs, leaves, and other disparate signs of life. As if from a murky fog, we hear the officer in charge of the firing squad give orders in a slow sound that appears as if a hand grabbed hold of the record player. What follows is a sequence dominated by a strong mood of realism: The protagonist swims away, somehow evading bullets scattering about him from a firing squad on the river bank above. We hear an officer barking orders to fire additional rounds at him. Whirling overhead pan shots of the sky and tree branches impart a feeling of the embattled man moving desperately through the now swiftly flowing currents—shots that provide an incredible surrealistic mood to the well-crafted escape scenes. When he drifts toward shore, we hear no music or dialogue as the sound track is turned off again. His triumphant laugh on reaching the sandy beach rings hollow after he turns it into a brief frenzy of exultation for simply being alive. His understandable reaction is to go lie on the beach and laugh aloud, a scene rendered all the more bizarre through the combined impact of the music and the whirling camera in the sky.

Yet the narrative of *Owl Creek Bridge* continues: The frantic protagonist hears a bomb detonate nearby and begins once again to move quickly in retreat—this time along a path toward home. The soundtrack resonates with beating drums of the firing squad. The hero runs into a grove, the firing squad drumbeat pursuing him all the way. As the drumbeats rise in intensity, he collapses onto a tree and then runs toward a more remote destination. As if from a long tunnel, he runs directly toward the camera (situated close to his wife and family), moving faster with each step. He finally drops from total exhaustion and slows his stride as he walks barefoot along a tree-lined country lane. In the dim predawn light, we see his feet approaching the long-awaited destination, at which point he walks through opening iron gates and quickens his pace into a run. With only a background of birdsongs, followed by the introductory theme song, he notices his wife moving toward him and runs in her direction full speed. Just as he seems ready to clasp her in his arms, tears running down her cheeks, the director abruptly returns the action to the gallows, where in a quick instant the protagonist is killed, his neck broken by the thrust. All that happened before this grand finale was, as it turns out, a wild flight of the prisoner's racing, vivid imagination. What the audience observes, thanks to sophisticated editing in the postmodern style, is a cinematic experience wherein time is fundamentally and surrealistically reconstituted, slowed down—where a split second can be deftly transformed into what seems like an eternity.

FILM CULTURE TRANSFORMED

Since the late 1960s, Hollywood directors have experimented with an enormous variety of innovative cinematic techniques—open-ended shots, imaginative and nonlinear editing sequences, oblique camera angles, creative montages, freeze frames, intricate crosscutting, and, of course, the digital imaging that shapes so much contemporary filmmaking. Many have looked to reinvention of film canons and techniques to suit their idiosyncratic creative impulses. The preoccupation with technique, however, means that film culture responds just as much to the input of cinematographers, writers, and editors as to that of producers and directors; the end product is inevitably more collaborative. And it is often left to film editors to bring vital technical and stylistic flourishes to the cinematic enterprise. The aesthetics of film production are rarely static, depending instead on the work of free-spirited directors whose vocation is unthinkable without creative editing. With the New Hollywood generation, one can readily glimpse the main constituent elements of postmodern cinema; editing was always central to this shift, even where it was left unacknowledged.

A distinctly "postmodern" cinema first appeared as the self-conscious repudiation and transcendence of the Hollywood system run by formula-driven studio executives obsessed with profits, market share, and mass consumer appeal. Skeptical of conventional invisible editing and other long-established techniques, the new filmmaking generation—inspired by the French New Wave, 1960s counterculture, end of the Hollywood film code, and increased availability of new techniques—was able to carve out new creative terrain. The stock-in-trade of New Hollywood directors was a cutting methodology based on chaotic juxtapositions, discontinuity, fragmentation, and highly distorted images, visible in such films as Altman's *Nashville*, Coppola's *Apocalypse Now*, Allen's *Stardust Memories*, Scott's *Blade Runner*, and Tarantino's *Pulp Fiction*. Throughout this period, technical and stylistic experimentation was the sine qua non of creative filmmaking; in some cases, however, experimentation was more closely associated with sloppy efforts that called attention to the trivial and the bizarre disconnected from any meaningful thematic or narrative framework, inhibiting the prospects of genuine storytelling.

The influential New Wave film Agnès Varda's *Le Bonheur* (1965) adopts a variety of highly innovative editing devices—for example, the framing of actions that can be perceived as alternately being repeated, moving backward, and moving forward in time. Varda constructs a scene in which a husband discovers his wife's dead body, picks her up in his arms, and then lays her back down. We see him repeating this action several times, with Varda cutting off the sound track so that we end up with dead silence for underscoring, thus undercutting the viewer's conventional world of linear causality. Yet another New Wave device that came into vogue was the freeze-frame, employed by François Truffaut in *The Four Hundred Blows* (1959)—a film that ends with a frozen shot of Truffaut's young hero, Antoine Doniel (Jean-Pierre Léaud), dramatically gazing on his face as he looks pensively toward the ocean. Motionless in the freeze-frame, the boy's face seems to be saying that Truffaut's narrative is not yet over, the problems confronted by the boy never having been resolved. While the freeze-frame breaks the suspension of disbelief and stands out as a useful dramatic (these days often repeated) artifice, it further anticipates the postmodern idea that stable notions of truth and knowledge no longer have much validity or at least cannot be determined with much certitude.

In the United States, varied forms of "experimental editing" in the New Wave tradition became increasingly in vogue after the 1960s. What might have been dismissed as aesthetically risky or too avant-garde thirty years ago has been assimilated by a large number of mainstream and independent filmmakers alike. We have seen how postmodern cinema thrives on novel aesthetic and technical departures enhanced by new, increasingly fluid photographic and editing approaches. Editing that calls attention to the filmmaking process itself, that embellishes a certain self-consciousness, and that often celebrates a world of fragmentation and nonlinearity today permeates the work of such filmmakers as Allen, Altman, Kubrick, Lee, Stone, the Coen brothers, Nichols, Scorsese, Coppola, Wenders, and Tarantino.

More than suspense or drama, comedy lends itself to innovative photography and editing insofar as it thrives on the element of surprise and, by extension, tends to violate more traditional motion picture norms and motifs. The postmodern style seems perhaps most at home with the comedic impulse, as reflected in cinematic traditions going back to Charlie Chaplin,

Buster Keaton, Laurel and Hardy, and the Marx Brothers and extending through the more recent films of Woody Allen, the Coen brothers, and John Waters. Postwar comedy carried this same ethos forward, exemplified by Wilder's *Some Like It Hot* (1960), with its cross-dressing, gender-role confusion, cynical view of sexuality and marriage, and liberal use of montage. In the 1970s, Allen's *Annie Hall* may have conquered new terrain for the largest assemblage of innovative editing cuts made for any single film. Consider the very first shot, where Allen faces the camera and, looking it squarely in the eye, conducts a long prologue in the fashion of a comic routine probably inspired by Allen's own onstage experience. According to conventional Hollywood wisdom, looking directly at the camera is regarded as such a clear violation of accepted filmmaking protocol that it is rarely used by even the most daring auteurs. When characters position themselves frontally at the camera, the audience is likely to respond as if it were being addressed directly, meaning that the illusion of unseen observers watching other people's actions is far more difficult to sustain.

In one scene from *Annie Hall*, the two main characters, Alvie (Allen) and Annie (Diane Keaton), are replaced by cartoon images of themselves. In another scene, the families of both Alvie and Annie simultaneously celebrate Passover and Easter on split screens, Annie's mother speaking to Alvie's family across the screen as if they were seated at a neighboring table in the same restaurant. Still another now legendary scene unfolds on Annie's balcony, where Alvie and Annie have their first "intimate" conversation. The cinematographer (Gordon Willis) shot the conversation in a familiar-enough manner, using two-shots and shot-reverse-shots of Annie and Alvie throughout their interaction, but when the inevitable close-up shots appear on screen, Allen inserts subtitles beneath their auditory exchanges as if the subtitles were designed to translate the dialogue of a foreign film. Of course, the subtitles furnish nothing so obvious as a different language but rather the deep, unspoken thoughts of Alvie and Annie during the exchange, conveying a strong relational (and slightly erotic) undertone to an otherwise prosaic conversation. By means of expert cutting, we are able to observe an interaction that turns out to be far more intimate (at least potentially) than appears on the surface. Open-ended scene construction of this sort would never occur, of course, in a more conventional dramatic film. The comedic status of *Annie Hall* permits Allen to introduce what is generally considered a simple technique (subtitling) in a satirical and slightly absurd manner, bringing in emotional subtext as well as verbal narrative. The result is superb ironic twist with a powerful message about the inevitably dual nature of first encounters—indeed perhaps *all* human encounters—in which words themselves can be a treacherous measure of what is actually going on in people's minds. Surface appearances usually tell us little about underlying social and psychological dynamics, a premise underlying virtually all of Allen's films and characteristic of the broader postmodern style.

A widely used editing technique befitting postmodern cinema is the "match cut," which refers to shots of disparate locales or settings that share crucial features. A good example is contained in Peter Weir's *The Last Wave* (1977), which relates the story of a young Sydney attorney (Richard Chamberlain) who defends an Aborigine man accused of murder. As the title might suggest, the film revolves around water both as physical setting (for example, rainstorms) and as a metaphor, with water sometimes meant to indicate an elevated sense of distortion achieved through dreamlike sequences rendered, for example, when the sound track shifts to tribal-sounding music and animal-like calls. The protagonist is visited in his dreams by Aborigines. At the same time, images of apocalyptic destruction wrought by flooding appear and reappear in the film, lending its narrative a frightening, highly prophetic quality. In certain scenes, Weir depicts sunlight reflecting off a building paralleled by electric lights shining through a grate; in other scenes, we see cloudy sky matched by sporadic, brilliant patches of sunlight. Elsewhere, he matches water running from an overfilled bathtub with rain pouring against a window. In creating such provocative montages, Weir combines skills as both director and editor to establish visual matches that bring added layers of meaning to the frames. Near the end, Weir fashions a sequence of shots focused on a cataclysm in which bodies are seen floating underwater where, as in the dream sequences, "reality" is left behind in favor of surrealism. In the final scene, Chamberlin has a prophetic vision at the edge of the ocean as he sees waters cresting toward a mammoth wave destined to engulf everything before it. In a nod to Truffaut, Weir brings *The Last Wave* to a powerful conclusion with a freeze-frame of a huge wave sweeping across the vast terrain, seemingly bound to annihilate everything in its path. The match-cut technique, postmodern in its inspiration, would reappear widely in films by Altman, Allen, and Lynch, among others.

Still another editing technique friendly to postmodern cinema involves the insertion of an unmatched frame within a larger montage, visible, for example, in Ridley Scott's *Blade Runner*. The opening scene develops through an establishing shot of Los Angeles in the year 2019, revealing a familiar dystopic urban nightmare where, among other visible effects, fiery infernos erupt from massive towers. True to convention, the camera shifts toward a large office building, but then Scott abruptly inserts an extreme close-up of an eyeball—a shot that clearly does not "belong" to the invisible montage viewed by the audience. There is a flash-forward to the next scene, in which engineer Leon Kowalski is being given a psychological test in which a machine carefully examines his retina. Although Scott's bold inclusion of the eyeball into the Los Angeles 2019 montage is a breach of standard Hollywood invisible editing, here it makes abundant good sense and conveys both abstract and concrete (social) meaning within an emergent postmodern sensibility.

Lynch's postmodern thriller *Blue Velvet* introduces a variety of unmatched cuts, all violating standard Hollywood editing conventions. The film opens with an elaborate montage that unfolds on a sprawling suburban front lawn—the perfect image of well-scrubbed, friendly, conservative small-town America. What Lynch does here, however, is to render this idyllic setting disturbingly unreal or, more accurately, *surreal*. With only a few strategically placed frames, he transforms the imagery of contented middle-class suburbia into a grotesque setting of violence and death. Shots in the opening montage are cut in such a way as to demonstrate a harmonious, peaceful, integrated tone (white picket fence, congenial people, and tranquil neighborhood), but they soon give way to images of intense *conflict* festering beneath the surface (black insects feeding voraciously underground and the kink in the water hose that foreshadows a man's seizure). The emotional impact of *Blue Velvet* is achieved, most of all, through the creative use of jump cuts in the editing room.

In his 1975 film *Barry Lyndon*, Kubrick uses diverse editing techniques to establish a deep psychological gulf between the main protagonist and the audience, techniques that have proved essential to postmodern directors. In this eighteenth-century costume picture, the director presents the narrative of a duel between the young hero (Lyndon) and an English army captain named Quin. Instead of framing the epic duel scene through a typical "master" or establishing shot—a panorama of the total setting—Kubrick begins with just the opposite: a close-up of the two antagonists' pistols. As the camera pulls away in a somewhat quixotic manner, we observe the two antagonists standing on a riverbank. By reversing the expected sequence of shots, Kubrick leaves the audience feeling somewhat befuddled and unsettled. The riveting question here is, Why not simply frame the scene in accordance with the conventional pattern? Only much later does the audience finally discover the real basis of this reversal—namely, that the duel was rigged with blank bullets in order to fool Barry Lyndon (and the audience). Here we find an example of editing techniques introduced in a way as that imparts a postmodern ethos to a variety of scenes and montages—indeed to the entire film project.

Blue Velvet (David Lynch, 1986)   *Dennis Hopper and Isabella Rossellini become involved in a tormented relationship replete with bizarre sexuality, intrigue, drugs, and acts of sadomasochism that descends into psychological and moral chaos.*

Yet another fine example of postmodern visual eclecticism can be found in Tony Scott's *Enemy of the State* (1998), which succeeds in blending an enormous variety of visual media. Along with the standard thirty-five-millimeter format, Scott's film contains footage from retail surveillance cameras, satellite photographs, video and handheld camera footage, and a variety of computer-enhanced images. He weaves all these visual sources together to tell the story of an out-of-control National Security Agency (NSA) official (Jon Voigt) who directs the agency's formidable human and technological resources against U.S. citizens who stumble on evidence that a prominent congressman has been assassinated. The fast-paced political thriller stars Will Smith as Robert Dean, a Washington, D.C., labor attorney, and Gene Hackman as a former NSA agent turned rogue surveillance operative. Dean suddenly finds himself jobless, homeless, and penniless after he inadvertently receives a tape recording of the assassination, and he must go undercover himself in order to avoid being killed. Scott employs a dizzying array of special effects as NSA agents stop at nothing in their desperate attempt to locate and destroy the tape. Scott's use of so much visual surveillance media leaves the audience filled with feelings of angst and paranoia, faced with an Orwellian universe in which privacy seems rather obsolete, making this movie one of the most powerful statements within the postmodern idiom in both technique and thematic content.

Lynch's *Mulholland Drive* (2001) further incorporates strong elements of the postmodern visual style: neo-noir lighting, campy retro costumes, surrealistic makeup, miniature characters, weird juxtaposition of frames, and so forth. Lynch alternates between daytime sets bathed in postcard-quality California sunshine and dimly lit night-for-night shots replete with fog-shrouded vistas and flickering lightbulbs. The film opens with a pretitle assemblage of dancers gyrating to 1950s rock and roll, even though the picture is set in the present. At later points, singers dressed in 1950s costumes sing classic rock songs, reinforcing the film's distinctly retro look. Characters adorned in campy thrift-shop costumes reappear throughout, as does an incongruous parade of bizarre figures. A sinister-looking homeless man with surrealistic facial makeup appears as a stand-in for Satan, while an ominous, diminutive cowboy enters as the dialectical opposite of the familiar John Wayne–style Western hero. At the end, two characters from an early scene at the Los Angeles airport reappear as miniatures that literally slip under the door of the protagonist's apartment in order to terrorize her. Such visual ^elements—and more—stamp Lynch's film as indelibly postmodern.

The Coen brothers' *The Man Who Wasn't There* (2001) is quickly recognizable as a postmodern visual effort from the very first black-and-white shots. The brothers chose to locate their film in the 1940s, which gives it something of the look of a classic film noir. The small-town setting, replete with art deco shops and buildings, helps reproduce the campy feel of the movie, much along lines of *Raising Arizona, Blood Simple,* and *Fargo.* The majority of the film is composed of expertly framed night-for-night shots. There are slatted venetian blinds emitting bars of light into the shaded interiors. The cast (including stars Billy Bob Thornton and Frances McDormand) is adorned with vintage costumes. Water icons of various types abound, from a bathtub in which McDormand soaks to a placid lake that hides a car with a dead body. Both Thornton's deadpan voice-over narrative and classic swing music combine to re-create an unmistakable neo-noir ambience, much along the lines of earlier films like *Body Heat* and *The Last Seduction.*

SPECTACLE AND CHAOS

A survey of contemporary Hollywood films can illustrate just how postmodernism departs thematically and aesthetically from modernism within the cinematic enterprise—a shift dependent perhaps most of all on the task of editing. Modernist cinema, as we have seen, gains much of its definition from "invisible" editing, with cameras riveted on action and movement, generating a style consonant with narratives revolving around conventional heroes struggling to triumph over terrible odds. The modernist camera is most often set up to follow the trajectory of a protagonist whose string of actions and maneuvers dominates the mise-en-scène. Repeated endlessly during the studio era, the modernist formula takes a more or less straightforward, linear path, discrete shots giving expression to standard plots literally and sequentially and scenes connected in a distinctly logical fashion. This format discourages flamboyant representations of directorial craft, that is, the tendency to glorify the aesthetics of editing and cinematography at the expense of dialogue, character development, and action.

Films in the postmodern style, on the other hand, move along an entirely different trajectory with their aesthetics tied to the auteur's reliance on surprise, hyperdrama, spectacle, and the surreal, which can transform a seemingly harmonious world into a terrible nightmare of violence, chaos, and cataclysm. No better example of this can be found than Stone's epic *JFK*, which offers a complex, tightly interwoven melange of powerful visual images derived from documentary footage, overpowering dramatic scenes, and staged reenactments of historical events, all marked by extreme rapid pacing and unrelenting emotional intensity. With the brilliant editing of Joe Hutshing (and cinematography of Bob Richardson), Stone was able to portray a universe of unbelievable fluidity, conflict, and turmoil within a larger coherent cinematic structure.[8] *JFK* emerges as a pioneering effort in the development of a postmodern visual style, building on previous films that Stone directed (above all *The Doors*). Stone and Richardson labored to provide the film with the look of a superdocumentary, blending standard thirty-five-millimeter footage with sixteen-millimeter black-and-white shots, handheld video scenes, and myriad special effects. *JFK* comprises no less than 2,000 different special effects, along with roughly the same number of individual shots and a script encompassing 200 speaking roles. As one writer noted, "*JFK* breaks on through to the other side; it uses all those techniques, but it subverts melodrama with its pyrotechnic editing and varied film stocks, frame sizes, and processes into a starburst narrative. The seamless reality of Hollywood narrative explodes, and the viewer confronts the speculative nature not only of film but also of history."[9] To handle such complexity, Stone hired Hank Corwin, then a respected editor of television commercials, to assist in editing precisely because Stone felt he possessed a "highly chaotic mind."[10] *JFK* marks Stone's final use of traditional editing equipment; from that point on, he would come to rely on digital editing systems that were coming into vogue by the early 1990s.

As with *JFK*, postmodern-style editing celebrates the graphically illusory, bizarre, and baroque, hoping to illuminate the social relations of anxiety, despair, paranoia, and chaos—one reason the classic noir visual style is so often favored by directors like Scorsese, Coppola, the Coen brothers, Cronenberg, De Palma, and Kubrick. Their films often begin with long takes of the sort that furnished the signature of many noir classics, including *Touch of Evil, Double Indemnity, Sunset Boulevard,* and *Gun Crazy.* What these films depict is a social environment teeming with corruption, violence, and powerlessness, usually inhabited by doomed protagonists trapped in a Hobbesian jungle where the darkest, most perverse elements of human existence seem to prevail—qualities we have come to regard as standard within postmodern cinema.

6

POSTMODERN CINEMA IN A CORPORATE WORLD

The American film legacy was rooted from its very origins in a complex interplay of traditional, modern, and postmodern motifs, suggesting that distinctly "pure" expressions of cinematic discourse are virtually impossible to locate. Many features of what we have defined as postmodern cinema turn out to be part of emergent trends that in different ways connect with the modern style: thematic emphasis on chaos, intrigue, and paranoia, death of the hero, disjointed narrative structures, dystopic vision of the future, and so forth. Postmodernism is a perpetually shifting, complex, ambiguous field of cultural expressions in which, however, it is possible to delineate fundamental developments shaped by an uneasy coexistence of styles, techniques, genres, and narratives with particular films, directors, and other creative forces seen as the product of multiple (sometimes contradictory) influences. And such influences resist simple categorization, which becomes obvious with any attempt to critically evaluate individual films, genres, or subgenres. In a society where what might be understood as postmodern culture becomes increasingly pervasive, resonant, and faddish, we know that labels, generalizations, and meanings become fluid and unpredictable, open to multiple readings and interpretations. This state of affairs is made all the more overpowering insofar as images, motifs, and symbols so often wind up detached from stable points of reference in a world of commodity production and media culture.

Yet postmodern cinema has become undeniably part of a universe of "stable references" in the form of highly integrated structures, a vast network of economic arrangements, and a global communications system tied to expanding corporate media empires. It is this labyrinthine framework—profit driven, oligopolistic, global, and ideologically dominant—that so thoroughly establishes and delimits Hollywood filmmaking agendas. This system has dramatically extended and rationalized its operations through the workings of global competition, technological refinement, and assimilation of immensely diverse markets and "constituencies"—a process just taking off at the start of the twenty-first century. The growth of autonomous spaces available for independent or semi-independent cinema within this huge corporate aegis can be understood as part of such a historical context. It is a reality that contrasts with the common view of media culture as monolithic, rigidly commodified, and totally resistant to incursions from outside the fortress. A more nuanced and contextualized understanding of film production (and viewing) can help explain why postmodern cinema, though often culturally subversive, turns out to be so economically assimilated and politically ambiguous—why it can be simultaneously progressive and regressive, experimental and conformist, novel and mainstream. If media culture in its varied representations can be said to colonize most spheres of everyday life, in actuality postmodern cinema occupies a terrain of explosive cultural and ideological energies where little is taken for granted beyond the (always incessant) pressures of market calculation and success.

If modernity historically meant a break with traditionalism and a gradual shift toward a system defined by industrialization, monetary exchange, urbanism, bureaucracy, and mass culture, then the later postmodern turn suggests a rather profound, indeed, epochal but always uneven movement away from that established paradigm. We know that in the advanced capitalist world, economic growth depends on intensified concentration of corporate power along with a thoroughgoing process of commodification tied to the perpetual search for domestic and global markets. With such a globalizing economic framework, however, the *cultural* reality has turned out to be something altogether different: Grounded in what George Ritzer calls "new cathedrals of consumption,"[1] popular culture is shaped by an expanding universe of leisure, entertainment, consumerism, and mass communications, where struggles over autonomy, localism, and even populism come readily to the surface. Viewed thusly, postmodernism (as both ideology and social relations) takes shape according to a transformative dynamic that works in many ways to reconfigure the public sphere. Above all, the postmodern turn involves a breakdown of fixed modes of aesthetic representation, institutional hierarchies, Enlightenment beliefs, and stable forms of personal and social identity. One consequence of such breakdown is a pluralizing and decentering of human life experiences in a way that corresponds to those new modes of consumption now so integral to media culture—and to the increasingly significant terrain of postmodern cinema.[2]

THE NEW CULTURAL REVOLUTION

Media culture in general and Hollywood filmmaking in particular have emerged as critical arenas for the diffusion of values, beliefs, attitudes, and myths that influence popular consciousness in the realms of work, family, sexuality, politics, art, and so forth. From its earliest days, the film industry embellished system-sustaining ideas such as patriotism, the work ethic, competitive individualism, and Puritanism, all the while generating positive attitudes toward big business, government, and the military—all part of what Antonio Gramsci called mechanisms of ideological hegemony. The modernism of the classical studio system merged neatly with this ideological dynamic, allowing for a few exceptions here and there. Modernist cinema would leave an indelible imprint on American public opinion in the areas of class relations, power, and culture, defined, as we have seen, by what Girgus labels the "Hollywood consensus."[3] It was a liberal-democratic consensus that gave definition to American popular culture, in many ways consonant with the Middletown syndrome explored in chapter 2, of which a film like *Mr. Smith Goes to Washington* (1939) was exemplary. Referring to Capra's famous montage of Jimmy Stewart touring Washington, D.C., Girgus writes that it "provides a powerful representation of a prolonged scene of ideological consensus. The montage works on two levels combining both myth and history. A sequence of shots of monuments, historic sites, and documents in combination with the patriotic music of the sound track forms a mythic narrative of American culture and character. . . . [It] thereby functions as a powerful visualization of the ideology of consensus."[4] As American society grew more economically mature and differentiated and, indeed, far more inclusionary, the role of cinema—always situated within the broader contours of popular culture—expanded in its ideological functions, helping sustain evolving liberal-capitalist structures and beliefs that achieved undeniable preeminence over time.

With the postmodern shift of the 1980s and 1990s, however, fissures in this once seemingly invulnerable hegemonic system became sharper and more visible: Values integral to earlier capitalist development came under mounting assault in the post-Fordist milieu, which began to take shape after World War II. This milieu was one of growing social fragmentation, breakdown of family life, widespread revolt against bureaucracy, decay and atomization of urban life, environmental crisis, and the ever present threat of nuclear war—tendencies contributing to the rise of the New Left, the counterculture, and new social movements of the 1970s and later. Historic tenets of the American Dream (and the American Century) would begin to unravel amid mounting turbulence and change. Filmmaking along with other artistic forms mirrored these developments in the extreme, made possible by the simultaneous decline of stuffy, conservative, obsolete studio regimes that had ruled Hollywood since the turn of the century. A new creative openness linked to the growing mood of ambiguity, chaos, and dystopia that would become vital to postmodern culture served to profoundly influence and reshape the entire filmmaking enterprise, grounded in the emergence of an innovative, nonconformist, often progressive stratum of auteurs willing to push the boundaries of artistic integrity.[5] Within a postmodern milieu, the power of long-cherished myths, traditions, and identities could no longer be merely assumed within or outside the Hollywood orbit. Themes of alienation, rebellion, and mayhem now entered film culture, easily visible even in such commercially successful pictures as *The Godfather*, *Nashville*, *Annie Hall*, *Blade Runner*, *JFK*, and *Pulp Fiction*. In certain ways, these films—and dozens of others fitting loosely within the postmodern ethos—reflect a society in the throes of social crisis and political decay, phenomena seemingly endemic to contradictions at work within post-Fordist capitalism. Beneath the appearances of an orderly, rationalized, calm, technically calculable world of "modernization," beneath the veneer of organizational cohesion and economic prosperity, we encounter a society riven with conflict and turbulence where the popular mood of anxiety, paranoia, and fear seems increasingly commonplace.[6] At the same time, while postmodern cinema often deftly explores the pulses and rhythms of this world, furnishing dramatic critical insights into the crises of liberal-capitalist society, it has so far projected little understanding or vision beyond the contours of that Hobbesian state of disorder.

In a system overrun by large-scale corporations, the ascendant "post" mode of discourse is organically connected to elements of *cultural* subversion that can readily be seen as the logical outgrowth of historical conditions and social contradictions produced by that system. Postmodernism, after all, coexists rather comfortably with a global corporate structure at the very same time it celebrates movement toward "local" knowledge, social diversity, and cultural eclecticism along with devotion to autonomy, innovation, and aesthetic exploration. The "post" dimension consists precisely in this stark and uneasy dualism, where creative independence flourishes alongside commodification while the dynamics of change and novelty interface with requirements of corporate stability. What this historical moment introduces, above all, is a new dialectic between cultural production and social reality where the boundaries separating art and daily life are now more blurred than ever. The process of economic (indeed also cultural) globalization—and with it increasing U.S. hegemony—inevitably contributes to this historical moment.[7]

On one side of a reconstituted film industry in the 1980s and 1990s lies the well-worn phenomenon of blockbusters, spectacles, and hypercommodified fare featuring mindless and formulaic action narratives, disjointed visual images, cartoonish characters, threadbare plots, and unnerving sound levels—the output of a corporate-defined culture industry thirsting for profits and acclaim on the basis of what Biskind calls "big-screen infantilism."[8] Such filmmaking offers a bizarre combination of retro fantasies, goofy scenarios, and pseudorealistic attachments to conventional heroes even as the "product" itself may be surrounded and deeply influenced by the postmodern spectacle.[9] A mixture of both modern and postmodern, this cinema thrives on a milieu of passive spectatorship in which the audience ends up reduced to the status of manipulable consumers, appropriate to an era when movies are so often geared to young viewers.

On the other side of this rather murky divide lies the kind of postmodern cinema explored here—one involving a recasting and renewal of the classic Hollywood auteur, a creative force dedicated to innovative pictures that call into question a variety of mainstream ideological discourses. What separates this semi-independent stratum of directors from earlier generations is the great facility with which they, as boldly innovative filmmakers, somehow manage to operate simultaneously within and outside the Hollywood structure, keeping alive the auteur tradition while maneuvering (often with great difficulty and frustration) through the vast network of corporate film production, marketing, distribution, and exhibition. If the once perhaps overly glamorized auteur, in whatever revitalized form, remains more alive today than at any time in the past, this new possibility owes everything to an immense cultural opening carved out within an otherwise tightly integrated commodity system. It is easy enough to see that postmodern cinema departs significantly from the classical studio system where significant local or diverse creative spaces were rarely permitted to exist. Within Hollywood film culture, economic structure and aesthetic sensibilities converged around a number of dominant themes: the idea of historical progress, sense of national purpose, work ethic, individual heroism and redemption, the essential goodness and stability of American social life, and, perhaps above all, the moral validity of U.S. foreign and military policies. Cracks in this modernist edifice first became visible, as we have seen, in the work of such influential directors as Welles, Hitchcock, Lang, and Wilder—all of whom bore the stamp of European cinema and worked within or on the fringes of the film noir tradition.

The more expressive side of postmodern cinema was the work of a new generation of auteurs able to forge creative purpose and social identity along the borders of mainstream commercial and independent filmmaking: Coppola, Altman, Scorsese, Allen, Lee, Stone, the Coen brothers, Tarantino, and, to a lesser extent, directors like Pollack, Nichols, Cronenberg, and Levinson. Moving into this space, a younger group of quasi-independent directors came to the forefront in the 1990s—Bryan Singer, Ed Burns, Steve Soderbergh, John Singleton, Paul Thomas Anderson, Danny Boyle, and Peter Berg, among others—all inspired by fresh ideas derived from youth culture, hiphop music, and distinctly postmodern approaches to fashion, sexuality, violence, and indeed history. Having little to do with the film school generation, this innovative stratum of auteurs typically employs flashy photographic techniques, novel special effects, and rapid-fire nonlinear modes of storytelling, taking postmodern sensibilities well beyond what had defined the earlier generation of "new auteurs." A film like Berg's *Very Bad Things*, for example, takes postmodern themes of Hobbesian chaos and dystopia to levels transcending anything found in *Blade Runner* or *Pulp Fiction*, although the work of Scott and Tarantino surely had its impact on younger directors like Berg. These cinematic trends reveal the powerful imprint of television (most notably MTV), video games, the video revolution, digital technology, and the increasing globalization of markets that fosters novelty and experimentation built into the very logic of economic diversity integral to globalization. Postmodern auteurs seek broadened autonomy, control, and creativity essentially *within* (and not against) the global corporate economy.[10]

The new cultural revolution creates a situation where forms of ideological hegemony are questioned and sometimes contested within the mass media and popular culture, within the rapidly shifting arena of symbols, images, and messages. It involves a perpetually uneasy coexistence of affirmative and critical, regressive and progressive, traditional and modern elements of ideological discourse; the culture industry (above all, cinema) is today far less monolithic or one-dimensional than the bulk of earlier Frankfurt school theorizing or various propaganda models assumed. Postmodern cinema introduces a variety of codes, narratives, and techniques that in many ways embellish an ever more atomistic and chaotic world, and we may be seeing just the beginning of such trends. Postmodern culture, as we have argued, cannot be reduced to a collection of theories and concepts but instead corresponds to deep historical forces at work in contemporary society: post-Fordism, the communications revolution, social fragmentation, growth of media culture, globalization, and so forth. In this setting, mass media and popular culture greatly expand in scope at the very moment their general ideological functions become more diffuse and in some ways more contradictory. As James Lull points out, the popular media not only furnish mass publics with particular views of "reality" but also work to reshape the very popular experience of time and space.[11] For postmodern cinema, this development opens up terrain for critical opposition against ideological representations of the dominant culture, reflecting many of the fissures and conflicts endemic to the larger order. In a certain touch of irony, conservative observers like Michael Medved who bemoan Hollywood's jaundiced view of such institutions as the family, religion, big business, the police, the military, and the national government do not really veer too far off the mark.[12] The crisis and eclipse of modernism, with its celebratory, optimistic view of American history and social life, are hastened by yet another phenomenon: Prevailing ideologies of the past century (nationalism, liberalism, socialism, and communism) no longer provide unified narratives and political directions, their capacity to address and explain historical reality having been exhausted.[13]

With postmodern cinema recently on the ascendancy, therefore, the idea of coherent ideological guideposts seems obsolete, indeed unfathomable—nowhere more than in Hollywood, which, after all, is located in the corridors of the giant entertainment corporations. Postmodernism affirms rapidly flowing images, technological wizardry, thematic eclecticism, cultural pastiche, and nostalgia, not to mention the power of the media spectacle itself. While media culture saturates ever larger regions of daily life, so too does daily life saturate the media with "life," as Gabler suggests, becoming itself a kind of "movie" engulfing larger zones of popular consciousness.[14] This is simply another way of arguing that boundaries between art and reality have become obscured beyond any easy recognition. The power of the commodity to create, sustain, and impose cultural (not to mention political) meaning in a turbulent, post-Fordist, globalized society is not what it appears in the wake of unprecedented corporate media consolidations of power. The new cultural revolution lies precisely in this epic breakdown of hegemonic discourses and novel openings made possible for plural, nonconformist, and even subversive cultural expressions that, at the same time, are largely devoid of familiar ideological references and influences. In this sociohistorical context, the immensely wide range of feelings, desires, hopes, and identities entering cultural life remain profoundly unsettled and often confusing—surely one of the defining features of the postmodern age—and nowhere is this more visible than in recent American cinema.[15]

This postmodern shift augurs broadening space for increasingly plural, difficult-to-chart audience responses to film products, one result of the growing corporate requirements for diversity and adaptation in an era of globalization and informational technology. The mammoth and complex media apparatus is not today—and probably never was—the vehicle of a totally administered system.[16] With the ebbing of an undistilled modernity, it is today possible to identify the spread of fluid, eclectic, critical discourses that do not always fit ready-made ideological paradigms—the very same discourses helping to shape the postmodern ethos in filmmaking.

Viewers and audiences bring their own range of experiences, tastes, preferences, and outlooks to cinema, endowing the intricate process of "seeing" and interpreting films with a strongly interactive dimension calling into question the simple inculcation thesis that presents a one-way impact of art or culture on popular consciousness. As with graphic arts, literature, music, and television, motion pictures are always subject to multiple readings and interpretations, cultural meaning always being dependent on variable social contexts, structural mediations, and individual perceptions. The phenomenology of mass media and popular culture is such that the number of prospective filters, schemas, and mediations is seemingly endless—a dynamic that applies to both the production and the consumption of cultural goods.[17] This explains the surprising proliferation of indie and quasi-indie films during the 1990s as well as the rapid growth of postmodern fare at the very moment corporate media power is more concentrated than ever. Rather than the specter of audience entrapment, we encounter a wide spectrum of aesthetic choices accompanying a more "dialectical" relationship between film and audience, producer and consumer, and cultural object and psychological response. Surely the innovative and influential work of directors like Coppola, Stone, Allen, Lee, Altman, and Waters occupies a special niche encompassing discrete rather idiosyncratic audience preferences, backgrounds, and outlooks. The one-dimensional view of media culture that informs the culture–industry, propaganda, and ideological inculcation model of hegemony has less and less resonance in the postmodern setting, just as grand modernist narratives attuned to mass publics have eroded under the onslaught of new historical trends. This hardly means that a genuinely open, two-way process of communication exists or is even possible within the present corporate structure, but it does suggest that creative and experimental local spaces can develop and even flourish. Media culture in post-Fordist society is probably more vulnerable to subversive incursions at the start of the new century than at any time in the recent past.[18]

As modernism loses its capacity for cultural (and no doubt political) expansion, giving way to and coexisting with the postmodern turn, long-established connections between economic and cultural life become more oblique and diffuse. The apparently solid, hierarchical, and commodified matrix of corporate capitalism unfolds alongside the dramatic pluralization of social and cultural forces intrinsic to the developmental patterns of advanced (post-Fordist and globalized) industrial society, and this is nowhere more true than in the United States. A tense and uneasy dualism is pushed forward by the Internet, video, cable television, and other outlets of informational technology. The postmodern ethos flourishes mainly *within* the modern edifice and thus does not typically expand in direct opposition to the structures of corporate power. Yet it could signal a qualitative break with modernity insofar as crucial aspects of Enlightenment rationality—universal discourses, faith in historical progress, and attachment to norms of industrial and bureaucratic order—can be expected to yield to a culture of ambiguity, pessimism, fear, dystopia, and other features of the famous Hobbesian state of nature.[19] In the meantime, however, we can be sure that a postmodern *cultural* shift does not necessarily signify equivalent changes in the formation of economic critiques or political strategies—a dualism reflecting the sharply uneven trajectory of American society.

CORPORATE POWER AND POSTMODERN FILM

Film culture cannot be dissociated from the realities of class structure and power relations that define the entire historical landscape. The influence is surely dialectical to some degree: Cinema exerts a pervasive impact on society and vice versa. To speak of this phenomenon is to focus on the growing concentration of economic power, not only in Hollywood but in the larger domestic (and global) system as well. Here we argue that postmodern cinema reflects nothing less than a new developmental phase, a break with the past in which modernity corresponded to an earlier paradigm of liberal capitalism and corporate studio system that lasted well into the 1960s. This historic break has encouraged broadening spheres of auteurial independence befitting the New Hollywood era that built on the energies of 1960s radicalism, the counterculture, and European filmmaking, not to mention far-reaching changes elsewhere in popular culture (television, music, graphic arts, architecture, and literature). Nourished by this creative environment, filmmaking carved out new aesthetic freedoms largely *within* an expanding culture industry, relying on technological wizardry, alternative music, diversification of global markets, cable television, and the video revolution to force a deep rupture with established canons.[20] Yet if the appearance of a "New Hollywood" was made possible by disintegration of the "Old Hollywood"—allowing for some radical cinematic departures in the 1970s—the truth is that the studio-based film industry never actually disappeared; in disarray for a while, it merely reproduced itself under new guises, reconsolidating even more power than before. Studios like Fox, Universal, Paramount, MGM, and Warner Brothers maintained their preeminent role in film production and distribution, their fortresslike presence joined by emerging giants like Sony, Disney, Viacom, and Dreamworks.[21]

Hollywood business empires remained very much alive, expanding their scope of operations throughout the 1980s and 1990s in the midst of rapidly growing and diversifying global and home markets—all the while dedicated to product expansion, managerial control, and profit making within a stable economic environment. Their ambitious designs were merely refocused with advancing globalization that helped stimulate a wave of corporate mergers and consolidations among entertainment media giants. At the same time, however, such concentrated power did not block the spread of independent cinema and directorial autonomy fueled by sophisticated technology, globalization of markets, and the pluralization of American culture that converged with those other transformations mentioned earlier. We suggest that the logic of commodification and the power of the spectacle did not fully envelope filmmaking in its postmodern embodiment despite the renewed emphasis on blockbusters, expensive action films, and assorted peripheral marketing ventures.[22] Oddly enough, cultural trends favoring pluralism, freedom, creativity, and local experience—all preconditions of innovative cinema—now seem to widely coexist with the heightened commodification and managerial control we have come to expect in advanced capitalist society. Post-Fordist development combines two crucial ingredients that help explain this seeming paradox: a relatively stable institutional matrix and managerial system combined with a fragmented, turbulent *social* milieu in which the popular mood of alienation, cynicism, and insecurity becomes the norm—a Weberian system of rationalized organizational routine that is frequently counterposed to a Hobbesian state of disorder and chaos. Postmodern cinema is shaped and delimited by this dialectic.

As in the heyday of the classical studio system, Hollywood filmmaking today is governed by the priorities and dictates of business culture, with the proviso that enterprises are now larger, more concentrated in their economic power, and more integrated into *global* media conglomerates. Following lines well established throughout American film history, present-day cinema stresses commerce over art, profits over aesthetics, and form over substance at a time when the bulk of Hollywood remains committed to many of the tried-and-true formulas, spin-offs, managerial conservatism, fear of politics, and obsession with cost cutting that is so elementary to the outlook of producers, studio executives, and others involved in the business side of filmmaking. Corporate heads, always cautious by temperament, want to avoid costly and/or risky ventures, even at a time when rather mediocre pictures (for example, the James Bond action movies) can cost upwards of $100 million. Yet even with all these studio imperatives fully intact, independent filmmaking has thrived as never before, carving out new creative niches on the margins of a corporate structure that finds itself forced to seek out (or at least engage) local centers of innovative film production in order to sustain a dynamic presence among film audiences, now far less homogeneous than before.[23]

The corporate media behemoths are able to diversify their global reach through the twin processes of economic internationalization and technological restructuring fueled in part by the computer-based communications revolution. It is often forgotten that Hollywood has become a major center of technological renewal, advertising, managerial efficiency, export of cultural products, and general economic dynamism.[24] It is a major source of employment, with roughly 150,000 new jobs generated in Los Angeles alone during the 1980s and 1990s. Encouraged by neoliberal deregulation policies, the film industry has reinvigorated itself as an oligopolistic system dominated by several huge companies: MGM, NewsCorporation, Sony, Disney, Time Warner, Universal, and Polygram. These corporations exercise remarkable power over the American economy, social life, and popular consciousness with their endless output of blockbusters, action films, horror movies, and other commercial fare that intersects with an enormous variety of consumer goods available at retail outlets, restaurants, theme parks, and so forth—all of which enter into the hallowed, nearly sacred "cathedrals of consumption" analyzed by Ritzer.[25] Films like *Star Wars*, *Batman*, *Jurassic Park*, *Titanic*, and *Pearl Harbor* exemplify this (hugely successful) kind of strategic cross promotion tied to ancillary markets. At the same time, thoroughly commodified as it is, the new entertainment oligopoly falls considerably short of the cultural uniformity we are led to believe will flow from such concentrated economic power—one piece of evidence for this being the significant growth of postmodern cinema since the 1970s. More than that: From a distinctly *cultural* standpoint, there can be little doubt that film today is far more diverse in both its production and its consumption than at any time in the past, with far-reaching consequences for the larger society.

Of course, the main offerings of contemporary Hollywood filmmaking—not just blockbusters but also mainstream action films, thrillers, horror films, comedies, and dramas—are given shape by the risk-averting, formulaic norms of corporate executives interested mainly in garnering the largest audiences, a mission that favors mediocre product. From this standpoint, surely little has changed over the past century beyond greatly improved technical and production values (notably in cinematography, sound, and special effects); the commodity still reigns, usually through the mechanism of overpowering images and spectacles, now enhanced by digital imaging and new forms of animation.[26] Here a convergence of film culture and consumer culture seems to have been total, with rather devastating consequences for motion picture aesthetics. The result is that glitzy images, surface eroticism, fast-paced action sequences, and technological wizardry reinforced by mind-numbing soundtracks wind up as the stock-in-trade of filmmaking, relegating more well-crafted, socially meaningful, literary narratives to the trash bin. As Thomas Schatz argues, "Well beyond the convergence of moviegoing and shopping, we are witnessing the confluence of entertainment, information, and advertising at a rapid and alarming rate."[27] All of this is true enough. Yet while generalizations of this sort obviously apply to the dominant strands of Hollywood cinema, they fail to account for important and surprisingly widespread *countertrends:* the pluralization of film production and consumption, growth of independent cinema, resurgence of auteurial creativity and status, and diffusion of critical motifs that often get expressed in *opposition* to mainstream culture and corporate values. A dismissive stance by critics toward the established film industry, valid enough for most of what is produced and viewed, is too facile and overdrawn when looking at the full range of aesthetic trends at the beginning of the new century.

Underlying such postmodern countertrends is the twin impact that globalization and the new technology has brought to bear on markets: Today, viewers are no longer restricted to major U.S. theaters, where distribution and exhibition facilities are typically owned and managed by giant entertainment corporations. On the one hand, the globalizing process means that U.S.-made films can expect large enough audiences around the world to make a profit, enabling even the weakest performers in domestic box office to recuperate their initial losses through foreign sales. Meanwhile, the video revolution permits continuous and almost limitless sales for home and classroom viewing, extended over many years, further improving the marketability of even relatively small-scale, independent, politically off-center pictures.[28] Given these outlets, along with cable television, it follows that filmmakers today can afford riskier ventures—and more innovative works—since their investment is virtually guaranteed to reap solid financial returns. Many films rely on more than 70 percent of their revenues from sources beyond the domestic box office, and these sources are frequently more geared to adult viewers at a time when the bulk of mainstream films are pitched to the youth market. This development is all the more significant at a time when the *costs* of movie production are skyrocketing. As video, cable, and DVD formats become more available, film consumers gain increased autonomy at the very moment filmmakers are gaining far more options and flexibility. The point here is not only that more independent cinema is likely to be forthcoming under these circumstances but also that such films (more experimental in style and noncommercial in substance) will be seen by much larger audiences both in the United States and abroad.[29] In this way, epic historical processes tied to globalization and media culture set the parameters for, and simultaneously feed into the ascendancy of, postmodern cinema.

The new cinematic technology, relying heavily on computer-based graphics and editing programs, brings filmmaking into a broadened public realm, allowing for a new kind of local, popular access. Feature films like *The Blair Witch Project*, *Time Code*, and *Run, Lola, Run*, not to mention the James Bond extravaganzas and other spectacular productions, owe much of their raw edginess and freshness of style to the use of low-cost digital cameras and editing devices, a form of technology that is becoming less and less expensive, paving the way toward an even greater explosion of indie films. Digital cameras and handheld DVD players have had the effect of opening up new creative space for directors, writers, and editors.[30] We have reached the point where talented filmmakers can shoot their own movies and, utilizing a website, broadcast the work over the Internet, totally bypassing normal production and distribution channels (paralleling what is happening in the realm of popular music).

It hardly needs to be emphasized that digital technology threatens to alter (indeed, has already altered) many basic formulas that enter into the enormously complex production of motion pictures—a developmental process still in its infancy. Audiences viewing such films as *Zelig* and *Forrest Gump* could see archival footage interspersed with new footage placing, for example, Gump (Tom Hanks) adjacent to Richard Nixon and Leonard Zelig within the entourage of none other than Adolf Hitler. Rita Hempley of the *Washington Post* predicts that it will soon be possible to substitute difficult or recalcitrant actors with computer-generated versions of them, replacing live performers with technological creations. Should this come about, there is nothing to stop a filmmaker with superb technical skills from casting future movies exclusively through computer-generated images that would be impossible to distinguish from real-life persons or situations. These would be expertly digitalized images that, in the future, are likely to be more readily and cheaply available. Beyond that, there will be nothing to keep future cinema from being "shot" exclusively inside a computer, thereby allowing for the jettisoning of movie sets, studio lighting, and, of course, expensive actors; editing, too, would be thoroughly revolutionized. Such "virtual films" could be released over the Internet or cable television, with the most successful of them released to large theaters across the country. While innovations of this sort might give new impetus to postmodern cinema, such a high-tech scenario could produce chaos for the Hollywood studio system, already experiencing competition from independent producers, films made for television, and the Internet.

Observers of the film scene have identified two broad categories of digital image processing: removing unwanted, tarnishing elements from a frame, such as a jet streaking across the sky in a period-piece film, and the computer modeling of scenes as the basis of cinematography. In actuality, digital technology refers mainly to the latter process of creating and photographing digital images. Within this epochal shift, there is the increasingly popular usage of "morphing," involving the transformation of one shape or image into another, as used in such films as *Terminator 2* (1991) and *Sleepy Hollow* (1999). Digital manipulation can be used to eliminate part of an image, such as part of a figure's legs in *Forrest Gump*, or to combine images as in the previously mentioned examples of *Forrest Gump* and *Zelig*. Through computer technology, actors can be filmed in front of a blank screen and then placed in virtually any setting the director chooses.[31] In any case, digital image processing forces us to rethink even further the familiar distinction between "realism" and "formalism," indeed between actuality and fantasy in films—a demarcation that, as we have seen, has already been blurred within the spreading contours of postmodern cinema. The question can be posed as follows: Can motion pictures be regarded in any sense as "realistic" where they contain abundant digitally enhanced (or animated) images? Historically, even moderate reliance on special effects was usually understood as "formalism," but what happens when technological wizardry is designed to further a more compelling sense of realism? Earlier critics like Charles Pierce, Roland Barthes, and Siegfried Kracauer likened film to the field of photography, that is, to the technical reproduction of actual life events and situations. Kracauer observed that "the redemption of physical reality rests upon the assumption that film is essentially an extension of photography and therefore shares with that medium a marked affinity for the physical world around us. Films come into their own when they record and reveal physical reality."[32] But digital imaging now separates film from photography for the first time and allows filmmakers to create a vast realm of "alternative realities" with minimum effort and cost. The blurring of definitions and interpretations through technological innovations upsets the long-standing notion that viewers tend to make sense of motion pictures largely on the basis of assimilating "real-world informational cues."[33] In this fashion, the new technology renders traditional definitions of cinematic representation obsolete.

Yet another revolutionary development is anticipated in the collapsing of new technologies into a unified system integrating the functions of a computer with those of a video player, allowing viewers to do away with the necessity of possessing a computer, a VCR, and a television set. Separate processes would be combined into one superappliance capable of performing a complex multitude of tasks and functions. As Edward Herman and Robert McChesney observe, "Virtually all forms of data and information will be produced and stored in interchangeable digital bits," a process that threatens to overtake film production and viewing as we know it.[34] At the same time, it would be hard to imagine any kind of home appliance or technological system becoming an adequate substitute for an actual, spacious, interactive movie theater. "Going to the movies," as in going to the theater, has for many decades been a deeply ingrained part of American cultural life, and this experience will never be duplicated by or on a computer screen, however large, clear, and "realistic" its digitally generated images. As we write, cinematic engineers are drawing up plans to replace the standard thirty-five-millimeter prints with digital versions that can be beamed to theaters directly from satellites orbiting around the earth, while cable transmissions of film products are also on the horizon. The larger impact of such revolutionary technology on the trajectory of postmodern cinema remains impossible to predict.

POSTMODERNISM: A DUAL LEGACY?

The technical and cultural transformations associated with postmodern cinema can be said to have a dual legacy—a subversion of certain dominant values associated with modernity combined with an aesthetics celebrating mayhem, ambiguity, and chaos that inevitably results in a collapse of human subjectivity. Such duality, of course, captures much of the general essence (and paradox) of the postmodern cultural shift. There is an undeniably radical temperament but one that ultimately possesses little coherent social meaning or transformative vision despite its obviously profound impact on contemporary American cinema and popular culture in general. Familiar themes of alienation, cynicism, and rebellion, cast in new contexts and defined in altogether new ways, depart from Hollywood modernism and its conventional formulas, but they rarely transcend a dystopic, often cynical or pessimistic spirit that infuses films so widely separated in time as *The Graduate* and

American Beauty, *Easy Rider* and *Thelma and Louise*, *Bonnie and Clyde* and *Pulp Fiction*, or *One Flew over the Cuckoo's Nest* and *Blade Runner*. Postmodern cinema is shaped by a milieu of harsh social relations, civic decay, and generalized alienation and powerlessness, upholding few aesthetic or political embellishments beyond artistic fashion and little hope of moving beyond that milieu—much less overturning it. Practically everything remains trapped within the Hobbesian social immediacy it so compellingly (and often brilliantly) illuminates.[35] It is frequently observed that postmodern culture can be made compatible with virtually *any* political ideology—or just plain cynical retreat—but our understanding of postmodern *cinema* is that it articulates more than anything an exhaustion of the established ideologies drawn from the modernism of Enlightenment rationality.[36] The defining features of postmodern cinema feed into this dual and sometimes conflicted legacy: disjointed narratives, rapid or chaotic camera movement, speedy flow of images, explosive special effects, themes revolving around social chaos, death of the hero, dystopic scenarios, and so forth. Such a complex trajectory is no doubt inevitable given the status of postmodern films as equally commodities and art forms, commercial enterprises and aesthetic works, and entertainment and social or psychological statements (whether intended or not). Caught as it were between two worlds, postmodern cinema can be seen as both calling attention to and undermining the idea of a "self-sufficient subject as the source of meaning or action."[37] Today, of course, the two sides are increasingly difficult to separate, just as corporate studio power and thriving enclaves of independent filmmaking turn out to be integral to the same media culture.[38]

One might argue that postmodern cinema should be viewed as more expressly "radical" than the bulk of modernist fare grounded in well-understood production formulas, established genres, cinematic realism, linear narratives, worship of the hero, and neatly resolved endings—a tradition going back to the work of D. W. Griffith and other early Hollywood auteurs. Modernism in the old-fashioned studio system gravitated toward conformism, order, and predictability, even where its social messages here and there might have been critical of the status quo—witness popular and critically acclaimed films like *Gone with the Wind*, *Mr. Smith Goes to Washington*, and *The Grapes of Wrath*. Postmodernism, as we have seen, winds up resisting or subverting conventional rules, canons, and motifs, moving toward forms of technical experimentation and stylistic openness that easily coincide with ambiguity and opaqueness of film content. We know that the postmodern turn gave rise to a series of challenges to an Enlightenment rationality that emphasized historical progress, social hierarchy, cultural uniformity, and individual reason. Yet while postmodernism as a general outlook might be described as critical-oppositional, it can hardly be said to be transformative, or counterhegemonic in the familiar Gramscian meaning, insofar as its celebration of cynical detachment, dystopia, and alienated subjectivity runs counter to the very idea of an alternative *politics*.[39] Where all identities, loyalties, and meanings lack ideological mooring, they are inevitably fluid and elusive. Moreover, as the linkage between postmodern cinema and the media spectacle grows ever closer, we enter into an out-of-control world that seems to confound rational analysis, a world filled with an endless variety of misfits, losers, grifters, and doomed heroes of the sort found in *Zelig*, *Bugsy*, *Thelma and Louise*, *The Doors*, *Barton Fink*, *The Grifters*, *The Last Seduction*, and *JFK*. A searing cynicism and mocking critique directed at the established order is simultaneously pointed toward anything and anyone that might challenge or transform it: The "end of the subject" reflective of postmodernism calls forth a kind of historical quagmire from which there is no likely exit. In his *A World without Heroes*, George Roche writes of precisely this sort of monumental impasse, akin to the Marcusean concept of one-dimensionality, that takes hold in the arena of social discourse and public action.[40]

The steady rise of postmodern cinema since the 1970s demonstrates a profound ambivalence toward the Hollywood studio system among creative filmmaking people: directors, writers, actors, cinematographers, and many producers. Never a majority of the entire industry, they struggle to carve out spheres of (limited) autonomy within relatively fixed corporate parameters.[41] Many on the creative side of film are disillusioned with traditional business and family values, religion, patriotism, and glorification of the military and law enforcement—historically staples of mainstream cinema, especially during its "golden" period spanning the 1920s to the 1950s. At the same time, while these established values might be generally scorned, one finds little in postmodern cinema that calls into question basic operating structures and norms of capitalist society itself. The critical spirit sooner or later dissolves as it runs up against strong currents of postmodern relativism and ludic playfulness that, while appealing to mass audiences, reinforces the popular mood of impotence and cynicism and with it a sense that the dysfunctions and problems of the larger social system lie far beyond the reach of human intervention.[42] The violence, corruption, greed, and alienation that pervade everyday life become, in the postmodern setting, largely a taken-for-granted reality. This new cultural milieu has given rise to an emergent critical public intelligentsia (composed mostly of postmodern auteurs) surely more influential than any comparable stratum in politics, literature, or academia—but this is emphatically no *radical* intelligentsia dedicated to transforming social life.

The subversive element of postmodernism, in film as elsewhere, is tempered if not altogether negated by its emphasis on fetishism of ambiguity, indeterminacy, and pessimism, its failure to confront large-scale social and political discourses, and its ambivalent stance toward social change.[43] There is, moreover, a sense in which postmodernism never defines itself in clear opposition to modernity; it can better be understood as evolving within and alongside modernism, especially in its *cultural* expressions. Both modernism and postmodernism have taken a somewhat tortured path through the various discourses grounded in urban industrial society, with no clear break from one to the other—a generalization especially true of film culture.[44] Still, a number of postmodern currents in filmmaking are transformative insofar as specific conventions are overturned, hierarchies are questioned, an eclectic spirit is upheld, and populist sensibilities are affirmed. At its extreme margins, postmodern cinema embellishes a cultural shift in which everyday life is approached in a mood of diffuseness and even anarchy, made possible by the gradual decline of long-established discourses: preindustrial values, religion, and political ideologies such as nationalism, liberalism, socialism, and communism. The great expressions of corporate power today—media culture, commodification, technological restructuring, globalization, colonization of daily life, and so forth—work incessantly to undermine traditionalism and modernity alike, all the while reinforcing the (postmodern) trend toward increasingly fluid modes of communication. While this tendency converges with and strongly encourages innovative cultural departures, its cynical and dystopic mood blocks any radical break with the past.

If modernism is grounded in classic Enlightenment ideals of reason, scientific certitude, faith in historical progress, and individual self-activity, the countermovement linked to postmodernism sooner or later runs up against its own limits. Lacking any notion of a stable or centered self, postmodern cinema checkmates any prospects for social or political stability. In the end, postmodern cinema constructs a Hobbesian universe filled with a colorful assemblage of antiheroes, drifters, outcasts, marginals, and just ordinary losers. It is enough to revisit any Woody Allen or Oliver Stone film or neonoir movies like *Taxi Driver, Chinatown, The Grifters, The Last Seduction,* and *The Usual Suspects* to fully grasp this point. The "postmodern" characters framed in these films seem perpetually—and furtively—in search of an elusive personal integration and identity in a world overwhelmed by psychological turbulence and social meaninglessness; subjectivity is deflected or undermined at the very moment it is freed from constraints of traditionalism and modernity. As Hutcheon argues, "The postmodernist is in this sense less radical than the modernist; it is more willfully compromised, more ideologically ambivalent or contradictory. It at once exploits and subverts that which went before, that is, both the modernist and traditionally realist."[45] In an environment shaped by commodified, superficial images and spectacles, the spread of disrupted personal and social identities seems inescapable. It is a small leap from a situation where space and time orientations are profoundly unsettled to one where social existence is engulfed by purposelessness and atomized chaos. Insofar as this is true, we can expect the once-awesome power of ideological hegemony (that is, liberal capitalism) to partially lose its grip since elites themselves come increasingly under the spell of pure instrumental efficiency, devoting less and less attention to popular beliefs at least up to the point where oppositional discourses begin to coalesce.[46]

The argument that postmodern cinema coincides with deep structural and cultural transformations in a post-Fordist globalized setting does not imply that modernism (or the studio system that long embraced it) is now actually moribund (far from it) or that postmodernism exhausts all that might be understood within the sphere of independent or subversive filmmaking. Mass audiences in the United States still seem to prefer familiar modernist cinema or at least those with some postmodern veneer (such as blockbusters) that carry strong modernist themes. While postmodern cinema (including most of neo-noir, dystopic adventures like *Blade Runner* and *Pulp Fiction*, some Oliver Stone pictures, and the films of Woody Allen) often enjoys a measure of critical and/or box office success, other strains (such as the ludic films of John Waters) still hover on the margins. Meanwhile, the bulk of independent filmmaking has not been strongly influenced by the postmodern shift as conceptualized here. Thus, the work of John Sayles, always on the cusp of mainstream and indies, fits squarely within the modernist paradigm because of its linear narratives and mostly docudrama structures (*Matewan* and *Eight Men Out*) highlighting struggles against corporate power. More to the point, the 1990s witnessed the growth of a thriving U.S. documentary scene that would not usually be described as postmodern but that nonetheless represents an important cultural development. Dozens of film and video producers carry on work that is often of highly professional quality and that is critical, experimental, and even relatively free of big-business largesse or influence. And the new technologies mentioned previously, like cable television, video, and the Internet, permit the flourishing of such neomodernist trends, for which there is no end in sight. Significantly too, indie cinema has provided a venue for many creative artists otherwise underrepresented: the anticorporate and culturally insurgent films of Michael Moore, the investigative work of Errol Morris, Barbara Trent's exposés of U.S. foreign policy, Barbara Kopple's portraits of American workers, and documentaries ranging from anti–World Trade Organization protests in Seattle to the Chiapas uprising in Mexico to events surrounding the federal assault on the Branch Davidian compound in Waco, Texas. Indie productions by minority filmmakers have likewise been on the increase since the 1980s, as in the work of Charles Burnett, Ang Lee, John Singleton, Gregory Nava, Carl Franklin, and Malcolm Lee, most of whose work lies outside the strains of postmodern cinema as defined here. Throughout the 1980s and 1990s, the various indie productions have been dramatically strengthened by the same twin processes of globalization and technological change that foster postmodern cinema.[47]

THE STIRRINGS OF BACKLASH?

By dint of its departure from the Hollywood mainstream, postmodern cinema runs up against plenty of obstacles and contradictions of its own: cultural resistance to novelty, the eccentric reputations of many directors, viewers' preference for structure and coherence, media indifference, and the familiar problems of raising money. For these and other reasons, it is possible to detect glimpses of a backlash against the sort of motion pictures we characterize as postmodern among producers and consumers alike. From the time that independent or quasi-independent films first appeared in the United States, mostly in art houses but occasionally in major theaters, the reception among both critics and viewers has been decidedly mixed. Allen's films, often criticized for being either too New York centered or too "intellectual," have been met with popular indifference outside major urban centers. Spike Lee's work was commonly viewed as too "controversial" or too "militant" (*Do the Right Thing* and *Malcolm X*) from the outset, a reaction also greeting some of Stone's best work (*Born on the Fourth of July*, *The Doors*, and *JFK*). Except for limited cult audiences, Waters's films have been received with amused bafflement or even derision—that is, where they have been received at all. Scott's *Blade Runner* faced much controversy when first released, and this stigma has remained even through the director's cut version of 1993. While critics paid homage to the film's innovative set designs, powerful visual imagery, and bold narratives, the controversy arose over Scott's bleak dystopic portrayal of a society in which technology looms as a threat to all forms of planetary life. Of course, *Blade Runner* does generate anxiety and discomfort among many viewers, but that is precisely what the picture's most ardent defenders find most fascinating about it—and what gives it a unique postmodern cinematic quality. The point here is that quixotic, experimental films, like virtually all postmodern cinema, have only rarely elicited broad critical and/or popular acclaim whatever their potential social or aesthetic impact.

By emphasizing severely compromised or doomed heroes and by dwelling on repressive, dark, dystopic scenarios, postmodern filmmakers (though never clearly identified as such) risk the wrath of critics and viewers, thus jeopardizing the artistic integrity and commercial viability of their projects. Studio executives, ever eager to maximize returns on investment, tend to prefer straightforward, formulaic, less risky modernist projects replete with linear narratives, conventional themes, standard cinematography, successful and appealing heroes, and, of course, happy endings. When offered scripts departing radically from such approaches, producers usually become queasy, fearing box office disaster. Thus, Terry Gilliam's *Brazil* (1985), an early postmodern retro-futuristic sci-fi film closely resembling *Blade Runner* in content, frightened executives at MCI/Universal, who were appalled by the film's excessively bleak motifs set in a futuristic Brazil. They did everything in their power to alter, soften, and render more "accessible" Gilliam's innovative picture, including attempts to take over the film and reedit it to fit the preferred modernist format. Eventually, Gilliam's darker version won out over the studio's more conventional design, but explosive legal and ethical battles ensued.[48] David Cronenberg's *Videodrome* (1983) and David Lynch's *Blue Velvet*, among others of this genre, were at first treated mercilessly by both critics and mass audiences. Whether in the form of critics' attacks, viewer hostility, or determined studio opposition, earlier films with distinctly postmodern themes and styles encountered stiff obstacles, and such obstacles remain in force today.

Even the highest quality postmodern films are likely to get a mixed reception at best, quite in contrast with the bulk of Hollywood fare crafted for mainly young audiences. It would normally be expected that films immersed in the dark side of life, that depict bleak characters and settings, and that embrace a mood of cynicism and despair would be unpopular with mainstream critics and audiences. There is also an abiding question of style: Postmodern films can be thematically abstruse, disorienting and hard to follow, and even more difficult to interpret. Dahl's *The Last Seduction*, a skillfully directed neo-noir, is so mordant and pessimistic that writer Leonard Maltin has described it as engendering a mood of "unrelenting meanness." Much the same could be said of a good many other films explored here, including even such commercially successful pictures as *The Grifters*, *Thelma and Louise*, *The Doors*,

Pulp Fiction, and *Blue Velvet*. Stone's *JFK* occupies its own niche in the pantheon of mordant, pessimistic, dystopic films, overlaid with strong elements of paranoia and conspiracy.[49] No doubt the "unrelenting meanness" identified by Maltin in *The Last Seduction* refers to a deeper pessimism about social existence in advanced industrial society and the capacity of human beings to make their way in a disorienting Hobbesian world—a world that is (directly or indirectly) the inspiration for so much postmodern cinema. Interestingly enough, Dahl's film was first released on cable television, a medium now more receptive to offbeat, independent films than the major theaters. Cable networks like Bravo, independent film channels like A&E, and some PBS networks provide important venues for the kinds of postmodern films normally screened at the art-house theaters. Such outlets as film festivals often celebrate the work of directors like Allen, Waters, and Cronenberg—opportunities rarely provided by major theaters. Television gives independent directors wider exposure than they might otherwise expect within the general orbit of media culture. This is true because studio executives, driven by fear of box office failure, continue to veto the bulk of postmodern filmmaking—a situation that forces directors to find their own funding sources and search for ways to reduce costs of their projects. Only well-entrenched filmmakers like Allen, Stone, and the Coen brothers seem to have been able to resist the pull of this commodified logic.

As for mass audiences, their inclination is more often than not to avoid what we have identified here as postmodern films, preferring instead new cycles of action–adventure, light comedies, romance tales, horror pictures, coming-of-age films, and the always popular blockbusters, mostly featuring modernist heroes (attractive, charismatic, macho, and so forth) who today still manage spectacular victories against great odds. Pictures like *Star Wars*, *Jaws*, *Superman*, *Aliens*, *Schindler's List*, *Saving Private Ryan*, *Titanic*, *Pearl Harbor*, and the latest James Bond episodes prove that an enormous viewing public can still be targeted for well-worn modernist narratives, themes, and styles, suggesting a powerful backlash against postmodern cinema that has waxed and waned since the mid-1970s. These audiences serve to encourage and legitimate the work of filmmakers like Lucas, Spielberg, Ron Howard, James Cameron, and Michael Bay (good directors all) in their quest to explore and expand neomodernist formats, now constantly upgraded with ever more elaborate, sophisticated, computer-generated special effects. (Here the new technology, as we have seen, is both vital to the postmodern turn and constitutes a certain subversion of it.)

In yet another sign of backlash, some directors initially drawn to postmodern motifs began to defect, opting to move in the direction of safer, more conventional approaches. Thus, Scorsese's *Kundun* (1997), an upbeat, modernist story about the rise of the fourteenth Dalai Lama, marks a radical departure from the director's general oeuvre, which, going back to the early 1970s, helped establish the foundation of neo-noir and postmodern cinema. In his commentary on *Kundun*, Maltin writes that viewers must "search in vain for a Scorsese edge." Likewise, David Lynch's Disney-produced *The Straight Story* (1999) can hardly be confused with such influential post-modern works as *Blue Velvet, Eraserhead, Dune, Lost Highway,* and *Mulholland Drive.* The story of an elderly Iowa farmer who sets out by tractor to visit his ailing brother in Wisconsin, *The Straight Story* was met by critics with such adjectives as "heartwarming," not a description we normally associate with postmodernism or with Lynch. Writing in the *New York Times,* Brendan Lemon referred to Lynch's film as "Disney's cleanest non-animated picture since *Son of Flubber.*" David Mamet, the architect of such postmodern films as *House of Games, Oleanna,* and *The Spanish Prisoner,* elected to write and direct *The Winslow Boy,* described by one critic as a "verbally buttoned-up English period piece." Next, he directed *State and Main* (2000), an ironic comedy about a motion picture crew on location in a small New England village, also on the light side (for him). In similar vein, Stone directed the modernist sports picture *Any Given Sunday* (1999); Allen made the classical, no-frills jazz biography *Sweet and Lowdown* (1999); and Steven Soderbergh, author of *Sex, Lies, and Videotape* along with *Kafka,* moved onto new modernist terrain with *Erin Brockovich* (2000) and *Oceans 11* (2001). Of course, these and other departures might well be ephemeral, but it is more likely they represent a larger backlash against postmodernism in both substance and technique.

The pull of commercialism in Hollywood is difficult to resist even for committed auteurs deeply immersed in the independent scene: There is always the seductive lure of big budgets, mass audiences, and public status that is frequently denied to postmodern filmmakers.[50] Erstwhile independent or quasi-independent directors like Scorsese, Coppola, Altman, Lynch, Ridley Scott, Stone, and Lee now make few pretenses along those lines, in part because they generally seek larger-budget, big-production ventures requiring high-level investments needed to fund star casts, sophisticated technology, and first-rate production values. While many small indie filmmakers refuse to go along with this countertrend, their audiences remain pitifully small—one of the reasons why established directors with strong critical recognition are inclined to yield to the temptations of commercial filmmaking. Take the example of John Sayles: For nearly two decades one of America's leading independent (and unabashedly political) filmmakers, in 1999 he decided to cast his lot with Sony Pictures in the making of *Limbo*, a picture set in Alaska revolving around a series of highly conventional narratives. While never really postmodern in outlook, Sayles was consistently and fiercely antistudio, protecting his creative autonomy with a vengeance, but, in the words of *Premiere* magazine (July 1999), he finally "learned to stop worrying and love the studio." Still other directors, like Tarantino and Cronenberg, seem to have partially or at least temporarily withdrawn from the pressure-laden film scene altogether. Allen, for his part, signed a contract in 2000 with Dreamworks that would carry him through three (presumably more) mainstream pictures.

An interesting recent development in European filmmaking—and in both European and North American television—is the "Dogma" movement, which has self-consciously challenged some basic tenets of what we understand here as postmodern cinema. The trend dates back to 1995, when Danish film directors Lars von Trier and Thomas Vinterberg established what they call "pure cinema" rules outlined in the *Dogma 95* manifesto. They insist upon a "vow of chastity" in which they bid farewell to the assorted "sins" of disjointed narrative structures, stagey and expensive sets, flashy lighting and musical underscoring, computer enhancement, and even postproduction dubbing. (Of course, some of these methods are just as compatible with "modern" as with postmodern filmmaking.) The resulting film style aims to re-create the look and feel of a "real" narrative replete with documentary-style methods. Dogma rules aim to encourage "purer" or more authentic cinematic production shorn of its reliance on high-powered, expensive, flashy Hollywood techniques. The movement is surely as much a reaction against blockbuster formulas as against the stylistic elements of postmodernism. Inspired by this countertrend, a few Dogma films have appeared in Europe, including Vinterberg's *The Celebration* (1998), Christof Kieszlowski's *Camera Buff* (1998), and von Trier's *Idiots* (1998)—works that appear to have influenced some television productions but that, to date at least, have not caught on within the U.S. film industry. The Dogma backlash against postmodern cinema consists mainly in its embellishment of "natural" sources of lighting, sound, music, and so forth—a methodology, paradoxically, that often endows these films with a bleak, mordant emotional tone characteristic of noir, neo-noir, and even a good deal of postmodern filmmaking. Taking all this into account, we argue that any cinematic revolt anchored to Dogma rules is likely to be at best partial and uneven. The particular form of "backlash" most likely to gather momentum might be found in the continued vitality of U.S. independent filmmaking—notably documentaries and docudramas—that seeks a more *critical* reconstruction of cinema along essentially neomodernist lines. As indicated earlier, these filmmakers, including such accomplished professionals as Kopple, Moore, Trent, Morris, Lee, and Ken Burns, view cinema or video mainly as a mechanism for *reflecting* and *interpreting* social problems in American society and throughout the world: social inequality, poverty, rampant corporate power, environmental crisis, and the harsh impact of economic globalization. Expensive in comparison with what they would have cost two or three decades ago, such films are still inexpensive enough for filmmakers and their backers to gather sufficient nonstudio financial support for both studio and nonstudio distribution over time. These directors, while innovative and often even quirky in their techniques, shy away from such postmodern indulgences as disjointed narratives, cynical or pessimistic motifs, characters with whom few viewers can empathize, and dystopic scenarios. The more time-honored radicalism many of these filmmakers bring to their work runs counter to the familiar postmodern mood of pessimism and despair, even if exceptions such as Moore's *Roger and Me* or *Bowling for Columbine* and Kopple's *American Dream* can readily be found.

The development within indie filmmaking toward neomodernist, critical, documentary-style works has strongly influenced recent mainstream Hollywood cinema—witness the release (and popularity) of pictures like *Dead Man Walking*, *Ghosts of Mississippi*, *A Civil Action*, *The General's Daughter*, *Cradle Will Rock*, *The Insider*, *Erin Brockovich*, and *Frida*, all based on actual historical events with critical social messages and the feel of docudramas that even the Dogma movement might appreciate. Even *Titanic* and *Pearl Harbor*, notwithstanding their many historical flaws and omissions as well as their status as blockbuster extravaganzas, can be said to have followed neomodernist impulses as shown, for example, in Cameron's elaborate reconstruction of the ocean liner, his patient attention to historical detail, and his breathtakingly graphic depiction of the ship slowly going down in the Atlantic. It would be ironic indeed, though perhaps not very surprising, if the main countertrends against postmodern cinema were to come from the left rather than from the mainstream part of the ideological spectrum.

CONCLUSION

Hollywood and the
Decline of Political Culture

In his best-selling book *Ecology of Fear*, Mike Davis writes of a "Blade Runner" society where environmental catastrophes, mounting social crises, and the plain misery of everyday urban life will converge to produce an impending nightmarish future for sprawling, fragmented cities like Los Angeles. Reflecting on historical conditions rooted in a post-Fordist, globalized capitalist system, Davis pointedly asks, "Is there any need to explain *why* fear eats at the soul of Los Angeles?"[1] Los Angeles, of course, was the city of Raymond Chandler, James L. Cain, and the rich Hollywood noir tradition—not to mention the upheavals surrounding the bombing of the *Los Angeles Times* building prior to World War I, the Black Dahlia murder, two major riots (in 1965 and 1992), the Rodney King episode, the Charles Manson killings, the O. J. Simpson spectacle, and the more recent exploding Los Angeles Police Department scandal as well as periodic earthquakes, fires, and floods. The unsettling scenario painted by Davis far transcends anything imagined by the great architects of noir or even standard dystopic postmodernism, but it does suggest a milieu (within and far outside of Los Angeles) in which contemporary film directors like Tarantino, the Coen brothers, John Badham, Bryan Singer, Mike Figgis, Peter Berg, and the Oliver Stone of *Natural Born Killers* and *JFK* will easily discover abundant nonfictional material. Today, Los Angeles is the main locus of a renewed noir tradition—fueled above all by the work of African American writers like Walter Mosley and Gary Phillips. Although an important mission of film directors is to bring a semblance of order and meaning to artistic projects, the dynamics of both Hobbesian society and postmodern culture tend to work in opposition to this: Disorder and chaos define much of the social and political landscape, occupying and helping shape the very center of the filmmaking enterprise we refer to as postmodern. Deeply influenced by the growing impact of both economic globalization and media culture, this powerful convergence of historical developments and creative elements of filmmaking mirrors yet another phenomenon, namely, the profound and astonishingly rapid disintegration of American politics.

Here we arrive at one of the historically central meanings of postmodern cinema in the United States—its transcendence and, in certain ways, subversion of the vital world of political thought and action. We have already seen how postmodernism in general represents a broad shift away from the very idea of fixed discourses, identities, and meanings, away from the familiar Enlightenment faith in the blessings of modernity and a progressive vision of the future generally shared by liberals, conservatives, and socialists alike. In some fashion, the crisis of modernity translates into an escalating crisis of politics, with postmodernism assuming the character of the "postpolitical."[2] Well before the events of 9/11, the future appeared to American film audiences as an increasingly murky, threatening, hard to decipher realm much like those dystopic scenes in *Blade Runner, Brazil, Zelig, Natural Born Killers, Seven,* and *The End of Violence.* Within this cultural milieu, the character of social life appears more and more destabilized, purposeless, dominated by images of chaos, and thus quite at odds with the requirements of rational ideological discourse and political organization. This is one reason why the work of many postmodern filmmakers is so elusive politically, so difficult to locate along the ideological spectrum; it can be simultaneously "conservative" and "radical" or "liberal," critical of the status quo (and film industry) yet impotent to identify any constituent elements of collective action or social change, any visionary alternative to the present corruptions and nightmares. Postmodern film narratives and styles are commonly broken, discontinuous, and pastichelike—aesthetically compelling yet scarcely consonant with anything but the most surreal discourses and images. Nietzsche's famous nineteenth-century "death of God" proclamation turns into a more contemporary statement about the "death of the hero" and finally the "death of politics" as we begin the twenty-first century.

By the 1990s, American society had surely become more thoroughly depoliticized, more bereft of political energy, than at any time in recent historical memory—ironic given the extremely high levels of affluence, education, and media and communications literacy, not to mention access to computer technology. Remedies for the most difficult social problems seem increasingly out of reach within the existing public sphere, in part because of expanded corporate colonization, in part because of the erosion of civic culture and the decline of citizenship that seems to mark the postmodern era. The formal shell of democracy barely conceals this process of disintegration, reflected in persistently low voter turnout, loss of community, political and bureaucratic corruption, eclipse of the party system, the spectacle-like (yet exceedingly boring) nature of electoral campaigns, and the narrowing of public debates. What might be called the triumph of antipolitics constitutes a predictable response of millions of people to a system that is actually *designed* to trivialize political discourse and block significant debate while marginalizing dissent or opposition. Alienation from government, politicians, and the public sphere is inevitably accompanied by a generalized mood of cynicism and passivity and, sooner or later, a severe devaluation of citizenship. Thus, "politics" in the United States has deteriorated into a mixture of interest-group machinations, bureaucratic intrigues, and electoral rituals even as corporate agendas and social crises remain largely unchecked. Meanwhile, public dialogue revolves mainly around an interminable series of false promises, empty gestures, media sound bites, official posturing, and soap opera–like scenarios. It follows from this state of affairs that the most dramatic crisis of American society today is one of *citizenship*, or collective empowerment, since this crisis lies at the heart of a society's capacity (or incapacity) to adequately face all the other ones.

The historical trend toward depoliticization finds its expression in present-day Hollywood filmmaking just as in other arenas of cultural life. Not surprisingly, the vast majority of studio executives, producers, and directors want little to do with projects that might be labeled "political," even though the film industry "consensus" remains staunchly liberal with strains of progressivism generally quite visible. Antipolitical attitudes of one stripe or another have now become one of the defining motifs of postmodern cinema. (One highly visible countertrend here is the neomodernist/documentary revival discussed in chapter 5.) Even films that engage politics in a specific, usually critical fashion—such as *Bob Roberts*, *Wag the Dog*, *Enemy of the State*, *Primary Colors*, and *Bulworth*—usually present views of the government, politics, and politicians that are unmistakably jaundiced and alienated. Other pictures with clearly progressive agendas—such as *A Civil Action*, *The Insider*, and *Erin Brockovich*—offer images of collective action that fall considerably short of *political* engagement; they uphold the idea of citizen initiatives only within a localized, delimited (usually legal) sphere.

Here as elsewhere, postmodern cinema inherits and builds on a long tradition of American hostility to politics, feeding on such currents as noir and neo-noir where suspicion, fear, and paranoia rule, where political ideals and good works are scoffed at, and where the public sphere is riddled with corruption, distrust, and cynicism.[3] A good many other films in the pre–New

Hollywood era echoed this motif, including *Dr. Strangelove*, *The Manchurian Candidate*, *Seven Days in May*, and *Easy Rider*. Later, films like Brian De Palma's *Blow Out* (1981) and Alan Pakula's *All the President's Men* (1976) embellished themes of political skullduggery, conspiracy, and cover-ups that, in the Vietnam and post-Vietnam periods, became virtual staples of American political mythology. De Palma's work, including also *Obsession* (1976) and his more recent *Snake Eyes* (1998), dwells especially on themes of paranoia, voyeurism, and surveillance made commonplace by the advent of new technology. While in no sense postmodern, the familiar *Rambo* series of the 1980s—endowing Sylvester Stallone with his signature role—carries the motif of antipolitics to new heights, portraying Stallone as a macho, self-righteous, lonely underdog frustrated with bureaucratic paralysis and political cowardice, taking on "enemies" of the U.S. government at a time when all seems lost. The upper echelons of the American political system are depicted as spineless—incompetent yet scheming in their failure to mount decisive, all-out operations against communists, the Soviet Union, insurgents, and other "enemies." The Rambo character is shown as impervious to risk and danger, manly, heroic, fiercely devoted to military weaponry, and forever willing to lock horns with corrupt politicians and government officials.

Only with the postmodern turn, however, do we fully encounter the spirit of antipolitics in its most developed form—one that reveals (and often seems to celebrate) a Hobbesian world of social turbulence and violent conflict in which official political statements, claims, and discourses are far removed from the actual experiences of daily life. Here *JFK* stands as an ideal expression of this modality—Stone's masterpiece that sets out to disentangle (not always successfully) the myriad complex plots, narratives, conspiracies, and cover-ups surrounding the first Kennedy assassination, by any definition a watershed in postwar U.S. history. Stone (Jim Garrison) indicts a broad network of groups for the murder, including the Mafia, the CIA, anti-Castro Cubans, and other elements involved in the cover-up: the Warren Commission, politicians, journalists, and sectors of the military–industrial complex. The brilliant cinematography employed by Stone reinforces a pervasive mood of chaos, fear, and paranoia, characterizing not only events of the moment but, by extension, much of contemporary American history as well. Politics here amounts to little more than a cesspool of immorality and futility. A number of other Stone films convey similar antipolitical motifs, including *Salvador*, *Born on the Fourth of July*, *Talk Radio*, and *Nixon*.

In the wake of *JFK*, many postmodern-style films of the 1990s featured, indeed championed, this kind of antipolitical sensibility, which began to reflect deep trends at work in American society: decline of civic culture, eroding public trust in government and politicians, privatization of social life, trivialization of political debate, ideological convergence of the two major parties, and the corrosive impact of money in both elections and legislative activity. Where modernist cinema had largely celebrated the (however flawed) liberal-democratic legacy, pictures strongly influenced by the postmodern ethos—mainstream and independent alike—offered a profoundly jaundiced image of American politics and public life. Tim Robbins's satirical treatment of the electoral process in *Bob Roberts* (1992) provides an excellent case in point. Roberts (played by Robbins, who also directs, writes, and sings) is a popular right-wing folk singer running against the liberal Brickley Paiste (played by Gore Vidal) for the U.S. Senate. The embodiment of Citizen Kane–type hubris, Roberts uses his celebrity status and undaunted confidence to assault liberals and their big-spending social programs as the source of virtually every problem faced by the country. The "campaign" unfolds along surrealistic lines, replete with contrived debates, phony scandals, candidate pratfalls, silly manufactured crises, and even a desperate try at Roberts's assassination. In the end, both Roberts himself and his supporters turn out to be bland middle-class citizens with only superficial interest in policies and issues that matter to ordinary people. We have already seen how *Wag the Dog* (Barry Levinson, 1997) satirizes both the political system and media culture, depicting the machinations of a U.S. president who, needing to worm his way out of a White House scandal, establishes a team of advisers and media/political consultants hired with the aim of creating a phony foreign "crisis." A patriotic campaign is orchestrated against a suddenly demonic enemy (in this case, tiny Albania), in the hope of distracting public attention away from the scandal, thereby ensuring the president's reelection just two weeks hence. The main figure behind this bold stratagem is Hollywood producer Stanley Motts (Dustin Hoffman), whose manipulative and propagandistic skills are so well honed that he is ultimately able to dupe an entire nation.

The outright contempt for American politics evoked by these films— indeed, the very substance of their narrative flow—seems at times to have been borrowed from actual historical events. While *Primary Colors* (Mike Nichols, 1998) may lack the extreme cynicism of *Bob Roberts* and *Wag the Dog* (not to mention such documentaries as *American Dream, A Perfect Candidate*, and *The Big One*), its story line appears even closer to real-life history, which in this case involved Bill Clinton's tortured yet successful first campaign for the presidency. More than anything a docudrama, *Primary Colors* reveals in depth the candidate's (and his advisers') endless schemes, machinations, and obsession with money to the virtual exclusion of real policy concerns as the president keeps moving along the road to power. Playing the role of Governor Jack Stanton from a "southern state," John Travolta is able to uncannily impersonate the actual president in a fashion anticipating the White House sex scandal of 1998–1999. An even more scathing indictment of American politics is depicted in Warren Beatty's *Bulworth* (1998), the bizarre story of Senator Jay Bulworth (played by Beatty), who suddenly rebels against his own tepid "conservative Democrat" persona and begins speaking the blunt truth about social issues, in the process immersing himself in the rap music culture of South Central Los Angeles. The film turns out to be one long, protracted, surreal assault on virtually everything that corrodes the body politic: empty promises, boring and meaningless public exchanges, stuffy personalities, corporate deceit, media manipulation, and racism. Beatty's approach to American politics is nothing short of farcical, a Brechtian motif appropriate to the general spirit of postmodern cinema.

This "postpolitical" aspect of American filmmaking today goes beyond any direct appropriation of politics as such, extending also into the sphere of media culture, where the power of images and spectacles contributes so mightily to the depoliticization of post-Fordist society. It is worth emphasizing that those films mentioned previously generally dwell on the famous marriage of politics and the media, which throughout the 1990s had become more solidified than earlier media theorists like Marshall McLuhan had ever imagined. Pictures like *Being There* (Hal Ashby, 1979), *Zelig* and *Network* (Sidney Lumet, 1976), and *Videodrome* (David Cronenberg, 1983) had to some degree already established this terrain, though mainly on the fringes of Hollywood. Allen's *Zelig*, in particular, seemed to offer a McLuhanesque view of media culture, showing how the boundaries between "media" and "reality" had become increasingly obscured, how individual subjectivity and identity were so completely engulfed by the electronic spectacle. This theme was more fully elaborated in the 1990s by a series of widely viewed films that appeared to hit a deep collective nerve: *Forrest Gump* (Robert Zemeckis, 1994), *Natural Born Killers* (Oliver Stone, 1994), *The Truman Show* (Peter Weir, 1998), *Pleasantville* (Gary Ross, 1998), *Celebrity* (Woody Allen, 1999), and *Summer of Sam* (Spike Lee, 1999), to name the most recognizable. While these pictures exhibit diverse narrative content, style, and thematic intent, they share much the same views regarding a mass media that is today virtually indistinguishable from people's daily experiences, where "art" and "reality" achieve the ultimate convergence. Some depict a media culture where violent images, trivialized discourses, and the specter of doom, fear, and paranoia hover over the social life-world. Others present a world in which ordinary people are trapped within a manipulative order made possible by a convergence of technology, media, and popular culture. The general thrust is a deep skepticism regarding people's capacity for critical thinking, self-directed activity, and collective empowerment in a universe where genuine, interactive public discourse turns out to be elusive.

At the beginning of the new century, this embrace of antipolitics by the architects of postmodern cinema has shown no signs of disappearing, all the more understandable given the depressing state of American politics marked above all by expanding corporate power over the government process. Some of these pictures dwell on the seeming loss of national innocence traced back to the John F. Kennedy assassination and the Vietnam War, others depicting a world in which the search for truth and knowledge—not to mention justice and democracy—is frustrated and denied. Thus, *Conspiracy Theory* (Richard Donner, 1997) features a New York City cabbie (Mel Gibson) whose head is filled with assorted paranoid delusions of far-flung conspiracies, who sees vague and mysterious plots everywhere, and whose wildest fears at times even come true. A failed thriller, the film nonetheless depicts with technical efficiency a society dominated by fear, voyeurism, violence, and one harebrained scheme after another. *Absolute Power* (Clint Eastwood, 1997) lays out the sleazy tale of vast criminal plans and cover-ups at the top levels of American government based on David Baldacci's novel, in this case following essentially a modernist format. De Palma's *Snake Eyes*, another frenetically paced but often disjointed thriller, portrays the complex investigation led by a corrupt police officer (Nicolas Cage) into the brutal assassination of the U.S. secretary of defense during an Atlantic City boxing match. This picture too is filled with abundant intrigue, paranoia, and technological surveillance while also plumbing attitudes of cynicism toward public officials. Tony Scott's *Enemy of the State* is presented in the form of an intricate cautionary story about the ominous threat of government and police surveillance, starring Will Smith as an innocent figure framed for murder by a corrupt intelligence officer for unknowingly possessing vital information. Scott's paranoia-laden narrative contains plenty of nefarious schemes, calculated violence, cover-ups, and flashes of technological wizardry to the point where the viewer is immobilized by feelings of a world spinning out of control. Finally, *The Beach* (Danny Boyle, 2000) depicts the furtive quest of a young man (Leonardo DiCaprio) for sanctuary from the chaos and dehumanization of modern society, only to find an even more intolerable living hell in the paradise he seeks on a remote island off the Thailand coast. While the film illuminates the loss of self and meaninglessness of life in the urban, technological setting, its portrait of a quasi-countercultural existence on the island retreat is even more harshly dystopic. Boyle's message seems to be that, horrible as conditions might be in the modern urban quagmire, efforts to create any kind of alternative are doomed to failure given the terrible frailties of the human condition. Put in other terms, we might conclude that the public sphere has become so corroded, even in the remotest corners of social existence, that it has become *universally* bereft of hope and vision.

This rather significant body of films—and a good many others comparable in their dystopic spirit—might be referred to as a cinema of political cynicism. In this context, postmodern filmmaking, like postmodern theory and culture in general, is shaped by elements of discontinuity with the recent past, when larger narratives, discourses, and ideologies furnished a guiding framework for social and political life, and themes associated with the Enlightenment (human reason, universal truths, social progress, and modernity) held sway throughout the advanced industrial world. The result is a collapse of sweeping intellectual claims linked to all-encompassing or totalistic belief systems at a time of rapid change, social fragmentation, depoliticization, and exhaustion of old ideologies, all entering into the aesthetics and social matrix of postmodern cinema. And the ethos of antipolitics fits this universe perfectly.

At its deepest level, the postmodern shift markedly undermines discourses related to the macrorealm of institutional power, governance, and public life; the motif of antipolitics seems to be built into the very logic of "post" interpretations, with large-scale power relations essentially vanishing from sight. Postmodernism reflects and feeds into a generalized mood of pessimism and defeat associated with widespread popular retreat from the public sphere—a trend visible in film as well as society as a whole. In the splintered, discontinuous world of postmodernism, social bonds linked to community and collective action are severely weakened, further undoing the linkage between the personal and public arenas. Targets of suspicion and hostility, governing institutions suffer eroding legitimacy—a phenomenon not troubling in itself for people dedicated to *changing* those institutions but connected to a larger fracturing and devaluing of politics that *is* indeed troubling. Contemporary American society is flooded with a vast array of symbols, images, codes, and spectacles that sooner or later come to dominate the political landscape, distorting issues and discourses in a way that can benefit only the already well-entrenched privileged interests. The advancing corporate colonization of politics is thus left only feebly challenged at best in a milieu where great tributes to such murky notions as populism, diversity, identity politics, and multiculturalism turn out to be yet another cover for postmodern amorphousness and localism.[4]

These developments force us to confront the gargantuan power of media culture in the United States—a media culture that in itself has brought into being a reconstituted public sphere that surely incorporates but goes beyond Baudrillard's theory of simulations and Debord's earlier concept of the "society of the spectacle." In such a media-saturated public sphere, politics begins to lose its crucial element of specificity, meaning any capacity for transformative vision or action; politics unfolds, as it were, in a widening civic or social vacuum, degenerating to the level of spectator sport at best and to corrupt and/or authoritarian practices at worst. Citizens are reduced to the status of "viewers" who are conditioned to absorb and somehow process a constant barrage of ready-made images and formulas that gives rise to some combination of political rituals, soap operas, carnivals, spectacles, and conspiratorial intrigues. Postmodern cinema, as we have seen, takes up these motifs with a vengeance, the inevitable result being that it both appropriates and caricatures the antipolitical mood of the times while trivializing the major social problems that dominate the lives of ordinary citizens. As Neal Gabler argues, an important outgrowth of media culture has been the transformation of popular consciousness into its own theatrical image of illusions, fantasies, myths, and larger-than-life spectacles; life has in fact become a "movie" and vice versa. Thus, "The total cinema world exists in and consists of reality."[5] In this milieu, politics, now more than ever part of the burgeoning entertainment culture, is translated into something akin to Hitchcock's famous MacGuffin—a purely symbolic exercise that is staged, contrived, manipulated, and made elusive, with no distinctly instrumental role in solving urgent problems at hand.[6] Following this script, in many ways American politics has taken on a "ludic" dimension not far removed from the narrative content and style of John Waters films.

Yet this hardly exhausts our concern with political atrophy in the postmodern era: While politics may well be part theater, part ritual, with elements of conspiratorial myth thrown in, the postmodern social landscape remains Hobbesian in its atomized interpersonal relations as well as its pervasive mood of fear, anxiety, and dystopia—and in its sense of impending crisis, breakdown, and doom. Again, Mike Davis's trenchant critique of (postmodern) urban life seems appropriate here insofar as it takes up a noirish "Blade Runner" view of sprawling, fragmented cities as havens of poverty, crime, violence, anomie, corruption, and powerlessness—all the stuff of a mordant outlook informing the noir, neo-noir, and postmodern film traditions. A cruel social world and atrophied political world coexist with and reinforce each other. As reflected in the proliferation of gangs, militias, cults, urban enclaves, and Mafia-style groups, civic strife more frequently takes the shape of narrow self-interest, turf wars, and ethnic conflict, with broader political goals and ideologies winding up submerged on both the left and the right. Of course, elite power (and politics) remains fully intact, but there is a precipitous decline in the *popular* capacity to lay hold of politics for the purpose of forging collective identities, establishing notions of the public good, and carrying out social change. This is surely even more true of the international scene, reflected in the chaos and breakdown of Yugoslavia, persistent strife in areas of the former Soviet Union, ongoing warfare in the Middle East and Africa, and intensified social conflict in many of the largest "world cities" where "civil wars" often assume the form of armed mobs, tribal conflicts, Mafia-type intrigues, and ethnic and religious strife—a situation that, as Hans Magnus Enzensberger writes, is one of the strong legacies of the post–Cold War era.[7] On one side of this dialectic is a shrinking public sphere in which old rival forces stand in naked opposition to each other, lacking transformative potential. On the other side is a world run by multinational corporations and megafinancial empires, governed by no effective planning mechanisms or compelling moral and social principles. Of course, this is global antipolitics with a vengeance, the violence and chaos of which find their way into the scripts, cinematography, and techniques of both postmodern and mainstream Hollywood cinema.

Turning to the apocalyptic events associated with the terrorist attacks of 9/11, we have already argued that the deadly cycle of U.S. militarism and international terrorism has given rise to an unprecedented milieu of chaos, instability, and violence likely to engulf the United States and its citizenry in ways largely unthinkable until fairly recently. Anarchic violence seems to have become a daily fact of global social and political life. Reverberations from 9/11 will surely continue well into the future, just as the war on terrorism promises to be endless, costly, and bloody. The cultural and psychological blow of 9/11 was almost unimaginable, resulting in great disruption of the routines of daily life, economic downturn, political turmoil, and deep transformations in the sphere of international politics. Here again it might be suggested that 9/11 has actually *reinforced* conditions of postmodernity exemplified by a world of heightened atomization, chaos, violence, and dystopia—themes that for many years have been salient to postmodern cinema as we have analyzed it throughout this book. (One impact of 9/11 on Hollywood film culture was already discernible within the first year of the attacks, reflected in the spate of superpatriotic, in some cases xenophobic and racist, combat movies that have gained wide popular appeal, especially among youth.)

Many of the films we have encoded as postmodern engage the present historical context, including such important works as *Blade Runner*, *The*

Grifters, House of Games, JFK, The Player, Pulp Fiction, Wag the Dog, Enemy of the State, and *Bulworth.* While such movies do not fit conventional Hollywood formulas, they nonetheless stand at the critical edge of contemporary film culture today; their "postmodernity" equates with their graphic illumination of fundamental social and intellectual trends. Such trends are undeniably Hobbesian insofar as they lead toward, and perhaps help intensify, those phenomena we associate with the post-Fordist, globalizing, consumer-oriented capitalist order: gross material inequities, social polarization, possessive individualism, civic fragmentation, and impending chaos. Each of these social realities contributes to the erosion of a dynamic public sphere, community life, and collective forms of social and political action.[8] The narrowing of politics, a legacy of liberal-capitalist development that is especially visible in the United States, coincides with loss of moral and public vision and with it the absence of viable countervailing forces or planning mechanisms that might work against growing corporate colonization of the world. The American populace is left with what it can observe through the medium of motion pictures, namely, graphic images (often rather accurate) of the current predicament rooted in the endless pursuit of material self-interest, wealth, and power by corporate elites. Michael Rogin points out that it was precisely this complex, often confusing overlap between life and film that set the stage for a convergence of Ronald Reagan the man and Ronald Reagan the Hollywood image that found its expression in the 1980s presidency. Here the big screen evolves into a massive, glorified, mythological portrait of American life that winds up embedded in the very rhythm and flow of politics.[9] This historical script amounts to yet another restatement of the Hobbesian "state of nature" addressed in chapter 4 and referred to throughout this book. Such a ruthless (and precarious) state of affairs, however, can reproduce itself only as long as the awesome Leviathan (authoritarian state power) has not yet been brought into play as a means of holding centrifugal tendencies in check—a rather frightening prospect for "resolving" the postmodern quagmire. Viewed in this way, the thrust of possessive individualism (tied to a purportedly "free" market) converges perfectly with the requirements of elite control, furnishing what turns out to be a crucial linchpin of the contemporary political wasteland. In this fashion, postmodern cinema and the eclipse of politics represent opposite sides of the same historical logic.

FILMOGRAPHY

Selected Postmodern Films

In the following section, we present a carefully selected list of postmodern films, alphabetically by title. In a brief annotation, we identify postmodern elements contained in each film, consistent with the overall thematic development of this book. Each film illuminates a slightly different aspect of the postmodern condition insofar as each film constitutes a rather unique blend of features including urban chaos, dystopic sense of the future, descent into violence and mayhem, death of the hero, demise of the family (actually or metaphorically), ludic playfulness, and tormented sexuality. For the most part, the tone of these films strikes the viewer as cynical, pessimistic, and mordant, at times fatalistic—especially in their orientation toward established structures and discourses. We recognize that few films exhibit all these attributes. Indeed, the majority of postmodern films can be seen as "hybrids" involving dimensions of modernism as well as of postmodernism, though, of course, the films will contain at least one (and usually more) of these characteristics. The annotated filmography we have compiled here offers a large sampling of postmodern works—most of them by well-known directors—that we view as having the greatest long-term cultural influence.

AMERICAN BEAUTY

Sam Mendes's *American Beauty* (1999) depicts a middle-class suburban family caught hopelessly in a cycle of frustration, disillusionment, chaos, violence, and, ultimately, destruction. The trouble begins when Lester Burnham (Kevin Spacey) enters into a midlife crisis when he quits his job, falls in love with his teenage daughter's best friend, starts smoking marijuana, buys a sports car, and, in short, behaves very much like a man undergoing a severe midlife crisis. His wife Caroline (Annette Bening) soon enters into her own midlife crisis, at which point she has an affair with a married man, takes up target shooting, and finally decides to kill her husband. Alas, she arrives too late: Burnham has already been murdered by a homophobic but, in fact, closet homosexual neighbor, Colonel Fitts. The Burnhams' teenage daughter simultaneously experiences a coming-of-age trauma in which she rejects her parents and falls in love with a neighbor boy. While the entire family disintegrates, Mendes's film contains some elements of redemption that occur only after Burnham is dead, having discovered the intense beauty that life holds. There is redemption in this chaos-ridden film, but it takes place only after Burnham's murder amid powerful currents of family turmoil, sadism, homophobia, and adultery.

ANGEL HEART

Alan Parker's *Angel Heart* (1984) remains one of the more absorbing, if also cynical and mordant, of postmodern thrillers. The film costars Mickey Rourke as Harold Angel, a film noir–style private detective, and Robert De Niro as Louis Cypher, a shadowy character who is actually Lucifer or Satan in disguise. The action begins in Brooklyn during the 1950s after Cypher hires Angel to investigate a missing person, then heads south to New Orleans, eventually arriving at a small Louisiana village. Strange things are afoot from the very outset as the seemingly routine missing persons case opens the gate to multiple murders—each one implicating Angel, who believes he is being framed for the crimes. With a cast of characters that includes an angel and a devil, strange things are likely to occur, and they eventually do. With nearly everyone in the movie murdered in some particularly violent manner, the film descends into random, chaotic violence. Lucifer finally reveals that Angel himself is actually the missing person they are both seeking. It turns out that Angel is controlled by a certain Johnny Friendly, who has stolen Angel's soul to escape from a bargain with the devil in which Friendly pledged the soul in return for musical talent. This bargain is reminiscent of the legendary deal supposedly struck between blues singer Robert Johnson and the devil, on similar terms. Angel emerges as a devil in disguise, or at least he is controlled by a devil, and he becomes the film's ultimate villain (along with the devil, of course). The audience is forced to conclude that Angel will go to hell with Lucifer to make good on Friendly's unholy bargain, leaving everyone with a profound sense of meaninglessness and hopelessness.

ANNIE HALL

Woody Allen's *Annie Hall* (1975) served as an early model for the offbeat, satirical postmodern comedies that followed during the coming decades. Allen's film stars himself as Alvie Singer, a self-absorbed stand-up comedian who falls in love with Annie Hall (Diane Keaton), providing viewers with a prime example of angst-filled relationships that continue to obsess Allen and other postmodern filmmakers. The two appear mismatched from the start: Hall's suburban middle-class WASP world juxtaposed against Singer's urban Jewish lower-middle-class origins. Their lifestyles and personality types seem so contrasting that viewers cannot help wondering why the two ever linked up in the first place. Of course, the explanation is complex, stemming in part from the physical attraction they share for each other—an attraction, however, that fades in the light of their inability to simply get along. While rather cynical about the prospects for man–woman relationships, the film nonetheless exudes a good-humored though ironic whimsy. The families depicted here are dysfunctional, replete with moody, disturbed son and rabidly anti-Semitic grandmother, but still less pathogenic than what would be depicted in his next two films, *Interiors* (1977) and *Manhattan* (1979). Most of all, *Annie Hall* embellishes a quite weak, powerless "dead" hero, not to mention a tortured, ambiguous sexuality as Annie and Alvie discover that even therapy cannot alter the downward trajectory of their relationship.

BARTON FINK

The Coen brothers' *Barton Fink* (directed by Joel Coen, produced by Ethan Coen, and coscripted by the two in 1991) features the title character (John Turturro) as a successful Broadway playwright who makes the fateful decision to write a film script for a Hollywood producer named Lipnick (Michael Lerner). Nineteen-forties Hollywood turns out to be nothing less than urban chaos, as Fink winds up enmeshed in a bizarre postmodern nightmare redolent with urban chaos and descent into what might be called the "cinema of mayhem." Fink is shown as a weak, powerless postmodern hero suffering from an acute case of writer's block. Arriving in Hollywood, he lives in an eerie, almost empty hotel: His only neighbor is an overly talkative salesman named Charlie Meadows (John Goodman), who turns out to be a psychotic killer. Fink finds himself in a typical postmodern conundrum, pitted against the corrupt venality of Hollywood on the one hand and the dark, violent side of the contemporary human condition on the other. Soon after arriving, Lipnick informs Fink that his sole purpose is to tell the simple story of a prize fighter, but Fink never fulfills Lipnick's expectations as he discovers that his only local friend is a self-absorbed neighbor who turns out to be a full-blown psychopath. Laced with mordant irony as Fink is pulled relentlessly to a noirish conclusion, the film ultimately and inevitably descends into a whirlpool of turmoil and violence.

BILLY BATHGATE

Robert Benton's *Billy Bathgate* (1991) adheres to the postmodern tradition of dead, or at least powerless, heroes who fail to resolve the challenges presented by overwhelming forces pitted against them. Based on the novel by E. L. Doctorow and adapted to the screen by Tom Stoppard, the film represents New York mobster Dutch Shultz's decline from gangster kingpin to federal prisoner. Benton, known from his neo-noirs like *The Late Show* (1977), deviates from the modernist formula by having the protagonist fail miserably and then further distances the main characters from the audience by featuring a youthful initiate–hero also called Billy (Loren Dean), who serves as a flunky to Bathgate (Dustin Hoffman) and is never able to work entirely free of mob control. The younger Billy is assigned to watch over beautiful Drew Preston (Nicole Kidman), the girlfriend of Bathgate's top enforcer (Bruce Willis), whom we see being executed by Bathgate (by drowning in the East River) as the film begins. Preston exercises pragmatic flexibility as she abandons her doomed boyfriend and unites with the younger Billy. These characters inhabit a world of urban chaos from which none of them can emerge. Bathgate himself descends further into violence and mayhem as he frenetically beats an innocent policeman to death in his crowded office.

BLADE RUNNER

Ridley Scott's seminal sci-fi thriller *Blade Runner* (1982) is one of the first examples of films crafted in the postmodern style. Scott's film tells the story of Deckard (Harrison Ford), a former special "blade runner," an undercover policeman hired to seek out and kill (deactivate) errant androids who will stop at nothing to escape death through planned obsolescence. Deckard is cold and detached by nature, having inspired the nickname "sushi" given to him by his ex-wife. He combats menacing "replicants" (and the film contains many hints that Deckard is himself a replicant), desperate androids bent on arresting their self-destructive design that renders them inactive after a predetermined number of years in service. Deckard's dangerous pursuit takes him through dirty, crowded streets teeming with mixtures of exotic, mostly Asian ethnic groups. Bereft of most ordinary emotional responses, Deckard is a spiritually dead hero from the very outset. Scott's Los Angeles of the year 2019 emerges as a dark, dystopic sci-fi urban setting that goes back at least as far as Fritz Lang's *Metropolis* (1926). The film depicts urban chaos—crowded, cluttered, rain-soaked streets where neon signs flash their sleaze in several languages. Eerie floating vehicles point toward awesome technological developments, yet it is precisely such technology that poses a threat to everyone alive at the time. Urban chaos, doomed futures, mayhem, and a semiliving hero: This film has everything.

BLOOD SIMPLE

The Coen brothers' *Blood Simple* (1984), their first feature film, affords a preview of their innovative postmodern films that followed, each one now recognized as a classic of the neo-noir genre. Here the brothers present an offbeat, satirical thriller oozing with sleazy atmosphere centered around a small-town Texas bar owned by Marty (Dan Hedaya). Frances McDormand plays Marty's wayward wife, who has an affair with one of Marty's bartenders (John Getz). Marty hires Visser (M. Emmet Walsh) to murder the pair, but Visser double-crosses Marty and murders him instead, at which point Visser goes after the adulterous couple. The resulting struggle plunges this film into an unforgettable "cinema of mayhem" and presents a disturbingly hopeless image of human corruption and social chaos, though in this case the turmoil is located in a small Texas town rather than a dark, sleazy urban setting. The film is defined by gloomy, noirish settings and is brimming with postmodern cynicism along with a sense of mordant, ironic black comedy. It portrays the "death of the hero" as deeply flawed characters murder each other without a trace of remorse, leaving at the end only Marty's cheating though engaging wife.

BLUE VELVET

David Lynch's *Blue Velvet* (1986) takes its audience through a long moral and spiritual descent into social and moral chaos, replete with tormented sexuality, drug binges, and myriad acts of sadomasochism. The young, innocent hero Jeffrey Beaumont (Kyle MacLachlan) discovers a severed ear near his home in the small town of Lumberton, where the local motto is "Let's get those chain saws running." Beaumont soon encounters Dorothy Vallens (Isabella Rossellini), who likes to sing "Blue Velvet" and also enjoys sadomasochistic relations with villain Frank Booth (Dennis Hopper), who sucks down drugs through rubber masks and then likes to carry out acts of violence against individuals. Beaumont is attracted to Vallens, pulled downward into her world of violence, chaos, and, ultimately, death. The savage aggression and utter moral disintegration revealed in these characters can be associated with what might be called the "cinema of mayhem." Beaumont, with his naïveté and inability to ward off the menace of Frank and his sadistic friends, fits the postmodern concept of a rather pathetic, ill-fated, "dead" protagonist, although he ultimately survives by killing Frank in the final scene. In the film's last line, Vallens exclaims to Beaumont, "It's a strange world, isn't it?"

BODY HEAT

Lawrence Kasdan's *Body Heat* (1981) served as both model and inspiration for a cycle of neo-noir films made since. In his directorial debut, Kasdan also scripted the film in the style of James M. Cain's roman noir works that figure prominently in earlier film noir. William Hurt plays a small-time lawyer who meets Mattie Walker (Kathleen Turner) in a coastal Florida town during a heat wave. They become romantically involved even though Walker is presumably happily married. In the time-honored noir formula of treachery, adultery, and murder, Walker proposes that the two lovers kill her husband (Richard Crenna). This film focuses on heat and humidity, both the heat of sexual attraction (as the title implies) and the physical heat and humidity of a scorching Florida summer. The familiar hero's fall and ultimate demise, along with the general descent into chaos and violence, qualifies this film as one of the first postmodern cinematic efforts.

BOOGIE NIGHTS

Paul Thomas Anderson's *Boogie Nights* (1997) examines the pornography industry from what might be considered a postmodern viewpoint. The film stars Mark Wahlberg as teenage porn star Dirk Diggler and Burt Reynolds as Jack Horner, a porn producer and pseudo-father figure to a motley assemblage of hangers-on who include Amber (Julianne Moore) and Horner's female porn star and Rollergirl (Heather Graham), a sex-addicted groupie who demands "respect" from her varied sex partners. Horner, Diggler, Amber, and Rollergirl form a surrogate family, featuring Horner as the father and Amber as the mother, while Diggler and Rollergirl take on the roles of children. Matters end tragically as Anderson employs noirish lighting and icons to give the production a highly cynical tone. Dead, powerless heroes and a crisis-ridden "family" endow this film with postmodern qualities, as does the descent into mayhem and violence that occurs later in the film. Anderson's chronicle of the 1970s porno industry resonates with great irony and pessimism—yet another sign of the postmodern style.

BULWORTH

Warren Beatty's *Bulworth* (1996) takes an irreverent look at American politics after Senator Jay Bulworth (Beatty) enters into a dramatic midlife crisis. First, Senator Bulworth, running for reelection in California, discovers that he cannot stand the sound of his own voice along the campaign trail. Suddenly realizing that his life has been one of endless compromise and self-deceit, Bulworth finally decides to take out a contract on his own life. After taking this step, he visits an African American church in South Central Los Angeles, shocking the congregation with blunt remarks about why politicians ignore the needs of African Americans. He invites three beautiful African American women to accompany him in his limo on a drive, then takes all of them on a wild romp through an after-hours nightclub. Bulworth's old smarmy WASP self begins to evaporate under these exciting conditions, and he metamorphoses into a dedicated, down-to-earth rapper. During this transition, the old Bulworth perishes, to be replaced by an altogether new persona. This film exemplifies a kind of death of the hero as well as postmodern dystopia with all its deceptions and myths.

CAPE FEAR

Martin Scorsese's *Cape Fear* (1991) is a distinctly postmodern remake of J. Lee Thompson's 1962 film noir classic of the same title. It chronicles the story of attorney Sam Bowden's (Nick Nolte) encounter with a psychotic ex-con named Max Cady (Robert De Niro) who has an obsessive grudge against him. Jessica Lange is Bowden's wife, while Juliette Lewis plays his sexually blossoming daughter. The Bowden family in Scorsese's version is not the clean, all-American suburban middle-class family of Thompson's earlier version (played by Gregory Peck, Polly Bergen, and Lori Martin). In Scorsese's version, Bowden commits the crime of withholding evidence in a criminal trial. He is also guilty of having extramarital sex with a young legal secretary (Illeana Douglas). Bowden's high school daughter too is presented as far less than innocent in this version, being strongly attracted to both marijuana and older men. The inevitable descent into violence is typically postmodern, and though the Bowden family survives its ordeal, it winds up compromised again and again, reduced in the final scenes to a lower, primitive form of existence. Scorsese's version contains much postmodern cynicism about personal relations in general and the nuclear family in particular.

CASINO

Martin Scorsese's *Casino* (1995) depicts the rise and fall of two Las Vegas gangsters: Sam "Ace" Rothstein (Robert De Niro) and Nicky Santoro (Joe Pesci). Contrary to a modernist approach, which might follow the trajectory of obviously successful protagonists, Scorsese's film depicts their inexorable decline and, in the case of Santoro, physical demise. Rothstein goes to Mafia-controlled Vegas to oversee a money-skimming operation that systematically drains profits from a casino run by Mafia kingpins. Santoro carries out old-fashioned Mafia retribution, enhanced with a generous dose of postmodern sadism, to enforce Rothstein's harsh and unsparing regime. The two become involved with femme noir Ginger McKenna (Sharon Stone), a high-priced call girl who marries Rothstein for money and then turns to Santoro when the relationship goes sour. All these characters disintegrate by the end, as the film portrays a social milieu that is gradually engulfed by scheming and violence. Here it is not just criminals and gamblers who are depicted as evil, but also local politicians and civic leaders who are shown as no better morally than the mobsters running the casino, thereby reinforcing the relentlessly hopeless spirit of the picture.

CHINATOWN

Roman Polanski's *Chinatown* (1974) qualifies as an early postmodern film that has influenced a number of politically charged detective thrillers of the 1980s and

1990s. Everything works well in this neo-noir picture, which introduces a strong element of urban chaos as the hero, J. J. (Jake) Gittes (Jack Nicholson), encounters a shadowy, murderous, child-molesting tycoon named Noah Cross (John Huston), who teaches him that under the right circumstances an individual should not hesitate to commit even the most grisly crime if it means survival. If the stakes are high enough, Cross assumes, everyone will succumb to the lure of money and power—just as he has done in his own life. The Los Angeles of the 1940s that Cross dominates epitomizes urban chaos, sleaziness, and corruption. Throughout the film, Cross pursues his daughter Evelyn Mulwray (Faye Dunaway), who also happens to be the mother of his incestuous daughter. Forced to give up sexually molesting his daughter, Cross actively pursues his granddaughter out of the same incestuous desire. Incest here takes on new meaning as Cross ends up abducting his underage granddaughter to satisfy his wanton sexual lust. Not only does Polanski present the audience with a "dead" hero powerless to prevent the crime of child rape, but he also furnishes a portrait of the family as crisis-ridden and decaying.

CLUELESS

Amy Heckerling's *Clueless* (1995) is a comedy that chronicles the myriad daily trials of an upper-middle-class teenage girl named Cher (Alicia Silverstone) as she attempts to create her own persona within a Beverly Hills high school milieu where values of possessive individualism are pursued by all means available, where rules are made to be broken. Cher's corporate lawyer father, played by Dan Hedaya, teaches his daughter that she can manipulate and argue her way out of any predicament. He seems to get more pleasure knowing that Cher has cheated to get high grades than he might if the grades had been duly earned. Against this background, Cher attempts to assist her new girlfriend Tai (Brittany Murphy), who, Cher believes, is fashionably challenged and needs to find a special niche in the high school culture along with an appropriate boyfriend. Much like her father, Cher sets out to control her friends but soon discovers that youthful affairs of the heart are quite unpredictable. She begins to doubt her own powers of manipulation when she finds her best plans going awry, and she ends up falling in love with her stepbrother, an older, more "intellectual" college boy, and through him ultimately discovers her own identity. Cher turns out to be far more complex and fascinating than the shallow valley girl audiences encounter earlier in the film. Instead of urban decay, the film portrays an abundance of suburban chaos and moral aimlessness that seems to infect locales such as Beverly Hills. In the end, Cher, as clueless protagonist, emerges with some identity and purpose intact, but she—like most characters in the film—is forced to undergo a serious psychological makeover.

CRASH

David Cronenberg's *Crash* (1996) explores the bizarre world of people who get themselves sexually turned on by watching, participating in, or simulating automobile crashes. The hero, James Ballard (James Spader), discovers that his beautiful wife Catherine (Deborah Unger) fantasizes about being in car crashes. Ballard too develops a strange attraction to automobiles and violent crashes after he himself suffers serious injuries in a nasty collision. During recovery, Ballard encounters an attractive physician (Holly Hunter) in the hospital who also fantasizes about crashes. The two wind up involved in an intense sexual relationship consummated inside (stationary) cars. The car-and-sex-enthralled couple next encounter an improbable "benign psychotic" crash researcher named Vaughn (Elias Kotias), who introduces them to a demiworld of former crash victims who have an aberrant fascination with crashes. Addicted to viewing and, at times, to participating in "auto-eroticism," these people refer to themselves as "benign psychotics" who become sexually aroused by automobile violence. Soon the film moves into the realm of surrealistic car crashes juxtaposed with heated, offbeat sex between various people inside the cars. Ballard and the others proceed to have car sex with each other, crossing gender lines in what turns out to be a car sex serial orgy that brims with blood and gore. Another powerless hero, Ballard begins as a passive recipient of female sexual overtures in backseats of cars and quickly advances from passive neophyte to passionate devotee. Urban chaos certainly describes the crash-strewn setting, with automobile and body parts littering the mise-en-scène. The world of crash enthusiasts constructed by Cronenberg reveals yet another kind of dystopic vision that is so ubiquitous in postmodern films.

CRIMES AND MISDEMEANORS

Woody Allen's *Crimes and Misdemeanors* (1989) marks a certain departure from Allen's earlier postmodern comedies. In this psychological thriller, Allen tells two stories by using two protagonists. The main story features Judah Rosenthal (Martin Landau), a prominent physician who becomes involved romantically with a flight attendant (Anjelica Huston). After some hesitation and partly out of desperation that his mistress will reveal their relationship to his wife, Rosenthal decides to accept his outlaw brother's offer and have his mistress murdered. After the murder occurs, Rosenthal has some difficult moments wrestling with intense guilt, but he manages to overcome his conscience and somehow reconcile himself with his horrible deed. The other protagonist, independent film producer Cliff Stern (played by Allen), reluctantly takes on a job of creating a documentary about his brother-in-law, a self-important comedy maven named Lester (Alan Alda). Stern cannot stand Lester, who adds insult to injury by seducing a young television editor (Mia

Farrow) with whom Stern had fallen in love. In this rather mordant film, the less merit a character has, the more it appears he or she succeeds. Hence, the vacuous Lester wins the beautiful woman, while ruthless Dr. Rosenthal gets away with having his girlfriend murdered. In many respects, both characters embellish the moral chaos of flawed, "dead" heroes. Because of the dark cynicism surrounding this film, it ranks as one of the most disturbing yet provocative of postmodern works.

CRY-BABY

John Waters's *Cry-Baby* (1990) contains all the vital elements of a postmodern musical comedy. Set in the 1950s, this film features no less than eleven dance numbers staged around the hero, Cry-Baby (Johnny Depp), so named because he is constantly reduced to tears at the thought of his parents being executed in the electric chair. Depp plays a lovable juvenile delinquent who falls for a beautiful rich girl (Amy Locane). The plot follows the Romeo and Juliet thwarted-romance formula, but the action between Depp and Locane is subsumed by the rock-and-roll dance aspects of the film. Consistent with other Waters films, the light treatment of romantic conflict, coupled with the Elvis Presley–like song-and-dance performances of Depp and other characters, gives this film a satirical or ludic postmodern dimension. The film demonstrates perfectly the postmodern undercutting of "serious" cinema through the medium of satire—in this case the teenage-exploitation genre. *Cry-Baby*, like most Waters pictures, ridicules the modernist hero quests through use of abundant humor and irony.

DEAD RINGERS

David Cronenberg's *Dead Ringers* (1988) features two ill-fated heroes who happen to be identical twins, both of them successful gynecologists played by Jeremy Irons. The twins function almost as one person, suffering from their tragic failure to differentiate themselves and form viable (separate) personalities. In this case, the characters never become fully independent, unified persons but see their filial bonds stretch to the breaking point when they fall in love with the same well-known actress (Genevieve Bujold). Failing to settle the matter of romantic competition, the brothers fall under the influence of drugs and find their lives gradually imploding all the while. Their self-destruction occurs in typical postmodern style, eventually leading to their mutual suicides as they use surgical tools to "separate" themselves from each other as if they were physically conjoined twins. Their confused identities lend a strong air of chaos to this exceedingly dark film. The society they inhabit, furthermore, exhibits all the earmarks of a postmodern dystopia. A darkly pessimistic tone, mordant dialogue, and theme of doomed heroes make this film one of the best examples of postmodern cinema.

DECONSTRUCTING HARRY

Woody Allen's *Deconstructing Harry* (1997) is a postmodern tour de force, beginning with its very high-sounding philosophical title. Allen's hero is a writer named Harry Block, who has a terrible case of writer's block as the movie begins. Block experiences a jarring midlife crisis brought on by a series of problems, including his girlfriend's (Elizabeth Shue) decision to marry his best friend (Billy Crystal). Like many Allen protagonists, Block lives in Manhattan. In a plot bearing strong resemblance to Igmar Bergman's *Wild Strawberries*, the hero has been invited to a small college in upstate New York that wants to honor him for his writing. At this point, he decides to kidnap his son from his ex-wife's legal custody, then picks up a brash hooker (Judy Davis) to accompany him on his upstate trip. As usual, things fall apart, at which point he is arrested on charges of kidnapping shortly after he arrives at the college. Pervasive elements of social chaos, dystopic images of social life, and a weak, tormented hero make this film easy to identify as postmodern.

DEVIL IN A BLUE DRESS

Carl Franklin's *Devil in a Blue Dress* (1995) extended the neo-noir genre to African American culture in southern California. Based on the work of Walter Moseley, the film centers around Easy Rawlins, a down-and-out private detective (Denzel Washington) hired by a sleazy underworld figure (Tom Sizemore) to find Daphne (Jennifer Beals), a mysterious white woman who is somehow implicated in a series of crimes. The hunt leads to an African American district of Los Angeles, around Central Avenue, in 1948. Rawlins goes in search of Daphne but instead encounters a world of violence, murder, and deceit. He epitomizes the postmodern hero who is forced to come to grips with the city as an evil, treacherous environment where nothing is as it seems and all manifestations of danger lurk everywhere. Franklin's work is rife with a mood of urban turmoil with its decent into a social Darwinian ethos and tormented sexuality. Washington's Rawlins is presented as a weak postmodern hero who is all to easily seduced, tricked, and manipulated by ruthless individuals who seem to appear around every corner.

THE DOORS

Oliver Stone's *The Doors* (1991) deconstructs what might be considered a quintessential postmodern hero—1960s rock star Jim Morrison of the Doors, a man pushed by social pressures of his time and by inner demons to a downward trajectory leading to a tragic, premature death. Morrison (Val Kilmer) develops at an early age into an extremely talented songwriter, poet, and performer, but the influence of the counterculture, along with his own unrestrained egoism and hedonism, lead to his downfall and self-destruction. Stone graphically and brilliantly depicts Morrison's fall from unparalleled rock icon to a self-absorbed alcohol- and drug-abusing wretch of a human being. Morrison's seemingly predictable fall from grace—beyond any possible redemption—epitomizes the harrowing condition of some postmodern heroes, reflecting a loss of innocence for both the individual and American society as a whole (a familiar Stone motif). Stone's treatment of the rock culture evokes postmodern cynicism, but in this case it also calls into question not only Morrison's lifestyle but also the entire socioeconomic system that creates, lionizes, destroys, and then romanticizes such tragic heroes.

DO THE RIGHT THING

Spike Lee's *Do the Right Thing* (1989) brings all the elements of postmodernism together in a film highlighting racial and ethnic conflicts in contemporary New York City. Lee's main protagonist, Mookey (played by Lee himself), is a pizza delivery man for an Italian restaurant located in Harlem. The pizzeria setting develops into a focal point of rising conflict involving African Americans, Puerto Ricans, and Koreans as well as Italian Americans. The strife revolves around such sensitive issues as whose cultural icons will be displayed in the restaurant and who will determine what brands of consumer items like beer will be carried in the local grocery store. It all intensifies during a summer heat wave that symbolizes a number of deep tensions that seem to define community life. Powerfully felt differences ultimately erupt into violence as outraged residents destroy the pizzeria in one of the crucial scenes in the film. With its graphic depiction of urban chaos, violence, cultural strife, tortured sexuality, and heavy cynicism regarding the future, Lee's seminal film constitutes an ideal example of postmodern filmmaking.

DOUBLE JEOPARDY

Bruce Beresford's *Double Jeopardy* (1999) is a postmodern thriller about a young woman named Libby (Ashley Judd), who seems happily married to Nick (Bruce Greenwood). The two have a young son, but trouble erupts after Libby awakens on their yacht covered with blood. She picks up a bloody knife just in time to be spotted by the Coast Guard and then finds herself charged with her husband's murder. Six years later, she gets paroled, then sets off to recover her son and avenge herself against her husband. During her stay in prison, however, Libby discovers that her husband has moved away and changed his name. At last catching up with him, she provokes a confrontation that ultimately ends with Nick attempting to murder

Libby, then being killed himself in a shootout with a probation officer (Tommy Lee Jones). Although Libby finally prevails in her protracted struggle with her husband, she is forced to give up nearly everything she values, including her freedom and her reputation.

DREAM LOVER

Nicholas Kazan's *Dream Lover* (1994) expresses the strongly postmodern fear of dangers that lurk within personal relationships and intimacy. Recently divorced architect Ray (James Spader), intent on finding a new relationship, finds seemingly warm, vivacious Lena (Madchen Amick). After a brief courtship, the two marry, but Ray is plagued by recurring nightmares in which carnival performers laugh at him for having married Lena. Doubts about his wife begin to creep into Ray's consciousness until he finally realizes that she has been deceitful and adulterous (with one of his closest friends). Exploding into rage, Ray falls directly into Lena's trap and finds himself a declared lunatic imprisoned in a mental institution. Later, Ray is able to save himself by resorting to Lena's own ruthless methods of trickery and deception when he lures her to visit him in the institution, then strangles her to death while he calmly explains that he cannot be found guilty of her murder because he is legally insane. "In a year I'll be cured, and they'll have to let me out," he tells her in the midst of the murder. Through this violent act, Ray manages to redeem himself and thereby save his life, although he pays an extraordinarily high price for survival: He descends to the villainous level of Lena in order to prevail. In this film, therefore, the hero survives only by becoming a despicable villain himself—a condition of remarkable postmodern irony.

ED WOOD

Tim Burton's *Ed Wood* (1994) stars Johnny Depp as Edward D. Wood Jr., voted by the Motion Picture Academy of America as the "worst Hollywood director of all time." This fact alone makes Wood the ideal postmodern hero who, thanks in part to Depp's outstanding performance, manages to keep audiences laughing at his cluelessness in directing such notorious bombs as *Glen or Glenda* and *Plan Nine from Outer Space*. At one point, Wood, beset with self-doubt after being scolded by his own film crew, retreats to a local bar hoping to drown his sorrows, where he encounters none other than Orson Welles. Wood asks Welles, generally considered among the best directors ever, whether he should give up in the face of strong opposition and surrender his "vision" of the film (*Plan Nine*). Welles ironically encourages the younger, far less talented filmmaker to persist in his work. Bolstered by

Welles's counsel, Wood continues to make films devoid of artistic value. Wood, falling into a miserable life of frustration, defeat, and alcoholism, eventually winds up a "dead" hero in more ways than one.

THE END OF VIOLENCE

The plot of Wim Wenders's *The End of Violence* (1997) revolves around an ultrasecret government project that places a network of high-powered cameras capable of photographing every single inch of Los Angeles from a secret base in the Griffith Park Observatory. The chief computer scientist at work on the project (Gabriel Byrne) e-mails a Hollywood film producer (Bill Pullman) a top-secret file containing detailed information that, if leaked to the press, would cause the whole enterprise to be scrapped. The unsuspecting producer receives the file, labeled "Top Secret," and immediately orders his secretary to delete it—but not before its discovery by government cyberspies. The producer is kidnapped by two hit men who plan to kill him, but before they can execute their plan, the two break out into a violent quarrel over whether they should go ahead with the murder. We soon discover that the hero has escaped after apparently overpowering the two thugs and literally blowing their heads off. It turns out that shadowy security forces have killed the two hit men from afar, while the hero remains alive and is redeemed but not before losing his current work in progress and nearly losing his wife (Andie MacDowell). The Los Angeles cityscape depicted in this film is filled with urban chaos, much as in the noir classics. More than that, the city emerges as an Orwellian dystopia where individual privacy and home security are almost entirely lacking.

FARGO

Fargo (1996) extends and refines the postmodern careers of director Joel Coen and writer/producer Ethan Coen (*Blood Simple, Barton Fink*). In this film, the Coen brothers depict a "perfect crime" that goes tragically wrong: Minneapolis car dealer Jerry Lundegaard (William H. Macy), having badly overextended his credit with the factory that supplies him, decides to have his wife kidnapped for ransom by a pair of ordinary crooks. The plan is for Lundegaard to obtain the ransom money from his wife's wealthy father, pay off the thugs, and pocket the rest with the intent of saving his credit and dying business. In typical postmodern fashion, the plan quickly unravels when the thugs are stopped by a highway patrolman. One of them shoots and kills the officer, at which point the crooks have a falling out that results in one murdering the other and destroying the body in a woodchopper. Frances McDormand plays a quirky, pregnant rural police officer who is able to solve the grisly crimes and capture the at-large crooks. Although her character proves victorious, the underlying thrust of this film is the Coen brothers' portrait of the criminal mind-set and lifestyle. Like some other Coen brothers films, *Fargo* has achieved nearly cult status among audiences fascinated with this genre of offbeat thriller.

FATAL ATTRACTION

Adrian Lyne's *Fatal Attraction* (1987), considered a shocking exposé of the contemporary nuclear family when first released, continues to generate intense debate today, having become probably the most widely discussed film in recent history. What fascinates viewers and critics most about this film is, of course, the deep sexual intrigue of an affair the produces sexual obsession and ultimately self-destruction. This film explores a favorite theme of recent films—the "one-night stand" sexual encounter, which usually begins at a bar or party, along lines of *Looking for Mr. Goodbar*. Here the key actors include Dan Gallagher (Michael Douglas) and Alex Forrest (Glenn Close), who meet at an office party and quickly take advantage of the fact that Gallagher's wife (Anne Archer) is out of town, dropping by Alex's apartment for a bout of steamy sex, including a heated though furtive encounter on a freight elevator. Douglas and Close inject an initial element of playfulness into their rendition of frenzied sex, but the mood quickly sours when Alex refuses to leave the affair gracefully once Gallagher's wife returns. Instead, she sets out to wreck the Gallagher marriage, finally deciding to murder the wife, who she is convinced stands in the way of her goal of winning over the husband. The film portrays the family as violent battleground between the husband's desire for sexual pleasure outside marriage and his wife's fierce determination to keep the marriage intact despite her husband's philandering. Lyne's message seems to be that it is the very permissiveness of society that is so menacing—hence the aptness of the title. It suggests that extramarital sexual encounters are never worth the threat they pose to the nuclear family structure.

THE GRIFTERS

Stephen Frears's *The Grifters* (1990) stars John Cusack as Roy, a small-time hustler who comes into conflict with his girlfriend Myra (Annette Bening), a sex-obsessed con artist, and his mother Lily (Anjelica Huston), who works for a Baltimore gang leader. Frears's setting is Los Angeles, mainly the neighborhood bars where Roy operates his cons and the racetrack where Lily collects mob gambling money (and diverts some for her own personal use). Roy must fend off Myra's attempt to interest him in joining her for a "long con," a riskier enterprise than the "short con" that is Roy's specialty but one for which there is a greater payoff at the end. Roy is compelled to fend off Lily, his own mother, who has come to beg for his secret stash of cash, the loot from his hustler schemes. Lily attacks and murders Roy after killing Myra in self-defense, at which point the film descends rapidly into a cycle of murder and mayhem. Greed, deception, and violence underlie the entire film, giving it an overall mordant aura. In failing to survive Lily's attack, Roy becomes very much the dead hero, while, in good postmodern style, the future is shown to be extremely bleak as Lily flees the scene of her son's killing in order to escape the certainty of mob reprisal.

THE HAND THAT ROCKS THE CRADLE

Curtis Hanson's *The Hand That Rocks the Cradle* (1992) is the story of a ruthless, vengeful attack on the Bartel family, an innocent young couple with a new baby. The Bartels hire a nanny, Peyton Flanders (Rebecca DeMornay), who harbors a secret grudge against them stemming from Claire Bartel's sexual assault charges against Peyton's gynecologist husband—charges that were factually based. The totally ruined doctor subsequently commits suicide, at which point Peyton tries everything in her power to destroy the Bartel family out of misplaced revenge for her dead husband and baby. The family eventually finds the resources to survive and defeat this force from hell. The film depicts an apparently peaceful social world that turns out to be criminal, vengeful, and duplicitous, the Bartels becoming innocent victims of a postmodern world where smiling faces conceal duplicitous, violent assaults on the supposedly peaceful, harmonious inner sanctum of the family.

HANNAH AND HER SISTERS

Woody Allen's *Hannah and Her Sisters* (1986) is one of the director's more complicated and serious films. It depicts the romantic lives of three attractive sisters, beginning with a mise-en-scène at a family Thanksgiving dinner they attend and concluding with a similar Thanksgiving dinner two years later. Hannah (Mia Farrow), the oldest sister, is married to an agent named Elliott (Michael Caine), but Elliott falls madly in love with Hannah's youngest sister, Lee (Barbara Hershey). By the end of the film, Allen's character (a television producer) winds up married to the middle sister (played by Carrie Fisher). In its brilliant depiction of intricate sexual affairs along with the tendency of present-day couples to follow the path of frequent partner dumping and serial monogamy, the film is one of the seminal representations of family pathos, disintegration, and possible renewal.

HOUSE OF GAMES

David Mamet's *House of Games* (1987) was the initial foray into filmmaking by writer Mamet. Here Dr. Margaret Ford (Lindsay Crouse) finds herself drawn into a criminal con game of manipulation and deceit perpetrated by Mike (Joe Mantegna), a persuasive con artist who feeds on Dr. Ford's attraction to the dark side of human existence. Dr. Ford extricates herself from a con scheme by noticing that the gun a gambler threatened to use against Mike was only a child's squirt gun filled not with bullets but with water that drips out of the barrel. Although she escapes with her $6,000, Dr. Ford is compelled to return the following day, at which time she becomes ever more deeply involved in a shadowy world of duplicity and illusion. Dr. Ford soon discovers that she is hopelessly attracted to the world of crime and scheming herself, seduced most likely by the adventure and risk. The film's unyielding cynicism about human behavior endows it with a distinctly postmodern motif.

JFK

Oliver Stone's epic *JFK* (1991) focuses cinematic attention on two quintessential postmodern heroes—President John Kennedy and New Orleans District Attorney Jim Garrison (Kevin Costner). Garrison investigates a shadowy right-wing underworld of homosexuals and anti-Castro Cubans, including wig-wearing David Ferrie (Joe Pesci), mysterious businessman Clay Shaw (Tommy Lee Jones), and gay prostitute Willie O'Keefe (Kevin Bacon). His investigations uncover a vast, byzantine conspiracy to murder Kennedy that eventually leads to the Mafia, anti-Castro Cubans, and the military–industrial complex itself. Stone presents nothing less than a government-centered conspiracy to assassinate its own leader—a corrupt, venal, and out-of-control apparatus posing a threat to anyone brave enough (or foolish enough) to challenge it. Perhaps more than any other film of the 1990s, *JFK* exudes paranoia about every face of the power structure, so that viewing it can easily generate feelings of immense powerlessness in the face of insuperable forces. "Justice" and "democracy" within such a perverted system can only be mythical, illusory. *JFK* contains all the elements of postmodern cinema analyzed in the text, including death of the hero, demise of the family, and dystopic sense of the future.

L.A. CONFIDENTIAL

Curtis Hanson's *L.A. Confidential* (1997) is probably the most celebrated neo-noir since *Chinatown*. Winner of two Academy Awards (best actress—Kim Basinger, best screenplay adaptation—Brian Helgeland and Curtis Hanson), this film, revolving around police department culture in the 1950s, received seven other Academy Award nominations. Kevin Spacey plays Sergeant Jack Vicennes, who made his professional reputation by arresting Robert Mitchum on marijuana charges in the late 1940s, and Danny DeVito plays Hollywood gossip editor Sid Hudgeons, while Russell Crowe and Guy Pearce play other Los Angeles cops. Everyone is caught up in an era of Hollywood glamour, with Sergeant Vicennes serving as adviser to the *Badge of Honor* police television series and Basinger taking up the role of a Veronica Lake look-alike. Hanson shows the Los Angeles Police Department as being totally corrupt, with the media not far behind. In the end, the police force loses out although not before the film is overcome by protracted flashy images of violence and mayhem that point toward a familiar Hobbesian state of urban chaos and dread.

THE LAST SEDUCTION

John Dahl's *The Last Seduction* (1994) offers a bleak picture of human greed, corruption, deceit, and propensity for cruelty and violence. Linda Fiorentino plays Bridget, an attractive but ruthless insurance executive who convinces her physician husband, played by Bill Pullman, to sell large caches of illegal drugs to criminals. Once her husband secures the loot, however, Bridget absconds with it to a small town where she hides from her husband's inevitable quest for vengeance. There she picks up Mike, a weak-willed local man (Peter Berg) who comes under her sway and agrees to murder her husband even though he does not know his potential victim's true identity. Once Mike discovers the true identity of his intended victim, however, he refuses to go through with the murder, at which point Bridget calmly sprays a lethal dose of Mace down her husband's throat and then frames Mike for the crime. This film presents a chillingly bleak view of the American family, shown not only as dysfunctional but as highly toxic and dangerous. It embraces a social dystopia populated by weak-willed men and one obsessively strong-willed femme noir.

MAGNOLIA

Paul Thomas Anderson's *Magnolia* (1999) explores the demise of the postmodern family. Dying tycoon Earl Partridge (Jason Robards) is tormented about his past sins, including cheating on and later walking out on his first wife and their only son, Frank Mackey (Tom Cruise). Partridge is married to a much younger woman named Linda (Julianne Moore). Events force the abandoned son Frank, now a slick workshop organizer teaching men how to appear "sensitive" and "sincere" enough to seduce women, to visit his estranged father on the latter's deathbed. Other characters include Jim (John C. Riley) and Claudia (Melora Watters), a drug addict who eventually agrees to date Jim. The seemingly mismatched couple become involved, while the Partridge/Mackey family eventually reconciles—though it is on Partridge's deathbed. The film depicts the postmodern family, replete with all its conflicts, abandonments, and odd pairings—a far remove from the *Leave It to Beaver* culture.

MANHATTAN

Woody Allen's *Manhattan* (1979) represents a significant development in the shift to-ward postmodern cinema. Themes here include a series of tormented sexual relation-ships in which the entire cast of characters becomes involved. We have the angst-ridden middle-aged television writer Isaac Davis (Allen) having an affair with seventeen-year-old Tracy (Mariel Hemingway), along with Davis's philandering college professor friend Yale (Michael Murphy). Both men become enamoured with Mary, a would-be in-tellectual played in glib, pretentious style by Diane Keaton. In an unusual twist, even for Allen, the only relationship in this film that has any chance of survival is the rather bizarre affair between Davis and Tracy. As in *Annie Hall* before it, this film captures all the fragility and superficiality of romantic relationships viewed from the perspective of existential angst. Shot in campy black and white, *Manhattan* depicts New York City as a sexual dystopia filled with shallow, vexed, corrupt relationships, yet Allen seemingly cannot avoid revealing his love for the city by showing its bohemian charm and spec-tacularly beautiful vistas. Beneath these vistas, however, lies the darker side of contem-porary urban life, which Allen also depicts with brilliant insights.

NASHVILLE

Robert Altman's *Nashville* (1975) was one of the earliest postmodern films and is considered one of the director's greatest achievements. As the title suggests, the film chronicles the country music scene in Nashville, featuring Ronee Blakely, Ned Beatty, Karen Black, Keith Carradine, Geraldine Chaplin, Shelley Duvall, Henry Gibson, and Lily Tomlin. With his reputation as a brilliant if iconoclastic and unconventional filmmaker, Altman has little difficulty attracting a large caste of talented actors, at one point even having Elliot Gould and Julie Christie play-ing themselves on a public relations tour. The film takes a hard, critical look at country music production in the 1970s, with Altman striking a highly ironic tone throughout—a mood reinforced by songs from the Grand Ole Opry to the ama-teur nights at taverns and roadhouses. Established country singers like Barbara Jean (Blakely), shown as a woman on the verge of a nervous breakdown, and Haven Hamilton (Gibson), a conservative older singer with a repertoire of semi-patriotic ballads, epitomize those who have arrived in the Nashville music busi-ness. Others, like the waitress (Gwen Welles) who sings badly off key and is forced to perform a humiliating striptease at a stag party, represent the wanna-bes flocking to Nashville with hopes of becoming stars. *Nashville* is essentially a cross between a country musical and a sociopolitical satire on the music business. Alt-man's scattered narrative overlays both elements with a thick layer of postmodern cynicism, which really settles in after Barbara Jean is assassinated by an angry young man in a military uniform.

NATURAL BORN KILLERS

Oliver Stone's *Natural Born Killers* (1994) features Mickey (Woody Harrelson) and Mallory (Juliette Lewis) as a sex-and-blood-crazed young couple who embark on a crime spree where, in the pattern of *Gun Crazy* and *Bonnie and Clyde*, they murder no fewer than fifty-two people—a crime spree begun after the two cold-bloodedly murder Mallory's parents. They murder her father, played by Rodney Dangerfield, on the pretext of his abusing and molesting his daughter, then kill her mother for failing to report the daughter's abuse by her father. After these murders, the couple moves off into an orgy of violence and sex virtually unmatched by any other contemporary film, graphically exhibiting serial murders in gory detail. In keeping with Stone's aim, the film turns into a satire of violence both in films and in society as a whole. There are harsh criticisms of the mass media, shown in the vehicle of television producer Wayne Gale (Robert Downey Jr.), who in fact glorifies the outlaw couple. This film appears to set a record for dead bodies on screen, while characterization of the sex–violence linkage is chillingly postmodern.

THE OPPOSITE OF SEX

Don Roos's *The Opposite of Sex* (1998) is a postmodern comedy about a rather atypical family: the Truitts. At the beginning of the film, teenaged Deedee Truitt (Christina Ricci) decides to run away from home and live with her gay half-brother Bill (played by Martin Donovan). Truitt quickly falls for Matt (Ivan Sergei), Bill's youthful live-in lover, only to later reveal that she is pregnant, at which point they run away to Los Angeles with a chunk of Bill's money. They are pursued and eventually discovered by Bill and his friend Lucia (Lisa Kudrow), a spinsterish schoolteacher with a hopeless crush on Bill. Matters become even more outlandish as Deedee Truitt's former lover shows up and Matt's would-be boyfriend also comes into the picture. This film presents the turbulent contemporary family as charmingly dysfunctional.

PECKER

John Waters's *Pecker* (1998) features Edward Furlong as Pecker, a likable amateur photographer who loves shooting events and people he encounters in his Baltimore neighborhood. After some of his photos are displayed in a local pizza parlor, Pecker is discovered by a New York art critic who sets out to make him the newest star of the glitzy New York art scene. Pecker's pics surprisingly take New York by storm, but he longs to return to plain old Baltimore, where he feels more at home. As he sees the people around him turn into distorted images of their former selves because of the corrosive influences of the New York art world, Pecker decides to abandon everything and return to Baltimore. He turns down the offer of a one-man show at a major New York gallery, but that notoriety only results in his making the cover of a popular art magazine. Waters's film portrays urban dystopia and social chaos with a kind of Baltimore provincialism that only Waters can muster. The characters from his hometown seem sweet and somehow vulnerable in the brutish world of New York cultural life.

A PERFECT MURDER

Andrew Davis's *A Perfect Murder* (1998) chillingly depicts the postmodern family as adulterous, scheming, and murderous. The film is based on a play by Frederick Knott that served as the basis for Alfred Hitchcock's thriller *Dial M for Murder* (1954). Davis's version lacks some of Hitchcock's touch but does become a splendid revision of the original. In Davis's film, wealthy commodities trader Steven Taylor (Michael Douglas) discovers that his wife Emily (Gwyneth Paltrow) is having an affair with young, bohemian artist David Shaw (Viggo Mortensen). Soon aware of his wife's treachery, Taylor confronts Shaw, who it turns out is a felon living under an assumed identity. Taylor's aim, however, is not to get rid of his competitor; instead, he offers Shaw $500,000 to murder his wife, who is wealthy in her own right. Shaw accepts the offer, immediately putting Emily in grave danger—but he manages to bungle the murder attempt. Growing suspicious, Emily is ultimately forced to confront her husband, who finally murders Shaw on a train, with the idea of destroying him (which she does). Davis's film depicts nothing less than the death of the nuclear family as we have come to know it.

THE PLAYER

Robert Altman's *The Player* (1992) scathingly indicts the film industry as greedy, shallow, violent, power mad, and ultimately absurd. Tim Robbins's Griffin Mill is a far remove from the modernist hero pattern. He is a successful Hollywood producer who, we soon discover, is very much an antihero who lies, cheats, and then murders to further his own ambitions, finally marrying his murdered victim's girlfriend Uune Gudmunsdottir (Greta Scacchi). Mill epitomizes the postmodern hero who acts according to the ethics of social Darwinism. In *The Player*, the descent into mayhem is already visible in the first scene, when Mill reads a card that says, "I HATE YOUR GUTS, ASSHOLE." Mill later confronts screenwriter David Kahane (Vincent D'Onofrio), who dismisses him with a similar-sounding "See you in the next reel, asshole." Mill struggles with Kahane, whom he kills in a parking lot outside a movie theater. Mill strives to make the crime scene look like a robbery and a mugging, then manages to seize control of each difficult challenge he faces. In Altman's film, crime surely does pay since we see Mill in the final scenes as a now promoted studio head with a limousine who finally cuts a deal with his screenwriter–tormenter (not Kahane, whose killing served no legitimate purpose). In the end, the monstrous evil that Mill embodies does triumph over good, as portrayed through the courageously honest Kahane. The film can best be understood as a wake-up call to the viewer—cinema that presents Hollywood as it really is, not in its typically idealized version.

PULP FICTION

Quentin Tarantino's *Pulp Fiction* (1994) can be said to have brought postmodern culture to a mass audience. This quixotic, entertaining, bloody film features two gangland hit men, Vincent (John Travolta) and Jules (Samuel L Jackson), who run into some formidable characters, situations, and events during the course of their assorted "business" activities. Early in the movie, the two are sprayed with gunfire from a youthful criminal, although miraculously none of the bullets hit their targets even as the wall behind them is shown to be riddled with many bullet holes. The two killers embark on a series of misadventures after Vincent accidentally blows the head off a captive riding in the backseat of their car, splattering the entire vehicle and everyone in it with blood. The two inform their boss, who orders a specialist in solving "mob emergencies" (Harvey Keitel), and he proceeds to handle the problem with professional aplomb. Then, as a favor, Vincent takes his boss's girlfriend (Uma Thurman) on a date, only to have her lapse into a coma after overdosing on drugs. The heroes romp through this film committing one crime after another, providing a kind of campy, comic book atmosphere. There is the usual postmodern descent into chaos and violence, but strong elements of redemption are also present as Jules ultimately decides to renounce his outlaw ways. Vince, however, fails to survive this film, being shot and killed by his own gun while emerging from the bathroom.

RESERVOIR DOGS

Quentin Tarantino's debut film *Reservoir Dogs* (1992) epitomizes the descent into total mayhem characteristic of many postmodern films. In this effort, Tarantino depicts a botched diamond robbery and its protracted violent aftermath. The main figures, known only by code names like Mr. Blue, Mr. White, Mr. Brown, and Mr. Blue, return to a hideout after the robbery, only to find that one of them (played by Michael Madsen) has captured a policeman and brought him to the hideout. The Madsen robber proceeds to torture his captive—shown graphically in the film—but this merely opens the floodgates to more violence, which continues until the picture finally staggers to its pitiful, depressing conclusion. Here we have a group of essentially powerless, dead heroes who live and die violently, one perfect example of the culture of violence that has become so common in postmodern cinema.

SALVADOR

Oliver Stone's *Salvador* (1986) chronicles real-life journalist Peter Boyle (James Woods) as he returns to El Salvador during that country's violent civil war in search of work and a woman he left behind. Boyle manages to antagonize the Salvadoran government, which at the time was being supported by the United States. He works to expose killings and corruption, including the murder of pro-rebel Catholic Archbishop Romero and the gang rape/murder of several Catholic nuns (crimes still unsolved). Consistent with many of Stone's films, *Salvador* exposes the twisted, dark side of American political culture and foreign policy. The film shows the Salvadorean government to be militaristic and ruthless, creating one of the more searingly dystopic narratives in postmodern cinema. Every character in this film is caught up in a web of intrigue, violence, and death—surely a metaphor for events in Central America during the 1980s and beyond.

SERIAL MOM

John Waters's *Serial Mom* (1994) celebrates the "ludic" quality of hilarious chaos revolving around seven murders committed by Beverly Sutphin (Kathleen Turner), a seemingly normal suburban housewife who is married to a dentist (Sam Waterston). The couple have two children, a daughter attending college (Ricki Lake), and a teenage son addicted to horror and slasher films (Matthew Lillard). Sutphin exhibits murderous impulses toward anyone violating the norms of what she considers socially correct public behavior—for example, a boy refusing to wear a seat belt, a couple stuffing themselves like gluttons, and even a juror (Patty Hearst) who has the audacity to wear white shoes after Labor Day. By film's end, all these "villains" wind up murdered. After dispatching her seventh victim, she becomes a media celebrity who will be the subject of a feature film starring Suzanne Somers. Waters satirizes not only the mass media, which, of course, pays obsessive attention to violence, but also suburban middle-class life with its phony, hypocritical, old-fashioned morals and politically correct norms. *Serial Mom* illustrates more than anything the tendency toward playfulness and irreverence that shapes so much postmodern cinema.

SEX, LIES, AND VIDEOTAPE

Stephen Soderbergh's *Sex, Lies, and Videotape* (1989) achieved near cult status with film critics when it was released. The screenplay received an Academy Award nomination, while performances by James Spader, Andie MacDowell, Peter Gallagher, and Laura San Giacomo also won critical acclaim. Soderbergh's film examines the extent to which each individual is a product of larger social relations or, as Leonard Maltin puts it, "how a quarter of the people are defined by their erotic impulses and inhibitions." Every scene involves sexuality in some fashion, most containing intimate conversations about personal and sexual life. The mood of postmodern despair and futility is summed up early in the film as Ann Millaney (MacDowell) confides to her therapist that she has been obsessed with images of garbage for a week. "Garbage. All I've been thinking about all week is garbage. I mean, I just can't stop thinking about it." The film's plot revolves around sexuality and sexual relationships, as Graham Dalton (Spader) drifts into town, upsetting the relationship between a married couple and the wife's youngest sister. Viewers learn that the husband (Gallagher) is having an affair with his wife's sexy, wild younger sister (San Giacomo). Dalton shares his private videotape collection of frankly sexual interviews with Millaney. In the end, viewers can only be left with the impression that contemporary sexuality is fraught with duplicity and frustration. It is a film that does for personal relationships what Altman's *The Player* does for the Hollywood film industry: It is thoroughly irreverent as well as entertaining.

SNAKE EYES

Brian De Palma's *Snake Eyes* (1998) demonstrates that evil and corruption are ubiquitous, suggesting (in the Hitchcock tradition) that terrible things can happen under the most "normal" of circumstances. The action centers around a high-ranking official, the U.S. secretary of defense, who is assassinated while attending a boxing match in Atlantic City. The murder is witnessed by homicide detective Rick Santoro (Nicholas Cage), who is so close that he finds himself wiping blood off his clothes. Cage plays Santoro as a flamboyant, publicity-seeking, cynical police officer on the take. He finds himself pitted against Navy Commander Kevin Dunne (Gary Sinise), although until the end he looks on the commander, his lifelong friend, as the epitome of honesty and propriety. In De Palma's film, however, little turns out as it first appears. The prizefight seemed to result in a knockout, until Santoro plays all the tapes, discovering that one fighter took a fall from a phantom punch that never connected. The audience soon becomes aware that Commander Dunne, far from being the hard-working, dedicated colleague Santoro believes him to be, is actually involved in the conspiracy. Eventually, Santoro discovers that his friend is actually the mastermind of the assassination as well as other murders. The whole criminal enterprise was hatched in order to keep the secretary from changing his mind about an expensive new missile defense system being developed by a military contractor. Santoro fails to discover the truth about his friend until late in the film—not until he has fallen into the villain's hands. Miraculously, Atlantic City police burst on the scene, rescuing Santoro and a young woman from being killed by Commander Dunne. Santoro becomes a media hero for solving the case, yet he is soon investigated for corruption and will predictably wind up ruined and imprisoned. Santoro emerges as the perfect postmodern hero who is so terribly flawed, so much a part of the general malaise and corruption, that he is ultimately reduced to the most abject social and psychological existence.

THE SPANISH PRISONER

David Mamet's *The Spanish Prisoner* (1997) features Campbell Scott as Joe Ross, a brilliant computer scientist who has invented a program that is projected to earn billions of dollars. While visiting a Caribbean island, Ross encounters Jimmy Dell (Steve Martin), an engaging con artist who talks Ross into an elaborate con game with the idea of stealing Ross's computer program. The characters become involved in a world of duplicity that leads down the path of violence and destruction. Mamet plays with the juxtaposition of appearances and "reality" in this thriller embellishing typical postmodern skepticism regarding positive intentions. Mamet appears to be saying in this film (as in *House of Games*) that beneath the surface of ordinary life lies a deeper layer of deceit and seduction, where smiling-faced, affable criminals stalk naive victims who could be anyone walking the streets. *The Spanish Prisoner*'s descent into violence begins with Dell holding a gun to the head of an incredulous Joe Ross and calmly mentioning how much he enjoys his con-artist job that, among other things, calls for murdering people. Ross himself winds up killed by an undercover policewoman posing as an elderly Asian woman, which, of course, only further enhances the macabre nature of this postmodern thriller.

THE TALENTED MR. RIPLEY

Anthony Minghalla's *The Talented Mr. Ripley* (1999) depicts the murderous shenanigans of personable young New Yorker Tom Ripley (Matt Damon), who is hired by a wealthy businessman to find and retrieve his son Dickie (Jude Law), living in southern Italy. Ripley finds Dickie and his beautiful writer girlfriend Marge (Gwyneth Paltrow) and quickly wins the couple's confidence, especially Dickie's. One day, however, while on a boat trip with Dickie, Ripley suddenly erupts into violence and murders his wealthy friend. He then sets out to assume the identity (and bank account) of his dead friend. Ripley is shown to be a true psychopath, ready and willing to kill again if it suits his nefarious purposes. This film extends the increasingly harsh postmodern critique of the family to human relationships in general. You can never be too careful in choosing your friends, it turns out, even when their surface appearances exude trust and friendship.

TALK RADIO

Oliver Stone's *Talk Radio* (1988) dramatizes the story of Alan Berg, the Denver talk show host murdered by neo-Nazis in 1984. Barry Champlain (Eric Bogosian) plays Berg, an in-your-face commentator who enjoys confronting listeners of all races, creeds, and political outlooks; Champlain cannot resist lacing his on-air remarks with biting satire and acerbic wit. Here he delights in his Howard Stern–like role as a provocative gadfly, even after receiving death threats from people who claim to belong to a specific hate group. Champlain begins negotiations with an agent who hopes to syndicate his show nationally, at which point his ex-wife Ellen (Ellen Greene) arrives in town. By the time Champlain is murdered by right-wing thugs, he has already attacked their hate-filled ideology on the air. A talk show personality so acerbic and contentious might have had difficulty winning over a national audience, but on second thought it seems he might well have succeeded beyond his greatest expectations given the present-day appetite for guest bashing on American television and radio. Champlain represents yet another in a long line of postmodern heroes whose self-destruction and inevitable demise parallel certain trends at work in American society.

TAXI DRIVER

Martin Scorsese's *Taxi Driver* (1976) was one of the first and most influential postmodern films. Here Travis Bickle (Robert De Niro) plies the rough-and-tumble New York City streets late at night in his Checker taxicab, providing a doom-laden film noir–style narration throughout. In the first scene, Bickle offers his shrewd perceptions of the city at night: "All the animals come out at night—whores, scum, pussies, buggers, queens, fairies, dopers, junkies. Sick. Venal. Someday a real rain will come and wash all the scum off the street." Bickle sets out to provide this "real rain" as he storms the den of Sport (Harvey Keitel), a pimp employing a teenage prostitute (Jodi Foster). In what would become a common postmodern theme—perpetual descent into mayhem and violence—Bickle follows the script and kills Sport, thereby "releasing" the prostitute. Despite the fact that Bickle's murderous outrage is induced by a psychotic mentality, he winds up venerated by the city's media as a hero. Heavy doses of irony, integral to a deeply mordant script by Paul Schrader, render this film one of the earliest (and harshest) depictions of the postmodern urban quagmire.

THELMA AND LOUISE

Ridley Scott's *Thelma and Louise* (1991) achieved wide distribution and critical acclaim, becoming one of the most widely viewed and discussed postmodern films to date. The picture features the two title characters, Thelma (Geena Davis) and Louise (Susan Sarandon), as waitresses from a small southern city who set off for a weekend without husband or boyfriend, only to wind up thoroughly enmeshed in rape, murder, and robbery. The trouble begins when the two pull up at a country-western bar for drinks and fun: A drunken, lecherous man proceeds to get Thelma drunk and attempts to rape her in the parking lot. Louise arrives just in time to save Thelma, but when she orders the rapist to desist at gunpoint, he challenges her to "suck my dick," at which point Louise shoots and kills him. The women then embark on an outlaw escape adventure extending into Arizona and terminating at the Grand Canyon. They end up as dead postmodern heroes when, surrounded by police, they commit suicide by driving their car over the rim of the Grand Canyon. Despite this dramatic ending, however, the women remain potent symbols of female rebellion against patriarchal domination. They have their finest moment when they deal with a sexist truck driver who had been harassing them along the road with crude advances and sexually explicit gestures. They lure the truck driver into stopping alongside the road, shoot up his tires, and then set fire to his entire rig, flames shooting high into the air. Thelma and Louise are powerful symbols of women ready to sacrifice their lives so they can live free from the prisonlike conditions of male-dominated society. Scott's film resonates with negative images of the family, sexual relationships, men in general, law enforcement, and a society where the ultimate redemption appears to be suicide.

TIME CODE

Mike Figgis's *Time Code* (2000) broke new ground in that it was filmed by four cameras using continuous long takes. The entire cast, including Salma Hayek, Holly Hunter, Stellan Skarsgard, Saffron Burrows, Steven Weber, Kyle MacLachlan, and Jeanne Tripplehorn, improvised their parts from sketchily predetermined plot elements. Figgis divided his screen into four equal parts, presenting different scenes simultaneously from multiple cinematic perspectives. The loosely connected plotlines revolve around a Hollywood production company, Red Mullet, and the sexual trysts and interactions of its staff. Figgis alternates between his cameras, often showing only a kind of graphics on one or two of the screens. Nothing could better serve to distance the audience from the characters, however, than this device, unless someone were to divide the screen into eight or more tiny screens. As it is, the viewer is burdened with the task of piecing together the narrative from four separate cameras and interwoven subplots. In the end, a jealous female (played by Tripplehorn) shoots and kills her actress girlfriend's male seducer, a producer at Red Mullet. One of the cameras follows her as she walks away from the scene, sharing screen space with another woman escaping from a troubled relationship. *Time Code* features dead, flawed heroes; unusual cultural and sexual diversity; a graphic descent into violence; fragmented narratives; and constantly improvising actors. Viewers will find it nearly impossible to identify with any of the characters, but this is precisely the intention of such postmodern format and thematics.

TITANIC

James Cameron's *Titanic* (1997) contains many postmodern elements, including descent into chaos and oblivion, an overlapping and fragmented narrative, and, in particular, emphasis on the spectacle as mode of filmmaking and entertainment. The romantic, schmaltzy plot, with its Manichaeistic good guys/bad guys mentality, and even the performance of the actors (including Leonardo DiCaprio, Kate Winslett, Billy Zane, and Kathy Bates), is dwarfed by the special effects and set designs of the famous luxury liner, which provides the setting for the first ten minutes, and its equally famous sinking, which takes a staggering eighty minutes. Cameron's film cost $200 million, much of it spent on enormously lavish sets and special effects. The sinking scenes are pure action–adventure, and they succeed in capturing audience attention, but these turn out to be little more than techno-thrills. The film is essentially an expensive, dressed-up romantic adventure story featuring Jack (DiCaprio), a boy from the wrong side of the tracks who meets Rose (Winslett), a beautiful but helpless damsel from the right side of the tracks, and the two get together despite Rose's exceedingly class-conscious father. But the plot really does not matter because it is the awe-inspiring technology of the final third of the movie that infuses the production with its aura of spectacle. *Titanic* is not so much a film as a special "event" or a sophisticated video game in which viewers are taken along for sense-rocking adventures while they surrender their interest in the characters—a shame given the actual complex history of the *Titanic* and its fatal voyage. *Titanic* boasts some outstanding performances, however, with Winslett receiving an Academy Award nomination for best actress and Gloria Stewart for best supporting actress, but the other performances are generally wooden and hackneyed.

THE USUAL SUSPECTS

Bryan Singer's *The Usual Suspects* (1995) paints a graphic picture of duplicity, deceit, and murder surrounding the robbery of a ship tied up at a pier. Kevin Spacey plays Verbal, who secretly masterminds two robberies while posing as a crippled member of the gang. Verbal and the other gang members, played by Stephen Baldwin, Gabriel Byrne, Kevin Pollak, and Benicio Del Toro, hijack an ammunition truck, then turn their attention to a docked freighter that serves as the setting for most of the violence permeating this film. The police investigation of a fire aboard ship focuses attention on Verbal, who narrates for police the events leading up to the shipboard inferno. The action cuts back and forth from the police station to enactment of the crimes, presented through flashback scenes. Having masterminded the entire scenario, Verbal is eventually released by the police, who realize just minutes too late that the man they were interrogating is the villain behind the robberies and killings. This film quickly descends into violence and mayhem as it leads viewers incessantly toward chaos and darkness. The opening scenes set the stage for arson and murder, with much more to follow. Verbal emerges as the protagonist but hardly the hero. In real life, he is Keyser Soze, a murderous antihero who earlier killed his wife and children in Turkey to prevent his enemies from doing it themselves—and to demonstrate his cold-blooded ruthlessness as a warning to others who might want to attack him. This lawless villain succeeds in the end, leaving with a fortune and very little likelihood he would ever be apprehended. The film concludes with Keyser/Verbal gradually dropping his phony limp as he strides away from the New York police station where he was interrogated.

VERY BAD THINGS

Peter Berg's *Very Bad Things* (2000) is a black postmodern comedy depicting how the lives of several friends become destroyed after an ill-fated bachelor party held in Las Vegas. The gathering starts to get out of hand after the men consume vast amounts of drugs and alcohol; they accidentally kill a prostitute who joins them at their hotel room. One member of the group, Kyle (Christian Slater), then murders an inquisitive hotel detective, at which point the friends dismember the two bodies and bury them in the desert. At this juncture, the real conflict erupts, as the men go berserk under the strain of guilt and treachery and proceed to murder each other. By the end of the film, nearly everyone gets sucked into a vortex of ruthless killings, with only paraplegics and a mad woman (Cameron Diaz) left at the end.

YOUR FRIENDS AND NEIGHBORS

Neil LaBute's *Your Friends and Neighbors* (2000) relates the story of three young men in Los Angeles who enjoy spending their free time in each other's company doing things like working out at a gym, meeting for drinks or dinner, or playing sports. The trouble begins when one of them, played by Jason Patric, seduces the wife of one of his friends, with her husband eventually learning of the treachery. Most of the film graphically charts the slow, painful destruction of every friendship and relationship that crosses the screen. Partners flirt with anyone available and cheat on their lovers. The family as depicted here is little more than an atomized, dysfunctional, irrelevant social unit, while the great fragility and ephemeral quality of all human relationships emerge with dramatic clarity.

ZELIG

Woody Allen's *Zelig* (1983) gives us a version of the postmodern hero as Leonard Zelig (played by Allen), something of a human chameleon who takes on different personas, depending on his surroundings, emerging as a 400-pound fat man, a Chinese man, an African American musician, an aid to Adolf Hitler, and a guest of William Randolph Hearst at his San Simeon Castle—to name just a few. The film is done in pseudo-documentary style, covering the span of the 1920s and 1930s. Zelig has the neurotic urge to blend in with his environment, to be liked and admired—an extremely weak-willed person whose character is so poorly defined that his very identity becomes murky and questionable. Obsessed with fitting neatly into every conceivable situation, Zelig becomes the ultimate conformist in a world saturated with media images and spectacles. There is a sense in which he has never fully and completely lived, the victim of a highly fragile selfhood.

NOTES

CHAPTER 1: THE NEW CINEMATIC SOCIETY

1. Norman Denzin, *The Cinematic Society* (London: Sage, 1995), 13.

2. George Ritzer, *Enchanting a Disenchanted World* (Thousand Oaks, Calif.: Pine Forge Press, 1999), xi.

3. See Steven Best and Douglas Kellner, *The Postmodern Turn* (New York: Guilford, 1997), introduction.

4. Mas'ud Zavarzedeh, *Seeing Films Politically* (Albany: State University of New York Press, 1991), 1.

5. Mike Davis, *Ecology of Fear* (New York: Henry Holt, 1998), 278.

6. See William Ophuls, *Requiem for Modern Politics* (Boulder, Colo.: Westview, 1997), especially chap. 1.

7. See Francis Fukuyama, *The End of History and the Last Man* (New York: Free Press, 1992), chap. 1, and John Schwartzmanatel, *The Age of Ideology* (New York: New York University Press, 1998), 9.

8. Fredric Jameson, *Postmodernism, or the Cultural Logic of Late Capitalism* (Durham, N.C.: Duke University Press, 1995).

9. Linda Hutcheon, "Postmodern Film," in *Postmodern After-Images*, ed. Peter Brooker and Will Brooker (London: Arnold Press, 1997), 39.

10. Denzin, *The Cinematic Society*, chap. 1.

11. Chalmers Johnson, *Blowback: the Costs and Consequences of American Empire* (New York: Henry Holt, 2000), 7–8.

12. Johnson, *Blowback*, 8.

13. Tariq Ali, *The Clash of Fundamentalisms* (London: Verso, 2002), 253.

14. Rahul Mahajan, *The New Crusade* (New York: Monthly Review Press, 2002), 7.

15. Caleb Carr, *The Lessons of Terror* (New York: Random House, 2002), 229.

16. Carr, *The Lessons of Terror*, 223.

17. See, for example, William Blum, *Rogue State* (Monroe, Me.: Common Courage Press, 2000), and Noam Chomsky, *Rogue States* (Boston: South End, 2000), especially chaps. 10 and 11.

18. Walter Laqueur, *The New Terrorism* (New York: Oxford University Press, 1999), 274.

19. Laqueur, *The New Terrorism*, 272, 274.

20. Hans Magnus Enzenserger, *Civil Wars* (New York: The New Press, 1993), 20, 46.

21. Nicholas Christopher, *Somewhere in the Night* (New York: Henry Holt, 1997), 263.

22. Ray Pratt, *Projecting Paranoia: Conspiratorial Visions in American Film* (Lawrence: University Press of Kansas, 2001), 9.

23. Pratt, *Projecting Paranoia*, 11.

24. James William Gibson, *Warrior Dreams* (New York: Hill & Wang, 1994), 9.

25. Joel Dyer, *Harvest of Rage* (Boulder, Colo.: Westview, 1998), 251.

26. Ophuls, *Requiem for Modern Politics*, 234–35.

27. Christopher, *Somewhere in the Night*, chap. 2.

28. Robert Stam, *Film Theory* (Cambridge, Mass.: Blackwell, 2000), 229.

29. See Jon Lewis, ed., *The New American Cinema* (Durham, N.C.: Duke University Press, 1998), introduction.

30. Best and Kellner, *Postmodern Turn*, 136.

31. See Walter Murch, *In the Blink of an Eye* (Los Angeles: Silman-James).

32. On the approach, see Michael Medved, *Hollywood vs. America* (New York: HarperPerennial, 1993).

33. For a more developed treatment of the retreat from politics in American life, see Carl Boggs, *The End of Politics: Corporate Power and the Decline of the Public Sphere* (New York: Guilford, 2000).

34. For a discussion on the limits of auteurial status, see Gary Crowdus, ed., *The Political Companion to American Film* (Chicago: Lakeview Press, 1994), chap. 1.

35. See Thomas Schatz, *The Genius of the System* (New York: Henry Holt, 1988).

36. Peter Biskind, *Easy Riders, Raging Bulls* (New York: McGraw-Hill, 1998), chap. 6.

37. Michel Foucault, "What Is an Author?" in *Critical Theory since 1965*, ed. Hazard Adams and Leroy Searle (Tallahassee: Florida State University Press, 1986), 136.

38. See Thomas and Vivian Sobchack, *An Introduction to Film*, 2nd ed. (New York: Harper, 1987), 274–78.

39. Crowdus, *The Political Companion to American Film*, 38.

40. Hutcheon, "Postmodern Film," 40.

41. See the essay by Christian Metz on semiotics in Gerald Mast and Marshall Cohen, eds., *Film Theory and Criticism* (New York: Oxford University Press, 1985), 164–76.

42. Antonio Gramsci, *Selections from the Prison Notebooks*, ed. Quintin Hoare and Geoffrey Nowell Smith (New York: International Publishers, 1971), chap. 1.

43. Dudley Andrew, *Concepts in Film Theory* (New York: Oxford University Press, 1984), 71–72.

44. See Sam B. Girgus, *Hollywood Renaissance* (New York: Cambridge University Press, 1998), chap. 1.

45. Christopher Sharrett, in *The End of Cinema as We Know It*, ed. Jon Lewis (New York: New York University Press, 2001), 319.

46. See, for example, Max Horkheimer's analysis in "Art and Mass Culture," in *Critical Theory* (New York: Seabury, 1972), 273–90.

47. See Ritzer, *Enchanting a Disenchanted World*, chap. 5.

48. Douglas Kellner, *Media Culture* (New York: Routledge, 1995), 16.

49. Among other sources, see Jean Baudrillard, *The Consumer Society* (1970; London: Sage, 1998), chap. 7.

50. See Ritzer, *Enchanting a Disenchanted World*, 172–86.

51. Ronald Inglehart, *Modernization and Postmodernization* (Princeton, N.J.: Princeton University Press, 1997), 22.

52. See Biskind, *Easy Riders, Raging Bulls*, especially chap. 3.

53. Guy Debord, *Society of the Spectacle* (New York: Zone Press, 1995), 13.

54. Debord, *Society of the Spectacle*, 15.

55. Debord, *Society of the Spectacle*, 29.

56. Debord, *Society of the Spectacle*, 23.

57. Debord, *Society of the Spectacle*, 153.

58. Ritzer, *Enchanting a Disenchanted World*, 180.

59. Denzin, *Cinematic Society*, 201.

60. Denzin, *Cinematic Society*, 36.

61. See Stephen Powers, David J. Rothman, and Stanley Rothman, *Hollywood's America* (Boulder, Colo.: Westview, 1996), chap. 1.

CHAPTER 2: THE RISE AND DECLINE OF MODERNISM

1. See Richard Hofstadter, *Anti-Intellectualism in American Life* (New York: Vintage, 1962).

2. Thomas Schatz, *The Genius of the System* (New York: Henry Holt, 1998), especially chaps. 10–15.

3. Neal Gabler, *An Empire of Their Own* (New York: Doubleday, 1988), introduction.

4. Gabler, *An Empire of Their Own*, 4.

5. Gabler, *An Empire of Their Own*, 2.

6. Gabler, *An Empire of Their Own*, 6.

7. François Truffaut, *Hitchcock/Truffaut* (New York: Simon & Schuster, 1983), 27.

8. On Ford's directing style, see Andrew Sinclair, *John Ford: A Biography* (New York: Lorrimer, 1979), chaps. 8 and 9.

9. Sinclair, *John Ford*, 97–98.

10. Sam B. Girgus, *Hollywood Renaissance* (New York: Cambridge University Press, 1998), 15.

11. Girgus, *Hollywood Renaissance*, 176.

12. Girgus, *Hollywood Renaissance*, 39.

13. See Robert Lynd and Helen Merill Lynd, *Middletown: A Study in American Culture* (New York: Harcourt, Brace, Jovanovich, 1929).

14. Peter Biskind, "Blockbuster: The Last Crusade," in *Seeing through Movies*, ed. Mark Crispin-Miller (New York: Pantheon, 1990), 219.

15. See the excellent discussion on the Rambo phenomenon in Douglas Kellner, *Media Culture: Culture Studies, Identity, and Politics between the Modern and the Postmodern* (New York: Routledge, 1995), 65–72.

16. Kellner, *Media Culture*, 69.

17. See Susan Mackey-Kallis, *Oliver Stone's America* (Boulder, Colo.: Westview, 1996), chap. 4.

18. Gabler, *An Empire of Their Own*, 118.

19. Gabler, *An Empire of Their Own*, 119.

20. Gabler, *An Empire of Their Own*, 119.

21. See David Sterritt, *The Films of Alfred Hitchcock* (New York: Cambridge University Press, 1993), introduction.

22. Norman Denzin, *Cinematic Society: The Voyeur's Gaze* (Thousand Oaks, Calif.: Sage, 1995), 118–19.

23. Denzin, *Cinematic Society*, 128.

24. Pauline Kael, *Raising Kane* (Markham, Ont.: Fitzhenry and Whiteside, 1984), 23.

25. Robert E. Kapsis, *Hitchcock* (Chicago: University of Chicago Press, 1992), 226–27.

26. Sinclair, *John Ford*, 197–98.

27. Nicholas Christopher, *Somewhere in the Night* (New York: Henry Holt, 1998), 17.

28. Cited in an RKO documentary.

29. Cited in an RKO documentary.

30. Christopher, *Somewhere in the Night*, 16.

31. See Denzin, *The Cinematic Society*, 51.

32. See, for example, Peter Biskind, *Easy Riders, Raging Bulls* (New York: McGraw-Hill, 1998), chap. 2.

33. On the hostility of strong currents within Hollywood filmmaking toward the dominant social (and, to a lesser extent, political) norms of American society, see Stephen Powers, David J. Rothman, and Stanley Rothman, *Hollywood's America* (Boulder, Colo.: Westview, 1966), chap. 11.

34. Christopher, *Somewhere in the Night*, 29.

35. Christopher, *Somewhere in the Night*, 36.

36. Christopher, *Somewhere in the Night*, 179.

37. Christopher, *Somewhere in the Night*, chap. 4.

38. See Mike Davis, *Ecology of Fear* (New York: Henry Holt, 1998), chap. 7.

39. See Ray Pratt, *Projecting Paranoia: Conspiratorial Visions in America* (Lawrence: University Press of Kansas, 2001), 56.

CHAPTER 3: THE POSTMODERN REVOLT: A NEW ERA?

1. On the relationship between countercultural values and the New Hollywood cinema, see Peter Biskind, *Easy Riders, Raging Bulls* (New York: McGraw-Hill, 1998), especially chap. 1.

2. David Ashley, *History without a Subject: The Postmodern Condition* (Boulder, Colo.: Westview, 1997), 6. See also Terry Eagleton, *The Illusions of Postmodernism* (Oxford: Oxford University Press, 1998), especially chap. 4.

3. See, for example, Timothy Corrigan, "Auteurs and the New Hollywood," in *The New American Cinema*, ed. Jon Lewis (Durham, N.C.: Duke University Press, 1998), who calls attention to the phenomenon of the "displaced Hollywood auteur" (59).

4. Fredric Jameson, "The Nostalgia Mode and 'Nostalgia for the Present,'" in *Postmodern After-Images*, ed. Gary Crowdus (Chicago: Lake View Press, 1994), 23–35.

5. Biskind, *Easy Riders, Raging Bulls*.

6. Charles Champlin, *Hollywood's Revolutionary Decade* (Santa Barbara, Calif.: John Daniel, 1998).

7. Biskind, *Easy Riders, Raging Bulls*, 17.

8. This would be true of the postmodern condition generally speaking. See, for example, Barry Smart, *Modern Conditions, Postmodern Controversies* (New York: Routledge, 1992), chaps. 4 and 5.

9. Corrigan, "Auteurs and the New Hollywood," 42.

10. Biskind, *Easy Riders, Raging Bulls*, chap. 6.

11. David Mamet, *On Directing Film* (New York: Penguin, 1991), 4.

12. Jean Baudrillard, *Simulations* (New York: Semiotext, 1983), 2.

13. See the discussion of the hyperreal in Steve Best and Douglas Kellner, *The Postmodern Turn* (New York: Guilford, 1997), 100–3.

14. On the role of propaganda in helping set up U.S. intervention in the Balkans, see Barry Lituchy, "Media Deception and the Yugoslav Civil War," in *NATO in the Balkans: Voices of Opposition*, ed. Ramsey Clark (New York: International Action Center, 1998), 203–9.

15. On the antipolitical element within postmodernism, see Carl Boggs, *The End of Politics: Corporate Power and the Decline of the Public Sphere* (New York: Guilford, 2000), chap. 6.

16. Douglas Kellner, *The Persian Gulf TV War* (Boulder, Colo.: Westview, 1992).

17. "Nostalgia" works in rather complex ways within postmodern culture. See Jameson, "The Nostalgia Mode and 'Nostalgia for the Present,'" 23–35.

18. See Ray Pratt, *Projecting Paranoia: Conspiratorial Visions in America* (Lawrence: University Press of Kansas, 2001), especially chap. 10.

19. "David Cronenberg," in *Inner Views*, ed. David Breskin (New York: Da Capo, 1997), 238.

20. Joseph Campbell, *The Hero with a Thousand Faces* (Princeton, N.J.: Princeton University Press, 1949).

21. Max Weber, *Economy and Society* (New York: Bedminster, 1968), 241.

22. Sigmund Freud, *Civilization and Its Discontents* (New York: Encyclopaedia Britannica, 1952), 767.

23. Thomas Hobbes, from *Leviathan*, in *The Great Political Theories: Vol. 1*, ed. Michael Curtis, ed. (New York: Avon, 1981), 332–35.

24. For a discussion of this point, see Barbara Creed, "From Here to Modernity," in *Postmodern After-Images*, ed. Peter Brooker and Will Brooker (New York: Arnold, 1997), 46.

25. Interview with Clint Eastwood, in Breskin, ed., *Inner Views*, 380–81.

26. Nicholas Christopher, *Somewhere in the Night* (New York: Henry Holt, 1997), 235.

27. Stig Bjorkman, ed., *Woody Allen on Woody Allen* (New York: Grove, 1993), 85.

28. Sam B. Girgus, *The Films of Woody Allen* (New York: Cambridge University Press, 1993), 75–76.

29. Michael Medved, *Hollywood vs. America* (New York: HarperPerennial, 1993), 201.

30. On this point, see Allen's references to characters in many of his films, here referring mainly to *Interiors*. Bjorkman, ed., *Woody Allen on Woody Allen*, 105.

31. On the connection between noir sensibilities and later films, see Christopher, *Somewhere in the Night*, chap. 8.

32. Christopher Lasch, *Haven in a Heartless World* (New York: Vintage, 1979).

33. Alvin Toffler, *The Third Wave* (New York: William Morrow, 1980).

34. See Neil Gabler, *An Empire of Their Own* (New York: Doubleday, 1988), chap. 6.

35. Sam B. Girgus, *Hollywood Renaissance*, 86–107.

36. David N. Meyer, *A Girl and a Gun* (New York: Avon, 1998), 69–72.

37. On traditional family values, see in particular Stephanie Coontz, *The Way We Really Are* (New York: Basic, 1997). See also Jodi O'Brien, *Social Prisms* (Thousand Oaks, Calif.: Pine Forge Press, 1999).

38. Toffler, *The Third Wave*, chap. 1.

39. Coontz, *The Way We Really Are*, 4–7.

40. On radically changing patterns of childhood socialization, see Judith Rich Harris, *The Nurture Assumption* (New York: Free Press, 1998), especially chaps. 1–3.

41. On this point, see Denzin, *Images of Postmodern Society* (London: Sage, 1991), where he dissects the work of Lynch and others (chap. 5).

42. Medved, *Hollywood vs. America*, chap. 13.

43. Bjorkman, ed., *Woody Allen on Woody Allen*, 95.

44. Medved, *Hollywood vs. America*, 137.

45. Emanuel Levy, *Cinema of Outsiders* (New York: New York University Press, 1999), 346.

46. Coontz, *The Way We Really Are*, chap. 3.

CHAPTER 4: THE MANY FACES OF POSTMODERNISM

1. For an elaboration of this point, see Steven Best and Douglas Kellner, *The Postmodern Turn* (New York: Guilford, 1997), chap. 1.

2. See Sam B. Girgus, *Hollywood Renaissance* (New York: Cambridge University Press, 1998), chaps. 1 and 2.

3. Peter Biskind, "Blockbuster: the Last Crusade," in *Seeing through Movies*, ed. Mark Crispin-Miller (New York: Pantheon, 1990), 112–49.

4. See Jean Baudrillard, *The Consumer Society* (New York: Routledge, 1995), chap. 4.

5. Paula Parisi, *Titanic and the Making of James Cameron* (New York: Newmarket Press, 1998), 216.

6. David Anshen, "Out of the Depths and through the Postmodern Surface," *Cineaction*, no. 50 (1999): 23–29.

7. See Daniel Allen Butler, *"Unsinkable": The Full Story* (Mechanicsburg, Pa.: Stackpole Books, 1998), 137–38.

8. Butler, *"Unsinkable,"* 221.

9. Butler, *"Unsinkable,"* 222.

10. Anshen, "Out of the Depths and through the Postmodern Surface," 29.

11. Biskind, "Blockbuster," 120–21.

12. Biskind, "Blockbuster," 147.

13. Sam B. Girgus, *The Films of Woody Allen* (Cambridge: Cambridge University Press), 2.

14. Girgus, *The Films of Woody Allen*, 58.

15. Stig Bjorkman, ed., *Woody Allen on Woody Allen* (New York: Grove, 1995), 50.

16. Bjorkman, ed., *Woody Allen on Woody Allen*, 105.

17. Erich Fromm, *Escape from Freedom* (New York: Avon, 1965).

18. Bjorkman, ed., *Woody Allen on Woody Allen*, 154.

19. Bjorkman, ed., *Woody Allen on Woody Allen*, 156.

20. Girgus, *The Films of Woody Allen*, 78.

21. See Norman Denzin, *The Cinematic Society* (London: Sage, 1995), 32.

22. Bjorkman, ed., *Woody Allen on Woody Allen*, 223–25.

23. *Los Angeles Times*, May 31, 2000.

24. *Los Angeles Times*, May 31, 2000.

25. *Los Angeles Times*, May 31, 2000.

26. Girgus, *The Films of Woody Allen*, 1–2.

27. Susan Mackey-Kallis, *Oliver Stone's America* (Boulder, Colo.: Westview, 1996), 22.

28. Mackey-Kallis, *Oliver Stone's America*, 24–25.

29. For a general historical discussion of the Salvadorean conflict in the 1980s, see Noam Chomsky, *Turning the Tide* (Montreal: Black Rose Books, 1987), 101–27.

30. For a fuller discussion of this point—that Kennedy was indeed the main architect of more extended involvement in Vietnam—see Bruce Miroff, *Pragmatic Illusions* (New York: David MacKay, 1976), chap. 4.

31. This argument is made with great force by Robin Ramsay in *Who Shot JFK?* (London: Pocket Essentials, 2002).

32. Mackey-Kallis, *Oliver Stone's America*, 44.

33. Chris Salewicz, *Oliver Stone: The Making of His Movies* (New York: Thunder's Mouth Press, 1998), 54–55.

34. Salewicz, *Oliver Stone*, 84.

35. Michael Ryan and Douglas Kellner, *Camera Politica* (Bloomington: Indiana University Press, 1988), 190.

36. Hobbes, from *Leviathan*, in *The Great Political Theories*, ed. Michael Curtis (New York: Avon, 1981), 330.

37. Curtis, *The Great Political Theories*, 333.

38. Curtis, *The Great Political Theories*, 334–35.

39. Gerald Peary, ed., *Quentin Tarantino Interviews* (Jackson: University Press of Mississippi, 1998), 126.

40. Peary, ed., *Quentin Tarantino Interviews*, 31.

41. Peary, ed., *Quentin Tarantino Interviews*, 33.

42. Peary, ed., *Quentin Tarantino Interviews*, 59–60.

43. Peary, ed., *Quentin Tarantino Interviews*, 200.

44. Jami Bernard, *Quentin Tarantino: The Man and His Movies* (New York: HarperCollins, 1995), 53.

45. Emanuel Levy, *Cinema of Outsiders: The Rise of American Independent Film* (New York: New York University Press, 2001), 125.

46. Cited in Salewicz, *Oliver Stone*, p. 103.

47. Bernard, *Quentin Tarantino*, 82.

48. Dana Polan, *Pulp Fiction* (London: BFI, 2000), 79.

49. For an example of such references, see Polan, *Pulp Fiction*, 18–23.

50. John Waters, *Shock Value* (New York: Thunder's Mouth Press, 1995), 167.

51. Tom Corlis, *Time*, March 3, 1997.

52. Waters, *Shock Value*, 85.
53. Denzin, *The Cinematic Society*, 79
54. Waters, *Shock Value*, 2.
55. See Dawn Ades, *Dali* (London: Thames and Hudson, 1990), 119.
56. Ades, *Dali*, 202.

CHAPTER 5: THE POSTMODERN VISUAL STYLE

1. For a discussion of the "syntax of cinema" as it relates to editing, see Louis Giannetti, *Understanding Movies* (Englewood Cliffs, N.J.: Prentice Hall, 1996), 133–70.
2. Walter Murch, *In the Blink of an Eye* (Los Angeles: Silman-James, 1995), 6.
3. David Mamet, *On Directing Film* (New York: Penguin, 1991), 104.
4. Murch, *In the Blink of an Eye*, 58.
5. See Fredric Jameson, "The Nostalgia Mode and 'Nostalgia for the Present,'" in *Postmodern After-Images*, ed. Peter Brooker and Will Brooker (London: Arnold, 1997), 23–35.
6. François Truffaut, *Hitchcock* (New York: Simon & Schuster, 1984), 6.
7. Mamet, *On Directing Film*, 4.
8. See Linda Seger and Edward Jay Whetmore, *From Script to Screen* (New York: Henry Holt, 1994), 267.
9. Gary Crowdus, ed., The Political Companion to American Film (Chicago: Lake View Press, 1994), 422.
10. Chris Salewicz, *Oliver Stone: The Making of His Movies* (New York: Thunder's Mouth Press, 1998), 84–85.

CHAPTER 6: POSTMODERN CINEMA IN A CORPORATE WORLD

1. George Ritzer, *Reenchanting a Disenchanted World* (Thousand Oaks, Calif.: Pine Forge Press, 1999), chap. 2.
2. On media culture in the postmodern era, see especially Douglas Kellner, *Media Culture* (New York: Routledge, 1995), 2–8, and Janet Wasko, *Hollywood in the Information Age* (Austin: University of Texas Press, 1994), chap. 1.
3. Sam B. Girgus, *Hollywood Renaissance* (New York: Cambridge University Press, 1998), 1–18.
4. Girgus, *Hollywood Renaissance*, 16.
5. See Timothy Corrigan, "Auteurs and the New Hollywood," in *The New American Cinema*, ed. Jon Lewis (Durham, N.C.: Duke University Press, 1998), 38–63. See also Wasko, *Hollywood in the Information Age*, chap. 3.
6. Ray Pratt, *Projecting Paranoia* (Lawrence: University Press of Kansas, 2001), especially chap. 1.

7. See Edward S. Herman and Robert W. McChesney, *The Global Media* (London: Cassell, 1997), 8–22.

8. Peter Biskind, "Blockbuster: The Last Crusade," in *Seeing through Movies*, ed. Mark Crispin-Miller (New York: Pantheon, 1990), 137.

9. On the phenomenon of spectacle in the Hollywood blockbuster, see the excellent discussion in Paula Parisi, *Titanic and the Making of James Cameron* (New York: Newmarket Press, 1998), chap. 18.

10. Lewis points out the corporations in their profit seeking are driven to exploit *different* media outlets and sources of creativity, enabling them to coexist with postmodern cinematic trends. See Lewis, "Money Matters: Hollywood in the Corporate Era," in *The New American Cinema*, 97.

11. James Lull, *Media, Communication, Culture: A Global Approach* (New York: Columbia University Press, 1995), 27.

12. See Michael Medved, *Hollywood vs. America* (New York: HarperPerennial, 1993).

13. On the eclipse of modern ideologies, see John Schwartmantel, *The Age of Ideology* (New York: New York University Press, 1998).

14. Neil Gabler, *Life the Movie* (New York: Random House, 1998).

15. See Linda Hutcheon, "Postmodern Film?" in *Postmodern After-Images*, ed. Peter Brooker and Will Brooker (New York: Arnold, 1998), 36–38.

16. This theme is developed within Frankfurt school theorizing and is elaborated perhaps most clearly in Herbert Marcuse's classic *One-Dimensional Man* (Boston: Beacon Press, 1994), intro. and chap. 1.

17. On this point, see David Harvey, "Time and Space in the Postmodern Cinema," in *Postmodern After-Images*, 62–64.

18. Lull, *Media, Communication, Culture*, 174.

19. The Hobbesian theme is contained in Pratt, *Projecting Paranoia*, chap. 1, and in Mike Davis, *Ecology of Fear* (New York: Henry Holt, 1998), chap. 7. For these writers, as for us, the expression of postmodern cultural themes are perhaps most visible today in Hollywood cinema.

20. See Wasko's discussion of the relationship between Hollywood filmmaking and the informational revolution in *Hollywood and the Information Age*, chaps. 5–7.

21. The strength of such film studios has been enormously magnified by their incorporation into *global* media empires. See Herman and McChesney, *The Global Media*, chap. 3.

22. On this point see Corrigan, "Auteurs and the New Hollywood," 38–63.

23. Powers, Rothman, and Rothman suggest that the indie phenomenon was able to gain more freedom and flexibility because of distinctly *cultural* changes that made it increasingly difficult for corporate heads to exercise total control over filmmaking processes. See Stephen Powers, David J. Rothman, and Stanley Rothman, *Hollywood's America* (Boulder, Colo.: Westview, 1996), 29.

24. William H. Phillips, *Film: An Introduction* (New York: St. Martin's, 1999), chap. 9.

25. Ritzer, *Reenchanting a Disenchanted World*, 8–11.

26. Wasko, *Hollywood in the Information Age*, chap. 3.

27. Thomas Schatz, "The Return of the Hollywood Studio System," in *Conglomerates and the Media*, ed. Erik Barnouw (New York: The New Press, 1997), 102.

28. Wasko, *Hollywood in the Information Age*, chaps. 6 and 7.

29. Justin Wyatt, "Marketing/Distribution Innovations," in *The New American Cinema*, 87–124.

30. On the new film technology, see Phillips, *Film*, chap. 9.

31. See Phillips, *Film*, 398–401.

32. Sigfried Kracauer, "True Lies: Perceptual Realism, Digital Images, and Film Theory," *Film Quarterly* 49, no. 3 (1996): 27–37.

33. Paul Messaris, *Visual Literacy: Image, Mind, and Reality* (Boulder, Colo.: Westview, 1994), 166.

34. Herman and McChesney, *The Global Media*, 106.

35. On the complex relationship between modernity and postmodernity, see Barry Smart, "Modernity, Postmodernity, and the Present," in *Theories of Modernity and Postmodernity*, ed. Bryan S. Turner (London: Sage, 1990), 14–30.

36. On the exhaustion of classical ideologies associated with modernity, see Schwartzmantel, *The Age of Ideology*, chaps. 7–9.

37. See Hutcheon, "Postmodern Film?" 37.

38. Corrigan, "Auteurs and the New Hollywood," 38–63.

39. On the limits and contradictions of political discourse within postmodernism, see the discussion in Steven Best and Douglas Kellner, *Postmodern Theory* (New York: Guilford, 1991), 283–94.

40. George Roche, *A World without Heroes* (Hillsdale, Mich.: Hillsdale College Press, 1987).

41. See Chuck Kleinhaus, "Independent Features: Hopes and Dreams," in *The New American Cinema*, 307–27.

42. On the potentially corrosive impact of postmodernism on human subjectivity, see Terry Eagleton, *Illusions of Postmodernism* (Cambridge, Mass.: Blackwell, 1996), chap. 4.

43. On the "postmodern paradox" here, see Barry Smart, *Modern Conditions, Postmodern Controversies* (New York: Routledge, 1992), chap. 5.

44. On the continuity from modernism to postmodernism, see Best and Kellner, *The Postmodern Turn*, chap. 1.

45. Hutcheon, "Postmodern Film?" 36.

46. See Eagleton, *Illusions of Postmodernism*, 62–63.

47. On the role of globalization in this process, see Herman and McChesney, *The Global Media*, 189–205.

48. Jack Mathews, *The Battle of Brazil* (New York: Crown, 1987).

49. On the film *JFK* and its powerful embodiment of themes of paranoia and conspiracy, see Pratt, *Projecting Paranoia*, 221–29.

50. See Lewis, "Money Matters," 87–124.

CONCLUSION: HOLLYWOOD AND THE DECLINE OF POLITICAL CULTURE

1. Mike Davis, *Ecology of Fear* (New York: Metropolitan Books, 1998), 363.

2. Carl Boggs, *The End of Politics: Corporate Power and the Decline of the Public Sphere* (New York: Guilford, 2000), chap. 7.

3. See the excellent discussion of paranoia in American public life in Ray Pratt, *Projecting Paranoia* (Lawrence: University Press of Kansas, 2001), chap. 1.

4. This point is developed further in Boggs, *The End of Politics*, chap. 7.

5. Neal Gabler, *Life the Movie* (New York: Knopf, 1999), 56.

6. Gabler, *Life the Movie*, 123.

7. See Hans Magnus Enzensberger, *Civil Wars* (New York: The New Press, 1993).

8. See William Ophuls, *Requiem for Modern Politics* (Boulder, Colo.: Westview, 1997), 25–28.

9. Michael Rogin, *Ronald Reagan the Movie* (Berkeley: University of California Press, 1987), 3.

PHOTO CREDITS

INDEX

ABOUT THE AUTHORS

Carl Boggs is the author of numerous books in the fields of contemporary social and political theory, European politics, and popular movements, including *The Impasse of European Communism* (1982), *The Two Revolutions: Gramsci and the Dilemmas of Western Marxism* (1984), *Social Movements and Political Power* (1986), *Intellectuals and the Crisis of Modernity* (1993), *The Socialist Tradition* (1996), and *The End of Politics: Corporate Power and the Decline of the Public Sphere* (2000). His most recent book is an anthology titled *Masters of War: Militarism and Blowback in an Era of American Empire* (2003). With Tom Pollard, he has written extensively on themes related to the politics of cinema. He has taught at Washington University in St. Louis, University of California, Los Angeles, University of Southern California, University of California, Irvine, and Carleton University in Ottawa. For the past fifteen years he has been professor of social sciences at National University in Los Angeles.

Tom Pollard is professor of social sciences at National University in San Jose, where he has taught since 1986. He received his Ph.D. in American Studies at the University of Kansas. He is a screenwriter and researcher for documentary films, with productions including *Paradise Bent* and *Maya Pompeii*. He also has been involved in creating several television documentaries over the past several years. With Carl Boggs, he has written extensively in the area of film and politics and is currently engaged in a project titled *The Hollywood War*.